The Cup, the Gun and the Crescent:
Social welfare and civil unrest in Muslim societies

**Critical Studies
in Socio-Cultural Diversity**

Editor-in-Chief: Dr Sara Ashencaen Crabtree

Current and future titles in the same series

*Practice Research in Nordic Social Work:
Knowledge production in transition*
Edgar Marthinsen and Ilse Julkunen

*Rainforest Asylum
The enduring legacy of colonial psychiatric care in Malaysia*
Sara Ashencaen Crabtree

*Active ageing?
Perspectives from Europe on a vaunted topic*
María Luisa Gómez Jiménez, and Jonathan Parker (Editors)

Men and Masculinities in Europe (2nd edition)
Keith Pringle, Jeff Hearn, Harry Ferguson, Dimitar Kambourov,
Voldemar Kolga, Emmi Lattu, Ursula Müller, Marie Nordberg, Irina
Novikova, Elzbieta Oleksy, Joanna Rydzewska (Editors)

The Cup, the Gun and the Crescent:

Social welfare and civil unrest in Muslim societies

Edited by

Sara Ashencaen Crabtree,
Jonathan Parker
& Azlinda Azman

Whiting & Birch
MMXII

Published by Whiting & Birch Ltd,
Forest Hill, London SE23 3HZ

ISBN 9781861771322

Printed in England and the United States by Lightning Source

To Isabel, Milly and Ruth
for making it all worthwhile
SAC & JP

Special thanks
to my husband, Suffian Siman, son, Hafiy Daniel,
and both of my parents for their continuous support
and encouragement in my career development
AA

Contents

I

Warfare and welfare: Civil strife and the humanising imperative in contemporary Muslim societies

Jonathan Parker

Alms shall be used only for the advancement of Allah's cause... for distribution among the poor, the destitute, the wayfarers, those that are employed in collecting alms, and those that are converted to the faith. (Sura ix, 60)

Fight for the sake of Allah those that fight against you, but do not attack them first. Allah does not love the aggressors.

Kill them wherever you find them. Drive them out of the places from which they drove you... fight against them until idolatry is no more and Allah's religion reigns supreme. But if they mend their ways, fight none except the evil-doers. (Sura ii, 190)

Introduction

War, civil strife, dissension and political violence, all contentious concepts in themselves, permeate contemporary lives throughout the world, being channelled through local, global and social media and reflected through the lenses of senders and receivers alike. Position statements are made through these various media (whether written, visual, aural or social) and enacted through the actions of individuals, interest groups and States seeking to promote or protect cherished beliefs and cultures, or at least perceived constructs of such. The verses from the Qur'an, at the outset to this chapter, may be open to different levels of theological interpretation, but indicate well many of the humanitarian concerns championed by Islam as well as the fraught socio-political contexts into which the faith was born. They provide a useful corrective to some of the more crass binary distinctions between 'good' and 'evil' promulgated by different contenders within contemporary conflicts, and militate strongly against some Western assumptions of Islamic violence and aggression as unquestionable givens.

Although political and religious tensions and conflicts are not new, since the al-Qaeda attacks of 11th September 2001 a heightened and often polarised set of assumptions have layered perspectives taken in respect of faith groups and political regimes. For instance, beliefs in US disdain for non-American human life have increased since the invasion of Iraq, the 'war on terror' and 'collateral damage' to Pakistani families resulting from US operations against Afghan insurgents. Deaths in these countries have increased in significant proportions to those killed in the horror of 9/11 (Rogers and Sedghi, 2012), purportedly as a result of the West having to protect itself from substantial and imminent attack (Fisher and Wicker, 2010). Distrust, fear and the search for a sense of 'righteous' purpose inform political relations and popular perceptions as we live in a shrinking and co-dependent global world.

It is this rather pessimistic context which acts as a landscape to our, sometimes, more optimistic (at least potentially so) portraits of the ways in which social welfare organisation responds through and within these tense and violent social worlds. What we offer is not a 'pollyannaish' view, nor do we focus necessarily on the political or theological rights and wrongs of conflictual actions – although as authors we all have our views, some of which are expressed throughout the chapters of this book. We place a range of alternative and balanced perspectives on the easel - a *Via Media*–that examines the harsh realities of violence and conflict alongside the social welfare regimes, its organisation and individuals' needs, that flower in the contemporary world's brutal landscape.

We specify the context of the book as countries which by majority population or national expression are Muslim. We must state at the outset, this does not imply Muslim countries are more likely to engage in conflict or violence any more than it suggests non-Muslim countries are likely to attack those that are Muslim. The book is multi-authored comprising people with a range of faith and non-faith positions, but all of us having practice, political and academic interest in the ways in which welfare and psycho-social help is enacted in world settings and on a global stage, how it is influenced and shaped by faith and non-faith and by experience – violent or otherwise.

Comparative social welfare policy has since Titmuss (1956), and followed by Esping-Andersen (1990), been a contested area, but, as is clear from the literature and the locus of authors, it has been led by Western academic traditions. Approaches have centred on the ideal-typical, in a Weberian sense, types of social welfare system providing a globalised view but without the nuanced granulation of real-typical accounts (see Deacon, 2011). These typical approaches have been seen in terms of the Scandinavian universalist/social redistributionist, the Christian Democratic approaches of Northern Europe, and the liberal/neoliberal of UK and US. Aspalter (2002) adds substance to the development of Asian perspectives to welfare that reflect the globalised world, the isomorphisms of social protection, care and welfare and the cultural differences underpinning its organisation. Aspalter (2011) adds the perspectives of the Latin-American and East Asian pro- and anti-welfare approaches. However, the comparative social welfare discipline is young and much work is needed to ensure the perspectives of all are included. What is perhaps also clear is that it is no longer tenable to support a polarised critique between indigenous welfare practices on the one hand and Westernised impositions on the other. The global perspective demands, again, a *Via Media*, a system of welfare that is appropriate and authentic but practised on a global stage.

This introductory chapter explores differing social welfare models and negotiates the ways in which the processes of political violence, conflict and regime change operate on the development of localised morphologies of welfare, offering a modest contribution to understanding social policy and welfare regimes across an underdeveloped area. It is recognised that, often we are comparing 'oranges with lemons' and generalising knowledge may, therefore be limited. However, the book builds a range of experiences from varying perspectives that helps us understand particular aspects of some of the ways in which Islamic principles and social welfare may be interconnected when responding to those needs resulting from conflict, violence and disaster. The ways in which Islamic countries (those which sport a majority of citizens, or subjects, who are considered Muslim, or those countries whose political drivers result from Islamic belief and its localised interpretation) develop and practise welfare, form the focus of this book. Also, perhaps a little more controversially in the world of social protection, the embodiment of welfare as a proselytising, or at least, loyalty-inducing political act is analysed. How these models and processes intertwine throughout the chapters of the book and its rationale will be presented at the end of this chapter.

Modelling social welfare and comparative social policy

The concept, or rather concepts, underlying social welfare represent a range of options for helping individuals and communities, sponsored or not by governments, international or national or faith-based charitable organisations that can be broadly subsumed under this banner. Rather than exclude, however, we wanted, in this volume, to extend the inclusivity to gain a flavour of how different groups and organisations operating in different Muslim countries across the world respond to people in need resulting from conflict, disaster or violence. Of course, comparative social policy offers us guidance in understanding welfare positions, and whilst we do not exclude descriptions of welfare, we do examine this through positions on State social welfare, including those States in which there is little formalised provision and where NGOs and other organisations predominate. There is no single model of social welfare preferred in this book, and the presentation in this chapter reflects only one interpretation.

Ideal-typical models for understanding welfare assist us only in so far as they are representative of the ideal welfare regime within nations (Deacon, 2011). This works for understanding the approaches taken by the Governments and State-sanctioned arms of the various countries represented in the chapters. There is, of course, an implied direction in these models suggesting concern only for State-approved welfare, and models built on resistance to the State or on agitating or proselytising for change are excluded. Therefore, in countries where current conflict has disrupted people, communities, countries from a solid politico-traditional base a real-typical approach is warranted in which the warp and weft of tradition, conflict and change create a new fabric to clothe those in need in a particular society. The processes of conflict are analysed throughout this book in terms of psycho-social impacts, the relationships that create the conditions leading to fragmentation, groupings and politically violent power struggles. They are less understood in respect of the ways in which war and political violence is integral to the development of actual social welfare and protection and the construction of real-typical welfare models. The religio-social systems and political aspirations combine becoming embodied within social supporters of particular groups and played out as a weapon of war, a protest against violence or a cry of hope as social darkness descends, such as Emdad in Iran, the social welfare concerns of Hamas, or NGOs in Afghanistan.

Deacon (2011) argues for a shift away from the alleviation of poverty as a model of global social policy, suggesting that reliance on aid to NGOs and

INGOs and/or private welfare contractors reduces the capacity building role of the State. This is something he believes is beginning to be recognised in government and international policy circles, such as the UK Department for International Development (2006), United Nations Chief Executives Board for Co-ordination, UNICEF, the International Labour Organisation and even in G20 and World Bank debates. The shift has moved towards a more global response based on a global social floor or minimum social protection package, 'a step appears to have been taken in the direction of the ONE-UN lining up behind the Minimum Social Protection Package or Global Social Floor' (Deacon, 2011, p. 93). Evidence from welfare programmes, and exacerbated by the fiscal crisis of 2007 and beyond, the need for an educated middle-income population that identifies with more vulnerable populations has been recognised. Of course, these approaches result mainly from the hegemonic Global North, and it must questioned how they square with political tumult and ideological or religious policy drivers but Deacon's cautious optimism is to be welcomed as a changed approach to global social policy and social protection that promotes humanitarian concern:

> 'Certainly, the endorsement of this policy by UNICEF is an important indicator of the growth of support for this idea. Whether there will be global funds available to back this policy up in impoverished countries is another matter' (Deacon, 2011, p. 98).

Barrientos (2011) would agree that social protection must be wide but believes that social assistance programmes for those in poverty, not as in the West built around income maintenance but on cash transfers to aid consumption and take up of basic utilities is fundamental. A long term rather than emergency based approach is needed in which social protection and welfare policies are embedded into the fabric of the state. Barrientos draws on learning from welfare and social protection after the East Asia Crisis of 1997. Social assistance programmes have demonstrated gat capacity for reaching poor households in a variety of ways dependent on circumstances and needs but these are hindered by national debts, for instance in Sub-Saharan Africa where reliance in international aid rather than state support has hindered development and self-sufficiency. Low-income countries are also affected by migration flows if not directly affected by the fiscal crisis in the West. Restrictions and debts reduce the potential for social assistance and poverty alleviation. Understanding the interaction of social welfare policies and the potential for political conflict is important, whilst contentious. However, the potential for offsetting internal and external predilections for political violence appear to have some credence (Burgoon, 2006).

The important influence of religious values on social welfare is recognised by Jawad and Yakut-Cakar (2010) reporting the contribution religion has made in the Middle East and developing on the established model of the 'Rentier State', and is shown in Clark's (2004) study of Islamic charities. The role of Islam in welfare is not exclusively formulated around political Islam's patronage so as to create a kind of dependent legitimisation but is considered more broadly in respect of religion's ideals and principles in shaping human well-being. Jawad and Yakut-Cakar believe historical analyses of welfare policy in the Middle East is inadequate when constructed around ideas of natural resource revenue financing social welfare whilst retarding the growth of social or citizenship rights-based welfare, and the necessary piece of the jigsaw to explain this concerns the role of religion, notably, Islam. Traditional Rentier State ideas suggested that natural resource revenues eliminated the need to develop economic capacity and competences or the technological skills of the population and thereby undermined citizen development, but this ignores the ways in which social order is negotiated, conflicts take place over welfare and social organisation and the role of religion.

Islam has a rich history in providing welfare echoed in the current development of Islamic welfare associations. *Zakat* is important to the redistribution of welfare means in Middle Eastern States, and the Shi'a tradition of *khums* funds social welfare organisations. *Zakat* represents an obligatory tax on Muslims of certain means, but it is also supplemented by voluntary donations – *sadaqa* - however small, that is recommended to all Muslims (Singer, 2005). *Zakat* and *waqf* (a form of *sadaqa*), religious endowments, underpin the voluntary nature of Middle Eastern welfare and social protection, which, suggest Jawad and Yakut-Cakar (2010) have not been backed by State engagement. Thus, 'it is precisely the lack of State engagement and responsibility for social welfare in the region of the Middle East which has fuelled popular political protest that has found a ready ally in Islamic social movements' (page 665).

Social welfare is enmeshed within Islamic social movements where States have failed to provide or are perceived as corrupt and over-secularised. Jawad (2009) indicates that social welfare is central to such politically controversial organisations as Hizbullah and Hamas. Singer (2005) points out that this is not new and underpins the obligation Muslims carry to contribute to those engaged in all aspects of the work of Allah. Jawad (2009) illustrates that concepts of social justice underpin these politically religious approaches to social welfare. However, Islamic typologies of welfare are more varied than current political Islamic welfare, including religious order provision, philanthropy from elite families, international humanitarian organisations and para-State organisations such as *Emdad* in Iran.

Islamic provision is not restricted to Muslims, however, as Qureshi (2011) points out that *Zamimis*, non-believers, are protected and afforded security and welfare under Hanifi jurisprudence. The long history, and capacity for tolerance, is again demonstrated by bin Talal (2004), in his examination of the Jewish scholar, Musa ibn Maymun, and his potential contribution to Islamic education.

Singer (2005) describes the historical association of charity, philanthropy, welfare and Islam through her examination of Ottoman public kitchens or 'imaret, from the fourteenth to the nineteenth centuries. In her analysis she explores the concepts of giving and the rationale behind it finding that it is not only associated with voluntary giving, *sadaqa*, through religious endowments, *waqf*, but is necessarily associated with political power. Imperial giving reinforced support for the Sultanate and ensured continuity. Welfare and charitable giving is always complex and is unlikely to be informed by a single purpose and we should expect a melange underpinning the rationale behind social welfare ventures in contemporary societies.

Political violence, conflict and other concepts

The title of this volume may be a little contentious but it is chosen to reflect the profound relationship between offering succour to those in need, social, civil and political unrest, disruption and violence. In the context of our book, we are particularly interested in its interaction with religion, specifically Islam. The relationship is nuanced and plurivocal. It concerns help and protection offered to those experiencing unrest or violence; it focuses on those being asked to engage in struggle and conflict from whatever position; it centres on the wish to provide as part of a State's aim to circumvent resistance or the rise of radicalism; it relates to human and/or religiously motivated desire to heal fractured lives. Two things are clear: firstly, welfare and social protection and the desire to help are intrinsically bound with socio-political upheaval and in a range of ways. Secondly, the definitions used to describe the various positionings held by actors in these contexts are complex and contested, and require some discussion. This section introduces some of the diverse understandings and definitional problems with which we are faced.

During the process of editing this collection, the world has witnessed, yet again, profound social uprising against sustained political violence and the subsequent jockeying for power as regimes change. Nowhere has this been as starkly portrayed as in the 'Arab Spring'; those social and popular as well as religious protests that led to the fall of Hosni Mubarek's thirty year rule of Egypt; the fall, capture and death of secular leader Muammar Gadaffi in Libya; and the hope for a future reflected in secular and religious positions simmering out in ripples from a local Islamic tradition to a globalised, and still predominantly Westernised, world. Indeed, as this book was coming together an email from the UK's *Guardian* journalist, Jack Schenker, puzzled at the significance of changes in Egypt after a short time travelling in North Africa and out of reach of the world (personal communication, 2011).The timeliness of the analysis of welfare and conflict, to which this volume adds a modest amount, was strongly reinforced by the continuing bloody uprising in Syria in which estimates suggest at least 7,500 people have been killed (Borger and Pease, 2012). As this chapter was written, the Syrian president, Bashar al-Assad, held talks with the former United Nations secretary general, Kofi Annan, aimed at securing a political solution to what is rapidly becoming a humanitarian crisis. Al-Assad refused to entertain a political solution for the conflict using an argument befitting of former US President George Bush in stating that negotiation was not possible as long as 'terrorist' groups were destabilising the country (Borger and Pearse, 2012). Around the times of the talk, the northern region of Idlib was coming under ferocious attack exposing the contest of ideologies underpinning the concepts of terror and terrorism, and raising questions of the role of international, State and philanthropic welfare in these contexts; whether welfare and social protection stems from within communities and interest groups or from States or the international community; whether it is spawned of religious or secular humanitarian concerns or politically and ideologically motivated.

Political violence is not an easy concept to define, drawing as it does on two slippery terms, 'political' and 'violence'. Is an action political only when undertaken by or on behalf of an administrative region, or can groups jostling for power-positions also act politically? Is violence a physical act or can psychological and even welfare-generated acts be deemed violent? There is also an element of the moral that underpins the term suggesting that perpetrators of such are at best misguided, and certainly to be halted, whilst those who halt in brutish and violent ways are excused from the same definition. This is confusing and leads to partisan appreciations that may occlude wider learning. Theologies of political violence developed in the Leftist liberation movements of Central America. Kee (1974), an important, early theological commentator, recognised that the term represents an ambiguous phenomenon with the actions of revolutionaries being condemned by States and those in power, whilst the revolutionaries seek to justify their actions as a campaign against unjust and oppressive regimes.

War may perhaps appear to bean easier concept to determine as it has an overt political rationale to it. Wars are conducted by nations or States against other nations or States, and the actions of war have been mandated by at least one of the States' governments. Warfare concerns engagement in the prosecution of war. However, wars can be large or small, historical and perhaps not always ended by treaty (for instance the, possibly apocryphal, story of Berwick-upon-Tweed on the English-Scottish border remaining at war with Russia because of its omission from the peace treaty signed in respect of the Crimean war [see Kiely et al., 2000]). It is also the case that war, whilst concerned with open expression of hostilities by States is also enacted between stateless peoples, for instance nomadic peoples, and is prosecuted in multiple ways. Dinstein (2011) exposes many of the tensions in this slippery concept from his analysis of war in the context of international law, concurring that State-prosecuted armed conflict comes within its purview.

Civil war represents a particular subset of the category 'war' and is representative of discord and strife for populations and groups within States; however, its meaning is still contested. For instance, the uprising in Syria in 2011-12 has been debated as both constituting a civil war and not doing so. Of course, the contestation is often political, and in the case of Syria represents those who believe those rebelling against the regime are an organised group seeking political change and power, and those who would describe them as a disorganised rabble without cause. On the basis of usual numerical definitions of civil war, however, the situation sports the hallmarks of one – over 1000 people killed, and over 100 killed on each side as seen above (Collier and Hoeffler, 2004).

Anderson (2011) exposes the definitional dilemmas further highlighting the shifting lines between war and terrorism in his examination of the wars in Iraq and Afghanistan, which presents both the duplicitous reasoning cited for the removal of Saddam Hussein and the catalogue of abuses perpetrated at Abu Ghraib. Terrorism is extremely hard to define and remains contested. Contemporary definitions of terrorism are linked to discussion about political violence, its legitimacy or otherwise, and those with the power to constitute definitions. Allen (2007) points to the partisan character of definitions of terrorism, suggesting that using the concept 'evil' as a descriptor tends to demonise and 'other' the person to whom the label is applied. The simplistic construction that contrasts the two (at least) protagonists at a level of 'good guy' and 'bad guy' is unhelpful and constructs allegiances that are difficult to break down. Sweifach et al. (2010) suggests that definitions of terrorism concern violence against a State in which the status quo is challenged; however, this has not always been the way in which terrorism has been seen with others seeing the violence of the State against individuals or groups within it constituted terror such as during the French Revolution, or more recently in the era of Stalin in the former Soviet Union.

Dekel et al. (2007) recognise that the political and ideological ascriptions preclude an agreed international definition and make a distinction in this context between terror by a state or government and terrorism by an individual. This helps our understanding but it does not fully capture all nuances of deliberate actions to harm and intimidate. The central problem of divergence between definitions is related to the definition of the individual person as a terrorist which in turn relates to whom the definer views as the 'enemy' (Dedeoglu, 2003). Belonging is important (Atran (2010), and the responses agreed and negotiated by each group defines the terror and the terrorist and the ascription of 'ally' or 'enemy'. It must be remembered that concepts of Holy War and Christian theology has been highly influential in the political development of the United States, and in the underpinning rationale for the 'War on Terror' (Lock-Pullan, 2010). In the current context in which assumptions may be made about the affiliation of terror and religion or political perspective, it is important to recognise the complex arguments about defining terrorism does not become associated with one religious tradition alone.

Shah (2005) offers a useful corrective to the often automatically assumed interdependence of *Jihad* and terrorism, with the latter being used uncritically. He understands the Islamic *jihad* as representing a struggle for social justice and the maintenance of public order to protect all not to destroy and impose a particular viewpoint or social system. This idealistically framed interpretation leaves unanswered questions of interpretation or interpreter, and decision-making, but it does help in reinforcing the notion that most people have peaceful intentions regardless of religious and political background (Winter, 2010). Achtar (2010) argues more specifically in the current context that al-Qaeda represents a fringe group, that seeks, misguidedly, justification for its acts of violence; something that runs counter to mainstream Sunni theology. This is important given the 'Jekyll and Hyde image of Islam' portrayed by some Western Governments, against the backdrop of 9/11, 7/7 and the 'War on Terror', that calls for 'good' religious leadership and repression of 'bad' radical groups (Singh and Cowden, 2011, p. 360).

We may, with Vertigans (2011) be left with a need to move beyond the emotion and value-laden aspects of the term, considering terrorism broadly as intentional and often targeted use of violence, across the spectrum, that is used for political ends. It is not useful in a book of this kind to be prescriptive partly because of the disagreements over definitions, but also because of the emotional characteristics of many attempts and the direction in which they are positioned. Indeed, it is the practice and development of helping actions and welfare in troubled situations that forms our primary concern.

The human experience of political conflict and violence in all forms, and however defined, creates a range of psychological, emotional and social needs that social welfare organisations seek to address. Many of these are not dissimilar to those resulting from natural disaster and, in many cases, those organisations – international, State, NGO and religious or secular philanthropic – provide similar understandings and practical approaches to those experiences and their impacts.

This edited text seeks to make a modest contribution to theorising the enactment of welfare in contexts of political violence, civil unrest and Muslim societies. It does not purport to develop a coherent sociology of conflict, violence and its interaction with social welfare, but provides glimpses from a range of perspectives into a dynamic, sometimes troubled and sometimes humane world, exposing diverse responses to civil conflict and political violence in the context of Islam.

The humanising influence of religion represents a well-known adage, even where its converse is equally accepted. Islam promotes traditions of alms-giving, hospitality and welfare for marginalised and vulnerable people, whether Muslim or not. Where the contemporary focus of media attention concerns acts of violence and terror enacted in the name of Islam, or associated with Islam because of the religion of perpetrators, their countries of origin (or possibly simply employing a convenient media device), assumptions are made by people in East and West that reinforce traditional senses of injustice and wrath and allow us to forget the centrality of concern for people's welfare that permeates the religious life and the tenets underpinning it.

The current volume

This book came about through discussions concerning socio-political foment and its interactions with social welfare, the way this fabric acts as an idiom of a particular culture, a visceral reaction to civil strife and/or the tangible outputs of ideological and/or religious expression. We were not aware at the time of its nascence of the fundamental shifts occurring on the world and the rise of popular, person-centred anti-autocratic protests that have led to the overthrow of oppressive regimes and the call for 'democratised' structures (a contested political concept, of course that requires careful use to avoid association with received Western wisdom that may be inappropriate in many of the countries we are concerned with in this book.)

Architecturally, the book sports a scaffolding of three comprehensive sections; the current chapter introduces the global context in which localised welfare responses to political violence are framed, providing an introduction for the subsequent three sections of the book. The focus of this volume also concerns the Islamic roots and socio-cultural expressions of the countries considered. These are enacted in the lives of those living through conflictual events (in potential and actuality). Therefore, the first section, *Religion, sectarianism &identity*, explores these issues in some depth. This section leads directly to an interrogation of the *impact of direct civil conflict* in part two. The social forces of political violence representing a pressure for social action and welfare response can be framed within a humanising effect of societal and religious expression. In this volume we look in particular at countries that profess Islam, either through the number of people within that country of the Islamic faith or through that State's explicit assimilation of Islam as part of government. However, the third section expands the view, exploring the global context in which socio-political developments occur. In *globalisation, urbanisation and social transformation* the wider contextual settings and meanings are considered. The final chapter of this work draws together the ways in which welfare, conflict and Islam have interacted in various countries to form bespoke responses to social problems and needs and embroiders conclusions reflecting the title *The Cup, The Gun and The Crescent: Social welfare and civil unrest in Muslim societies.*

The sections are not considered in equal length or given equal treatment. This is quite deliberate and reflects the ways in which these subject areas have been tackled. The gaps identify further areas for research, one of the purposes of any academic text.

The chapters within this book are representative but not exclusive. Again, this reflects the particular interest and expertise of the authors. The range of countries included, however, offers insights into core aspects at a real-typical level of welfare discourse. In the thirteen countries considered, discussion is contextualised and reflects authenticised perspectives illuminating some of the ways welfare and Islam interact with turbulent political settings.

In the first of five chapters comprising part one of this volume, Alean Al-Krenawi identifies the wide spread of Muslims throughout the world and the large proportion of Muslim-majority countries in the Middle-East and North Africa, whilst recognising that the numerical majority of Muslims live outside of this region. Al-Krenawi challenges and dispels some of the myths that have developed in the West concerning Muslims and their links with terrorism and presents a humanitarian portrayal of Islamic values and championing of human rights. The second chapter in this section, chapter three, concerns the understanding and analysis of social policy in the Arab world, focusing on the importance of religion in the development of social welfare and social protection initiatives in the Middle East. Rana Jawad presents research based on her in-depth empirical work in Lebanon and Egypt, expanding this by reviewing the social policy literature and research of other Middle Eastern countries. She builds on her important typology of religious welfare, contributing to the theorisation of welfare policy within a region of significant political and social conflict.

In chapter four, Taghi Doostgharin examines the more specific issue of social welfare and the Islamic revolution in Iran. The chapter contextualises the revolution and the social welfare and social protection initiatives that derived from and underpinned it. The focus illuminates the religious imperative in Islam to tackle inequality and injustice in society and the positive interweaving of welfare and radical action.

In the subsequent chapter, Parin Dossa draws on her powerful ethnographic research on the lived realities of the women in war-torn Afghanistan. The chapter makes an important methodological plea for 'ethical listening' to the stories of women that can serve to illuminate not only lived realities but also global challenges and perspectives and expose the tensions arising within a global world stage. As we watch from our various positions within the world the stories of women cry to be heard and Dossa provides a platform from which these cries can be presented. In the final chapter in this part of the book, the voices of seldom heard and marginalised groups are again promoted. Hew Cheng Sim and Sara Ashencaen Crabtree explore the unheard ramifications of *the Islamic resurgence in Malaysia and the implications for multiculturalism*. Considering that Malaysia has been viewed and, often, promoted itself as paragon of multicultural harmony dealing equitably with and between the multiple ethnic and faith groups that comprise it, Hew and Ashencaen Crabtree expose some of the controversial realities of a system that privileges certain ethnic groups over others in respect of land rights, education and employment. These ethnocentric approaches to social policy are interlinked with Islamic revivalism that commands political power and is beginning to permeate the civic arena. The impact and implications of these phenomena are considered in relation to vulnerability and opportunity among individuals, families and communities.

The impact of civil conflict is explored more directly in the seven chapters of part 2 of the book. In chapter 7, Christopher Candland and Raza Qazi Khan explore the connections between army operations, subsequent displacement of peoples and the Islamic charities that offer succour to those affected in their chapter *Civil Unrest and Islamic Charities in Pakistan*. Candland and Qazi Khan ask questions about the learning we can gain from the tensions between civil disaster and crisis, national security and human protection and examines this in the context of Islamic chartable relief. The diversity allegiances of welfare initiatives and organisation is considered as are the gendered characteristics of welfare, acknowledging that outlawed Islamist groups also provide welfare and that State and Islamist welfare groups, albeit recognised that most groups are non-partisan, can highlight the violence of the other through ministering to human need. The impact of warfare and political conflict on the business sector, in which many welfare-oriented NGOs operate, is analysed by Andromeda Agnew in the eighth chapter. Agnew looks at the problems restricting business development in the West Bank and Gaza following the Second Intifada in 2000. She posits the importance of supporting economic development to be able to tackle the welfare needs of Palestinians and the constraints faced in an area of continued threatened conflict.

In chapter 9, Kevan Harris returns again to the development of comprehensive welfare systems in Iran following the Islamic revolution of 1979, focusing in particular on the State-sanctioned Imam Khomeini Relief Committee or *Komiteh Emdad*. The role of Islamic and State welfare from the revolution and throughout the Iran-Iraq war is detailed, showing the balanced stage on which conflict and social welfare are played. This chapter provides new insights from Harris' primary research and begins to elucidate the IKRC model of welfare, informed by religion and politics, as central to contemporary humanitarian relief in Iran.

Moving into the arena of international cooperation in developing welfare in the contexts of warfare and political conflict, Jane Lindsay's chapter examines the development of an educational programme for professional supervision for school-based psycho-social workers in the occupied Palestinian territories. The author was instrumental in training for, supporting and evaluating the worth of professional supervision for this central group engaged directly with young people affected by political violence and its ramifications.

In chapter 11, Martine van Bijlert takes us back to Afghanistan, an extremely complex situation which she portrays in different ways according to which view is taken. She explores the clash of ideologies, whether we can conceptualise of the situation in Afghanistan as an externally-led and manipulated State-building exercise led by the West or a grievance-based insurgency. Whichever viewpoint is adopted, international involvement has tended to overshadow localised developments in formal welfare and social protection. The strength of families and Islamic principles of hospitality and religious obligation to the needy are retained, and social welfare must be seen within this contested frame if it is to be understood.

Elise Kipperberg, considers the social policy challenges relating specifically to adolescents in Kurdistan, drawing on the last twenty-plus years since the Convention on the Rights of the Child (CRC) has become the major instrument of human rights monitoring the situation for children under 18 in most countries of the world. Kipperberg promotes the rights of children involved in conflict situations as enshrined within United Nations resolutions, seeing these as one of the most important aspects of NGOs working in regions where reconstruction is ongoing. Her chapter draws in her research and explores some of the social challenges concerning adolescents in the Kurdish region of Iraq, asking such questions as what hopes, fears and needs have they? How social welfare policy develops to meet their needs in the phase of reconstruction and transition, and how does this relate to Muslim culture and values?

In the final chapter in this second part, Mahood Messkoub considers whether welfare provision in the Middle East and North Africa is based on religious or secular principles. He recognises that religious and political authorities have used welfare or *refah* as part of the language of persuasion and discontent, promising to address gaps for allegiance and support. This is understood as no different throughout the world, whether Islamic or other. In the context of poverty, fighting oppression and striving for social justice, Messkoub asks us to consider, however, whether it will be the fundamentalist Islamic groups or secular politics, albeit underpinned by Islam such as in Iran, that appeal to the social welfare needs of disgruntled citizens.

Part 3 of the book focuses on the impacts of globalisation and transformations within societies from the rural to the urban, examining the ways in which social life plays out global realities within a localised context. In the first chapter of this section, chapter 14, Sara Ashencaen Crabtree, Margaret Wood and Belkeis Altareb explore juvenile delinquency and youth justice in the United Arab Emirates. Their chapter explores how delinquent behaviour is identified and understood in the United Arab Emirates (UAE). They consider the attitudes of professional practitioners working with youth offending towards rehabilitation and include an analysis of the perceptions of Emirati social work students towards perceived deviant conduct in young people. The chapter explores gender issues, social cohesion and tensions between a growing globalised and external-facing perspective and the socio-cultural, religious and demographic context of the UAE. The impact of urbanisation and globalisation processes is to the forefront of the chapter 15 in which Nabil Aboulhassan and Abdel-Ghany undertakes a critical analysis of social welfare policies in Egypt prior to the tumultuous changes resulting from the removal of Mubarak. The chapter considers some of the rapid changes in the Egyptian society at the economic, social and cultural levels that result from the processes of globalisation. Some of the social problems that have led to agitation for change are identified such as the high rate of unemployment, poverty, deprivation, social classes changes, increased rates of internal and external migration, integration of some ethnic groups and a high rate of crimes. The authors discusses how the NGOs and welfare organisations need to respond to strengthen citizenship and human rights in Egyptian society, something important to a post-Mubarak Egyptian society.

Hew Cheng Sim and Azlinda Azman provide the final chapter to part III in which we return to Malaysia and explore some of the implications of globalisation for women's health and vulnerability, recognising that maternal mortality has decreased. Gender relations are considered within this context and the global problem of human trafficking, predominantly sexually focused and concerning women, reflects the negative side of these otherwise enviable advances in women's health.

In the final chapter to this volume we bring together some of the central challenges and elements that arise from this collection of disparate views and perceptions and examine future lines of inquiry, weaving together fractures in social welfare and policy where conflict and dissension abound.

Part I

Religion, Sectarianism and Identity

The focus of this volume concerns the Islamic roots and socio-cultural expressions of the countries considered by chapter authors. These are enacted in the lives of those living through conflictual events (in potential and actuality). Therefore, the first section, explores these issues in some depth through five chapters.

In the first chapter of this section, Alean Al-Krenawi sets the scene, identifying the wide spread of Muslims throughout the world and the large proportion of Muslim-majority countries in the Middle-East and North Africa. The context is enhanced when it is recognised that the numerical majority of Muslims live outside of this region. Some of the myths that have developed in the West concerning Muslims and their links with terrorism are challenged and Al-Krenawi presents a humanitarian perspective of Islamic values and the championing of human rights. Rana Jawad undertakes a masterly analysis of social policy in the Arab world, focusing on the importance of religion in the development of social welfare and social protection initiatives in the Middle East. She presents her research in Lebanon and Egypt and expands this by reviewing the social policy literature and research of other Middle Eastern countries. Jawad's important typology of religious welfare offers a unique contribution to the theorisation of welfare policy within a region of significant political and social conflict.

Taghi Doostgharin employs a more focused lens to examine social welfare and the Islamic revolution in Iran. The chapter examines the revolution and the social welfare and social protection initiatives that derived from and underpinned it. Again, like Al-Krenawi, Doostgharin illuminates the religious imperative in Islam to tackle inequality and injustice in society and the positive interweaving of welfare and radical action.

In the subsequent chapter, Parin Dossa draws on her powerful ethnographic research on the lived realities of the women in war-torn Afghanistan, balancing perspectives with other political realities. The chapter makes an important methodological plea for 'ethical listening' to the stories of women that can serve to illuminate not only lived realities but also global challenges and perspectives and expose the tensions arising within a global world stage.

The final chapter in this part of the book, gives voice to seldom heard and marginalised groups. Hew Cheng Sim and Sara Ashencaen Crabtree explore the unheard ramifications of *the Islamic resurgence in Malaysia and the implications for multiculturalism*. Considering that Malaysia has been viewed and, often, promoted itself as paragon of multicultural harmony dealing equitably with and between the multiple ethnic and faith groups that comprise it, Hew and Ashencaen Crabtree expose some of the controversial realities of a system that privileges certain ethnic groups over others in respect of land rights, education and employment.

Islam, human rights and social work in a changing world

Alean Al-Krenawi

Introduction

Globally, Islam is the second-largest religion after Christianity. According to the latest comprehensive estimates, 1.57 billion people in the world today state that they follow Islam. This figure represents 23 percent of an estimated 2009 world population of 6.8 billion. Driven by immigration and high birth-rates, Islam is the second largest religion in Europe, where the number of Muslims has tripled in the last 30 years, and demographers expect a higher rate of growth in the coming decades (CFRPL, 2009). Although Islam is often associated with the Arab world and the Middle East, fewer than 15 percent of the world's Muslims are Arab and two thirds of the global Muslim population lives under a democracy of some sort (Ibrahim, 2005). Nevertheless, popular misconceptions about Islam include beliefs that all Muslims are Arabs, all Arabs are Muslims, all terrorists are Muslims and that all Muslims are terrorists. The assumption that Islam is at the root of terrorist activity results in fear and discrimination; widespread Islamophobia is a barrier to acculturation while fueling hate crimes against Muslims as well as extremism among Muslims.

Cultural competence is critical if social workers are to live up to the ideals of their profession through advancing human rights, advocating for minority groups and promoting understanding between social and cultural sectors. Social workers working with Muslim clients need to understand Islam and how Islam comprehend human rights in order to promote social justice for Muslims while encouraging pride in rich cultural and religious traditions. Muslim immigrants do not need to repudiate their faith in order to embrace principles of universal human rights, as these principles are, in fact, integral to Islam.

Principles of Islam

The holy grail of Islam is the Quran. It is the primary source of Shari'a (Islamic Law) that regulates all life affairs for devout Muslims (Renard, 1998). The Quran is understood to be the Word of God (Allah) as revealed to the Prophet Mohammad. Devout Muslims must believe in the existence of angels, the devil, the Day of Judgment, destiny, heaven and hell, and they must practice the five pillars of Islam during their lives (Azmi, 1991). Primarily, Muslims must believe in and recite the 'Shahadah'; 'there is no God except Allah; Mohammad is the messenger of Allah'. Secondly, Muslims must practice '*Salah*', which means they are required to pray five times a day taking the direction of their holy city, Mecca. Muslims may pray anywhere and at anytime of the day. The third pillar is '*Zakah*,' whereby Muslims are required to give money to charity for Muslims and non Muslims alike; this may go towards building new hospitals, schools, or assisting the poor and the needy. The fourth pillar is '*Siyam*' - Ramadan is a month during which Muslims must abstain from food, drink and sex during the daylight hours. Ramadan ends with a three-day celebration, the feast of '*Eid Al-Fitr*', the breaking of the fast. The final pillar is '*Hajj*' (Pilgrimage); Muslims must visit the holy city of Mecca, in Saudi Arabia, at least once in their lifetime if they are financially, mentally, and physically capable (Al-Krenawi & Graham, 2000; Azmi, 1991; Ashencaen Crabtree et al., 2008; Hodge, 2005).

Key Islamic values include charity, being kind to others, respect for parents, gaining knowledge, going to Friday prayer, reading the Quran and abstaining from violence against others regardless of their religion, gender, colour or origin. Unlike common mythology, Islam is a religion which praises peace and civilization and the Quran clearly prescribes equal rights for women and children. The paradox is that Islamic values, as set out in the Quran and the life of the Prophet Mohammed, often differ significantly from the morality endorsed in many Muslim communities. It is the practices of some Muslims that lead to prejudice in the West and the misrepresentation of Islam.

As with most religions, there is no one Islamic perspective; varying interpretations of religious texts are used to justify different standpoints. There are two divergent groups within Islam and within those who study the Quran and human rights: the literalists (textualists) and the contextualists (or humanists) (Akbarzadeh & MacQueen, 2008; Ibrahim, 2005). The textualists insist that the Quran, hadith and other holy texts are to be taken literally, reflecting the conditions that were present at the time of the writing of these documents. This is problematic, as it reflects some archaic practices and is used to justify human rights violations and violence against certain groups (Senturk, 2005). The contextualists/reformers or humanists interpret the Quran as fluid. This group incorporates current events and international rights in their interpretation of the Quran. By advocating human agency and acknowledging a changing context to the Quran, contextualists demonstrate that Islam supports universal rights and is not a stagnant religion (Akbarzadeh & MacQueen, 2008). It is the textualists who have misrepresented the principles of Islam in Western media through human rights violations and extremist practices under fundamentalist regimes. Hassan (2005: 56) argues that this group has 'hijacked Islam and distorts the perception of this religion in the Western world.'

Islam and human rights

God is the ultimate truth and the ruler of the universe. He is the sovereign Lord, the Sustainer and Nourisher, the Merciful, Whose mercy enshrines all beings; and since He has given each person human dignity and honour, and breathed into him of His own spirit, it follows that, united in Him and through Him, and apart from their other human attributes, people are substantially the same and no tangible and actual distinction can be made among them, on account of their accidental differences such as nationality, colour or race (WAMY, 2009). Every human being is thereby related to all others and all become one community of brotherhood in their honourable and pleasant servitude to the most compassionate Lord of the Universe. In such a heavenly atmosphere the Islamic confession of the oneness of God stands dominant and central, and necessarily entails the concept of the oneness of humanity and the brotherhood of mankind.

Although an Islamic state may be set up in any part of the earth, Islam does not seek to restrict human rights or privileges to the geographical limits of its own state. Islam has laid down some universal fundamental rights for humanity which are to be observed and respected under all circumstances, whether a person is resident within the territory of the Islamic state or outside it, whether he is at peace with the state or at war. The Quran very clearly states:

> O believers, be you securers of justice, witness for God. Let not detestation for a people move you not to be equitable; be equitable - that is nearer to god fearing (5:8)

Importantly, human rights have been given by the almighty Lord. In other words, it is not given by or manipulated by the human race. Human rights that are gracefully given by God are to remain unchanged (absolute). This is unlike this dynamic world, where the rights granted by the kings or the legislative assemblies, can also be withdrawn in the same manner in which they are conferred. The same is the case with the rights accepted and recognised by the dictators. They can confer them when they please and withdraw them when they wish; and they can openly violate them when they like. But since in Islam human rights have been conferred by God, no legislative assembly in the world or any government on earth has the right or authority to make any amendment or change in the rights conferred by God. No one has the right to abrogate them or withdraw them. Nor are they basic human rights which are conferred on paper for the sake of show and exhibition and denied in actual life when the show is over. Nor are they like philosophical concepts, which have no sanctions behind them.

The teaching of Islam does not allow the oppression of women, children, or of any other shape or form of the human race. One learns that women's honour and chastity are to be respected under all circumstances. Furthermore, feeding the hungry person, treating the wounded with dignity, the giving clothes to the naked, regardless of their view of Islam, are some of the true values of the Islamic community teachings.

Human rights, including respect for women, minorities and religious freedom, represent core values of Islam. Yet, paradoxically, States with a Muslim majority are among the countries of the world with the poorest human rights records, and some governments try to justify human rights violations by referring to Islamic cultural values or Islamic law (Baderin, 2007). In these repressive and autocratic regimes (such as Libya, Saudi Arabia and Iran), in many instances both universal and Islamic law are accepted; it is Islamic law, however, that trumps the charters of the United Nations and global human rights litigation. Although the Quran and the Sunnah, two of the holiest texts for Muslims condemn the mistreatment of any other humans, their message has been distorted to justify human rights violations. The misrepresentation, interpretation and application of Shari'a law by some Muslim countries lead to gross human rights violations and subsequent condemnation from the West (El Fadl, 2005). This practice demonstrates the clear division among the core values of Islam mentioned in the previous section and the way in which they are practiced by some Muslims. There is gradual transformation but further change is needed in order to implement the ideology of equal human rights in the Arab world (Almihdar, 2008).

Many factors contribute to the poor human rights record of Islamic countries. These include the type of leadership and form of governance as well as differing approaches towards interpreting Islam (contextualists versus textualists). The blatant disregard and repressive approach towards human rights under certain Islamic regimes is not due to the teachings of the Quran; rather these rulers are following their own political and economic interests (Hunter & Malik, 2005). Ibrahim (2005) identifies a backlash against Western influence as an important third factor contributing to human rights violations, suggesting that there is a 'very troubling challenge for democracy activists and civil society advocates whose message gets entangled in the process of resistance to Western hegemonic policies in the developing world' (2005: 101).

Current conceptualizations of global human rights are often perceived as reflecting a Western tradition. While the creation of the United Nations documents (such as the Universal Declaration of Human Rights, United Nations on Economic Social and Cultural Rights, the Elimination of All Forms of Discrimination against Women, and the Convention on the Rights of The Child) may be seen as rooted in Western conceptualizations of universal human rights (Mayer, 2005; Hunter & Malik, 2005), the tenets of all that they stand for have been ever-present in Muslim holy texts (Akbarzadeh & MacQueen, 2008; El Fadl, 2005). While some Islamic rulers dismiss the universalist approach, suggesting that these ideas are rooted in Western imperialism, which promotes neocolonial ambitions and undermines Islam, the Quran in fact endorses equality, justice and human rights for all (Akbarzadeh & Macqueen, 2008; Ibrahim, 2005). Since its creation, the Quran has advocated for equal human rights and the defense of women's rights (El Fadl, 2005). The Arab countries need only a fair interpretation of the Quran, one that puts aside the corrupt political interests and aspirations of despots, in order to promote equal rights and the fair treatment of Islamic citizens. The teachings of Islam directly match the United Nation's charters of right; therefore Muslim rulers should not view an acceptance of these rights as bowing to Western interests, but instead, as practicing the tenets of Islam as stated in the Quran.

Human rights conceptualized: An Islamic-West based approach

The Declaration of Human Rights (United Nations, 1948) addresses one fundamental point: human rights are universal for all people, regardless of ethnicity, race, gender, age, religion, political convictions, or type of government (O'Byrne, 2003). If human rights are universal, then they do not depend on a specific cultural or ideal model; they belong to all persons in all places, at all times, for all cultures. The application and interpretation of these rights is, however, subject to debate because of cultural differences. While Monshipouri (2002:97) suggests that modern Islamic scholars 'see a clear association between universal human right standards and Islamic ethical constructs', conservatives would suggest that Shari'a (Islamic law) defines and describes human rights, whereby '(m)oral obligations which are, therefore, religiously-based, take precedence over individual human rights' (Monshipouri, 2002: 97). Thus, while there should be no fundamental conflict between Islam and other beliefs regarding the universality of human rights (O'Byrne, 2003), it is almost a certainty that rights are applied differently in other cultures and religions (Ife, 2001). One cannot expect, for example, that traditional Islamic and modern Western approaches to universal human rights would be the same due to historical, cultural and religious diversities (Hayden, 2001; Shenker, 1995). This is another indicator of the complexity of the concept of universal human rights. The relationship between Islamic culture, the political system of Islam and universal rights have been hotly debated for some time.

Monshipouri (2002: 99) notes that conservatives, or orthodox Muslims, look to both 'classical and medieval periods of Islam for their worldview', and see their religion as immutable and perfect, transcending time, space, and political ideology. Proponents of this view may have objections to Article 16-1 and 18 of the Universal Declaration of Human Rights (UDHR) that delineate the right to gender equality and to freedom of thought, conscience and religion. Apostasy may also be deemed a threat to conservative Islam, as are matters relating to divorce, marriage, and child care (see Hew and Ashencaen Crabtree in this volume regarding apostasy in Malaysia). Global trends may be viewed with suspicion as a broader process of Westernization, something to be resisted by major proponents of this view, who include Hassan Al-Banna (1906-49, the founder of the Muslim Brotherhood), Ayatollah Ruhollah Khomeini (1902-1989, who led the Islamic revolution in Iran), or Muhammad Zia-ul-Haq (1924-88, a former president of Pakistan) (Monshipouri, 2002). A universalist approach to human rights requires a move away from this conservative form of Islam. An acceptance of the universalist approach does not, however, entail an acceptance of Western domination; but rather is a progressive step that illustrates the evolving legal and cultural practices of Islam.

Modernists, or semi-integrationists, seek the integration of modern and traditional Islamic views. This process has, in fact, been significant throughout the religion's history. As noted by Monshipouri,

> [m]odernization can be Islamic, but the paradigm of 'the West versus Islam' should be repudiated: far better to integrate Islamic traditions within an emerging notion of the modern. (Monshipouri,2002: 101-102)

These scholars do not reject modernization carte blanche. The late Ayatollah Hussein-Ali Montazari (2009) is a noted advocate of this view. While Islamic human rights are firmly rooted in the belief that God, and God alone, is the law maker and the source of all human rights, Hassan (2005) argues that being a Muslim warrants interpreting the word of God. Muslims do not need to accept the strict and archaic repressive practices such as some forms of *Shari'a* law (Hassan, 2005).

Gender equality in the Muslim world

As a religion, Islam is formally reflected in the constitutions of some Muslim states, which have also adopted conventions such as the Arab Charter on Human Rights, the Charter of the Organization of Islamic Conference (OIC), the OIC Cairo Declaration on Human Rights in Islam and the OIC Covenant on the Rights of the Child in Islam, all of which reference Islam as germane to human rights discourse in the Muslim world. Problems still remain, however, with regard to the treatment of women in particular. In the minds of the general public in the West, Islam is often associated with the oppression of women (Afshar, 1996), although cruel treatment of women is a problem of patriarchal societies generally, not exclusively one of Islam.

Conservative interpretations of Islam have meant that religious traditionalists have disputed the concept of universal rights by choosing to implement fundamentalist laws. It is, however, a myth that 'Islamization' necessarily includes repressive policies for women, the promotion of honour killings, and harsh punishments within Shari'a law. The Quran, Sunnah and hadith never advocate the mistreatment and brutal punishment of women; instead, the rights of women are defended. Nevertheless, textualists use a literal interpretation of Shari'a law and out of context reference to certain Quranic verses to justify human rights violations (Hassan, 2005). Muslim regimes that advocate these harsh policies falsely represent the followers of Islam as oppressive agents of a violent ideology. This is a distortion of Islam and needs to be rectified for future generations and the success of Muslim regimes. Violence against women and child abuse is not representative of all of Islam; it merely represents one interpretation of select Quranic verses (Akbarzadeh & MacQueen, 2008; Mayer, 2005).

The misrepresentation of Quranic law by some Muslims has resulted in numerous human rights violations. The rights of children have been ignored, the right to divorce (a Quranic right) is denied, women's sexual rights are restricted, and finally, honour killings are justified through faulty interpretations of the Quran (Hassan, 2004). Although prohibited in the Quran, domestic violence still occurs and is accepted in areas throughout the Middle East at an alarming rate. This is yet another example of distortion of the Quran, which makes no mention of allowing or even tolerating violence against women by their husbands or any other male. This violence has been allowed only through an interpretation of *Shari'a* law (Elsaidi, 2011). In fact, Hassan (2005) argues that in order for a society to be truly Islamic, there must be equality between males and females.

Gender inequality exemplifies the tension between religion and culture. While Islam promotes equality and prohibits violence, traditional cultural beliefs threaten the fundamental right to life of many Muslim women -- for example, so called 'honour killing' is portrayed in some Muslim communities as realization of 'Islamic law' (Baderin, 2007). The term 'honour crimes' describes the killing of a female relative caught in the act of adultery, or in a situation deemed immoral. Although prohibited by Islam, such crimes are encouraged by traditional tribal culture. Honour killing is rooted primarily in culture rather than religion. These 'honour killings' are strictly prohibited in the Quran (Hassan, 2004) yet continue to be encouraged by some Muslim sects and groups. Social workers need to discern that this is a practice of few Muslims, not a tenet accepted in Islam.

Progressive steps are evolving, albeit slowly, to advance human rights in the Middle East. Saudi Arabia, a country known for harsh punishment, has joined the United Nations Human Rights Commission. Women's rights have also been the subject of debates and legislative change in Iran, although this legislation has unfortunately since been repealed (Mayer, 2008). Through the work of Non-Governmental Organizations, increased education for females and the spread of information, women's rights are constantly growing in the Middle East. Although many corrupt despots and political parties attempt to justify the subjugation of women through their interpretation of the Quran, education, information and contextualisation combat this tendency (Mayer, 2008).

The future of human rights in the Middle East

Recent developments within the Middle East (the Arab Spring) are indicative of a step towards changes in human rights in Islamic regimes (see Jawad Messkoub, Ashencaen Crabtree et al., Aboulhassan and Abdel-Ghany in this volume for further discussion of the Arab Spring events). The more democracy flourishes the more it changes the political demographic of the Arab Spring States, however, the scripts (teaching) of shari'a or religion in politics are only rough indicators of what the real effect might be, especially on the fate of human rights in the future. Islamists must now work out how to integrate more Islam into new democratic systems. Many terms used in the debate are ambiguous and some, especially the concept of Shari'a, are often misunderstood by non-Muslims (Heneghan, 2011).

It is crucial that social workers recognize this as a positive step towards a process of democratization in the Middle East. Egyptians, living under one of the aforementioned despotic regimes under Hosni Mubarak, have recently witnessed the overthrow of their government. This Egyptian revolution followed a revolution and regime change in Tunisia. Algeria, Libya, Yemen and Syria are also witnessing unrest and an attempt by their populations to form democracies. These uprisings, revolutions and demonstrations are primarily driven by youth and signal a 'wake-up call' and desire for basic universal human rights and a representative voice.

Many factors are responsible for facilitating the timing of these protests, including increased political engagement by the populace, better education and broader access to the media, particularly social media. Of those communication sites, Twitter and Facebook have played a major role by enabling the populations of these oppressive regimes to communicate and connect with one another, thus creating new 'imagined communities' on the internet and throughout the nation (Hashemi-Najafabadi, 2010). Undoubtedly, these sites serve as catalysts in creating closer networks and bolstering the work of Non-Governmental Organizations and human rights groups (Hashemi-Najafabadi, 2010).

It is not yet fully understood what ramifications current events will have for the Middle East, where tensions between often polarized viewpoints intensify conflict in Muslim communities. Recent developments within the Middle East not only highlight regime shifts, but also serve to accentuate the divisions within Muslim society – for example, among the old, the young and those who push for democracy or for Muslim extremism. The pro-democracy protests in Egypt and other locations in the Middle East bolster existing tensions within Islam. While many in the West view these revolutions and protests as a sign of progress, the accompanying emergence of Islamic fundamentalism and extremism is a concern in this highly polarized region. The recent protests and movements towards democracy within the Middle East have added another dimension to the study of instability within the Middle East. While a process of democratization has begun, many questions remain for the region -- for instance, to what extent will democracy be instituted or embraced? Will extremist groups like the Muslim Brotherhood exert significant control in the new Egypt and change the political landscape?

At the time of writing this manuscript, the author notes uprisings in the Arab world. Seemingly, the protesters have grown, tired of repressive regimes and abuse of their human rights. It is crucial for social workers to be aware of the importance of social media and the ongoing political situation in the Middle-East and North Africa, as there will certainly be political, cultural and social implications.

The dynamics of a changing Middle-East and Islamic world affect not only the political climate of the Middle-East, but also the social and cultural fabrics of the regions. While touted as political revolutions, these shifts are just as ingrained in the social and cultural context. Social workers do not need to be experts on Middle Eastern foreign policy; nevertheless, understanding the demographics and political situation of their clients' home countries will be beneficial (Erickson & Al-Timimi, 2001). The current protests do signal a desire to move forward to a more democratic system where the people have a stronger voice. Nevertheless, this should not be viewed as a desire to become Westerners, but rather a desire to become twenty-first century citizens and supporters of universal human rights. Social workers can play a vital role in determining the extent that social changes in the Middle East have on their clients' ability to acculturate and feel comfortable in the West, to assimilate without losing their cultural identity (Erickson & Al-Timimi, 2001).

Islamophobia and prejudice in the West

Besides being familiar with the cultural, social and political situations in the Middle East, social workers should be aware of Islamophobia in the West. Some Westerners have constructed stereotypical view of Islam and increasingly perceive Muslims as enemies (Gottschalk & Greenberg, 2007). This has translated into increased prejudice in Europe, particularly in the UK (CRG, 2008). Unfortunately, many terrorist events around the world have been committed by Muslims, or in the name of Islam, which has exacerbated global Islamophobia.

The relationship between Islam and the West spans centuries (Zaqzouq, 2008), but many in the West are misinformed about the Islamic world, relying often on the stereotypes portrayed in some Western media for the benefit of political gain by their affiliate parties. A tendency to focus exclusively on issues such as terrorism, women's rights violations, Muslims, anti-Semitism and homophobia serves to increasingly institutionalize Islamophobia within the Western states, creating the perception that Islamic values are divergent from those held by Western cultures. Islam is also frequently equated with violent political ideology, instead of being seen as a religion.

Unfortunately, this position serves to provoke Muslims into adopting aggressive stances out of fear (ISESCO, 2008). Furthermore, some radical movements in Europe and the Muslim world do not wish this relationship to improve; they refuse to offer opportunities for moderate Muslim voices to shed light on the facts for the Western audience (Zaqzouq, 2008). This situation polarizes communities and prevents mutual understanding, tolerance (acceptance), thus promoting both Muslim extremism and discrimination against Muslims. Given the inherent compatibility between Islamic principles and Western values, there is no reason why Muslim immigrants could not maintain pride on their culture and heritage while becoming integrated into the fabric of their adopted homeland. Moreover, when Muslims are able to maintain and celebrate holidays that defines their identities, the West will benefit from a rich intellectual Islamic heritage, as well as from Muslim scholars and professionals.

Professional social workers are in a unique position to assist in bridging gaps between Muslim and Western communities and to broker solutions that address the needs of all parties through their understanding of how both worlds (the West and the Islamic) affect their clients (Hodge, 2002). Social workers can take on the role of advocacy for diversity, coexistence and multi-faith societies, while proffering a constructive relationship between Muslims and non-Muslims based on cooperation and shared values to issues of common threat.

It is important to ameliorate the relationship between people and the social environment by changing the social structures that limit human function (view) and aggravate human suffering. Religious values and principles have played a major role in the development of social welfare as an institution, and the emergence of social work as a profession. These values have encouraged people to perform good deeds to help the needy and the weak in society (Williams et al., 1998). The structural approach to social work practice that embodies Islamic principles is briefly described in the next section.

Human rights and Islamic social work

Social work as a profession has sought a framework of social legislation to safeguard women, children, prisoners, and the elderly. While protection of the rights of the marginalized is paramount to social workers, professionals also draw on knowledge of human growth and social development in an effort to promote resolutions of social conflict, community development and peace building, as well as the enhancement of individual and public welfare (Moshe, 2001). Social workers can utilize their culturally-sensitive awareness and professional competencies to serve their Muslim clients.

The International Federation of Social Workers (IFSW) stresses that the social work profession promotes the values of democracy, human dignity, and equality between human beings (IFSW, 2002). In Muslim societies, it is important for social workers to be familiar with religious values in addition to Muslim family structures to provide effective service (Hodge, 2005). The following verse summarizes the perspective of social work in Islam:

> It is not righteousness that you turn your faces towards East or West; but it is righteousness to believe in Allah and the Last Day and the Angels and the Books and the Messengers; to spend of your substance out of love for Him, for your kin, for orphans, for the needy, for the wayfarer, for those who ask;

and for the ransom of slaves; to be steadfast in prayers and practice regular charity; to fulfill the contracts which you made; and to be firm and patient in pain (or suffering) and adversity and throughout all periods of panic. Such are the people of truth, the God fearing. (Quran 2: 177).

This verse describes in religious terms the ideals of social service delivery and advises Muslims to believe that their worship of Allah is not perfect without helping the less fortunate; in fact the belief that Muslims should help people to meet their needs is fundamental to Islam. Muslim social workers, male or female, need to adopt Islamic principles to assist clients; these principles are to be god-fearing, give regularly to charity, be trustworthy, honest and conscientious (Siddiqui, 2007).

In addition, Islam is not opposed to women in the role of social workers; moreover, it is not forbidden for female (or male) social workers to serve a client of the opposite sex. Furthermore, non-Muslim clients, if they live in a Muslim society, have the right to receive assistance from Muslim social work organizations. Social workers can link Muslims with Western views and non-Muslims with Islamic views through like-minded organizations and programs that enhance and promote human welfare and social change. Using this method, there is an important role for Muslim social workers in improving human rights, mediating and bringing optimistic relationship between Muslims and non-Muslims.

Social workers must also recognize the dynamics and impact of the Arab Spring, especially in religion and spirituality. It is important to confirm that social workers who teach and practice social work in Islamic societies and the West must be prepared to work with people with different political ideologies. These new social work perspectives should emerge based on both Western Christian and Islamic Middle Eastern values; these approaches can have an enormous benefits for cultural collaboration with common grounds and shared values of Christian, Muslim, as well as Jewish traditions. A new social work perspective may be aptly positioned to fight against phobias in Islam, Christianity and Judaism. Through mutual understanding and respect of one another this may lead to effective outcome of the intervention; social workers and their clients can overcome the force that seeks to divide an increasingly integrated and interdependent world.

Conclusion

The place of Islam in social work – its meaning, its impact on problem definition and solutions, its influence on idioms of distress and the like – varies widely within and between communities. People's attitudes, values, and behaviours likewise vary substantively over time and place, and any religion, Islam included, is often a prism through which one understands the world. As Emile Durkheim insisted, religion:

> is never found apart from a collective. Religion unifies people; it links them to their common history and strengthens them in their common task. Religion is the source of social identification.... It is the symbolic representation of the vision and the values immanent in society. (Baum, 2006: 118, cited in Al-Krenawi & Graham, in progress)

To paraphrase one of Canada's leading scholars of religion, mainstream sociologists such as Durkheim and Weber understood that:

> there are no isolated humans: human beings are born into a community and come to be by participation in the language, the symbols, and the institutions of that community. They may start to doubt and use their reason to question the received wisdom, but they do this with presuppositions inherited from the cultural history. Human are never isolated thinkers: they are inevitably interdependent beings. (Baum, 2006: 218 cited in Al-Krenawi & Graham, in progress)

> The social construction of reality, as social scientists put it, is key. One can never transcend one's cultural and historic surroundings: the committed agnostic or atheist, invariably owes some assumptions of their thinking to the very religion they question or repudiate. (Al-Krenawi & Graham, in progress)

Understanding the true principles and teachings of Islam could lead Western practitioners and educators in social work to a deep recognition and appreciation of Islam and Muslims values. Future relationships supported through bona fide dialogue can serve to minimize Islamophobia and stereotypes, while enabling social workers to foster smoother transitioning and acculturation of Muslims within Western societies.

The Arab spring is the ice breaker towards a democracy that may be implemented solidly in the coming years and decades. The key players to bring oneness in the world by integrating the two ideologies, i.e. Western and the Islamic ideologies, are social workers. Hence, the Arab Awakening is a pre-condition for the factual implementation in bringing Islamic and other religious beliefs under one umbrella with a mutual benefit for one another.

The process of democratization and the recent developments in the Middle East adds another dimension to understanding Islamic human rights. It is essential that social workers do not confuse or blur the lines between Islam and Muslims. While Muslims are supposed to follow the teachings of Islam, they deviate and sometimes misrepresent or misinterpret Islamic practices. Undoubtedly, the Middle East is at a crossroads in regards to human rights and the future direction of the profession of social work.

Based on what is going on Egypt and the rest of Middle Eastern countries, can we anticipate the Islamization of social work? I believe the socio-political and religious aspects of today's activities in the Middle East may take one of two directions and each one may influence the practice of social work in the Muslim world. The first direction is leading to democracy, which will take time and perhaps generations, but during this process we may see an open dialogue among people in relation to human rights and, at a certain point, a changing of the discourse about adaptation of Western intervention social work models. The second direction may see various regions pushed towards a more conservative religious direction; possibly encouraging the practice of localization and the Islamization of social work. Though only time will tell which direction will prevail, either will have a major impact on how the West will perceive Islam and Muslim peoples in the future.

3

Reinstating social policy in the Arab world: Some new analytical perspectives on religion and social citizenship

Rana Jawad

Introduction

At a time of increasing interest in social protection and poverty-reduction in the Arab countries, driven since the early 2000s by multilateral aid agencies such as the UN and World Bank, and, since 2010, by the momentous 'Arab Spring' (see Messkoub, Al-Krenawi, Ashencaen Crabtree et al. and Aboulhassan and Abdel-Ghany in this volume for further references to the Arab Spring events), this chapter provides a critical examination of social policy in the Arab countries, a little researched and very poorly theorised area within Middle Eastern area studies. This chapter focuses on two key areas: the historical (under) development of social policy in the Arab countries; and the role of religion in shaping it, as well as discussing more broadly the experiences of citizenship. The chapter draws from the historical-institutionalism perspective as well as cultural analyses of social policy to examine the reasons why social policies in the Arab region are residual in character, and policy concerns with poverty and social deprivation have been slow in the making (Clarke, 2004; Manow and Kersbergen, 2009). This will serve to highlight the pivotal role of religious groups, both as political parties and civil society organisations, in shaping the development of social policy and social welfare provision (Manow and Kersbergen, 2009). The discussion offered here is based on in-depth empirical research in Lebanon and Egypt, and draws upon limited research and a policy desk review of other countries in the region, including the United Arab Emirates, Saudi Arabia, Palestine, Jordan, Kuwait and Iraq.

The chapter engages in a discussion on how religion provides an impetus for social action by introducing a typology of religious welfare, as discussed in more detail in a recent publication by Jawad (2009). This seeks to make a contribution to the theoretical literature in this area by departing from the conventional model of the Rentier State, which has traditionally underpinned political analyses of wealth generation and redistribution in Arab countries (Beblawi, 1990). The chapter argues that whilst religion forms a fundamental backdrop to political ideologies and political conflict in the Arab region, local empirical research, as well as international perspectives, help to add new analytical insights on the role of religion in social policy in the Arab region. This is based on two theoretical approaches that are inspired by a 'strengths-assets' based approach, which draws from participatory development policy, together with that of social work, to emphasise the existing coping strategies and resources of local people in solving local, social problems (Furness and Gilligan, 2010). In addition, to which the rich debate on social citizenship in Western social policy literature (Dwyer, 2004) contributes to this analysis, where, to some extent, it is possible to read into the future of welfare entitlements in the Arab countries through the current political mobilisations that are taking place in some countries there.

The chapter is made up of the following sections: the first provides a social and political profile of the Arab countries and the history of social policy there. Section two sets out the main theoretical approaches in the study of social policy in the Arab region. Section three looks at the role of Islam in social policy in the region, and how religious non-governmental organisations as well as formal religious authorities have come to shape social welfare. A typology of religious welfare based on the author's research in the region is also discussed. Section three considers the extent to the relationship between Islamically inspired populist social action and discourses of citizenship may be seen to form part of the emerging political landscape of the region (see Messkoub, Candland and Khan Qazi in this volume for further analyses on this point). The conclusion summarises the main arguments of the chapter.

A socio-political profile and history of social policy in Arab countries

This section offers an historical overview of the key developments shaping social policy development in the Arab region. For clarity, the Arab countries are geographically located in Northern Africa and Western Asia (see map below).

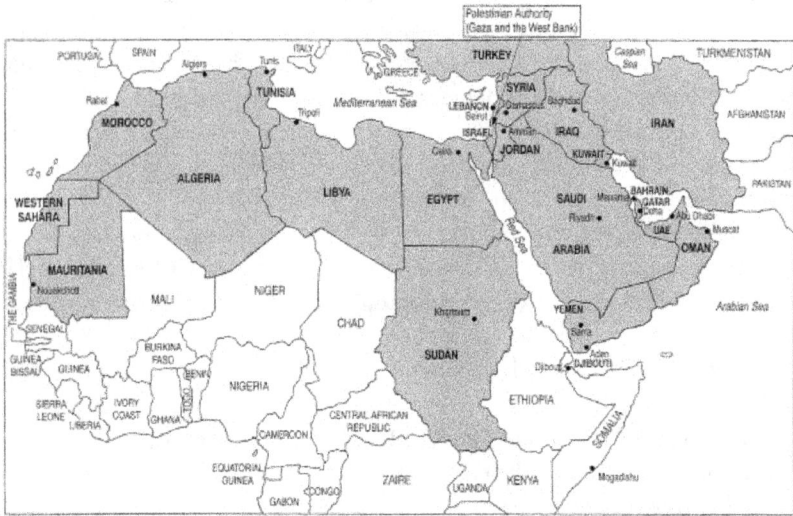

The Arab countries are a diverse group with equally diverse Human Development Index (HDI) rankings (see figure 1 below), and a variety of per capita income levels ranging from a high of US$27,664 to a low of US$ 930 (AHDR, 2009). Yet, a variety of social, political and historical factors make this one of the most problematic regions of the world. There are as a result, significant structural challenges facing the Arab countries relating to basic challenges of sustenance and survival.

To this end, it is noteworthy that the first Arab Human Development Report (2002: 26) described the Arab region as 'richer, than it is developed with respect to basic human development indicators'.

The region has been characterised by an oil-driven development strategy, which has resulted in substantial social and economic volatility due to the changing price of oil and over-dependence by Arab governments on oil revenues. This situation has created an insufficient number of social and economic opportunities to meet the needs of growing populations.

The Arab Human Development Reports have made important strides in charting the social situation of the Arab countries. The latest 2009 report argues that in several instances, social indicators in the Arab countries have worsened in spite of relative improvements in education or employment levels. The region continues to be characterised by a high degree of insecurity which encompasses all areas of life: jobs and income, the environment, health and education, as well as personal security. The recent global economic crisis is also expected to affect the social situation in the region, especially with regards to job opportunities in the Arab region, a situation further compounded by the effect of high population growth rates and rising female labour force participation.

Although the region is not considered to suffer greatly from income poverty, there are variations in the estimate of poverty in the region depending on which poverty line is used. The national upper poverty lines quoted above, contrasts with the average of 20% at less than $2/day for the year 2005, shown in Table 1 below. AHDR (2009) notes that based on the national upper poverty lines, the overall headcount poverty ratio would be closer to 40% in the Arab region. Poverty is also especially a problem in the rural areas.

Table 1
Middle East and North Africa Poverty Rates

(Percent of the population living below various poverty lines), 1981-2005

	1981	1990	1999	2005
$1/day	3.6	2.3	2.6	2.0
$1.25/day	8.6	5.4	5.8	4.6
$2/day	28.7	22.0	23.7	19.0

(Source: Chen and Ravallion, 2008)

Extreme poverty is especially acute in the low-income Arab countries reaching a level of 36.2% of the population. The UN's Human Poverty Index (HPI), which measures the deprivation of capabilities and opportunities, shows that the low-income countries of the region have an average HPI of 35% compared to 12% in the high income countries. The HPI measure has important implications for standards of living, health and education, particularly where children are concerned. In terms of income inequality, this is generally reported as being moderate in the region, although there are inequalities in overall wealth. The AHDR (2009) also argues that there are high incidences of social exclusion in the region, for example, on ethnic and religious grounds.

The 'Arab spring' has no doubt brought these issues into sharper relief, leading to the question of how social policy has developed in view of these challenges? Social policy in the Arab countries has been greatly influenced by international intervention. This include the opening up to the European-dominated economy since the 17th century through colonization and mandate rule, which set particular political and economic structures in motion. Furthermore, since the 1980s economic reform under the pressure of globalization and structural adjustment programmes has been led mainly by international development agencies, such as the International Monetary Fund (IMF) and World Bank. In all these instances, the groups that have taken control of State social policy have been mainly local elites made up of tribal, religious or ethnic leaders and wealthy merchants, whose privileged status during mandate rule and afterwards marginalized the interest of a primarily rural agricultural population.

The increasing market-orientation of Middle Eastern economies and the privatization programmes implemented under the present influence of globalization and those of actors within international development, has further retrenched the role of the State as principle provider of social services and employer in the public sector. Moghadam and Karshenas et al. (2003), El-Ghonemy (1998), Henry and Springborg (2003) and Clark (2001) have described how most States in the Middle East, especially the Arab ones, have failed or are failing to develop effective democratic institutions that can ensure representative government and political participation for all citizens. Whether over-sized and coercive (such as Egypt and Saudi Arabia) or weak and dysfunctional (such as Sudan and Lebanon), States are rife with corruption and the embezzlement of public funds.

State-led social and public provision is especially hard hit because of several factors such as:

1. the misallocation of resources and the prioritization of military spending over key social sectors such as health and education;
2. the narrow economic focus of public policy, which hinges social progress on economic prosperity;
3. the dominance of minority factions in Middle Eastern countries dating back to the colonial era;
4. political insecurity and military conflict, with the protraction of the Arab–Israeli conflict;
5. high levels of State indebtedness, which have taken away funds from social welfare services;
6. the introduction of structural adjustment programmes and the increasing privatization programmes, which have reduced the role of

the State further as provider of social services and public sector jobs.

The resulting social ills of unemployment, wealth polarization, and even malnutrition need to be addressed through the reform of public policy and State legislation, in the areas of labour laws for example.

The 1940s and 1950s in the Middle East saw high secular and socialist fervour, the vestiges of which can still be found in countries like Egypt and Syria. Until the 1980s, the Middle East experienced immense social and economic changes, due almost singlehandedly to oil windfall. This was used to establish and fund State social services, such as guaranteed government employment for graduates; new labour legislation (favouring workers in large public enterprises) in areas like health insurance, retirement pay, maternity pay; free education; free hospital care; and basic consumer subsidies, the most important of which were food and housing. Urbanisation and economic development were accompanied by significant attainments in education and enhanced female labour participation (Moghadam and Karshenas, 2006). These concessions, however, represented a short 'honeymoon' between State and citizens. The easy access to capital that resulted from oil revenues has led to the concentration of wealth amongst the urban elites, and left the majority of the populations poorly skilled and ruled primarily via patrimonial and tribal structures. This reliance on natural resource rents for social spending has earned the welfare regimes of the Middle East the label of 'Rentier'.

Another major factor hampering social policy is the politicisation of welfare and the instrumental use of social policy by the State to gain power and political legitimacy. Some argue that this is a historical factor as well. For example, the introduction of social benefits to workers and employment guarantees to university graduates in Iran and Egypt in the 1950s/1960s were motivated by the need to win the support of the working classes in the postcolonial States, and were not based on a civic discourse of social citizenship. Today, social benefits are channelled though clientelist networks, which link ruling governments to their supporters. Thus, social policy today in the Middle East, particularly in the Arab countries, lacks a sense of its own legitimacy, thus placing higher expectations for the 'Arab Spring' to change this. Heartening though this might be, it is important not to lose sight of the history and contemporary challenges for social policy that have been discussed in this section.

Theoretical perspectives on social policy in the Arab countries

Research conducted by Jawad (2009) indicates that State social policy is residual in character and is primarily focused on the provision of social safety nets and the reintegration of marginalized groups into society (Jawad, 2009). The most comprehensive employment-based insurance goes to urban public sector workers, particularly those who are unionized, with the best protection going to the army and security forces. At the heart of this residual social policy are key conceptual blockages, namely the overly economic focus of public policy and a corresponding lack of importance accorded to the social. A significant example of this residual or piecemeal approach to social policy is highlighted by the Egyptian case study in Karshenas and Moghadam (2006), where since the 1990s the State has not been able to cut back on key consumer subsidies, as it has wished, due to the outbreak of violent public protest. This situation is now under review with the fall of the Mubarak regime in February 2011.

Related to this narrow political-economic focus is the characterization of Middle Eastern states as 'Rentier' meaning that their primary source of revenue is from natural resources such as oil and natural gas (Beblawi, 1990). This is particularly the case for the oil-rich countries in the Gulf, as well as Iran, Iraq and Algeria. The reliance on oil revenues has meant that some States were able to provide social welfare and social insurance services to citizens during the oil boom era of the 1960s–1980s, without having to tax citizens on the basis of their civic membership to the nation. The easy access to capital and the sudden overnight affluence brought about by the oil windfall in the region is depicted as a curse by El-Ghonemy (1998), since it has directly undermined the structures of social citizenship and the need to develop the productive capacity of the local population, due to the over-reliance on foreign labour.

Some of the major challenges for social welfare provisioning in the Arab countries are not so much about the long-term structures of democratic participation and the sharing of decision-making by society, instead they are more about the urgent measures of wealth redistribution, income transfers, provision of basic needs and ensuring the support systems of basic survival (Karshenas and Moghadam, 2006). These are exemplified by basic indicators of wellbeing such as child morality, female literacy, sanitation and housing. At the heart of social policy, then, are key challenges of basic economic and social development. These concerns are also mirrored in much of the existing official government discourses on social and economic development in the Arab region, which remain focused on economic productivity such as creating more employment opportunities, reducing indebtedness, reforming property rights and the Islamic laws that dominate inheritance and family planning. This is not to say that social policies in the past did not bring about improvements in society in the Middle East. The immediate post-independence era in the 1940s and subsequently the oil-boom era, which lasted until the 1980s, saw rapid social transformation of the region with enormous improvements in education and health, including rapid urban transformation. However, these gains were rapidly lost, as States became more authoritarian in character and failed to develop adequate economic policies.

This has led to a sense of break-down in State and society relations in the Middle East, which we are now witnessing in the wave of political mobilisation, as mass populations seek to reclaim a political voice (Henry and Springborg, 2001). In many instances, this political mobilisation is being expressed in sectarian terms. For instance, the majority Sunnis population are rising against the Alawite regime, while the majority of Shi'a in Bahrain are rising against the Sunni regime. The sense of social unrest is exacerbated further by the notion within society that the State should take more responsibility for the welfare of citizens, and that the latter have the rights and entitlements over the State with regards to the provision of social services.

Competition between State and societal groups over the public sphere is most acutely expressed in the rise of Islamic groups in the Arab region, which are providing vital public and social services, and thus challenging the State not only as a provider of welfare but as a modern secular institution of government. Some of these groups are well-known political groups such as the Muslim Brotherhood (Egypt) and Hamas (Palestinian Territories), but others are more local and less political, such as the Islah Charitable Society in Yemen or the Mustafa Mahmood Health Clinic in Egypt (Clark, 2003). Under the banner of 'Islam is the Solution' (*Al Islam Huwal- Hal*), the poor and disgruntled middle classes in the Arab region have found a platform for mobilisation in political groups such as Hamas and Hizbullah.

Islam, populist social movements and social policy

Islam (like Judaism and Christianity) exercises an important cultural influence on personal status laws as well as general codes of moral conduct and charitable giving. Islamic teachings, it is also argued, may perpetuate wealth and gender inequalities, and as Tripp (2006) has argued, Islamic social reformers have failed to offer an alternative socially equitable vision to capitalism. Islam also underpins some important welfare institutions in the Arab countries such as *waqf* (religious endowments) and *zakat* (an obligatory 2.5% tax levied on assets) (Jourdan-Bellion, 2003). The giving of *zakat* has acted as a hugely important source of poverty-alleviation for the poor; and *waqf* has played a key role in the socio-economic development of the Middle East for quite sometime in the last few centuries prior to colonization.

To reiterate, Islamic values are important as an activating force for social groups and movements in society to engage in public and social service provisioning. They are underpinned by emotional and ideological ties of human fellowship and stewardship, as opposed to social entitlements of citizenship toward a nation-state. In Egypt, Yemen and Jordan, for example, Islamic movements or Islamic charity organizations use social welfare to challenge the basis of the secular modern State, and/or to protect the political status of the professional classes through the provision of employment opportunities and social networks. In the case of political Islamic groups, Wiktorowicz (2003) argues that organisations such as Hamas in the Palestinian Territories are social movements that have developed locally and are now supported by a comprehensive institutional basis, of which the provision of social welfare and public services is a vital component. The rise and popularity of Islamic welfare organisations may thus be understood in the following terms:

1. social groups, growing disenchanted with State corruption and failure to provide equitable social welfare services, have sought to fill the gap and social and public service provision themselves.
2. Islamic groups are disillusioned with the secular Middle Eastern State and are pursuing an alternative social and political option based on Islam.
3. Many Islamic welfare organizations, in Egypt, Yemen and Jordan, for example, are middle class organisations whose primary function is to provide economic and political opportunities for middle class professionals.

4. Social welfare provision is a constitutive dimension of the identity of political organisations such as Hizbullah and Hamas who act as social movements within their societies.
5. Not all Arab states are in conflict with Islamic (or religious) welfare organisations.

In Lebanon and Morocco for example, religious welfare NGOs are sub-contracted by the State to offer social welfare services. In these cases, common political goals underpin the relations between the state and welfare NGOs.

Jawad (2009) offers a typology of religious welfare made up of five 'types' which are discussed below, some of which overlap. The literature on faith-based organisations in the Western context also offers typologies of religious organisations, though they are specific to the role of faith in voluntary sector organisations (Chapman, 2009; Baker, 2009), as opposed to what kind of religious organisation gets involved in social welfare – which is the type of religious welfare discussed here.

Accordingly (Jawad, 2009), the first type of religious welfare organisation is the *religious order* which is clergy-based such as *Caritas*. This organisation has branches across the Arab world, particularly where there are substantial Christian populations such Lebanon, Jordan and Iraq. This organisation is part of a religious body, such as the Catholic Church or a religious order. It may employ lay individuals but the managerial tier is reserved for clerics who carry out the social services themselves. A second type is directly linked to the *elite families* of particular communities such as in the case of Dar Al Aytam in Lebanon, which was set up by prominent families. In the case of Dar Al Aytam, the Beirut families established an Islamic orphanage to care for orphans and widows living in the capital city and its suburbs. Some organisations are a joint endeavour between religious and political elites.

The charitable activities of upper-class families in the Middle East have a long history. Indeed, it was often under the banner of charity that such families engaged in public action across the Arab World and Middle East. In Egypt, for instance, in 1882, the first feminist movement mobilised was known as the 'Women's Educational Society'. The third type is a religious welfare organisation which is especially evident in the cases of the wealthy Gulf countries such as Kuwait, Saudi Arabia and United Arab Emirates, *the International Humanitarian Relief Organisation*. Organisations such as *The International Islamic Relief Organisation of Saudi Arabia* have also become well-known for their international relief efforts to emergency situations around the world. Some of these organisations may be seen as *para-State organisations* that are partly funded by the State and form part of its welfare infrastructure. This can be regarded as the fourth type of religious welfare organisation.

The fifth type is perhaps the most controversial and indeed the most politicised. It is *The Popular Political Movement*, examples of which can be found in Hizbullah in Lebanon and Hamas in the Palestinian Territories. This type can also be found in Egypt and Morocco in the example of movements with a clear Islamic ideology, such as the Muslim Brotherhood and the Justice and Development Charity Movement. Makris (2006) and Sutton and Vertigans (2005) have distinguished between 'radical Islamic movements' such as Al Qaida, and 'mass organisations' such as Hamas, the Muslim Brotherhood and Hizbullah. Here it is argued that a social welfare perspective is very important for understanding the character of Islamic groups, particularly those falling under the category of 'mass organisations'.

As argued in Jawad (2009), *The Popular Political Movement* resembles the 'mass organisations' referred to above, since a key facet of this type's identity is their populist character, expressed through their discourses on anti-imperialism and social justice and their active involvement in social welfare provision. Salamey and Pearson (2007) describe Hizbullah as 'a populist proletarian movement' that is part of an anti-imperialist international alliance. This, they argue, takes better account of the particular political discourse adopted by Hezbollah. In research conducted by Jawad (2009), this populist pro-poor discourse feeds into one of resistance, which is not just against neo-colonialism but also poverty and ignorance.

Jawad (2009) notes that viewing religion in a positive light in the Arab region is not driven by ideology, nostalgia or romanticism. Rather, it draws attention to the value of local, grassroots action of a kind similar to the assets-strengths based approach that British social workers, engaging with religious and ethnicity minority in the UK, now refer to (Furness and Gilligan, 2010). Indeed, as far back as 1980, Wilber and Jameson (1980) pointed to the critical role of religion and cultural values in Western social policy. Such arguments are relevant today to the Middle East, since they highlight the way in which populist mobilisation can enhance citizenship solidarity and participation.

In the Western context, populism is often regarded with suspicion for its association with conservatism and traditionalism (Hall and Midgely, 2004). However, populism can offer new ways of viewing social policy in the Arab countries, not just that enacted during and after the colonial era, but also with respect to the current involvement of Islamic social movements in social welfare in the region. Indeed, Hall and Midgely (2004) argued that populist approaches to social change have had a long history and a substantial record of achievements in low-income and developing countries. The social activism of Paolo Freire in Brazil, popular social movements in India and Latin America, and the expansion of social services in Argentina under President Juan Peron in the 1960s are all examples of populist mobilisation that rallied local populations around a sense of common identity and the common good (Hall and Midgely, 2004). Indeed, the more recent discussions of the success of social policy in the 'tiger' economies of East Asia is associated with Confucian values and the objectives of nation-building and political legitimisation that have underpinned them (Walker and Wong, 2005).

Populism here is seen not as a form of nostalgia for an Islamic society or a romantic vision of community life. Rather, our argument is to emphasise what is happening on the ground to ordinary people's lives in the Arab region and to look for examples of effective social action in the treatment of local social problems. Taking a historical look, Thompson (2001) documents how during mandate rule in Lebanon and Syria, populist movements flourished particularly in 1942-1943. Along with women's and communist movements, populist movements played an active role in challenging the European mandate, and in defining the terms of their subsequent citizenship by demanding the establishment of key political and social rights. Thompson (2001) calls these movements 'subaltern' because they were in conflict with the colonial rulers and the local elites, whose alliances with colonial rulers protected their privileges and power. It was through the combined efforts of these movements that the semblance of a welfare State based on citizenship rights was established in Lebanon and Syria in the post-independence era.

Jaber (1997), Shadid (2001) and Wiktorowicz (2003) also argue that Islamic groups such as Hamas in the Palestinian Territories, the Muslim Brotherhood in Egypt and Hizbullah in Lebanon have taken their social welfare role very seriously and are offering a genuine social agenda for large populations in their countries, many of whom come from the poor segments of society. While some of these organizations are also seen as politically threatening, they pose serious questions about the future of social policy in the region and more significantly, the enduring role of religious welfare organizations, with Islamic organizations at their helm.

To this extent, Shadid (2001) argues that these organisations have a genuine sense of social obligation and are not driven by political motives of self-interest. They see their social welfare work as an expression of their solidarity with deprived members of their population. To this end, Shadid (2001) advocates formal political support of these organizations, based on a culturally-sensitive analysis that places Islam at the heart of social policy in the region.

This cultural approach to social policy is also echoed in Clarke (2004), who describes the connection between culture and social policy where an understanding of what is happening to the welfare State begins with how we think about it. According to Clarke (2004: 36), culture means the 'politics of articulation', or put in a simpler way, it is the study of how social actors interact and enter into conflict with each other in order to define or control the environment they live in. This can bring important insights to how social policy works, particularly as policy making itself is a complex process, and has as much to do with the actors involved in making the decisions as with its actual content (Hudson, 2007). In this sense, Clarke (2004: 154) describes the Welfare State as a combination of 'institutionalised formations (apparatuses, policies, practices) and political-cultural imaginaries (symbolizing unities, solidarities and exclusions)'.

Based on this analysis, Clarke (2004) argues that from a cultural perspective, at the heart of the conflict over welfare and its meaning is the definition of nationhood and the construction of the 'people' in a nation as citizens. Thus, the current 'Arab spring' offers an important opportunity for studying the way in which the social order is itself being negotiated; and how States are seeking to keep their grip on the national formations and symbols of identity among Arab populations.

Conclusion

The history of the welfare State cannot be understood in a linear form that imposes a rational and objectivist approach to the study of social policy. Instead, as Clarke argues (2004: 5), our reading of history needs to be 'conjunctural', in that it should be sensitive to the variety of forces that come into play, in order to produce a particular event or definition of a concept. For our present purpose, this would mean supplementing the historical account of social policy from the point of view of the State through an analysis of the multiplicity of social actors and the polysemy of the concept of welfare itself. This is based on recognizing social policy as a discourse and as an anthropological phenomenon. The current 'Arab Spring' has brought this issue into sharp relief.

This chapter has engaged with the question of social policy and social citizenship in the Arab countries by first offering a broad mapping of how social policy has developed in this region, what the key social problems facing its populations are and how Islam has played a part in shaping public interventions in this landscape. The chapter has helped to offer a broad view of how Islamic values, actors and institutions have shaped social policy in the Arab region. The debate is still open with regards to the effects of such movements on the development of social citizenship and a broader discourse of universal social welfare entitlement. Religiously-inspired discourses of poverty alleviation tend to evoke moral sentiments of charity and obligation towards God. This intermingles with grassroots political mobilisation whereby Islamic groups champion the social cause of large, disenfranchised populations in the struggle for greater justice and equality in the Arab region. What is less clear is the wider more sensitive issue of the political legitimacy of some Arab states, especially in view of the uprisings that began in 2011 and the welfare functions that the secular nation-state can undertake in this struggle. Until this matter is resolved, some Islamic welfare groups will continue to pose challenges to social equity and political freedom - in some cases also entrenching exiting political cleavages.

Acknowledgement

I would like to thank the Economic and Social Research Council for supporting the research on which this paper is based.

4

Social welfare and the Islamic revolution in Iran

Taghi Doostgharin

Introduction

A prominent trigger of the revolution in Iran was an article published in one of the 1979 issues of *Keyhan*, a State-owned newspaper based in Tehran, which represented the late Ayatollah Khomeini in insulting terms. Many Iranians were outraged when they saw or heard about the article. A protest was initiated by some across Iran and soon spread further. This was followed by a strike by the majority of society, which including the closure of businesses, and the demonstration of hundreds of thousands of people on the streets.

However, the focus of the protests soon shifted from the controversial article to broader direct civil conflict. The demonstrators turned their aggression towards government buildings, demanding the resignation of the Shah's government. Among many issues, there were demands to improve the lives of poor people in Iran. Social welfare reform was a major contention for civil unrest in Iran. There was a prevailing idea that most of the Iranian assets and wealth were appropriated by minority groups who were close to the Kingdom family and their close supporters. In order to defuse the crisis and divert people's anger, the State authorities jailed some former ministers, who were allegedly part of the corruption, and also increased the salary of government employees. However, all these measures were not sufficient to stop the overthrown of the Shah's regime.

Moreover, before the Islamic Revolution, the Shah's government implemented a few social-economic reforms called the White Revolution, whereby some agriculture lands were transferred to the workers labouring on them. In addition, some welfare organisations were set up to look after needy people. However, this was not enough to prevent any socioeconomic-related unrest among the Iranian nation.

After the Islamic revolution, the new government set up new organisations and supported newly established charitable organisations such as the Immdad Committee to offer social assistance to the poor and needy.

Iran has always been a multi-ethnic and multicultural country. Islam is the official religion of Iran, but there are many other religious and ethnic groups living in Iran, including Christian, Jewish, Zoroastrian, Armenian, and Assyrian. However, since Iran is predominantly an Islamic country, where the State claims that all its social policy is based on Islamic principles, it is essential to explore Islamic perspectives on the nature of society and social welfare, before examining what is occurring in contemporary practice.

Social welfare from an Islamic identity perspective

The Islamic Identity is taken to mean the way of life of the Muslim: a broad set of beliefs, ideologies and practices as prescribed by the Quran and based on the example of the Prophet Muhammad, his family and close followers.

Here the importance of understanding questions about the nature of the Islamic identity and its concept of social welfare will be discussed. Moreover, an attempt will be made to locate Islamic identities in a community context, in order to recognise and appreciate the multiplicities and meanings that religion plays in social welfare. In addition, this section will engage with and unpick the theoretical understandings that are prevalent in the social sciences and humanities, so as to obtain a better recognition of the difference between contemporary theories and an Islamic perspective with a view to informing new and improved conceptual frameworks. Finally, the written recommendations of Imam Ali (Prophet Muhammad's son in law) to one of his commanders, the Governor of Egypt, will be examined to understand how they are structured to organise social welfare and social justice in the Islamic world.

Overall, there are two main rival perspectives about the role of the State in welfare; the first view argues that it is the responsibility of the government to support those who are marginalised and disadvantaged. The second view emphasises the belief that everybody should be responsible for their own welfare and should not be dependent upon the government (Oko, 2008).

However, it seems that overall an Islamic perspective involves 'collective action', which has been a central concern for social work practice, rather than leaning towards an individual rights and responsibilities discourse. Most verses of the Quran seek social change, as well as helping individuals to meet their needs for the duration of time that they may be experiencing difficulties.

In Islamic terms, it is the duty of the individual to look after those most in need. In other words, the overall essence of duties towards Allah is to worship Him only and to provide services to those in need. This emphasises the significance of duties and the accountability of people in society (Quran-AL-BAQR-177; AL-IMRAN-134; Quran-AL-DAHR-8).

In Islamic societies, the establishment of different forms of tax, including *Zakat, Oshr, Fai(Khoms)* and *Rekas*, can be considered as regular and active social institutions set up to provide social security to the people (AICMEU, 2009). However, Muslims are expected to pay them on a voluntary basis. Muslims from different branches of the Islamic faith have different views and regulations on these voluntary taxations.

Social welfare as a component of social justice

The Islamic perspective argues that where society is structured along lines of inequality, such as assets, revenue and health, it is the responsibility of others who are more fortunate to donate towards the welfare of those who are disadvantaged. The Islamic perspective emphasises the belief that social differences are less the result of an expression of individual deviancy or dysfunction, but instead represent the misbehaviour of the privileged who do not comply with the Islamic code to pay towards those in need. Moreover, it is the deviated action of man that results in the germination of ills and evils affecting individuals and societies (AICMEU, 2009). The Islamic perspective emphasises the belief that all troubles and hardships are abnormal events, which occur due to the twisting of manifestations created by Allah, away from their pure and righteous nature (AICMEU, 2009). Conflict theory is to some extent in line with the Islamic perspective (Oko, 2008). It argues that social differences represent differences in life chances and life experiences (Doostgharin, 2010b). From an Islamic standpoint, Allah is the creator and sustainer of all men; being His creatures, each and every one shares His bounties and boons. A number of people obtain their shares independently, but for those who are not able to do so, Allah arranges some support for them. However, it is here that the concept of social welfare appears more visibly for thought and action, in terms of advocacy and assistance towards those in need by those who are more privileged (AICMEU, 2009).

Social justice in Islam embraces a commitment to address and deal with the inequalities faced by underprivileged people, and subsequently supports the establishment of improved social equality (Doostgharin, 2010b). As Banks (2006) has pointed out, social justice includes equality in all senses, in terms of equal treatment, access to services and equality of outcome. In the Islamic perspective, everyone is equal before Allah (Quran-AL HUJURAT, 13.). Hence, this idea challenges the existing power structures and oppressive establishments and activities that do not treat people equally (Doostgharin, 2010b).

It appears that the Islamic point of view is to some extent concerned with supporting a discourse around individual rights and responsibilities that primarily support and inculcate individual liability. Additionally, this observation highlights a belief that individual responsibilities are as fundamental as shared obligations and responsibilities, and that each individual is obliged to take primary responsibility for their welfare rather than depend on State support. Nonetheless, such a view is not the characteristic of anti-collectivist or neo-liberal approaches to welfare. This abrogates the duty of privileged people, as well as the State, towards addressing welfare issues (Doostgharin, 2010b). On the contrary based on the individual rights and responsibilities discourse (Oko, 2008), the Islamic standpoint supports a belief towards individual responsibility, but it does not condemn them if they need some additional provision.

It can be understood that Islam also promotes social equality, but in practice it seeks to promote assistance through individual donations and voluntary Islamic tax. Furthermore, it can be seen that social exclusion is the result of a lack of personal and social, as well as political and financial opportunities(Mills, 1979, Oko, 2008). Therefore the strategies needed to support and encourage social inclusion need to be varied and adaptable (Oko, 2008).

Social welfare, justice, ethic and state responsibilities in Imam Ali's view

According to the Islamic point of view, justice is explained as the ethical virtue of enabling harmony among individuals and social structures by emphasising that people must live according to the principals of equity and equality (Bilgen, 2009). According to the Quran the essence of justice is in equity (see Al-Krenawi in this volume for an analysis of 'textual; and 'contextual' interpretations of the Holy Quran). Just as it is possible to reach out to divine inspiration through adherence to the 'right' i.e. the tenets of the faith, justice can also be obtained by obedience to the principles of equity (Quran-ARAF-159). Imam Ali's words and recommendations are very important and trustworthy to all Muslims, and in particular by Shiite Muslims, who are the majority in Iran. Hence by reviewing his beliefs and recommended instructions we can further examine the ideology of Islam and the ethics concerning the duty of the State towards society. The following quotations are based on a letter which was written by Imam Ali to Maalik al-Ashtar (Al-Islam, 2010) who was appointed as the Governor of Egypt when Imam Ali was the leader of the Muslim world approximately fourteen centuries ago:

The Letter of Imam Ali requesting the governor to be kind to all of his people:

> Maalik, You must create in your mind kindness, compassion and love for your subjects. Do not behave towards them as if you are a voracious and ravenous beast and as if your success lies in devouring them.

Islam rejects discrimination against people on the ground of religious beliefs. Imam Ali clearly states this in his letter to Maalik:

> Remember, Maalik, that amongst your subjects there are two kinds of people: those who have the same religion as you have - they are brothers to you; and those who have religions other than that of yours - they are human beings like you. Men of either category suffer from the same weaknesses and disabilities that human beings are inclined to, they commit sins, indulge in vices either intentionally or foolishly and unintentionally, without realizing the enormity of their deeds. Let your mercy and compassion come to their rescue and help in the same way and to the same extent that you expect Allah to show mercy and forgiveness to you.

In another part of his letter to Maalik, Imam Ali emphases treating people equally, regardless of the proximity to the rulers:

> So far as your own affairs or those of your relatives and friends are concerned take care that you do not violate the duties laid down upon you by Allah and do not usurp the rights of mankind. Be impartial and deal with them

justly, because if you give up equity and justice then you will certainly be a tyrant and an oppressor. Be fair, impartial and just in your dealings with all, individually and collectively, and be careful not to make your person, position and favours become sources of malice.

Imam Ali promotes practice based on the non-oppression of others. In his above mentioned letter to Maalik, he went on to say:

And whoever tyrannizes and oppresses the creatures of Allah, will earn the enmity of Allah along with the hatred of those whom he has oppressed; and whoever earns the Wrath of Allah loses all chances of salvation and he will have no excuse to offer on the Day of Judgement. Every tyrant and oppressor is an enemy of Allah unless he repents and gives up oppression.

Imam Ali condemns those who oppress people and believes that God will punish them sooner rather than later. The following passage of his letter to Maalik expresses this view quite explicitly.

There is nothing in this world more effective to turn His blessings into His wrath quicker than to impose oppression over His creatures, because the Merciful Allah will always hear the prayers of those who have been oppressed and He will give no quarter to oppressors.

When it comes to social policy and welfare, the message is very clear: Imam Ali points out that the Governor should consider the interests of those who may not be privileged as the core of his policy:

You must always appreciate and adopt a policy which is neither too severe nor too lenient, a policy which is based upon equity will be greatly appreciated. Remember that the displeasure of common men, the have-nots and the underprivileged outweighs the approval of the privileged; while the displeasure of the powerful few will be overlooked by the Lord, if the general public and the masses of your subjects are happy with you. Keep your mind on their affairs, be friendlier with them and secure their trust and goodwill.

Social welfare is the core duty of the State. Imam Ali explains this duty in very plain language. He observes that everyone has the right to expect that the ruler of the State will provide basic necessities for society's well-being and the contentment of the people. Imam Ali emphasises this issue especially in reference to poor and disabled people:

Then it comes to the poor and the disabled people. It is absolutely necessary that they should be looked after, helped and well-provided for. The Merciful Allah has explained the ways and means of maintaining and providing for each of these groups.

Imam Ali believes that the poverty of the masses is the actual cause of devastation and ruination of a country; and the main cause of the poverty of the people is the desire of its ruler and officers to amass wealth and possessions, whether by fair means or foul. That is why he reminds Maalik, as the governor, that he is made responsible for guarding the rights of the poor and for looking after their welfare:

> Fear Allah concerning their conditions and your attitude towards them. They have no support, no resources and no opportunities. They are poor, they are destitute and many of them are cripples and unfit for work. Some of them come begging and some (who maintain their self-respect) do not beg, but their conditions speak of their distress, poverty, destitution and want. For the sake of Allah, Maalik, protect them and their rights. He has laid the responsibility of this upon your shoulders. You must allocate resources for them from Baytul Mal (the Government Treasury).

In line with the above suggestions, Imam Ali asks the governor to be very careful of the welfare of the poor. He asks him not to be conceited or arrogant towards them and to remember that he has to take particular care of those who cannot reach him, those who are poverty-stricken and disease-ridden, whose sight who may be hateful to him, and those whom society treats with disgust, detestation and contempt. Imam Ali asks the governor to be a source of comfort, love and respect for them. In accordance with this charity, Imam Ali asks the governor to appoint a respectable, honest and pious person - a person who fears Allah and who can treat the underprivileged honourably, and to order him to find out everything about them and to submit a report to him.

When it comes to the welfare of the poor, positive action to improve their condition is a further concern for Imam Ali:

> Though every one of these poor persons deserves your sympathy and you will have to do justice to His cause to achieve His favour, yet you should pay more attention to the disadvantage of the young and old, orphans and cripples. They neither have any support nor can they easily come to you to beg. They cannot reach you; therefore, you must go to them.

Social welfare in the Iranian constitution

The Constitution of the Islamic Republic of Iran was adopted by referendum on October 24, 1979, and went into force on December 3 of that year, replacing the Constitution of 1906. It was amended on July 28, 1989. The Constitution states that the form of government in Iran is that of an Islamic Republic. It explains this form is due to the referendum passed by 98% of the eligible voters of Iran. An Islamic Republic is defined as a system based on the Islamic belief and in particular, stresses the understanding of God's divine nature to be fundamental to setting laws.

The Guardian Council of the Constitution, also known as the Council of Guardians, is an appointed and constitutionally-mandated 12-member council that exercises substantial power and authority in Iran. Arguably the Council of Guardians ensures that all articles of the Constitution as well other laws are based on Islamic principles.

We can see some of the effectiveness of changes in the approach to welfare as a result of the Islamic principles. In other words, we can identify some of the Islamic guidelines which have shaped government policies of the Welfare State. However, major welfare changes in Iran before and after the Islamic Revolution were more the result of Iran's exporting of petrol resources and economic wealth of the country (see Jawad and Messkoub in this volume for further analyses of this issue). After the Islamic Revolution and, in particular, after the end of the invasion of Iran by Iraqi forces, the Iranian Government increased the role of the State towards welfare provision, as well as supporting private insurance for health and promoting the increased privatisation of social care and education (Doostgharin, 2010a).

The preface of the Iranian Constitution states:

> The Constitution pledges anti-oppressive practice in all aspect of people's lives including social and economic affairs, so as to empower people to make decisions for their own lives. (Doostgharin, 2010b)

Based on the above mentioned principles, the Constitution emphasised the will to grant the nation social and economic justice (Doostgharin, 2010b).

In the next part the Constitution outlines social welfare provision:

1. Section 2: Helping mothers, especially throughout pregnancy and child rearing; and supporting foundlings.
2. Section 4: setting up insurance for widows and older people who have

no one to look after them.

3. Section 29: the government is required to provide the nation with the following: pensions: unemployment benefit, allowances for looking after older and disabled people, allowances for care of foundlings; and allowances for care of those affected by accidents or natural disasters. In addition, the government is obliged to supply the nation with health care through insurance or by any other means.

4. Section 43: 'The Government should assist citizens to meet their basic needs including: housing, food, clothing, health care, education; and providing facilities for every person to be able to maintain a family.

Furthermore, the *Social Welfare for Iran Within 20 Years Document*, has also set out government policies on the Welfare State. It states that the government is obliged to provide people with health care, welfare, judicial security, equal opportunities, distribution of appropriate income; and to assist families to remain intact, to eliminate poverty, corruption, discrimination and to promote the right of the population to enjoy high-quality living standards (Doostgharin, 2010b).

The implementation of government policy in providing social security benefits is the duty of two separate organisations:

1. the Ministry of Welfare and Social Security, which deals with different sorts of disadvantaged groups such as poor, single parents, disabled people and others;

2. the Immdad Committee which generally helps people in need.

The latter is a charitable organisation, however, 70 per cent of its money comes from the government (Doostgharin, 2002) (see Harris in this volume for an in-depth profile of charitable organisations in Iran).

The Ministry of Welfare and Social Security is responsible for the implementation of social welfare to a great degree and has a number of organisations to implement these duties at a variety of levels.

1. The State welfare organisation: deals with the different forms of insurance. The budget comes from insurance contributions.

2. The medical services insurance organisation: deals with medical insurance.

3. The civil servants pension organisation: deals with extending the pension insurance.

4. The social insurance corporation of villages and tribes: deals with

extending insurance to this group of citizens.

5. The rehabilitation and welfare organisation: deals with the underprivileged, destitute and disabled people (Doostgharin, 2010b).

Social welfare through the health care system

According to the Iranian Constitution and the *Social Welfare for Iran Within 20 Years Document*, all Iranian citizens have the right to access health care facilities (Doostgharin, 2010a; Hosseinpoor et al., 2007; Ministry of Health and Medical Education, 2005). This constitutional right has led to the improvement of the health network, which, it is claimed, covers the basic health care needs of 100% of the urban population and around 85% of the rural population (Hosseinpoor et al., 2007). Moreover, in Iran growth of the social services, educational opportunities and the establishment of the National Health Service have had positive impacts on the well-being of the nation (Doostgharin, 2010b).

The Ministry of Health and Medical Education is a regulatory body and mainly finances and delivers primary health care. Secondary and tertiary care systems are largely financed through the compulsory public sector and private insurance schemes (Hosseinpoor et al., 2007; World Health Organization-Country Office in I.R. Iran, 2004). General health and medical polices are made at a national level, but the facilities for delivering primary health care at district levels are localised (Hosseinpoor et al., 2007).

Whilst the private health sector plays an important role in the health care system in Iran, it has mainly been active in major cities, where it has a significant role in providing secondary and tertiary care, as well as drug distribution (Hosseinpoor et al., 2007; World Health Organisation-Country Office in I.R. Iran, 2004).

With regards to health insurance, there are three key health insurance bodies:

1. the Health Welfare Organization, which insures the formal sector employees, the self-employed and their dependents; and
2. the Armed Forces Medical Services Organisation, which covers members of the military and their dependents;
3. the Medical Service Insurance Organisation, which covers civil servants, rural households, and students.

The Iranian Government has made it a priority to increase its health insurance policy and to extend its benefits to those people living in remote rural areas (Hosseinpoor et al., 2007).

Redistribution of governmental assets and wealth amongst low-income groups

During the last four years the Iranian Government has initiated a plan to redistribute some of the governmental assets and wealth to low-income groups in the form of the shares. The main aim of this plan is to create social justice for those in low socioeconomic groups in society. In line with this aim, it is the government's intention to literally make many people owners of some assets, providing them with a long-term income and decreasing the dependency of these people on State hand-outs (see Harris and Messkoub in this volume for further references to this issue in Iran). In addition, the government wants to make its existing enterprises more competitive through privatisation, so that their activities can be more productive, reducing government involvement and the scale of service provision (see Messkoub on the pragmatic fiscal policies by Islamic States). According to government statistics as many as 60 per cent of Iranian people will receive some forms of shares. The first group of people covered by this plan were the most disadvantaged groups in society, including the clients of the Immdad Committee, service users of rehabilitation organisations and unemployed veterans of war. The second major group who have received shares were all people living in the rural areas. The plan has been extended to cover many more groups, including government employees and pensioners (Vase, 2010).

However, these shares are not free and the applicable groups need to pay for them. Having said that, the government has made it very easy for people to obtain them. They do not have to pay any money upfront to purchase them and will only pay the cost of them within ten years of being awarded. The instalment will be covered by the amount of gain that each share has achieved. For twenty per cent of the people who have the lowest income, there is a fifty per cent deduction of the share price (Vase, 2010).

As can be seen above, it will be a long term investment, so those applicable are more likely to gain from their shares in the future when they have paid off the full cost of each instalment. The amount of shares that each individual receives is very limited and the relevant income generated is not very significant. Furthermore, some shareholders will not gain any benefit at the end of some financial years. In such situations like this during the following year, if their shares make some gain, they must first pay for the previous year's payment which was not recovered from the gain of their shares in the past. At the present time, the shareholders are not allowed to sell their shares in any shape or form (Vase, 2010).

Social welfare through food provision

As mentioned above, according to Section 2 of the Iranian constitution and the *Social Welfare for Iran Within 20 Years Document*, the government must help mothers, particularly during pregnancy and child rearing. In 2007 the Iranian Government decided to tackle malnutrition in low-income families through food provision. For this reason, a committee was established within the Ministry of Welfare and Social Security, named the National Committee for Reducing Malnutrition of Families with Low Income (NCRMFLI). There are three main groups of service users who are covered by the duty of this committee:

1. Low-income pregnant women.
2. Rural children of 3-6 year of age who are in rural nurseries.
3. Families with a low income.

Food provision for low-income pregnant women

As part of this programme, the priorities are given to those low-income pregnant women who are mainly under the care of the Immdad committee or rehabilitation organisation. If a pregnant woman's Body Mass Index is very low and she is not gaining any weight during pregnancy, or weighs less than 45 kilograms, or is suffering from a severe major blood deficiency (anemia), she will be entitled to this provision. Each month such women will receive a basket of food worth about 150,000 Rial which is equivalent of $15 for one year along with the necessary vitamins and drug supplements. The programme starts when the mother is three months pregnant and continues for six months after the birth of the child. In addition, these women are required to take part in family planning classes after giving birth. They are obliged to follow the suggestions of the health professionals in regards to their health. Relevant women can only use these facilities once in their life time. Those families who comprise more than four people receive two baskets of food per month (NCRMFLI, 2010).

Food provision for children of 3-6 year of age who are in the rural nurseries

One course of warm food per day is provided for children of 3-6 year of age placed mainly in rural nurseries; this provision is designed to tackle malnutrition among such children. The aims of this programme are to improve their nutritional status; and to increase the awareness of these children and their families about the consumption of appropriately health foods through the running of different workshops (NCRMFLI, 2010). The evaluation of this programme, as reported by the Committee, shows a significant decrease (50%) in malnutrition of rural children after four years of programme implementation (NCRMFLI, 2010). However, although these kinds of provisions offer some useful support, the needs of these people far outstrip received provision.

Conclusions

As has been discussed, arguably the Council of Guardians ensures that all Iranian laws and policies are based on the Islamic values and principles. However, in practice how far these values and principles are implemented is another matter. On the whole, inequality and poverty have decreased in recent years in Iran. This confirms some gains in the quality of life for underprivileged people in terms of having access to basic services, such as electricity and clean water (Salehi-Isfahani, 2006). However, in comparison with many developed countries, Iran has still a long way to go.

In terms of the Iranian constitution and law, social welfare and welfare policies seem very promising, and appear to be based on Islamic principles, but in implementing them, there are numerous difficulties and barriers, which make it very difficult to put them into practice. One neglected area, which is the most important factor in the social welfare of the Iranian nation, is the issue of housing. Although, based on the Islamic principles, as adopted by the Iranian Constitution, it is the duty of the government to provide people with appropriate accommodation, there is very little provision in regards to housing. There is no universal housing benefit, for example. Only very few government organisations provide some form of accommodation for their employees. However, if someone is unemployed, there is almost no housing benefit for them. Only those who are extremely poor may receive a very small amount of help from charitable organisations, such as the Immdad Committee. Moreover, although this benefit is some help, it is far from able to meet all the needs of these families. Unemployment benefit, for example, is designed for those who had a job and contributed towards the unemployment insurance and then subsequently became unemployed. However, if an individual was not previously employed or has not contributed to social security insurance they will not receive unemployment benefit when they need it most.

As far as health care is concerned, whilst the health sector in Iran tends to provide equitable access to health services for different groups of people (Ministry of Health and Medical Education, 2005), regardless of its intended universal provision, in practice inequalities in health care between the different classes of people are vast.

5

Bearing witness:
Women in war-torn Afghanistan

Parin Dossa

Introduction

Trauma and human suffering have become a systemic part of our global reality. Yet it is shared unequally with the global South bearing the brunt of it. The global North, on the other hand, is the bearer of arms and humanitarian aid, a contradiction that is rarely brought to the surface. Our work as academics and readers is then cut out for us as we first need to explain this inequality. We have learnt that war results from the need on the part of the powerful nations to advance their economic and political interests. And that these interests are disguised under the banner of the white man's burden (colonial times) and the savior script (post-Cold War). Lulled into historical amnesia, we rarely receive the full picture. Violence in Iraq, Afghanistan or any other country in the South (it is invariably the South) is explained with reference to internal chaos and in-fighting. A case in point is the Taliban. Considered to bear the responsibility for the present-day violence in Afghanistan, the Taliban serves to subdue the causal links between the Cold War (1979-1989), the civil war (1991-1996), and the war on terror (2001– to date). It is the superpowers' war fought on the soil of Afghanistan that has made its streets and homes unsafe (see van Bijlert in this volume for further discussion of civil conflict and security issues in Afghanistan). It is important to note that violence does not rest at the level of physicality. It penetrates into the everyday lives of people forming an intricate web.[1]

As an anthropologist seeking to make a modest contribution to the body of literature on the 'ethnography of violence', I document the intricate ways in which violence weaves itself into the everyday lives of the people in Afghanistan.[2] At the same time I wish to make a case for witnessing, as opposed to merely observing suffering. I argue that the act of witnessing requires us not only to make the causal links between the local and the national/the global, but to identify how violence is woven into the everyday realities of people. This task is by no means simple as it calls for reversing the processes of political forgetting and historical amnesia deployed to maintain the status quo of stakeholders. I echo Lindqvist's comment:

> Everywhere in the world where knowledge is being suppressed, knowledge that, if it were made known, would shatter our image of the world and force us to question ourselves – everywhere there, *Heart of Darkness* being enacted. (Sanford 2006b:5)

In the case of violence on the scale experienced in Afghanistan and elsewhere in the South, it is time that we interrogate the world we live in.

Anthropologists have long asked the question: what makes us human? Conventionally, we focused on the diversity of peoples and cultures underpinned by our search for our common humanity. In the present times, this question is politicized. We pay greater attention to the fact that as human beings we are entitled to peace, shelter, food, access to medical and health services, and to a life of dignity lived in nurturing communities. Time and again we are reminded that a large number of people, especially in the South, are unable to attain what is basic to human life. The discrepancy is noteworthy. In one part of the world (the Occident), people consume coffee at the price of $2.00 or more; yet, in the East (the so called Orient), people are expected to survive on this rate per day.[3] Also, people from the South are on the move as a result of war, violence and suffering, an outcome of global geopolitics. While one may seek refuge in another country for a better life, this does not happen. Refugees and internally displaced persons are Othered, compromising their humanity. Public and media discourse suggests that displaced persons are undesirable because they disrupt our way of life: they take our jobs and (over)use our services, and on top of that they do not 'assimilate'. Though not part of the system, displaced persons are held responsible for its fault lines. People on the margins of society challenge our assumptions about life and take us out of our comfort zone. Their life experiences reveal uncharted territories that we do not wish to tread on. Furthermore, the sharp distinction between us and them creates a divided world, antithetical to nurturing a civil society. Global capitalism and U.S.-led militarization of our world are contributing factors in the displacement of people; this script has yet to be articulated in a manner whereby the North takes responsibility for rupturing the social fabric of the South, in alliance with the indigenous elite. It is then necessary to reverse the script of the west-as-the-saviour of the world because it masks the political agendas of stake holders. To secure the basic human rights, we need to work towards developing the script of entitlement that valorize the vision and aspirations of displaced persons. This is the new wave that critical anthropology seeks to address (For example, Dossa 2009, Sanford 2006[a]).

Ethnographic method lends itself to the concerns raised above. To begin with it captures the lived realities of people that otherwise go unnoticed. Here the mundane and the ordinary are given empirical and theoretical importance. In the case of violence - part of the weave of life – the method has assumed an ethical dimension of witnessing social suffering as opposed to mere observation. Here, we (the ethnographers) are obliged to establish and theorize connections between the local and the larger structures of power without diluting the former. Furthermore, the ethnography of violence must not lose site of the multiple ways in which survivors speak and remake their worlds. These aspects informed my research in Afghanistan (August-October 2008), part of a larger project on Afghan women at home and in the diaspora (Greater Vancouver and Pakistan).

This chapter is then divided as follows. I begin with my entry into the field site. My goal is to show how ethnographic research leads us into uncharted territories, salient among which is witnessing violence in the weave of life. In the second part I do a reading of the texts shared by women living in a shelter established by a German donor agency.[4] In the way of broader contextualisation, I include a discussion of two media documentaries. Also, I cite an example of a grassroot level initiative to make a case for witnessing at multiple sites. In conclusion, I argue that the story of the violence in the weave of life - gleaned through the ethnographic act of witnessing - must be told over and over again until it becomes part of our everyday vocabulary. I note the importance of discursive violence whose impact on the lived realities of people cannot be underestimated.

Entering the field

Since 9/11, the media has made its business to portray images and documentaries on Afghanistan on a daily basis. A closer look suggests one script: violence in Afghanistan is to be attributed to the Taliban and that military intervention will restore peace and introduce democracy to a country frozen by its backward culture.[5] In this scenario, the civilians encounter double-edged violence at a level that is difficult to imagine. Military tanks and helicopters loom large as you make your way into the city with its battered buildings, panhandling burqa-clad women and children working on the streets, anomalous sites. The visual physicality of violence contains another level: the intricate ways in which violence has become woven into the weave of life that escapes attention. The question of how to witness this deeper level of violence informed my research as I talked to dozens of women who worked with or were the recipients of services provided by donor-funded agencies (service organizations); women who had no access to services were also part of my research group. On my first day of research, I met the director of a service agency catering to children on the streets.[6] Our place of meeting and her matter-of-fact account on the work of the agency were telling; it was through this encounter that I began to understand how violence can penetrate the deep recesses of life.

Security is a huge concern in Afghanistan. Ironically, the military presence of the US and NATO has exasperated the situation, swelling the ranks of the insurgents/resistance fighters. My meeting with the director (Alaina) took place in the football field of a school, one of the few safe spaces for expatriates. While we had a designated space for ourselves, this is not the case with the Afghans. Walking or biking to work, the latter are vulnerable to bomb blasts or collateral damage. Unlike the expatriates (including myself) who travel in vans with a driver and a bodyguard, the civilians have no protection. Lives lost remain unnoticed and unrecorded in sharp contrast to the coverage given to an injury or a death of an expatriate. It was in this exclusionary and bounded space that Alaina relayed the story of her organization.

> 'It was the brain child of Kabir, an Afghan. As he went to work, he saw dozens of children working on the streets, selling water, plastic bags and food. He felt sad that these children did not have the opportunity for recreation. He approached a German agency and as the money required was not much, they agreed to fund the project. Gradually, it grew. Now we have four centers. Each center has 70 students who attend an accelerated learning program for half a day. The children must be under ten. The idea is to integrate them into regular schooling. You see they have missed the opportunity to go to school as they have to work on the streets to earn a daily wage of $1 or $2 for their impoverished families.'

The donor agency considers itself to be doing good work. They take pride in a few success stories such as girls going to school and boys moving ahead following their training. But we need to ask some hard questions. Why is it that so many children are working on the streets? It is indeed an anomaly. What about children who are not served by the agency, for example those who are over ten years old and others for whom there is no space? What is the family situation of these children? Why do they receive such little money after a hard day's work on the street in the hot sun or in the cold depending on the weather, notwithstanding the Kabul dust?[7] The response to these questions suggests gross inequality linked to the denigration of the lives of Afghans. Since the 1979 Soviet invasion of the country, Afghanistan has fought the wars of the superpowers. There is little regard for the lives of the people. As my participants informed me over and over again, their country has been destroyed and its people have been wounded. Children working on the streets for pittance to help their families put food on the table constitute a form of violence. It is woven into the fabric of their everyday lives where it remains hidden. The above extract brings home two points: violence entrenched in the deep recesses of everyday life is rendered invisible; without structural change, it will remain entrenched. For example, regardless of the number of children that the agency trains, there will be more children on the streets many of whom fall between the cracks.[8]

As we continued with our conversation, Alaina explained that the parents are reluctant to send their children to the agency's training program:

> as they are in the survival mode brought about by twenty eight years of conflict and destructiveness. They rely on their kids to bring whatever they can. There are 70,000 street children. Eighty percent of the people live on a dollar a day. Fifty percent of the kids work. We tell them [parents] 'we will provide your children with free lunch.' We explain to them the importance of education. We tell them that if their children are educated they will earn more. 'You are earning Afs. 50 now; in the future you will earn Afs. 2000.' You see, they do not think of the future. The mothers are illiterate and need to be educated. This is why we have a health program for mothers. Once a week they are required to attend our sessions.

Alaina has a good understanding of the embedded poverty the cause of which is prolonged war that uproots people and destroys lives. She realizes that her agency's work is limited to assisting a small number of children and their mothers. It does not have the capacity to effect structural change for the alleviation of poverty. Yet, she/the system deploys the saviour script assuming that Afghan's do not know any better and they have to be convinced to send their children to school. My conversations with

Afghan women revealed that they wanted nothing more than to send their children (including girls) to school. The donor agencies could initiate a conversation on the alleviation of poverty and concerns about security. But this is rarely the case. Their discourse reflects the international narrative with its omission of three points. First no mention is made of the fact that the suffering that the Afghans experience collectively is a result of the wars waged by the superpower in alliance with indigenous elite; second, there is no acknowledgement of the rich Afghan culture along with Afghan women's experiential knowledge of raising three to seven children (average). Third, it is eleven years since the 9/11 incident that led to the US-led invasion of Afghanistan. 'Remembering 9/11' has become an annual event. During this time we remember all those people who lost their lives in the attacks on U.S. soil. No mention is made of Afghans who have paid a heavy prize. Their lives do not count. This is a discursive form of violence, a subject to which I will return.

My entry into the field brought home how violence can become woven into the fabric of life at two levels, material and discursive. Ethnographic method lends itself to discerning these forms of violence as it compels us to look into the inner recesses of life and conduct a form of analysis to explain local realities in relation to the larger structures the impact of which cannot be underestimated. I continue to explore these themes in relation to the words and worlds of Afghan women.

Reading women's words

My multi-sited research in Kabul led me to women's shelter set up by a German agency. At its most basic, the shelter offers a safe space for battered women; owing to lack of resources it does not offer other services. Poorly funded agencies are largely the order of the day in Afghanistan. The shelter is not an exception. Women who had run away from their homes because of abuse were assured a safe space at a price; they were confined and were not allowed to go out on their own. Ironically this confinement won the approval of their families (natal and conjugal). The majority of the women planned to go back to their 'father's home' as they called it but under changed circumstances. In the words of one woman: 'because I was beaten so much in my husband's home my father said when you come back you can make your own decisions.' Inadvertently the shelter helped women to go back to their natal homes as their honor was preserved.

Of interest is the women's own take on their suffering that compelled them to take refuge in the shelter in the first place. Below I present their stories and validate their experiences that are otherwise dismissed by agencies as cultural pathology. The ethnographic project requires us to provide broader contextualisation for two reasons: to show the relationship between the lived realities and larger structures, and to ensure that women's words and worlds are taken note of in the interest of social justice. Our task therefore is to witness their stories

Zahra

> My life is bad. I was in a forced marriage with a paternal cousin. I have been married for three years. I am now waiting for my divorce. I am not happy with him. Paternal aunt is behaving badly towards me. After my marriage, she does not allow me to go to my parents. Better to be divorced. Husband is not happy with me. He is in love with somebody else. He says: 'Why did you come into my life?' We were in Iran for six years. Paternal aunt's husband came to the house. He forced my father. I was ten years old. Now I am thirteen years old. My husband is eighteen. Husband says until you get divorced, you must stay in the shelter. He will decide when he will grant me a divorce. Shelter is a safe and secure. No training is provided. We are counseled for good behavior. We are told to be patient and tolerant. No fighting.

A surface reading brings to the fore a script popularized by the international media. Zahra is an Afghan girl oppressed by her backward and barbaric culture. She is doubly victimized. She is forced into child marriage and then subject to domestic violence in the house of her in-laws. Her only way out is to seek the assistance of a foreign agency. In a country where community support has been eroded by prolonged war, the latter is constructed as 'only they can protect us from culture-based violence.' We need to acknowledge that if it was not for the shelter, 'preserving' the women's honor through confinement, familial doors (natal and conjugal) would have been shut. The women are not permitted to go out on their own. Being short of resources, not unlike other agencies, the shelter merely provides custodian care. There are no programs (especially skills development) to empower women. Out of fear of reprisal from conservative groups, the shelter advocates the status quo. It encourages women to go back to their families; in the words of one woman, 'be patient. Things will work themselves out'. The context of its work (material and discursive) is better understood through a reading of two documentaries *Afghanistan My Country* aired by BBC on August 18th and 19th 2009, respectively.

Documentaries

Feminized drug scene, the subject matter of the first documentary, portrays the lives of an addicted mother and her daughter. We are informed that there are one million addicts in Afghanistan, out of which one out of twelve are women. A problem of this magnitude calls for a structural solution, the starting point of which is identification of the root cause. In the not atypical mother-daughter case, it is unbearable suffering brought about by loss of husband, poverty and rupture of family and support system. At the risk of repetition, we need to continually emphasize the prolonged and ongoing war in the country. This reality of suffering however is not discussed. It is the pathologised images that register into our radar screens. Our hearts go out to the twelve-year old daughter, Gul Pari. To purchase drugs, she engages into the practice of pick pocketing. In response to the question as to whether she has been caught, she says: 'Yes. They let me go *because I am a child*' (italics added). If we were to put a context to this response, we would implicate the international community that fought its wars on Afghan soil and then abandoned the country. Its reoccupation post-9/11 is to wage yet another war: the war on terror. The majority of the funding (over ninety percent)[9] is spent on militarization that has given rise to increased resistance, categorized by outsiders as the 'resurgence of the Taliban'. The so-called humanitarian work has taken a back seat. The U.S. foreign policy, supported by the media, has put forward the rationale that militarization of Afghanistan will keep U.S. safe from further attacks. No mention is made of the safety and well being of the Afghans. The suffering caused to its people, the mainstay of which is drastic undermining of their livelihood, is not noted.

In the second part of the documentary we are taken to a rehabilitation centre where Gul Pari and her mother are admitted through the efforts of the film maker. The spotlight is on their non-compliance (they escaped and were then readmitted). A closer look reveals that the duration of the program is from one to three months, not sufficient for the purpose of rehabilitation. And second, its biomedical focus on the bodies and minds of people does not implicate the system. The onus is on the individual to get well.

Child marriage is the subject matter of the second documentary. The story line highlights extreme forms of abuse: forced marriage of girls to older men, spousal abuse and self-mutilation as the last resort of escape. At the burn unit, set up by the French charity, we are shown horrific scenes, captioned as: 'Disturbing. Viewer discretion is advised'. These are the scenes that call for an act of witnessing to collectively understand through history how such a situation can arise in any part of the world. Second, we need to take into account intersecting factors that give rise to gendered violence. The script of the interrelationship between class, poverty, displacement and patriarchal norms is yet to be articulated. Instead, our attention is drawn to the story line of the west-as-the-savior of the people of Afghanistan, evident in references such as 'Afghanistan is frozen into the dark ages, and that it has a barbaric culture'. We are also informed that the 'State' is lawless and corrupt; logically then it is not positioned to protect women. No mention is made of the fact that the Karzai regime was established by the international community with the drawing of the 2001 Bonn agreement. Covertly, the argument put forward is that U.S.-led 2001 military invasion and continuing occupation of the country is justified. The second part of the documentary covers conversations with the Ministry of Women's Affairs and other Afghan activists. They suggest women's education as the solution to their structural oppression. At the same time they highlight barriers such as security, distance requiring two-hour walk, and under-resourced schools (materials and teachers). They note that girls are not able to continue with their education because of the lack of colleges; existing ones are far away. Afghan activists implicate the international community for its inaction despite the fact that 'special funds are set up for women'. The documentary does not follow up on the suggestion of barrier-free education. Instead, the spotlight falls on 'the resurgence of the Taliban'. The latter is held responsible for its stance of opposing the education of girls and on the government, deemed to be weak and corrupt. The documentary ends with the comment: all the foreign aid given to the country along with the loss of the lives of British soldiers is wasted. The reader is left with the message that the West has done a lot for the people of Afghanistan; it is time that the Afghans 'got their act together'. Overlooked here is the fact that Afghanistan is an occupied country where suffering and injustice are the everyday realities of its people.

In the above discussion, I argue that it is necessary to bear witness to and interrogate the hegemonic narrative. This exercise requires delineating the causal linkages between the local, the national and the international. Only then can we witness the stories from the edges of society. We have a moral obligation to ensure that people's experiences of violence are not subdued by our analytical frameworks. In this vein, I continue to read women's stories from the shelter.

Mariyum

Mariyum began her story with the words: 'We are two sisters and two brothers, father and mother. We went to Pakistan. Father stayed in Ghazni [Afghanistan]'. This is not a mere demographic profile; it is politicized. Mariyum brings home the point that her once-intact family (father, mother and siblings) was split by war. When the father stayed behind in his home country to earn a living, he re-married. After a year, he brought the children from Pakistan. 'He was angry all the time and he started beating us. My grandmother took us back to Pakistan.' Meanwhile, the father entered into another relationship. The woman insisted that he give his daughter in marriage to her son or pay Afs. 300,000. The father complied with the first option. Mariyum was married at the age of eleven. 'For four months my mother-in-law kept me in the house, always beating me. I escaped from home and went to Kabul. I have been in this shelter for one and a half years'. The mother-in-law brought 'outside people to abuse me. I would shout. I did not allow them'. When she was asked to work in the house, Mariyum protested: 'I cannot do anything. I am a child.' Her twenty-five-year old husband has remarried.

Based on her grade ten education with some English, Mariyum teaches on a voluntary basis at the shelter. Her ambition is to become a doctor. She says: 'I have suffered enough. Society should help us to rebuild our lives, solve our problems and punish those who abuse us so that the abuse does not continue. Parents should be educated. In the Qur'an there is no discrimination between boys and girls. Girls have rights. They pray for everyone.' She continues: 'There has not been a happy moment in my life. Now I want to be away from problems. I do not want to marry again. I want to help other women who have suffered.'

There are two parts to the narrative. The story of abuse is of interest to the international media and donor agencies whose work rests on the narrative of the west-as-the-saviour of Afghan women. It is only by identifying a problem constituency that they can secure funding. This focus does not highlight the fact that domestic abuse is a function of structural factors (poverty, war, displacement, power). Also, by and large, the donor agencies do not take note of the absence of an infrastructure (legislation, support system, service programs and kinship networks) that could have protected Mariyum and other women in her situation. Emphasis on structural factors would compel a donor agency to adopt a different paradigm, one that would not exclusively attribute domestic violence to the patriarchal system. Moreover, it would take into account women's resilience and courage.

Mariyum is young and helpless; yet she frees herself from domestic abuse not underestimating structural constraints. By means of shouting she calls on the neighbors for moral support for the extreme abuse (prostituting her body). Her comment that she is only a child brings home the harsh reality of her life.

Narrative scholars have informed us that the moment we relate our experiences, we establish new contexts and reach out to new audiences (see Das 2007, Dossa 2005). By stating that she is only a child, Mariyum reaches out to society not just her in-law family. And the new audience is the researcher/reader. She challenges us to hear her story, not exclusively for the trope of resistance, but as witnesses: What do we do with the story once we have heard it? Mariyum leads the way. First, she shifts the story to a collective plane of 'we'. She does not only speak for herself but for the girls/women who are in her situation. She wants to become a doctor 'to help other women who have suffered'. She calls upon society to assist them (scarred girls/women) rebuild their lives and put an end to abuse. Consider the practical strategies that she puts forward: educating parents on the rights of the girl-child and learning the Quran's non-discriminatory stance towards women.

Mariyum's act of self-witnessing is nuanced and complex. She begins with her own story of abuse, not excluding the wider context of the rupture of her family life as a result of war. She highlights her acts of resistance and moves forward to alert society of its moral responsibility. She also makes practical suggestions as to how girls/women can rebuild their lives. But the shelter presents her as a victim a position that she must occupy for donor agencies to carry out their work. Women's unrealized rights provide justification for the military and 'humanitarian' intervention. Here we recall how the image of the burqa provided the rationale for the U.S.-led invasion of the country in 2001. The figure was prominently displayed during the August 2009 Afghan elections. The argument can be summarized as follows: Afghan women are oppressed and this is why the international community should assist them. The fact that not much has been done to reverse this structural oppressions (intersecting factors) remains unarticulated.

Khulsum

To relieve her father from poverty, Khulsum was promised in marriage to a fifty-year-old man when she was three months old. 'When it came time for marriage I refused. I took a knife and tried to kill myself. I stopped only because of my mother. She told my father not to do this. I would not be happy with him. He [father] did not listen. I ran away from home. I have been in the shelter for two and a half months. My father says I will kill you. Since I have come into this world, I have not had a happy moment. God should let you die.'

Khulsum went to school till grade five. Her education stopped when the Taliban came to power. She bemoans the fact that without education, she will not get a good job. She wants to change this. She is determined to study and establish a career. And she wants to marry the man she loves. 'Women should not be forced into marriage'.

This is a short but poignant account from a thirteen-year-old. Her childhood has been lost. Suffering has been her companion in life. Khulsum renders these experiences into a testimony that denounces violence and claims a future for herself and her peers as indicated in her closing remarks. A morally engaged ethnography of witnessing requires us to undertake a two-fold task: to validate and acknowledge her experiences keeping in mind that these are subdued in official narratives; and to delineate a broader context for envisioning a peaceful and a just society. Both aspects require reversing the historical and the political forgetting to identify the root causes of violence. Exploring its effects on the lived realities of people would be an important step that the participants have already undertaken. Khulsum explains her experiences of suffering with reference to the war (poverty equals forced marriage) and the Taliban (rupture of education) – structural factors. It is important to remind ourselves that the rise of the Taliban is not merely a local phenomenon; it is part of the global geopolitics. Khulsum's testimonial account (the context and the content) is an invitation to bear witness to her life and that of her peers.

Farida

Eighteen-year-old Farida yearned to get an education ever since she was young. She studied till grade eleven with great difficulty in the wake of her father's opposition. He disapproved of her goal to become a police officer.

She has sought refuge in the shelter: 'I feel that I cannot do anything right now. I am worried. I sleep most of the times. I don't know who I am. The shelter does not keep me busy. We are kept in a room and not allowed to go out. My father says, 'you make your own decisions. There is no place for you in our lives'. From the day I was born, I have not had good memories. I want to be a police officer so that I can help other women and girls.'

Farida's testimony is a plea for assistance, not as a victim but as someone who has endured suffering to achieve a service-oriented goal beyond gendered bounds. The image of a female police officer has not taken root in Afghanistan not because it is wrapped in the dark ages, as the official narrative would have it, but owing to structural factors. Farida and other women I conversed with highlighted the importance of education. They are held back not by tradition *per se*, but because of security, limited access to education, poverty and the lack of opportunities.

Farida's narrative then must not be read as a text but in the form of a life experience not uncommon for other women. The participants once again take the first step. Farida presents a narrative profile that contains juxtaposition of opposite worlds: suffering and efforts at relieving it; lost childhood and hope for the future. At the same time, there is no closure to her narrative. She is in a state of limbo. Her family has renounced her and the shelter does not offer her a future. She brings home the message of embodied violence.

Zahra

Zahra begins her story with a horrific event. She was kidnapped by the Taliban. She leaves it to the imagination of the reader to glean her experiences as a captive. She highlights two points: she was beaten and she escaped. But she does not have a home to go to. When she was three years old, she was separated from her mother. Her father abused her. She had complained to the police but they failed to protect her. 'My misery was made worse. I was locked in a room for one and a half years, tied up and beaten'. Zahra did not want to continue with her story. She showed us the scars in her body. 'I have been beaten too much. My whole body has scars and pain.' Zahra assumes the role of the wounded storyteller whereby her scars reveal how deeply violence is woven into her life.

The women have spoken. Starting with their personal experiences of violence in the weave of their lives, they touch on wider expanses: testimonial speaking, advocacy work, implicating the society and future plans. And they challenge us to witness their stories at two levels. To listen and validate their experiences and insights dismissed in the official narrative on the reconstruction of Afghanistan, and to weave their stories into wider contexts for progressive change. It is important to recognize indigenous initiatives governed by the need to weave a new tapestry where women's education and freedom from coercive practices (child marriage and domestic abuse) are salient. To complement what the women have said, I share the text from my interview (November 2nd, 2008) with Rahema, Minister of the Ministry of Women's Affairs.

Rahema

The Ministry of Women's Affairs is a constitutional body with no executive powers'. This means that it does not have the authority to implement programs and services that would benefit women. This constraint, however, is translated into activism on other fronts. First, the ministry has undertaken grass-root level mediation work involving husbands and fathers 'at the level of accountability. We challenge their behavior and encourage them to live peacefully.' Rahema noted that women face double victimization: they 'lack capacity and do not know what to do.' And second if 'we go through the judicial process it takes too long. Other problems exist in the system. There is corruption and women grow up without hope. They think what will be next. No job. No family. No support. They run away and the family shut the door. It is best that we work at the village and district level. We use traditional dispute mechanism. The *jirgas* [council for discussion] have power in the community. But we need to be careful. Women do not have a voice. They are victims of violence.

Rahema's comments on gender-based issues bring home structural factors. She feels that women are not given the opportunity to study. But she does not attribute this to tradition. She notes how women do not have access to schools either because of distance or there are no opportunities for further studies because of lack of secondary schools. She is concerned about security. 'You do not expect women to walk for hours to reach a school. With no other outlet, they are trapped in a marriage. This is the whole cycle of a girl.'

There are good stories too. There are some parents who give good education to their daughters. If you go deep into their lives, you will know how much discrimination they face. Poverty is the root cause of all the problems. And there is the culture of violence for thirty years. A little child is exposed to violent behavior. The whole environment is affected by war. People are shouting and beating each other. War has played a very significant role in introducing a violent culture. Also, there is lack of education, lack of services; there are no roads, no infrastructure and no jobs. Health and education are not for everyone.

We are trying to change their behavior. We emphasize the Islamic ways. We share references from the Qur'an. We tell them about the practice of Prophet Mohammed. We challenge the wrong interpretations that the community has. We need to find ways to challenge [not do it in a way that alienates the community]. We also let them know that we know Islam. If they use Islam to approve violence, we can also use Islam as a tool to decrease violence. We use the community level and the government level. We push the international communities. We remind them of the human rights treaties. Afghanistan has a constitution. They [the international community] have obligations. We work at the village level. We conduct workshops with the help of a volunteer. We invite *Mullah's* (religious figure) wife at women's gatherings. We influence people in the community. We work in three different phases. We first identify the problem. Second, we come up with a simple action plan. We talk about the harmful effects of child marriage. We present cases from the Qur'an. We tell them that if the girls do not get an education, what would be there future and the future of the village. Third, we facilitate the discussion in various places: home, school and meetings. And then we report back.

They were going to marry an eleven-year-old girl. Volunteers talked to both the families. The marriage was stopped. So we sensitize the community to reduce harm done to women and we encourage them to live peacefully. They must learn to respect the dignity of women and other minorities. We will go step by step. It is a slow process. Mullah started to change with his own daughter. We work with them using their channel of communication. We start at the bottom and then we expand. Good examples can be duplicated. We are lobbying with the government to revise marriage contract and family law. We have to do awareness-raising.

The main issue is that of livelihood and lack of resources, resulting in lack of capacities for action.

Referring to the unequal distribution of resources, Lindqvist notes:

Throughout this century, it has been clear that the standard of living enjoyed in industrial countries cannot be extended to the world's population. We have created a way of life that must always be limited to a few. These few can make up a broad middle class in a few countries and a small upper class in the rest. The members know each other by their buying power. They have a common interest in preserving their privileges, by force if necessary. They too, are born of violence (Sanford, 2006[b], 5-6).

In this schema, Afghanistan occupies the lower echelons. The country has been short changed by the international community. This does not absolve Afghan leadership and insurgents who have also perpetuated violence (includes structural) to advance their own interests. But the people of Afghanistan have not been rendered passive. Note how Rahima brings to the fore the civil spaces and suggests its reconfiguration for grater inclusion of women. Recognizing the slowness of the judicial system, she calls for family mediation, a delicate space as it is also a site where women in her words are 'discriminated'. She feels that through example such as that of the Mullah's wife and daughter, we can advance the cause of women. She also advocates re-reading the Qur'an to highlight women's rights. She desires to work within the *jirga* system while recognizing that its exclusion of women must be reversed.

She focuses on women's education, prioritizing the issue of access and lack of infrastructure. She links familial violence to the culture of violence the root cause of which is prolonged war. These observations fly in the face of the global narrative where Afghan women are deemed to be oppressed because of misogynous orientations. She reprimands the international community for not meeting its obligations towards Afghan women. Her pedagogy of working towards an expansive space is of value. This is reminiscent of the community-based approach that is gaining ground in the in the west; its long-standing existence in other parts of the world remains unrecognized. Note Rahima's three-fold approach to a problem: identifying it, taking action and discussion and reporting.

Straddling the boundaries between governance from the top (the Ministry), and the village and district level, Rahima's work is groundbreaking for a country with minimal infrastructure. Nation-states fail to deliver services to the vulnerable constituents except in the way of 'charity' rather than entitlement. In the case of Afghanistan, it is the US and its allies that have been instrumental in the formation of the nation-state, also funding its skeleton infrastructure. The foreign powers, including the International NGOs, do not attempt to capture nuanced grass-root level understanding of issues. While they may desire to acquire in-depth knowledge, their efforts are stalled by the official and hegemonic narrative of 'the backward and violent culture of Afghanistan'. They also do not acknowledge that they are implicated for 'destroying the country and wounding its people' (Dossa 2005). Furthermore, their paradigms rarely include indigenous ways of life. It is in this context that Rahima's work along with the initiatives (practical and discursive) taken by the women assumes significance.

In a situation of war and violence, Zarowsky (2004) emphasizes the need to tell the story straight from the heart. This is part of what I have endeavored to do. At the cost of repetition and what may appear to be an exaggeration, I have felt it necessary to bring home the reality faced by the people of Afghanistan. If I have kept in the forefront the official narrative, it is to bring home the message echoed by writers such as Johnson and Leslie (2004). They make three points. First, the impact of decades of war needs greater emphasis.

> The lives of Afghans changed dramatically during this period [1979 Soviet invasion to 2001 U.S.-led invasion]. Those who had always been poor, war pushed them to the edge of survival. Many of the urban middle classes were reduced to poverty, while others went into exile. There were also, of course, those who got rich on the spoils of war' (ibid, x). Second, '[t]he West has often seen Afghans as a war-like and exotic people, sifting its perceptions through the lens of its own world view. (ibid)

Third, the international community has failed Afghanistan. The aid promised to Afghanistan at various stages has not come through. I would add that the minimal amount injected into the country, compared with the military budget, is spent in a fragmented way, each agency doing its work under constraints but all adopting the west-as-savior script that undermines the dignity and humanity of women (and men) in Afghanistan. The ethnographic take is to take these narrative scripts further to show their impact in the weave of life, taking the form of nothing less than material and discursive violence. It is this level that we can engage into the act of witnessing violence.

Witnessing violence

In this chapter, I have explored violence at a deeper level to show how it becomes woven into the lives of people. I have suggested that the new wave of ethnography with its emphasis on engaged participation makes it possible for us to witness what we see, hear, and learn from the field. The act of witnessing requires delineating larger discursive and empirical contexts. I have alluded to the latter with reference to the recent history of Afghanistan. The story line is that for the last three decades the country has been subject to occupation and foreign interventions to the extent that the people of Afghanistan do not run their own affairs. Furthermore, their capacity for governance is undermined by lack of infrastructure and erosion of livelihood (for example, Kandiyoti 2005, Rubin 2000).

What is more difficult to access is the discursive context whose impact on the lives of the Afghans must be underscored. I want to begin by acknowledging the work of Edward Said. In *Orientalism* (1978) and *The Question of Palestine* (1979), Said bring home the power of ideas and discourses, respectively. He argues that the East is the creation of the West molding it in the image that it desires. The issue is not that of mere talk about the eastern world as inferior and backward compared with its counterpart: the civilized West. The image of the East, is, in fact, entrenched and kept alive in the West through it institutions (the mass media, academia, in policy and the public discourse) all of which coalesce to create a hegemonic narrative. This narrative, I argue with Said, suppresses other scripts in the interest of the colonial project. The power of this discourse is evident in the way in which it creates particular realities for example that the colonized territories were empty spaces waiting to be developed by the civilized West, and that its people had to be rescued from an unproductive and wasteful life and brought into the civilized world, defined according to the western criteria.

Militarization of their country is the harsh reality that Afghans encounter in their daily lives as they go about their business: work, shopping, school, celebration of weddings and festivals, or queuing for casual work in the cities.[10] This is not the end of the story. There are two other layers that engaged ethnography can help to identify. The first one concerns the impact of militarization on the everyday lives of people. Children do not feel safe walking to school, women are socially confined; militarization breeds a culture of violence that penetrates into the domestic sphere as noted earlier. This form of violence is rendered invisible as it is not given public acknowledgement. Woven into the fabric of social life, it does not form the subject matter of conversation among stakeholders. Second is the discursive level. Forms of violence that Afghan women (and men) experience are not given recognition because they are the Other. The security of the United States and the West is cited as the rationale for the militarization of Afghanistan. There is barely any space given to the suffering and violence that the Afghan people experience. They are socially non-existent.[11] Ethnography of witnessing makes it possible for us to understand violence in the weave of life.

Acknowledgments

I am indebted to the women who participated in the study. They were most gracious and generous with their time. Thank you to Yalda Noori for her assistance in translation from Dari to English. The research was funded by Social Science Humanities Research Council of Canada, Strategic Research Grant.

Notes

1. For background information, refer to Cooley (19991), Dupree (1997), Ghafour (2007), Goodson (2001), Johnson, C & Leslie, J. (2004), Kandiyoti (2005), Khan (nd.), Mamdani (2004), Saikal (2006).
2. Das (2003, 2007), Nordstrom (2004), Sanford & Angel-Ajani (2006) and Scheper-Hughes (1992), Sanford (2006a) Thobani (2003) are the forerunners of the growing literature on the ethnography of violence.
3. In the case of Afghanistan, Rubin (2000) notes that the daily calories supply per capita is 1,523 compared with 3,108 in Industrial countries.
4. All the names have been changed. My contact with the participants was established initially through international donor agencies along with my research assistant. My methodology was context specific depending on the comfort of the women: semi-structured interviews, conversations and participant observations were salient.
5. This script is portrayed in different ways. But the underlying message remains the same. Not a single day goes by when Afghanistan is not in the news. Despite this voluminous coverage, there is historical amnesia. The starting point is the Taliban as if Afghanistan has not had any history prior to this regime. If the recent history of Afghanistan is taken into account, the international community (read superpowers) would be implicated.
6. This meeting was arranged prior to my visit to Afghanistan. Given the relatively short period of my research, I had established prior contacts with

over a dozen aid organizations.

7. Kabul is famous for its dust. It is everywhere: roads, building, homes. To some extent, it presence can be attributed to the destruction caused by decades of war. The infrastructure that would take care of the dust, roads and social services are barely in existence.

8. Every day as I went to different districts in the city of Kabul, I came across panhandling burqa-clad women. They had become part of the city landscape. I did not see the women as pathetic beings. Their bodies symbolized the violence inflicted on them by society and their presence pointed to the political body that had failed them.

9. Sanford (2006[b]), Khan (nd.), Kandiyoti (2005), Moyo (2009).

10. See Johnson & Leslie (2004) for a good discussion of the current situation in Afghanistan.

11. Lest this is considered as an exaggeration, refer to E. Said (1979), *The Question of Palestine*. Said argues that the dehumanization of the people of Palestine through discourse has rendered them socially non-existent. In such a situation, people are easily subject to human rights violations. A similar scenario prevails in the case of Afghanistan. In the eyes of the international community, their lives are dismissed as less worthy as they have not stepped into the civilized world.

6

The Islamic resurgence in Malaysia and the implications for multiculturalism

Hew Cheng Sim and Sara Ashencaen Crabtree

Introduction

Malaysia has long promoted itself to the external world as a country at harmony with its multicultural heritage, and where, despite the State religion being Islam (Neo, 2006), other faiths are both well tolerated and accepted. So effective has been this message that Malaysia has often been regarded as an example of how the tensions of multiculturalism that exist elsewhere, and in particular in the West, as well as other developing nations, have been negotiated and accommodated in this youthful and energetic, industrialised Asian society (Balasubramaniam, 2006). Thus, in addition to its great natural beauties, the captivating mix of the hyper-modern and the eclectic traditional, together with the genuine charm and friendliness of local people, has ensured that Malaysia has become a very popular tourist destination.

The administration and rhetoric of Malaysia's charismatic and outspoken former Prime Minister, Datuk Seri Dr. Mahathir, demonstrated that Malaysia was to be regarded as a serious contender at the table of world politics; as well as economically: being a member of one of the 'Asian tiger' economies (Walker and Wong, 2005). The ills, corruption and general degeneracy of the symbolic West (including the UK as the former colonial master; the USA and Australia) was an oft-used motif in the Government's rhetoric, where stark comparisons were drawn between those countries and Malaysia, described as guided by so-called 'Asian values'. These values were constructed in Malaysia to reflect a fusion of Minimal State discourses,

Confucian principles and Muslim ethos, which, taken together, were by no means inappropriate given the national, polymorphous context. (Ashencaen Crabtree, 1999; Camroux, 1996). To underline the policy rhetoric viewing the West as morally and conceptually bankrupt, the Mahathir Administration promoted the 'Look East Policy', touting Japan and South Korea, as Asian nations worthy of emulation, in terms of work ethic and productivity, while overtly ignoring Malaysia's immediate and conspicuously successful 'tiger' neighbours: Singapore, Hong Kong and Taiwan (Case, 2000; Mauzy and Milne, 1983-1984).

This calculated snub carried both historical and 'racial' resonances in reference to the divergence between Singapore and the Federation in the 1960s (Liu et al., 2002), but also relating to the unavoidable fact that these are ethnic Chinese-dominated societies. Thus, the 'Look East Policy' sent a clear message of devaluing the Chinese contribution to developments in Southeast Asia to audiences regionally and at 'home', where the Chinese make up over 30% of the overall population (Camroux, 1996). Furthermore, this message could also be construed as overladen with historical and 'race'/ethnic overtones, in that the Japanese invasion across Asia during World War II had dealt unevenly with occupied populations. In Malaysia the Chinese had received brutal treatment at the hands of the Japanese, commensurate with the latter's notorious abuses in mainland China. However, the Malay population had received far more lenient treatment, were largely left unmolested and even promoted into administrative and paramilitary systems (Tan, 2001; Case, 2000).

With the defeat of Imperial Japan, the post-war years saw the temporary return of the colonial authorities to Malaya, but with the acceptance that the country would step towards an independent future and the sole management of its multicultural population, away from imperial British, paternalistic control. One of the primary concerns of the British government related to how the new Federation would manage its diverse ethnic population, made up of indigenous peoples and sojourner-turned-settlers (Tan, 2001). These negotiations proved difficult. Historically the British in Malaya had not attempted to overthrow the rule of the Malay sultans. Instead, they had expediently avoided challenging their status, preferring instead to use their influence over these leaders to advise on matters of local governance.

The British negotiating position in the move towards Independence, would hinge on the issue of establishing equal status and rights across 'race'/ethnic divides by giving full citizenship to the Chinese, which had been hitherto denied (Case 2000). In 1946 under the Malayan Union idea equal citizenship rights and dual citizenship were therefore proposed by the colonial authorities (Tan, 2001: 956). However, the Malayan Union was destined to be stillborn and its founding principles abandoned, since the birthright prerogatives of the Malay aristocracy and their own ethnic communities were so clearly threatened. The proposal was therefore energetically resisted. Accordingly under the newly formed United Malays National Organisation (UMNO) the colonial authorities were forced to accept the continuing status quo of Malay privilege (Case 2000).

Insurgency in the Malayan Communist Party in 1948 forced the five-year state of Emergency, where the country was placed under colonial martial law. Neo (2006: 98) claims that this insurgency was not driven specifically by 'ethnic imperatives'; however, Case (2000) argues that the disaffection by local Chinese communities owing to Malay resistance towards the Malayan Union principles initially added fuel. Ultimately, however, the internecine conflict between different ethnic communities was subject to a truce in order to tackle the threatened communist takeover.

Independence was finally achieved in 1957 in an amiable, peaceful manner, which had been the general characteristic of colonial rule in Malaya (Nah, 2003; Case 2000); leading the 'Father of Independence' Prime Minister, Tunku Abdul Rahman, to bask in civil calm, and declare himself 'the happiest prime minister in the world' (Case, 2000: 136). In 1963 the former Crown colony of Singapore joined the Federation of Malaya. According to Case (2000), the influx of ethnic Chinese brought in through the merger caused resentment among the Malays, thus necessitating the later acquisition of Sarawak and Sabah in 1963, to dilute this provocative ethnic ratio by greater numbers of indigenous populations. However, the Borneo States were only prepared to accede to the Federation after negotiating crucial terms with regards to the status of their indigenous natives in the newly welded country, now renamed Malaysia (Kheng, 2003).

Nonetheless, despite having been granted autonomy in internal governance, relations with Singapore were to be by no means easy. This was exacerbated by public riots when Singapore's elected leader, Lee Kuan Yew, refused to adhere to the policy of granting Malay privilege to its local population, 'arguing for a non-discriminatory, multi-ethnic society' (Liu et al., 2002: 7). Political tensions continued, until Singapore finally achieved full independence from Malaysia to form its own republic when it was duly expelled by Tunku Abdul Rahman from the Federation in 1963 (Stivens, 2010).

Political ferment in Peninsular Malaysia permeated ethnic relations, lighting the fuse for the subsequent explosion of the race riots of 1969, when the political coalition between the dominant UMNO and its lesser allies, the

Malaysian Chinese Association (MCA), performed poorly in the elections as many in the Malay community cast their vote in favour of the *Party Islam se-Malaysia* (PAS) (Pan-Malaysian Islamic Party) (Tan, 2001; Case 2000). In an atmosphere that was, to quote Guan (2000: 17), 'exceptionally racially charged', and despite claims of evidence to the contrary, the Chinese were accused by extremists in the Malay community of having abandoned their allegiance to the UMNO-MCA Alliance (Balasubramaniam, 2006: 76). Tensions escalated dramatically and the resulting riots rapidly fanned out from the capital city, Kuala Lumpur, resulting in thousands of deaths in the notorious 'May 13th incident', and the placing of the country once again under military law and order. Following the riots Tun Abdul Razak took power over the country from the Tunku (Case, 2000). The defection of Malay voters to PAS was reflected on and concluded to be a manifestation of an upsurge of Malay Nationalist feeling, which UMNO would also need to address. Thus UMNO's position was considerably strengthened within the metamorphosis that turned the Alliance into the powerful *Barisan National* (National Front) (Case 2000). From this elevated position of strength, UMNO initiated the New Economic Policy (NEP), which would serve to intensify Malaysia's ethnic woes, as will be discussed later in the chapter.

Race and ethnicity in the modern nation state

The contentious issue of 'race'/ethnicity has always provided the foreground for the formulation of politics in Malaysia. It has also carried deep historical resonances in relation to the country's colonial past, as well as having been usefully exploited in the post-colonial era.

The assumption of ethnic prerogative in Malaysia pivots on the issue of indigenous rights of native people, as opposed to any claims made by settlers groups, such as the Chinese and Indian communities. The arrival of these latter groups are firmly located in the colonial past, where the British authorities both in the peninsula and separately in the Borneo States, governed by the Brooke dynasty (the 'White Rajahs') in Sarawak and the British North Borneo Company in Sabah, encouraged an influx of such migrants. These were used to cheaply fill a skills vacuum in the mining and plantation industries, as well as in mercantile activities (Baba, 2011; Stark, 2006; Tan, 2001). The huge diversity of ethnic groups in the Malay archipelago, coupled with the Victorian preoccupation with taxonomy, manifested in both sound and pseudo science, encouraged the various colonial authorities to develop classifications based on race (Baba et al, 2011). At the same time, there was a deepening awareness that the rights of indigenous people would need safeguarding to avoid encroachment on traditional lifestyles by opportunistic sojourners keen to make their mark (Chua, 2007). Over a relatively short period of time the sojourners would establish themselves as permanent settlers and subsequently citizens, making a conspicuous contribution to the development of the region, as had been the intention of the colonial authorities (Tan, 2001). A feature of the colonial period in Malaysia related to the non-interventionist approach adopted, enabling ethnic groups to enjoy equal access to public spaces and to engage in cultural practices (Guan 2000). By contrast Guan notes that the struggle to impose Malay cultural forms in the social and civic sphere in postcolonial Malaya could only be achieved by suppressing those of other ethnic groups.

Consequently with the departure of the British and the rise of modern Malaysia the issue of racial demarcation did not disappear, but on the contrary was enshrined constitutionally through the concept of *bangsa* (race/ethnicity). This served to formally demarcate ethnic boundaries between the indigenous *bumiputra* (sons-of-the soil), which included Malays, Dayaks in Sarawak and the Kadazan-Dusun and others in Sabah, and the Orang Asli in the peninsula. However, it also served as a moral imperative to soothe the collective Malay 'experience of personal and collective disrespect', which demanded restitution through pre-eminence (Guan, 2000: 16).

The constitutional bargain

With the Malayan Union proposal jettisoned in the struggle towards confirming bumiputra privileges, a political bargaining point would be reached with the non-bumiputra residents of Malaysia. The Chinese and Indian population would make substantial concessions in several key areas in order to maintain certain prerogatives in their adoptive country. These concessions enabled the Malay aristocracy to retain their privileges; Islam would be the State religion, *Bahasa Malayu* (the Malay language) would be the national language, and that land would be reserved for the bumiputras, along with a raft of other privileges in relation to education, public service and other opportunities (Tan, 2001). In return, freedom to pursue their financial ends would not be constrained among the non-bumiputras; with a key point being that the privileging of the bumiputra was a finite concession in terms of duration (Neo, 2006).

Crudely therefore non-bumiputras were asked to cede their attempts to gain citizen parity by trading the crucial political clout held unyieldingly by the Malay elite, along with accepting an affirmative action policy targeting the bumiputra, for the right to pursue economic self interest. This constitutional bargain is one that Tan (2001) describes as ultimately 'Faustian'. Thus, the Chinese, Indian, Eurasian and all other non-bumiputra communities in the new Federation would need to accept a highly qualified citizen status; yet among the category of bumiputra, alpha citizenship would also prove stratified.

The New Economic Policy (NEP) and its aftermath

After the racial riots of 1969, the New Economic Policy (NEP) was effected in order to narrow economic disparities between the different ethnic groups in Malaysia and in this way to strengthen unity amongst its people. The twin objectives of eradication of poverty regardless of ethnicity, and the elimination of the identification of ethnicity with occupation were largely achieved by affirmative action. *Bumiputra* participation in the urban sectors of employment was to be increased commensurate with their population, and their share of capital in the corporate sector was targeted to increase to 30%. The NEP was to be implemented via four 5-year Malaysian Plans (over a time-frame of 20 years) focusing on industrialization, urbanization and education starting from 1970. Affirmative action for the *bumiputra* with respect to special quotas for entry into public universities, award of government scholarships and recruitment into civil service was the order of the day. This, according to Lee (2005: 212), was not social policy that was subject to open debate and possible dissent, as 'punitive laws', such as the Internal Security Art and the Sedition Act, were duly used to enforce public compliance. The NEP thus served to reinforce the sense of birth-right entitlement among the Malay community in particular (Neo, 2006).

By 1990, the objectives of the NEP were largely achieved through impressive economic growth and substantial public expenditure. Poverty declined from 49 per cent in 1970 to 16 per cent in 1990. The occupational structure was transformed and the *bumiputra* share of the eight highest paying professions (doctors, lawyers, engineers, dentists, accountants, surveyors, architects, veterinary surgeons) rose from six per cent in 1970 to 29 per cent in 1990. With the exception of agriculture and the civil service, which was *bumiputra* dominated, and wholesale and retail trade, which was Chinese dominated, it can be said that occupation and economic activity can no longer be identified solely by ethnicity. *Bumiputra* corporate equity share also increased from 2.5 per cent in 1970 to 30 per cent in 1990 (Jomo, 1994).

Despite these huge gains, there were many downsides to the NEP. Poverty reduction, although good, was achieved at the expense of a more equitable distribution of resources. For example, wealthy fishermen who owned bigger, high-powered boats were able to tap into bigger government diesel subsidies. Similarly, affluent farmers with larger acreages of land were better able to benefit from fertilizer subsidies. In other words, blanket subsidies benefitted the rich over the poor. To make matters worse, State expenditure on poverty eradication was used by politicians in the ruling coalition to benefit their own constituencies. This is particularly acute in Sarawak where the euphemism 'politics of development' is used to describe such patronage. There were also complaints that there was an ethnic bias in poverty eradication. It was merely poverty eradication of the Malays in Peninsula Malaysia and not an exercise regardless of race as originally touted. Poverty-stricken Indians in rubber plantations, poor Chinese in land-starved new villages, the Orang Asli in Peninsula Malaysia and the non-Muslim *bumiputra* in Sarawak and Sabah were all neglected in the poverty eradication programmes. In fact, the non-Muslim *bumiputra* in Sarawak and Sabah argued that they were in-fact second class *bumiputra* in comparison to the Malay *bumiputra* in Peninsula Malaysia.

Although the racial concept of *bangsa* was combined with indigenous birthright and political and affirmative action privileges, this is open to being problematised. The notion of equality is one that is highly disputed in contemporary Malaysia as is the self-representation of the Malay 'new self' (Nah, 2003: 513). Chua (2007) notes the tension for Bidayuh Dayaks (bumiputras) of Sarawak, pulled as they are between adherence to the traditional cultural knowledge and practices that define the construction of Bidayuh being, and the pull towards the *dunia moden* (modern Malaysia) where to 'get on in life' requires adopting a Malay Muslim identity and practices, which are seen as incompatible with their own, traditional one.

The 'new self' concept in modern Malaysia, hinges on indigenous rights, yet the Malay archipelago has historically been the crossroads, commercial, cultural and religious, for many ethnic groups over time. Nah (2003), for example, records how ferociously the Malay invaders oppressed and enslaved the aboriginal groups that today are now conflated to make up the Orang Asli, and who at that time had no recourse but to petition the colonial authorities for protection.

Although the category of 'bumiputra' appears to support the notion of a flattened hierarchy of privilege across the board, it is evident that this is far from being the case, particularly when we learn that the right to reservation land of indigenous people in Malaysia is not alienable; a matter of concern where rights to practise traditional life are integrally tied to rights to the land itself (Sharom, 2006). In Sabah, Doolittle (2007) observes a continuation of the unresolved colonial complexities of attempting to construct compromises towards imposed private ownership of land - and respecting cultural practices in relation to indigenous claims. The implementation of the NEP, it is argued, has served to further wrest control of native land from indigenous (bumiputra) peoples, like the Dusun, for profitable businesses, like logging. Here, as in Sarawak, 'crony capitalism' is conducted in alliances between the new wealthy business classes and politicians (Doolittle, 2007:478).

The restructuring of ethnic identification with occupation has been ethnically exclusive, for Malays enjoyed affirmative action in order to boost their numbers in areas where they were under represented. However, there was no similar action to increase Chinese participation in the civil service, nursing, police or military. Raising the question by Quek (2006):

> Why has there been a virtual monopoly by one race - numerically as a whole as well as in the top hierarchy – of the public sector, namely, the army, police, civil service, judiciary, public universities, semi- and quasi-government bodies, and government-controlled financial institutions and enterprises?'

Over 90% of the civil service, police, military, university lecturers and overseas diplomatic staff are Malay (Malott, 2011). The *bumiputra* quota for entry into public universities also saw their overwhelming presence in Malaysian campuses. As Jomo (1994) pointed out, there is now over-representation of Malays throughout the education system in comparison to the population ratio. *Bumiputra* privileges extend beyond recruitment into the civil service, military and police, corporate equity and university places. In the housing market, there is a quota for *bumiputra* purchasers who can obtain housing loans at a preferential rate. In other words, the social and economic welfare of the Malays took precedent over all the other ethnic groups, causing much resentment and dissatisfaction.

As a result, ethnic polarization has become worse than it was before 1970. Predictably the status quo has led to a 'brain drain' of Chinese and other non-*bumiputra* who have obtained an international education. The country has haemorrhaged talented human resource to the rate of half a million Malaysian émigrés between 2007-2009. John Malott, the US Ambassador to Malaysia 1995-1998 reported that those who emigrate were mostly

... skilled ethnic Chinese and Indian Malaysians, tired of being treated as second-class citizens in their own country and denied the opportunity to compete on a level playing field, whether in education, business, or government. (Malott, 2011: 2)

The regional grievances of Sarawak and Sabah were even more acute. The NEP was formulated as a result of the ethnic riots in Peninsula and hence did not take into account the specific needs of the Borneon States. The NEP was drafted without consultation with Sarawak and Sabah, resulting in the non-Muslim *bumiputra* in these States feeling clearly marginalized and alienated. In 1993, at the end of the twenty-year period of the NEP's implementation, the official incidence of poverty was 10.5% in Peninsular, 19.1 per cent in Sarawak, but was a staggering 33.2% in Sabah (Wee, 1995). However, the poverty rate in Sarawak eventually dropped to 5.8% in 2002. Amongst the bumiputra, the highest poverty rate was amongst the Iban at 10.5%. More alarming, in the year 2000, 17% of Sarawakians aged 6-years-old and above did not attend school at all when the national average was only 10% (Thien, 2004).

When the Federation was formed in 1963, Peninsula Malaysia and the two Borneon States of Sarawak and Sabah were seen as three equal partners but the treatment received by the Sarawak and Sabah relegated them to being a mere two States amongst thirteen others. Sarawak has rich oil reserves, the exploitation of which is left in the hands of the Federal-owned company, PETRONAS. The State gets only 5% in petroleum royalty and therefore there is a net transfer of funds from Sarawak into federal coffers. PETRONAS' appropriation of State oil revenues is a source of perpetual irritation in Federal-State relations, as perceived by ordinary Sarawakians, who remark on these practises and how far the goal posts have changed since joining the Federation. The economic growth of Sarawak and Sabah are mainly based on the exploitation of timber (now almost exhausted) and oil. The manufacturing sector in these States is weak and their economies are less diversified. Employment opportunities are fewer and additionally average household incomes are lower than in the Peninsula, while the incidence of poverty is, to reiterate, higher. It is therefore not surprising that both Sarawak and Sabah have a higher incidence of the 'diseases of underdevelopment' such as malnutrition amongst children and diseases caused by poor sanitation (Wee, 1995: 11).

The NEP's duration was initially presented as having a finite 20-year life span, terminating in 1990. Regardless of this agreement the NEP continued under the guise of a new policy known as the National Development Policy (NDP), albeit with some tweaking. The blanket subsidies for petrol, diesel, fertilizers and the like were gradually withdrawn and government assistance is now targeted at the hard-core poor. In order to release the pressure of limited public university admission of non-*bumiputra* students, the Government allowed the setting up of private institutions of higher learning. In 2002, the government also gave the non-*bumiputra* a nominal 10% for entry into the Malay preserve of government residential colleges. Foreign universities, like Monash University, Australia and University of Nottingham, UK, set up branch campuses in Malaysia and many others have twinning programmes for their undergraduate studies. This has led to a dual stream of higher education running parallel to each other - the publicly-funded universities, dominated by *bumiputra*, and the private-sector universities, dominated by non-*bumiputra*.

However, the policy of 30% *bumiputra* equity in corporate stocks is still firmly in place, although independent studies have shown that the target has long been achieved (Beh, 2006). The Government's argument is that the *bumiputra* share of corporate shares is only 18.9% and this has remained stagnant. Hence the preferential policies of the NEP have to be in place till 2020 (ibid). Critics have argued that the NEP has by and large served its purpose of nurturing a strong Malay middle class. The continuation of these policies would only exacerbate a rent-seeking attitude towards the non-bumiputra communities (Ong, 2006). For instance, the approved permit system to import cars meant only for *bumiputra* entrepreneurs have resulted in a monopoly by the politically well-connected few. As an opposition parliamentarian put it, 'It's not redistribution of wealth but reconcentration into a *bangsawan* (nobleman) class' (Teoh, 2008). Discriminatory policies have resulted in Malaysia losing competitive edge as one of the 'tiger economies'. According to data held by the United Nations Conference on Trade and Development (UNCTAD), Malaysia ranked fourth in the inward foreign direct investment performance index in 1990. By 2005, Malaysia's ranking has dropped to 62, provoking Anwar Ibrahim to remark,

> In the 1970s and 1980s our peers were Singapore, Taiwan and Korea – they are now far ahead of us. China and India have emerged as economic giants. We are now losing out to Indonesia and Vietnam and Thailand. (Ibrahim, 2006)

Anwar Ibrahim also pointed out that according to the Transparency International Corruption Perception Index, Malaysia has fallen from the 39th position to the 44th position in 2006.

Encroaching Islamisation

Religious freedom is enshrined in the Constitution, although, as noted, Islam is the official religion of Malaysia. Muslims are under the jurisdiction of the *syariah* (Islamic law) courts which rules over religious and family matters, while non-Muslims are served under the civil courts. The 1970s, witnessed an Islamic resurgence triggered by both internal and external events, resonating to some extent with political events that preceded the 1969 race riots. In the latter case this has been mirrored by the on-going aggressive ethnic persecution of the Chinese in Indonesia as non-*pribumis* (princes of the land) (Tan, 2001). In Malaysia the electoral success of Parti Islam Sarawak (PAS) in Kelantan and Trengganu meant that UMNO, the ruling Malay party in the coalition, had to be seen to be the champions of Islam in order to counter PAS accusations that UMNO is a secular party.

Externally, the Islamic Revolution in Iran emboldened some Muslim clerics in the country to call for the creation of an Islamic state (Jawad, 2012). The rise of the influential Malaysian Islamic 'study group', Darul Arqam, with its goal to find purification away from the corruptions of the West (and the patronage of complicit Muslim nations), sought spiritual inspiration through insularity from the nation State, at the same time as reaching out to a righteous Islamic world - until they were suppressed by the Malaysian government (Hamid, 2000).

By the late 1970s the *dakwah* (the 'call' to Islam) movement amongst university students grew apace and Muslim women's attire came under scrutiny with many starting to wear the *tudung* (head-scarf). Islamisation of the Government gained momentum when Prime Minister, Mahathir declared that his Administration would be infused with Islamic values, including an Islamic work ethic (Mauzy and Milne, 1983-4). What this meant was that Islam took on greater visibility. There was a proliferation of State-funded mosques, religious organizations and banking institutions. A new television channel dedicated to Islamic programmes was launched in 2007, Islamic prayers were recited at the start of official State functions, Islamic civilization given prominence in the study of history, in the secondary school curriculum, whilst simultaneously distorting the historical contribution of other ethnic groups to the region (Kheng, 2003); Muslim children had to attend compulsory Islamic classes; and the cultural practices of other ethnic groups, particularly the Chinese, were subject to increasing constraints (Guan 2000; 2005). In short, the annexing of the public domain by aggressive Islamisation foregrounded the direct, vigorous competition between PAS and UMNO to claim the electoral prize of being publicly regarded as the most Islamic party (Hew, 2010)

In recent years, the Islamisation process has become more entrenched and disturbing. Ethnic Malays are constitutionally defined as Muslims and are not allowed to leave the faith and convert to another religion. Apostasy is a crime and punishment can include not just rehabilitation but a fine, caning and a jail term. In Pahang, apostates can be caned up to six strokes of the *rotan* (cane). Former Islamic teacher Kamariah Ali (Kuppusamy, 2006a) and sales assistant Lina Joy (Kortteinen, 2007; Stivens, 2010) who were brought up as Muslims tried to renounce Islam and were denounced by radical Islamists who called for their death (Kuppusamy, 2006a; Kortteinen, 2007). Thus, apostates like Kamariah and Lina live in fear and secrecy (see Al-Krenawi in this volume for a discussion of apostasy and human rights).

It is also illegal to propagate other religious doctrine amongst Muslims, although the reverse is permitted (Tom Lantos Human Rights Commission, 2011). Muslim patrons of entertainment outlets were monitored for *haram* (illicit) activities such as alcohol consumption. In 2009, the Pahang *syariah* court sentenced Kartika Dewi to six strokes of the cane and a fine for consuming alcohol. Payments via Islamic credit cards are barred when used in bars, casinos and spas. In 2010, the National Fatwa Council issues a directive banning Muslims from practicing yoga, claiming that such an ancient Hindu practice may corrupt their faith. A fatwa is legally binding on all Muslims, although enforcement is uneven depending on the Islamic authorities of each State. The Council also issued another edict prohibiting girls from acting and dressing like boys in order to discourage homosexuality, which violated Islam.

State religious enforcement officials often act as zealous moral guardians of the populace, prowling quiet spots in the city to catch courting couples for *khalwat* (close proximity with the opposite sex). *Khalwat* is punishable with a fine of USD 940, two years' imprisonment or both (U.S. Department of State, 2011). Farish Noor (2002: 204) in Hew (2010: 204), an Islamic scholar put it succinctly:

> We now live in a country where the 'religious police' can enter your home at night, demand proof of your marital status, question your beliefs and persecute you for 'crimes' against Nature or God.

In December last year, a 14-year-old Muslim bride was discovered amongst 250 couples in a mass wedding in a Kuala Lumpur mosque. The Minister of Women, Family and Community Development immediately issued a statement that the Government did not condone child marriages.

In reply, the Law Minister argued that they did not ban child marriages as it was permitted by Islam, the rationale being that early marriages reduces adultery and babies born out of wedlock (U.S. Department of State, 2010).

Encroaching Islamisation has also meant that the civil liberties of non-Muslims are also being trampled upon. Approvals for building or renovations of churches, temples and other non-Muslim places of worship have become increasingly difficult with bureaucratic hurdles to negotiate, like imposed height restrictions on steeples, temple domes and statues (Guan, 2000). An example was that of a case brought by two Orang Asli Christians who alleged that their church's application for water and electricity was rejected by the Temerloh Land and District Office. The church was the only building in the Orang Asli settlement which was without water and electricity. The High Court upheld the decision of the Temerloh Land and District Office which argued that the church was an illegal structure as no prior approval was sought (U.S. Department of State, 2010).

In addition, since the 1980s, no less than ten Hindu temples have been demolished by local councils (Kannabhiran, 2007 in Hew, 2010), the latest of which was a 107 year old Hindu temple in the Muslim dominated city of Shah Alam. Another 19th century Hindu temple was demolished in the capital city of Kuala Lumpur (Kent, 2006 in Hew 2010). The local Indian community felt discriminated against and formed an unregistered NGO named Hindu Rights Action Force (HINDRAF) as a conduit for their concerns. In 2007, HINDRAF mobilized a mass demonstration in Kuala Lumpur and five members were arrested. HINDRAF is now an illegal organization. In August 2009, Muslim residents in Selangor placed a severed cow's head at the front gate of the Selangor government office and took turns stepping on the cow's head and threatened bloodshed if a Hindu temple was to be relocated to their neighbourhood. Twelve of those assembled were charged for illegal assembly and sedition as they had desecrated an animal sacred to the Hindus (US Department of State, 2010).

Christians also felt that they were under assault when in 2005, all Malay language Christian publications had to have the words 'Not for Muslims' printed on the cover. Later serial numbers were added onto Malay language bibles imported from Indonesia. The Government courted controversy when it banned the use of the word *Allah* (God) by non-Muslims in Malay language bibles and other Christian publications. The Catholic Church filled a lawsuit against the ban in February 2008 and continued to use the word *Allah* in the Malay language version of the Catholic Herald 'arguing that the Catholic Church had used the word in the country for more than 400 years' (U.S. Department of State, 2010). The High Court of Kuala

Lumpur ruled in the Catholic Church's favour and this angered Malays who launched a series of attacks on churches.

On 17 November 2011, Baru Bian, the State assemblyman from the opposition party alleged that non-Muslim children in government-run pre-schools in the rural areas were taught Islamic teachings and practices. A few days later, George Lagong, a Christian Dayak assemblyman, delivered an emotionally charged speech in the State Legislature with reference to Baru Bian's allegations. He was reported as saying '...we are morally-bound to regularly advise and guide the young Dayaks to be faithful in their Christian belief so that they will be resilient in the face of temptations and other forces of evil' (Anonymous, 2011). In recent decades, Christianity, and in particular the more aggressive Borneo Evangelical Mission, has grown in popularity amongst the indigenous communities in Sarawak. As greater numbers move away from a rural agrarian economy to an urban waged economy, many are turning to Christianity to counter what they see as encroaching Islamisation. Chua (2007) in Hew (2010) points out that by the 1990s, over 95% of Bidayuhs had become Christians of various denominations. She argues that urbanized Bidayuh adults turn to Christianity as a way of resisting peer pressure to convert to Islam in the cities. In other words, urbanization, modernity and an assertion of ethnic identity have led to increasing Christianisation of the indigenous communities in Sarawak.

For the Orang Asli in Peninsular Malaysia, the paradox of their status as *bumiputras* and their underprivileged material condition, has brought them into focus, as representing a challenging contradiction to prevailing ideology (Nah, 2003). Accordingly, they are the target of State intervention and management through the Department of Aboriginal Affairs, which involves itself in all aspects of their lives. Additionally, the Orang Asli are also constructed as forming a vulnerable group in need of social work intervention, where they are specifically mentioned in the social work curricula of some universities (Parker et al., forthcoming). For modern day Orang Asli people, it is no longer their bodies that are actively pursued, but rather their minds and their very souls, in terms of first, the pressure to comply with concentrated bureaucratic management (Nah, 2003), with inevitably disempowerment and learned helplessness following in its wake (Nah, 2003). Second *dakwah*, as policy is also aimed directly at the Orang Asli, whereby conversion serves to subsume them and thereby to eradicate the paradox to *bumiputra* ideology that they currently symbolise (Nah, 2003).

Across Malaysia there have been attempts to resist this process of Islamisation but efforts to open greater democratic space for discussion have been repeatedly thwarted by the Government. For instance, in 2006, a campaign was organized by the Bar Council involving 14 non-governmental organizations calling for a reaffirmation of the rights and freedom of Malaysians of all faith as guaranteed in the Constitution. The coalition was named 'Article 11' after the constitutional provision which guaranteed religious freedom in the country. The coalition was constantly harassed by Islamic activists and the Prime Minister finally put a halt to the activities of Article 11. In the previous year, plans to set up an Interfaith Commission came to naught when some Muslim quarters alleged that the Commission would 'interfere with the holiness of Islam' (Kannabhiran, 2007 in Hew, 2010: 206-207).

Interethnic marriages: Who is a bumiputra?

As mentioned earlier, Malaysia has a dual track legal system – the *syariah* courts for Muslims and the civil courts for non-Muslims, although some have argued for these to be synthesised as a form of legislative 'harmonization', but one where, seemingly, Islamic legal conceptualisations remain to the fore (Kamali, 2007).

Throughout the years, there has been a gradual erosion of the authority of the civil courts, which more often than not, cede control to the *syariah* courts in matters pertaining to marriage and family between Muslims and non-Muslims). Stivens (2010) argues that case of Massosai Revathi reveals how in Malaysia combined heritages and identities can lead individuals into religio-legal quagmires. Massaosai was raised as a Hindu by her grandmother, although her Indian parents had converted to Islam. In adulthood she and her Hindu husband automatically chose to raise their newborn infant as a Hindu. She was consequently prosecuted and sentenced to gaol (Stivens, 2010)

The growing dominance of religious legal bodies have been viewed with alarm by non-Muslims while moderate Muslims feel that their civil liberties are jeopardized by an increasingly oppressive brand of Islam. This is particularly problematic in the case of inter-marriages between Muslims and non-Muslims. Sharmala, an Indian Hindu, married her husband Dr. Jeyaganesh in a Hindu ceremony in 1998. Four years later, Jeyaganesh converted to Islam, changed his name to Dr. Muhammad Ridzwan and converted their children aged four and two-years-old without her knowledge. As they were still married at that time, Shamala applied to the High Court in Kuala Lumpur to annul her children's conversion but was told that the civil courts had no jurisdiction over matters pertaining to Islam. Shamala fled the country with her children after the civil court granted her custody (U.S. Department of State, 2010). Conversion to Islam is often used by estranged husbands to gain custody of their children as they are afraid that the civil courts will grant custody to their wives. Subashini is a case in point. Subashini's husband embraced Islam, annulled his civil marriage to Subashini and gained custody of his children. He converted his eldest son, aged four at that time without the consent of Subashini, a non-Muslim (Hew, 2010).

In yet another case, Moorthy an ethnic Indian, a soldier and well-known mountaineer, converted to Islam without the knowledge of his Hindu wife. When he passed away, the Muslim religious authorities took his body to be buried according to Muslim rites. However, his wife claimed that he lived as a Hindu all his life and wanted him buried according to Hindu rites (Kuppusamy, 2006[a] in Hew, 2010). The ensuing battle for his body had the entire nation riveted, to the extent that ten non-Muslim cabinet ministers submitted a memorandum to the Prime Minister, calling on him to protect the rights of religious minorities after the public outrage over the Moorthy incident. However, the memorandum was retracted a couple of days later, after the Prime Minister Abdullah Ahmad Badawi instructed them to do so (Beh et. al., 2006 in ibid). As a result of the adverse publicity these cases generated, the Government announced in 2009 that if a spouse converts to Islam, civil courts are to dissolve the marriage and not the *syariah* courts. In addition, the children would follow the faith of both parents at the time of their marriage (U.S. Department of State, 2010).

A further case is equally troubling. In October 2010, a ten-year-old boy by the name of Basil was canned in a primary school in Sarawak for bringing fried rice and pork sausages to school for lunch. According to the Muslim senior assistant who did the caning, Basil was a Muslim, yet both his parents were Iban, his father having converted to Islam a year before he was born. However, Basil's father argued that his son was brought up as a Christian. The senior assistant made a public apology but Basil's religious status is now under investigation by the State. For non-Muslim family members, the stakes are higher than the right to eat pork. Non-Muslim spouses and adult children lose all rights to inheritance when one partner in the marriage converts to Islam.

In Sarawak, the problem carries a different complexion where the majority of the indigenous population is non-Muslim, although they are still *bumiputra*. The Borneo Post daily newspaper in Sarawak frequently reports on cases where the children of a Chinese father and a non-Muslim indigenous mother are deemed to be Chinese because of their name and hence cannot inherit their mothers' Native Customary Rights (NCR) land. Similarly, children of mixed parentage are denied preferential selection into pre-university matriculation courses regardless of academic performance. Marina Undau of Iban-Chinese parentage and Teresa Clare Ratnam, who has an Indian father and an Iban mother, are examples in point, running counter to the Federal Cabinet administrative ruling that only one parent needs to be a *bumiputra* for the child to be accorded *bumiputra* status (Borneo Post, 10 May, 2011).

The issue of numerical strength and political power is germane to an understanding of Malaysia's apostasy laws. Malays are by definition Muslims and since Malays enjoy special privileges under the New Economic Policy (NEP), there is anxiety that if they should be allowed to leave Islam, their numerical strength would be reduced and this would be a blow not so much to Islam but to their political stronghold. Thus, some have argued that the way in which Islamisation has been played out in multi-ethnic Malaysia is not so much a reflection of religious intolerance but of the rise of right-wing Malay ethno-nationalism (Kent, 2006 in Hew, 2010). Accordingly, the primacy of Islam in Malaysia has meant protection of the economic privileges of the Malays and the well-connected Malay elites in particular. This inclusive cadre is one that the Indian Muslim community has long wished to join on the basis of common religious heritage, yet, unlike Malaysian Muslims of Arab descent (thus, of unimpeachable religious lineage), they remain excluded (Stark, 2006).

For non-Muslim *bumiputra* in Sarawak the situation is reversed in comparison with Malay Muslims For the former, their numerical strength is weakened through interethnic marriage, as their off-springs are deemed to be non-*bumiputra* in the first instance. The obvious lack of parity and concomitant discrimination manifested in this situation adds credence to the argument of racial and religious discrimination of the non-Muslim *bumiputra* in Sarawak.

The myth of '1 Malaysia'

Every successive Prime Minister introduces a slogan, the latest by the Najib administration is that of '1 Malaysia'. Admittedly this chimes with some research studies indicating that non-*bumiputra* citizens regard themselves as Malaysians first (*bangsa Malaysia*), and only secondly hold allegiance to ethnic identities (Banton, 1994; Stark, 2006). However, such studies are contradicted by one of the largest telephone surveys conducted of race relations in Malaysia in (2006, http://www.merdeka.org/pages/02 research. html), involving 1,200 respondents. It was found that 42% did not consider themselves to be Malaysian, first and foremost, instead, their ethnicity was held as more important to their identity. A further 46% claimed that ethnicity was important in voting; while 55% blamed politicians for racial problems and, finally 70% would help their own ethnic group first. What was more alarming was that half the population apparently did not trust each other (Kuppusamy, 2006[b]). Lamentably such attitudes can even be found in surprising quarters, where one small scale study of the attitudes of social work students in the late 1990s revealed the polarity of ethnic groups and how embedded was racial prejudice towards non-bumiputras (Ashencaen Crabtree, 1999).

The survey, commissioned by the New Straits Times newspaper and supported by the Friedrich Naumann Foundation, in turn graphically illustrates the extent of racism in Malaysia, causing the social scientist, Chandra Muzaffar to remark:

> 'The findings are not at all surprising. This is partly because ethnic boundaries are real in our society and almost every sphere of public life is linked to ethnicity in one way or another' (Kuppasamy, 2006[b]).

The Government remains well aware of these ethnic tensions and has initiated various measures to ameliorate the situation, such as integrating students of different ethnicities in schools, the national service programmes and in halls of residence at public universities. However, it would appear to be a case of too little too late. Ethnic-based political parties and the deeply entrenched affirmative policies for bumiputra that permeates all aspects of life from education, employment, housing and enterprise, have served to divide the nation.

Conclusion

In conclusion, it cannot be denied that the NEP did much to lift the Malay communities out of poverty and were successful in creating a Malay, urban middle class. The importance of this must be acknowledged, as any social harmony could not be achieved in a multi-ethnic society like Malaysia where wide economic disparities exist between different ethnic groups; and, moreover, where ethnic identity is tied to occupation. While the initial goal has been achieved by the NEP, the fact remains that after 40 years, this social policy has out-lived its purpose. Its continuation can only exacerbate ethnic tensions by handicapping and alienating large sectors of society, thus creating gaping social divisions that are highly corrosive to the social fabric, and ultimately damaging in making Malaysia less competitive in the face of globalization and an uncertain global economy. As Guan (2000; 2005) notes, a pragmatic government cannot overlook the inexorable rise of China as the millennium's next superpower, and accordingly where the Malaysian Chinese community, in particular, may need to be regarded as a valuable national asset. Nonetheless Tan (2001) offers a more pessimistic outlook in noting that, an increasingly Islamicised Malaysia, demonstrably antagonistic towards its non-bumiputra citizens, may take the equally pragmatically view that a diminishing and marginalised population of non-bumiputras inevitably yields to the dominant religio-cultural forms. However, in so doing, Malaysia, could no longer boast its credentials as striving to be a successful multicultural, multifaith, postcolonial nation. Instead it must acknowledge that it has renounced that claim as a result of the privileging of institutionalised, mono-cultural agendas implicated in ethnic and religious singularities.

Part II

Impact of Direct Civil Conflict

The second section of the volume offers an interrogation of the impact of direct civil conflict and interconnections with natural crises and disasters through seven chapters. The social forces of political violence representing a pressure for social action and welfare response can be framed within a humanising effect of societal and religious expression.

Christopher Candland and Raza Qazi Khan explore the connections between army operations, subsequent displacement of peoples and the Islamic charities that offer succour to those affected in this chapter, which asks questions about the learning we can gain from the tensions between civil disaster and crisis, national security and human protection in the context of Islamic charitable relief. Moving from Pakistan to Palestine, the impact of warfare, resistance and political conflict on the business sector, in which many welfare-oriented NGOs operate, is analysed by Andromeda Agnew. She looks at the problems restricting business development in the West Bank and Gaza following the Second Intifada in 2000. She posits the importance of supporting economic development to be able to tackle the welfare needs of Palestinians and the constraints resulting from international aid.

Kevan Harris, following Doostgharin, returns to the development of comprehensive welfare systems in Iran following the Islamic revolution of 1979, focusing in particular on the State-sanctioned Imam Khomeini Relief Committee or *Komiteh Emdad*. The role of Islamic and State welfare from the revolution and throughout the Iran-Iraq war is detailed, showing the balanced stage on which conflict and social welfare are played.

Moving into the arena of international cooperation in developing welfare in the contexts of warfare and political conflict, Jane Lindsay's chapter examines the development of an educational programme for professional supervision for school-based psycho-social workers in the occupied Palestinian territories, offering a more positive picture of local control to the entrepreneurial malaise reported by Agnew.

Martine van Bijlert returns us to Afghanistan, an extremely complex situation which she portrays in different ways according to which view is taken. She explores the clash of ideologies, whether we can conceptualise the situation in Afghanistan as an externally-led and manipulated State-building exercise led by the West or a grievance-based insurgency. The strength of families and Islamic principles of hospitality and religious obligation to the needy are retained, and social welfare must be seen within this contested frame if it is to be understood.

Elise Kipperberg, examines some of the social policy challenges relating specifically to adolescents in Kurdistan, drawing on the last twenty-plus years since the Convention on the Rights of the Child (CRC) has become the major instrument of human rights monitoring the situation for children under 18 in most countries of the world. Kipperberg promotes the rights of children involved in conflict situations as enshrined within United Nations resolutions, seeing these as one of the most important aspects of NGOs working in regions where reconstruction is ongoing.

In the final chapter in this second part, Mahood Messkoub considers whether welfare provision in the Middle East and North Africa (MENA) is based on religious or secular principles. He recognises that religious and political authorities have used welfare or *refah* as part of the language of persuasion and discontent, promising to address gaps for allegiance and support. This is understood as no different throughout the world, whether Islamic or other. In the context of poverty, fighting oppression and striving for social justice, Messkoub asks us to consider, however, whether it will be the fundamentalist Islamic groups or secular politics, albeit underpinned by Islam such as in Iran, that appeal to the social welfare needs of disgruntled citizens.

7

Civil conflict, natural disaster, and partisan welfare associations in the Islamic Republic of Pakistan

Christopher Candland[1] and Raza Khan Qazi

Introduction

The earthquake that hit Pakistan's Kashmir on October 8, 2005 lasted for 5 minutes, killed more than 73,000 people, and left 3.3 million people homeless. (*Philanthropy Today*, 2006) The victims criticized the Government harshly for not responding adequately. Social welfare associations, non-political and political, many operating in the name or the spirit of Islam, moved rapidly to assist traumatized people. The Pakistan army's operations against anti-government militants in Swat and South Waziristan in 2009 displaced more than two million people. Private welfare associations provided the displaced people with vital welfare services, including emergency transport, food, water, shelter, medical treatment, and funeral services. The heavy rains and floods of 2010 submerged one fifth of the country, led directly to the death of 1,750 people, and rendered 8 million people homeless. (Kronstadt et al 2010: i) Again, welfare associations organized in the name or the spirit of Islam provided most of the aid that the victims received. What can we learn from the work of these welfare associations about the nature of society, government, and state in Pakistan?

This chapter describes the work of three welfare organizations that were involved in aiding the victims of the 2005 earthquake, the 2009 military operations in Swat and South Waziristan, and the 2010 floods. These organizations are placed within the broader context of social welfare work, most of which is not related to party politics or to a specific religion or school or denomination of a religion. The three organizations considered each have a different relationship to party politics. A political party is a group of people who ostensibly seek to become a ruling party and to thereby form a government; the relations that each organization has with a political party might reflect differences in aspiration for state control.

The three social welfare organizations considered here are the *Jamaat ud Dawa* (Assembly for Propagation), affiliated to the *Lashkar i Taiba* (Army of the Pure), a banned militant organization; *Al Khidmat* Welfare Foundation, associated with the *Jamaati i Islami* (Islamic Assembly), one of the oldest 'Islamic 'political parties in Pakistan; and *Al Minhaj* (The Path) Welfare Foundation, associated with Brelvi, sometimes referred to as Sufi, thinking and the progressive *Pakistan Awami Tehreek* (Pakistan People's Movement).

Jamaat ud Dawa, *Al Khidmat* Welfare Foundation, and *Al Minhaj* are each related to a political party, but in different ways. Syed Abu A'la Maududi, a prolific theologian, co-founded the *Jamaat i Islami* in 1941 as an Islamic revivalist party. It established its welfare wing, *Al Khidmat* Welfare Foundation, only in 1992, 50 years after the *Jamaat i Islami* was established as an ideological party. (Nasr 1994) In 2004 the Shura of the *Jamaat i Islami* voted to officially separate *Al Khidmat* Welfare Foundation from the *Jamaat i Islami*.[2] But the leadership of *Al Khidmat* Welfare Foundation remains the same after the legal separation of the party and the welfare organization. The *Jamaat ud Dawa*, co-founded by Mohammed Hafiz Saeed during the war against the Soviet occupation of Afghanistan (1979-88), is affiliated to what has since 2002 been an illegal organization. It is not easy to distinguish the humanitarian work of *Jamaat ud Dawa* from its political work, which allegedly includes political violence outside Pakistan, in Indian Kashmir and Afghanistan. The *Pakistan Awami Tehreek* in contrast was created after *Al Minhaj* Welfare Foundation was established. Tahir ul Qadri is the leader of both the political party and the welfare foundation. But the party's work is dwarfed by the social welfare organization's work.

These three organizations are each related to different *masaliq* (denominations) of Islam. Pakistan's five major *masaliq* are Ahle-Hadith, Brelvi, Deobandi and Jaffria, and Jamaat i Islami. Jamaat ud Dawa is inspired by *Ahle-Hadith*, otherwise referred to as Wahabian thinking. *Al Minhaj* is associated with the *Brelvi maslaq* (denomination), often referred to as Sufi. And *Al Khidmat* Welfare Foundation is affiliated with the *Jamaati i Islami*, which claims to be above *maslaqi* (denominational) differences but has its own government-approved board that parallels the four dominant *masaliq* of Pakistan: *Brelvi, Deobandi, Jaffri,* and *Ahle-Hadith*. The *Jamaat i Islami* is often described as 'revivalist'.

It must be emphasized that the organizations considered are not representative of social welfare associations in Pakistan. We have focused on 'Islamic ' political party affiliated welfare organizations. But the vast majority of welfare work in Pakistan is non-partisan and not professedly 'Islamic.' Indeed, the vast majority of social welfare work in Pakistan is by individuals not organizations. This chapter's focus on the most political and some of the allegedly most militant organizations should not lead the reader to conclude that the vast majority of Pakistan's social welfare associations are not opposed to violence and effectively committed to ameliorating indignities and suffering of millions of people.

Government *versus* the State in Pakistan

It is important from the outset to have clarity on the distinctions between key concepts used here which elected leaders, media professionals, and scholars often conflate. The concept of the state, to have sufficient clarity to be used meaningfully, should be distinguishable from other related concepts, specifically those of the government and the nation. The state is a collection of institutions; government uses these institutions to exercise control over a territory and the people residing on it.[3] The state is a complex but inanimate object, incapable of initiating action. The state can act, but only in the way that a knife can cut. The state is an instrument. Martha Rosler describes the distinction between the state and the people who manage it with clarity:

> … the state and individuals must never be confused with one another. The state is not a person. It does not have an unconscious, a spouse, feelings, children, a house, pride, a body, sex organs. The state feels no pleasure, no pain. It does not experience ecstasy, love, depression, or hatred. It has neither rage nor passions. The state is not biological but social and historical. The state is not a worried, sleepless man. It is not a frantic mother. It is not a person or even a group of persons. The state does not have a right to do this or that. It has no right to seek revenge or retribution. The state has no personal rights. It has no personal opinions. (Rosler, 1983)

A government, on the other hand, is animate; a government acts. Indeed, a government is a group of people who manage a state. To model the world as if states were actors, often referred to as nations or as nation-states, is a theoretical exercise that might have heuristic benefits. But a model should not be confused with an empirical fact. The assumption that states are like very large individuals with their own preferences, thoughts, and wills, produces not only nonsense jargon, such as 'non-state actors, ' phantom phenomenon, such as 'national consciousness, 'but also justification for the denial of individuals' rights in the name of the greater rights of the nation.

National versus human security

It is also important from the outset to have clarity on the distinction between national security and human security. The concept of human security distinguished explicitly between the security of the state, ironically referred to as 'national security', and the security of the population of a country from whom government derives its legitimacy (UNDP 1994 22-23). The concept of 'national security' conflated the security of the state and of the people who live in the territory under the nominal *writ* of the state. The concept of 'human security' was designed to disentangle two senses of 'nation' -- the human element and the mechanical apparatus, or the state.[4]

Human security is the capacity of individuals and groups, such as families, to protect themselves from harm. Physical security refers to the integrity of the body; human security refers to the capability of individuals and groups to maintain that bodily integrity. Such capacity requires, foremost, the knowledge that one has a right to protect oneself. Knowledge of rights is thus vital to human security.

The Pakistan army's operations to fight the *Tehreek i Taliban Pakistan* (Pakistan Seminary Students' Movement) and Al Qaeda reveal a conflict between national security and human security. The attempt to protect the state itself ('national security') undermined peoples' ability to protect their selves from harm ('human security'). The more than two million people displaced in the Pakistan army's operations against anti-government militants in Swat and South Waziristan were not well equipped to accommodate social and physical destruction and indiscriminate violence. As a result of the operation to ensure national security, hundreds of thousands of people were displaced from their homes. Many died as a result.

Islamic charities and Muslim philanthropies

A third conceptual clarification needed before discussing the three selected organizations is that we avoid the phrases 'Islamic' or 'Muslim charities' and 'Islamic ' or 'Muslim philanthropies' because these are potentially misleading, for two reasons. The use of the adjective 'Muslim' or 'Islamic' tends to suggest that there is some authority that can determine decisively who is and who is not Muslim and what is and what is not in accordance with Islam, even as the Quran itself repeatedly cautions people to avoid assigning such authority to anyone other than God.[5] Indeed, those associations that make public pronouncements about their 'Islamic ' credentials are very often the least faithful to the spirit of Islam. Second, the donation of money or assets to the poor, charity [*khairat*] and philanthropy in the spirit of Islam is not merely to aid the needy but also to please God. Indeed, most funding for social welfare associations derives from *zakat* and *infaq*. *Zakat* is the obligation on Muslims who have a requisite amount of accumulated wealth to give 2.5% of those assets annually to designated eligible people [*mustahiqeen*]. *Zakat* is an obligation to God [*ibadah*] not an obligation to humanity [*mu'amalat*]. Accordingly, scholars of Islam discuss it as jurisprudence related to worship [*fiqh ibadah*] rather than as jurisprudence related to contracts [*fiqh mu'amalat*]. *Infaq* is an obligation to humanity. Failure to provide *infaq* cannot be forgiven by God but only by those whom one is denying God's blessings. 'Philanthropy ' (from the Greek *philos anthropos*). literally 'brotherly love of humans ' does not capture this concept of *infaq*, spending to please God, in its entirety.

The Swat-Malakand operation

The military operations began in May 2009 after a deadlock between the government and the largest insurgent group, the *Tehreek i Taliban* Pakistan, regarding the enforcement of Shariah in the Swat-Malakand region of Khyber Pakhtunkhwa province.[6] The military decided that for the operations to be successful the population of Swat, where *Tehreek i Taliban* insurgents had established a huge militant network, had to be displaced. The rationale of the military was that without such displacement insurgents could not be separated from the civilians. Consequently, the entire population of the mountainous Swat started moving towards the low-lying districts. The federal and provincial governments of the Northwest Frontier

Province (now Khyber Pakhtunkhwa) established makeshift camps for internally displaced persons in the districts of Mardan, Charsadda, Swabi, and Peshawar. In Mingora, the main city of the region, alone, more than 700,000 people registered with authorities as internally displaced people.

The arrangements for the internally displaced persons at the camps were relatively satisfactory but only because of the participation of private welfare associations. The government contributed in the setting up of camps and provision of electricity and water. The government was able to make this contribution with the help of international humanitarian agencies. Visits to these camps revealed that their dwellers faced many problems, including lack of food, clean drinking water, medicine, and sanitation facilities. Government authorities were incapable of meeting the needs of the displaced people.

One could see numerous volunteers associated with different welfare associations helping the affected people with enthusiasm and alacrity. One could see hordes of *Jamaat ud Dawa* workers busy in providing care to the internally displaced people just opposite *Al Khidmat* Foundation volunteers, who could be seen doing their utmost to reach out with food and other necessities to the affected people. Not far away, volunteers of the Edhi Foundation, the Umma Welfare Trust, Islamic Relief, and other welfare associations, would try to provide for the needs of internally displaced people lined up in long queues. Although secular political parties also had their kiosks at the relief camps for internally displaced people, the lack of enthusiasm among their workers could be plainly observed. Perhaps this was the reason that few of the internally displaced people thronged their desks at the camps for relief.

The military operation in Swat against the *Tehreek i Taliban* Pakistan continued from May to August 2009. During this period, private welfare associations provided rescue and relief to internally displaced people. Once the military defeated the insurgents and eliminated their command and control structure in the Swat valley, which the military had early allowed to be set up, these welfare associations also took the lead in helping the internally displaced people return to and rebuild their homes.

Jamaat ud Dawa

The militant *Lashkar i Taiba* and *Jamaat ud Dawa* have the same roots. General Pervez Musharraf, who took power in Pakistan and declared himself Chief Executive of the country in 1999, banned the *Lashkar i Taiba* and the *Jaish i Muhammad* in January 2002, as militants associated with these groups were accused by Delhi of being behind the attack on the Indian Parliament in December 2001. *Jamaat ud Dawa* is the name that the *Lashkar i Taiba* took when it was banned. Early in 2002, the founder of *Lashkar i Taiba*, Hafiz Saeed, adopted the name of *Jamaat ud Dawa* for his organization and took up charity work. The motive behind this seems to have been to distance itself from the militant *Lashkar i Taiba* and to evade the 2002 ban on the *Lashkar i Taiba*.

After the November 2008 attacks in India's financial hub, Mumbai, which the Indian government blamed on Hafiz Saeed, Islamabad vowed to extend cooperation to New Delhi to apprehend the accused. Pakistani analysts believe that the *Jamaat ud Dawa*, fearing that its leadership would be arrested and its network dismembered, thought it necessary to change its name to *Falah i Insaniyat* Foundation (Welfare of Humanity). In this way the resources of the organization could be saved from confiscation. Pakistani authorities arrested and tried Saeed in connection with the Indian Parliament attack in 2001, the Mumbai railway bombing in 2006, and the Mumbai city bombing in 2008 in the face of mounting Indian pressure; courts released him each time for insufficient evidence to prosecute. The *Jamaat ud Dawa* and *Falah i Insaniyat* Foundation claims that it activities are entirely humanitarian.

According to journalist Amir Mir, however, *Jamaat ud Dawa* predates the *Lashkar i Taiba*, and can be thought of as the original organization, formed in 1986. *Jamaat ud Dawa* was formed by academics at the University of Engineering and Technology, Lahore, to participate in war against the Soviet occupying forces in Afghanistan.[7] These teachers were associated with the Saudi-influenced *Ahle Hadith* sect. The motivation behind formation of *Jamaat ud Dawa* for the first time in 1986 seemed to be the promise of aid to the University of Engineering and Technology teachers from Madina University, Saudi Arabia. The *Jamaat ud Dawa*, also known by its full title *Markazul Dawa Wal Irshad*, formed *Lashkar i Taiba* to send young men for the Afghan war. (Mira 2007: 317)

Leaders of *Falah i Insaniyat* deny that the name of the organization *Jamaat ud Dawa* has been changed to *Falah i Insaniyat* to disguise the group's militant identity and operations. They argue that there has been no change of nomenclature:

In fact, Falah i Insaniyat is a long-registered welfare organization in Pakistan and its head is Hafiz Abdul Rauf. We have not changed its name. Jamaat ud Dawa is in fact an organization for Dawaat (invitation to Islam). Falah i Insaniyat is meant to carry out the work of falah (welfare) and rifah (reformation) and to respond to the needs of disaster-stricken people.[8]

Jamaat ud Dawa was a leading agency in the emergency aid to the victims of the October 8, 2005 earthquake, which left hundreds of thousands of people seriously injured or homeless. *Jamaat ud Dawa* also served the internally displaced persons from the civil conflict in Swat-Malakand in 2009 and the flood-affected people in the summer of 2010.

The Spokesperson for the *Falah i Insaniyat* Foundation in Khyber Pakhtunkhwa claims that the work of the foundation is entirely humanitarian:

> It is the teachings of Prophet Muhammad (may peace be upon him) that in the hour of trial every Muslim must respond to the woes of his Muslim brother. So as we are Muslims in this way it is a God-ordained entrusted duty to us to help people in disasters and catastrophes.[9]

Some analysts see political objectives behind the humanitarian work of *Jamaat ud Dawa* and *Falah i Insaniyat* Foundation:

> These so-called Islamic organizations in particular Jamaat ud Dawa or whatever other names it has definitely have a political agenda of winning a large number of supporters. To attain this aim the organization uses charity work as tool to reach out to these people.[10]

The criticism that *Lashkar i Taiba, Jamaat ud Dawa,* and *Falah i Insaniyat* Foundation have political objectives is true but not true only of these organizations. Many professedly 'Islamic' associations claim to want Pakistan to be ruled by Shariah, according to their own sectarian and doctrinal interpretation of the construct. Each group's leadership seems to want to be the sole spokesperson of Shariah and justifies this through verses of the Qur'an in which God commands that Muslims are Vicegerent of God on Earth and they would exercise state power as a sacred trust. The leadership of 'Islamic ' political parties in Pakistan argues that they and not the leadership of 'secular ' political parties, who they accuse of having no understanding of Islam and Shariah, meet the criteria for being the Vicegerent of God on Earth. Thus the Islamic party leaders lay claim to and take upon themselves the responsibility to rule Pakistan in accordance with the tenets of Islamic Shariah.

Irrespective of the motives behind the charity work of the *Jamaat ud Dawa* and the *Falah i Insaniyat* Foundation, discussed further below, these groups contributed significantly to improving human security for many vulnerable Pakistanis. These groups have been active in several sectors:

> At the moment one of the main focuses of Falah i Insaniyat Foundation is on health. In this regard we have built hospitals, dispensaries and have developed a vast network of ambulances. We also hold medical camps where people cannot afford medical treatment and medicines; we try to cater to their health needs. We also hold special camps for disaster-affected people. Apart from this our foundation is working on drinking water projects in areas like in Balochistan province, Tharparkar and D I Khan. In this regard we install water pumps, water tanks and hand pumps.

Al Khidmat Welfare Foundation

Al Khidmat Welfare Foundation is a registered charitable society. In 2004, the *Jamaat i Islami* separated it from the party. In response to the July and August 2010 floods, *Al Khidmat* Foundation attracted more than 20,000 volunteers in its 104 relief camps, according to *Al Khidmat* General Secretary Ahsan Ali Syed.[11]

Al Khidmat Foundation has the largest social welfare network of the 'Islamic' political parties in Pakistan:

> We have units of our Foundation in all districts of Pakistan; in FATA and Azad Kashmir we have separate units. Al Khidmat Pakistan is organized at the provincial, district, and union council level. We have both paid workers and volunteers at all these tiers. Al Khidmat has a separate organizational structure and is totally independent in its operations.[12]

According to the foundation's leaders the initial and continuing motivation behind the organization's charity work is the large-scale miseries of people in Pakistan.

> There are certain things which are beyond the state's potential in Pakistan. So the private charities like ours have had to play their role in alleviating the woes of the common man. The vision of Al Khidmat is to serve the nation; the priority sectors are health, education and emergencies or national disasters.[13]

Some critics of the *Jamaat i Islami* argue that the party started *Al Khidmat* because it failed to gain power through elections; because other political parties, such as its chief rival, the *Muttahida Quami* Movement, had their own social welfare programs; and because the governments were unable to meet the health and educational requirements of most Pakistani. To address the miseries of disaster and civil strife affected people gave the *Jamaat i Islami* an opportunity to gain public support through social service activities.

The *Jamaat i Islami* since its inception in 1941 has been taking part in Indian and subsequently Pakistani elections but failed to win a significant number of parliamentary seats. It only reached the echelons of political power by getting some if its leaders inducted as ministers in the cabinet of martial law ruler General Zia ul-Haq (1977-88) and joining the government with Pakistani Muslim League-Nawaz (PML-N) (1990-1993). Again when the alliance of Islamic parties[14] won a majority in Khyber Pakhtunkhwa province in elections of 2002 and formed the provincial government, the *Jamaat i Islami* was the junior partner of *Jamiat i Ulema i Islam*. Since the 1970s the *Jamaat i Islami* also formed an alliance with the country's military in a bid to Islamise Pakistan. It has largely failed but in the process has radicalized the military and the state's policy-making.

It appears that the *Jamaat i Islami* set up *Al Khidmat* Foundation with political objectives. The failure of state institutions to respond to the victims of natural disasters and civil strife or lack of government commitment to the educational and health needs of the population allows *Al Khidmat*, run by accomplished *Jamaat i Islami* leaders, to win public sympathy.

Nevertheless, *Al Khidmat* Foundation has provided vital services to desperate people. In particular, its contribution in the rescue, relief and rehabilitation won the foundation many admirers during the 2005 earthquake and during the displacements of millions of people from Swat in 2009 and from flood areas in 2010. Looking after the dire needs of thousands of displaced and devastated people was made possible by the services to *Al Khidmat* of hundreds of volunteers and donors:

> We have paid workers in routine times and we give them transport and daily allowance for the services they carry out in the fields. However, in emergencies we have many volunteers who take part in the rescue, relief and rehabilitation work.

Al Khidmat Foundation officials claim to receive generous donations:

> We have local donors. We organized provincial and district level donors

conventions. In these conventions we present our programmers, plans, and projects to the donors and tell them about their costs and impact. In this way we convince the potential donors of the needs of such projects. In one instance one donor gave Rs. 0.8 million (US$ 9,000) for the orphanages named as Aghosh Orphanages run by Al Khidmat Foundation.[15]

Like other welfare associations, *Al Khidmat* Foundation also depends heavily on the *zakat* money from its own communities. Hides and skins of animals, which are sacrificed on the occasion of *Eid-ul-Fitr*, are also given to the foundation in a large number to raise a large amount of money:

At the occasion of Eid-ul-Fitr, Al Khidmat Foundation especially organized skins collection points at every Union Council level in the country. Al Khidmat Foundation also runs independent hospitals. These hospitals charge the patients at the most the paltry sum of Rs. 50, which includes medical examination, laboratory tests and medicines. These hospitals are run on no-profit and no-loss basis while the additional costs are covered through charity money. We also receive cash and kind from international donors. To these donors we submit project proposals and then they assess and provide funds. In this connection we have especially received donations from Saudi Hilal-e-Ahmar [Saudi Red Crescent], Japan Government, UK Islamic Mission and Islamic Relief. Islamic Centre for North America and Islamic Centre for Canada have also provided significant funds to Al Khidmat Foundation. [The] Pakistan Army started using our data for rescue operations in Bamako after the 2005 Earthquake. In fact, Al Khidmat Foundation was the first to conduct surveys to assess needs of the affected people. Through this door to door and somewhat systematically carried out survey assessment we got the real situation on the ground.[16]

Al Minhaj Welfare Foundation

Mohammad Tahir ul Qadri is the charismatic center of *Al Minhaj* Welfare Foundation. Qadri is a passionate, animated, and full-throated speaker. He draws large crowds who are frequently moved to tears. Qadri's *fatawas* (religious opinions, plural of *fatwa*) about suicide bombings being contrary to Islam have made him the target of assassins. Qadri is a prolific Islamic scholar and broadcast personality. He founded Al Minhaj University in 1981 and *Al Minhaj* Welfare Foundation and a political party, the Pakistan *Awam i Tehreek*, in 1989. The party won one seat – Qadri's seat – in the 2002 national elections. The Pakistan *Awam i Tehreek* boycotted the national elections in 2008.

Al Minhaj Welfare Foundation maintains four societies in Lahore, each registered under the Societies Act. The Foundation provided relief services to the internally displaced people from the 2009 military operation in Swat. *Al Minhaj ul Quran* Foundation operates a maternity hospital. The Foundation also operates an FM radio station, *Awaaz* [Voice]. *Al Minhaj* Welfare Foundation has installed 1500 water pumps across the country costing Rs. 7 million. The Foundation performs collective weddings and wedding receptions, for one dozen families at a time. The Foundation thereby saves families from a considerable financial commitment. The Foundation has married three hundred couples.

Al Minhaj Foundation has offices at the *tehsil* and union council level, the lowest tiers of administration, in the four provinces of the country and in Azad Kashmir. The foundation also claims to have constructed 1000 schools and colleges in the country; the Minhaj Education Society claims to have set up 572 schools including 42 colleges and informational technology centers imparting education to 120,000 students through 5,000 teachers all over Pakistan.

For the past 20 years, thousands of Qadri's followers have assembled in Lahore for the last 10 days of Ramadhan. In 2010, with much of the country under floodwaters, Qadri requested those who were intending to attend to instead celebrate Eid by working for victims of the floods. He mobilized 15,000 volunteers. A day of training in emergency aid was given to the volunteers in Lahore, Faisalabad, Karachi, Multan, Rawalpindi, and Abbotabad. The Rs. 30 million that would have been spent on the *itikaf* [spiritual retreat within a mosque] was instead spent on emergency relief. The level and reach of rescue and relief work provided evidence of the organization's ability to mobilize volunteers.

Punjab and Sindh, where the 2010 flooding was worst, are the first and second most populous provinces and have *Barelvi* majority populations. As a result, the organization has concentrated its activities in these provinces. The conflict and disaster-hit provinces, the Khyber Pakhtunkhwa and Balochistan, have attracted less attention from *Al Minhaj* Welfare Foundation because people of the *Barelvi maslaq* are in a very small minority in these provinces.

Comparative reflections

The cases considered here are not representative of Pakistani social welfare associations. It must be emphasized that the better-known social welfare associations in Pakistan do not profess to be 'Islamic' and are not related to political parties. The *Edhi* Foundations, the best known and most extensive social welfare association in the country, maintain a studied distance from party politics. Its founder, Abdul Sattar Edhi, has been asked by political parties, in and out of government, and by the military, for support.[17] He has occasionally agreed, only to later regret his decision and leave party politics.

But when the October 8, 2005 earthquake struck, many were convinced that Judgment Day had arrived. Survives were convinced that God was punishing them for their distance from Islam. Under these circumstances, 'Islamic' welfare associations have a special appeal and a unique opportunity to win supporters to their theology.

Al Minhaj Welfare Foundation services for the relief, rescue, and rehabilitation of victims of the 2005 earthquake, 2009 civil strife in Swat, and 2010 floods were extensive but not as conspicuous as that of *Jamaat ud Dawa* and *Al Khidmat* Foundation. This might be attributed to *Al Minhaj* Welfare Foundation's concentration on education rather than relief to the victims of conflict and disaster. Moreover, the parent organizations of *Jamaat ud Dawa*, *Falah i Insaniyat* and *Al Khidmat* Welfare Foundation have run militant training camps in Azad Kashmir and Khyber Pakhtunkhwa. As a result, they had a ready local workforce to operate in those areas. The militant background of some of the volunteers of *Jamaat ud Dawa* and *Falah i Insaniyat* and their familiarity with the areas of the civil strife and natural calamities might have better placed them to help affected people. *Al Minhaj* and the *Edhi* Foundation did not have that kind of experience.

The decisions by *Falah i Insaniyat* Foundation and *Al Khidmat* Foundation to distance themselves from their parent organizations might have been taken with an eye to the general aversion of Pakistanis to politics, particularly to 'Islamic' parties taking part in politics. However, in the process of establishing their social welfare arms, 'Islamic' political parties have extended valuable services to the people affected by the October, 2005 earthquake; the military operations in Swat-Malakand of 2009; and countrywide floods of 2010. These welfare organizations after having the experience of working in these natural and man made disasters have matured as true welfare organizations. Herein lay their biggest merit. Perhaps first-hand experience of addressing people's sufferings and indignities can reconfirm the commitment to social service work and neutralize organizational political agendas.

Conclusions

What have we learned about the nature of the Pakistani state and Pakistani society from the work of these Islamic social welfare associations? Some general conclusions can be drawn.

First, the scope for faith-based welfare associations to emerge and work has been huge because the state in Pakistan has largely failed to provide human security to the majority of the masses particularly the vulnerable sections. The government's failure to adequately address the human security needs of the people during national emergencies such as civil strife and natural disasters have raised questions about the capacity of the state and the commitment of the government. Various state institutions particularly the civilian bureaucracy and military command and above all the governments themselves have been unable to rise to the occasion. This created a vacuum, filled by 'Islamic ' welfare associations. Before 2005 there had been no disaster management authority in the country. It was only in 2007 that the National Disaster Management Authority was established.

Pakistan has built the seventh largest military in the world and a nuclear weapons program. The state has enormous capacity but an over-emphasis on national security. But it not clear how the institutions for national security can be made to look after the human security needs of Pakistan. The biggest issue regarding human security in Pakistan is not state capacity but government will. Colossal allocations to national security both failed to address what are now grave educational and public welfare challenges and undermined the security of state institutions. Pakistan is now faced with two large-scale insurgencies, the insurgency of the *Tehreek i Taliban* Pakistan waged in the name of Islam and the insurgency of the Baloch nationalists for an Independent Baloch state.

Regardless of motivations and objectives, representatives of each of the welfare organizations considered here claim that they are involved in social welfare work because the government has failed to adequately respond to people's needs:

> Basically in Pakistan the government is not solving the problems of the people, thus shunning its primary responsibility. As Pakistan has been facing both internal and external threats therefore, all the Muslim NGOs are working with human spirit to alleviate the miseries of people.[18]

Second, reported motivations are diverse. It is difficult to confirm from behavior or words alone others' intentions. And intentions are often mixed and changing. We asked our interview subjects about their motivations. We often heard that the work suited a person or that the leader of an organization was an inspiration. We often heard that a Muslim should have a social consciousness, that it is an obligation to God to help the suffering, and that God would look kindly upon ones deceased parents if one did philanthropic work. At the same time, the philanthropic activities associated with 'Islamic' movements and political parties do seem to suit the aspirations of these movements and parties to secure the power of the state.

Our third finding is closely related to this point about diverse motivations. The commitment to the social teachings of Islam power many social welfare associations in Pakistan. It is only possible for Pakistani social welfare associations to provide services to millions of people in Pakistan because of the commitment of hundreds of thousands of social workers inspired by Islam, a sizable portion of which is female. The leadership of the organizations that we have examined is male. But women do the bulk of the work in these organizations.

Disaster-stricken people tend to accept aid from any who can provide it. As so-called Islamic welfare associations were in the forefront to provide vital services with apparent sincerity and sense of purpose, disaster-stricken people gravitated towards them. The political objectives of the charity organizations that attend to them might not be of central concern to people in dire need. And the state institution could not provide adequate rescue and relief. Pakistan's recent disasters created the opportunity for the cultivation of goodwill by 'Islamic' welfare organizations. At the same time, whatever the long-term objectives of these charities might be, in the short-run they outperformed every other state and non-state institution to help out the affected people. With the continued indifference of the state towards human security and with ever growing and complicating disasters, the role of 'Islamic' social welfare associations would increase and so as the people's reliance on them. Significantly this dependence of the people on the religion-based charity organizations would come at the expense of further erosion of the legitimacy of the state.

The Islamic parties have established welfare organizations after playing an active role in politics for decades without much success. They might have come to realize that they were more acceptable to the Pakistanis in the role of extending welfare services rather than as political parties. Generally, Pakistani politics are not about political ideologies but about loyalty to the leaders who can provide jobs, roads, and other resources to his or her supporters. To many Pakistanis, Shariah means good governance and speedy justice. In this context, the Islamic political parties' involvement in charitable activities is quite understandable. It might provide the support base for 'Islamic' political parties to gain political power.

At the same time, if governments fail to provide essential social welfare services but rather privilege the security of state institutions (misleadingly referred to as national security) and the security of those who control these institutions (at least as well as any can control an institution) over the security of ordinary citizens, then non-governmental organizations, including religious groups, will step in. They will provide public services and not only to meet real and dire need but also to challenge the government's claim to legitimacy. 'Islamic ' political parties are not merely using social welfare activities as a tool to gain political legitimacy as to gain control of the state. They are also striving to transform the state.

Notes

1. I am grateful to Raza Rehman Khan Qazi of the University of Peshawar for offering to contact and interview representatives of *Falah in Insaniyat* and *Jaamat ud Dawa*.
2. Candland's interview with Ahsan Ali Syed, General Secretary, *Al Khidmat* Welfare Foundation, Lahore, December 21, 2010
3. The definition of an institution in the social sciences ranges, but is concerned with conventional or standards practices and procedures, some under law, some by custom, even 'patterns of thoughts' (Veblen 1899).
4. Rabindranath Tagore's argument and distinction between the human and the mechanical dimensions of 'the nation ' in his 1917 lectures merits reading. (Tagore 1918 3-48)
5. We use the word 'God' rather than 'Allah' throughout this chapter, unless quoting others, because the word 'Allah ' is merely the Arabic word for the English word God. The use of the word 'Allah ' in English conveys wrongly that those who believe in the religion of Abraham and that Mohammad was a prophet, on the one hand, and those who believe in the religion of Abraham but do not regard Mohammad as a Prophet, on the other hand, are worshipping different Gods.
6. As Shariah has been defined and imposed in ways that are decidedly against the *Sunnah*, the *Holy Qur'an* and the *Ahadith*, we do not refer to *Shariah* as 'Muslim Law.'
7. These teachers included Hafiz Muhammad Saeed, Zafar Iqbal, Hafiz Abdul Rehman Makki, Hafiz Abdul Islam bin Mohammed, Sheikh Jamiluddin, and

Mufti Abdul Rahman.

8. Qazi's interview with Atiq Chohan, Khyber Pakhtunkhwa Spokesman for the *Falah i Insaniyat* Foundation, Peshawar, March 20, 2012

9. Qazi's interview with Atiq Chohan, Khyber Pakhtunkhwa Spokesman for *Falah i Insaniyat Foundation*, Peshawar, March 20, 2012

10. Qazi's interview with Ijaz Khan, Professor, University of Peshawar, Peshawar, February 25, 2012

11. Candland's interview with Ahsan Ali Syed, General Secretary of *Al Khidmat* Welfare Foundation, Lahore, December 21, 2010

12. Qazi's interview with Izzat Khan, Khyber Pakhtunkhwa Financial Chief of *Al Khidmat* Welfare Foundation, March 5, 2012

13. Qazi's interview with Izzat Khan, Khyber Pakhtunkhwa Financial Chief of *Al Khidmat* Welfare Foundation, March 5, 2012

14. This was the first time that Pakistani 'Islamic' parties rose above *maslaqi* (denominational) divisions. Parties of the Afghan Defence Council transformed their anti-NATO and anti-US platform into an electoral alliance.

15. Qazi's interview with Izzat Khan, Khyber Pakhtunkhwa Financial Chief of *Al Khidmat* Welfare Foundation, March 5, 2012

16. Qazi's interview with Izzat Khan, Khyber Pakhtunkhwa Financial Chief of *Al Khidmat* Welfare Foundation, March 5, 2012

17. The Pakistani media often refers to Edhi as *Maulana* as a term of respect. This gives the impression that his welfare foundations are working in the name of Islam. However, Edhi is not a religious scholar and does not claim to be. Indeed, he dislikes being referred to as *Maulana*, as he claims that most religious scholars in Pakistan are crooks. Candland's interview with Abdul Sattar Edhi, Karachi, December 27, 2010

18. Qazi's interview with Atiq Chohan, the Khyber Pakhtunkhwa Spokesperson for the *Falah i Insaniyat* Foundation Peshawar, March 28, 2010

8

An examination of ideological and practical approaches to small business development and social welfare policy in Palestine

Andromeda Agnew

Introduction

Micro small and medium size enterprises (MSMEs) are now widely recognised as a key driver of economic activity across developed and developing countries, fuelling job and wealth creation, and providing a litmus for the wider social and financial health of a nation.

Nowhere is their importance more manifest than in conflict zones, such as the Occupied Palestinian Territories (oPt), where the international community has long promoted economic development as key to the success of the peace process, and future Palestinian statehood, and flagged nurturing of small business activity as a crucial part of this aim. In the present, they also provide a platform for day today economic survival for Palestinians, at a time of widespread unemployment and poverty – as well as offering a framework for the stability of families and communities in an environment of violence, uncertainty, constricted support from the state, and barriers to inflow of remittances from abroad.

In the oPt, MSMEs employing less than 20 workers dominate the economic landscape, in 2008 making up 99% of businesses (Kawasmi and White, 2010).

Their importance has long been recognised by the Palestinian Authority, the oPt's administrative body who since their inception in 1994 has endeavoured to stimulate business through trade agreements and donor funded investment, with the ambition of turning these small, family-run and often unofficial businesses, into established, tax-paying corporations[1].

Results, however, have fluctuated wildly amid political instability, particularly after the second Palestinian uprising, or *intifada*, declared in September 2000. The intifada and was to last five years, with further violence throughout the decade; by 2008 killing an estimated 5000 Palestinians and 600 Israelis (B'TSELEM, 2012). But it was the following security measures imposed by the occupying government and the resulting economic fallout that would have the furthest reaching consequences on society that is still felt today.

Pre-Intifada, the economy had been expanding with gross national income (GNI) growing on average at 3.5% per annum (UNCTAD Secretariat, 2004). Despite growth, however, the private sector remained small-scale and under developed. Even in 1999 its largest growth year, micro-enterprises employing less than 5 people, accounted for 92% of all businesses, while the majority of employment (77%) was found within the production of basic consumer goods, particularly food and beverages, wearing apparel, non- metallic products, metal products and furniture (UNCTAD Secretariat, 2004). Amid such basic activity, the economy was neither able to keep up with population growth (growing at 4.5%) nor support itself with a trade deficit of 55.4% in 2000 (Khan and Naqib, 2006).

Arguably a principal reason for this under performance is the fact that the oPt is not a sovereign state but occupied by Israel, forcing the business community to operate in a highly restricted environment, over which they have little or no control.

Under a policy made during the Oslo Accords in 1993 it was agreed that while the PA would take over (at least in part) of the administration of the territory, to counter terrorism, security would remain in the hands of Israel.

Although Israel maintains that this policy of 'security first' was not initiated to submit economic and political control in the oPt, it is exerted as a de facto consequence. The PA's ability to assist its people is severely limited, as its only has jurisdiction in two out of the three areas (area A and B: the city of Ramallah and two small territories in the West Bank) set up in the Oslo Accords, with by far the biggest area (area C: 59% of the territory) still in the hands of the Israelis[2].

Border controls dictate the amount and types of trade that can exist. Israel controls all Palestinian imports, setting the tariff rates, while prohibiting the importation of over 200 goods that are considered to have a 'dual function' (usable in both industry and terrorism), preventing local businesses from gaining access to materials that enterprises elsewhere take for granted. In addition, Israel collects the duty on all imports, which represents around two-thirds of the PA's self-generated revenue. While these fees are nominally handed over to the PA, they can be, and are regularly, withheld (Guardian, 2011).

Likewise, Palestinians cannot directly export their goods, and must go through Israel – preventing local traders from making international contacts and expanding business opportunities abroad. The difficulties businesses face in exporting products keeps Palestine almost entirely dependent on Israel for trade (with Israel forming the destination 89% of Palestinian products in 2009 (Kawasmi and White, 2010)). This dependency has arguably contributed to an exploitative relationship between the countries, whereby Palestinian businesses have been locked into long-term agreements for manufacturing goods or construction materials, yielding a low income and offering little opportunity of turning a 'blue-collar' economy into a 'white collar' one (Khan and Naqib, 2006). Furthermore, across the territory, infrastructure cannot be built without the permission of the Israeli military authorities, creating barriers to investment and development (ibid).

The Second Intifada

These restrictions, and their suffocating effect on the economy, were amplified in the period following the second *intifada*. In addition to the widespread destruction of property and infrastructure – which is estimated to have cost the economy $3.5 billion (Khan and Naqib, 2006) – Israel stepped up security in an initiative that some academics have called a deliberate policy of de-development (Roy, 1995).

The principal strategy, that still exists today, is to exert a greater control over the movement of people and goods through a series of internal barriers. By 2008, over 600 of these 'physical obstacles', in the form of checkpoints, road gates, trenches, and other barriers, remained in place (Kawasmi and White, 2010). The effect on business has been disastrous; the territory has been turned into a succession of isolated enclaves, severing producers and traders from their markets. The movement of goods has become almost impossible, as at each checkpoint the contents of a truck must be unloaded to be inspected. There is no timeframe for these inspections, while checkpoints open and close arbitrarily, meaning that if goods are perishable they can spoil, and if they are not they can still be confiscated. The cost of transport has also doubled in some areas (UNCTAD, 2009).

Worst still, since 2002, under a new 'containment' policy, the Israeli government has been building an eight metre high separation barrier (also known as 'The Wall') to separate the oPt from Israel. This policy is estimated to have forced over 3,500 enterprises out of business (UNCTAD, 2009), as The Wall does not follow the old 'Green-line' set up in the 1949 Armistice Agreements that created Israel, but deviates inwards, cutting off 122 villages (274,000 people) from the rest of the territory, in areas now known as 'closed zones' (UNCTAD Secretariat, 2006).

To maintain their residency rights, the people living in these areas must apply for permits from the Israeli Civil Administration, while Palestinians who work in these areas must apply for a permit to enter. Permits last only six months and they are not easily granted – it is estimated that only 18% of Palestinians that worked in the closed zone in 2008 received permits (Human Development Report, 2010). Agriculture has been one of the sectors that have been worst affected by The Wall, with 30% and 20% of arable land in the oPt rendered inaccessible, and water supplies severely disrupted or limited (UNCTAD, 2009).

Amid such hostile business conditions by 2003 outside investment dropped by 90% (UNCTAD Secretariat, 2004), while access to finance became increasingly difficult, falling by 2002 by 24% (ibid) of its pre-2000 level. Unemployment, that had fallen in the previous 15 years from 26.6% to 21.2%, spiked to an all-time high of 41.2% in 2002 (Kawasmi and White, 2010).

Gaza

Gaza – which was to go on to suffer another military campaign lasting three weeks in December 2008–January 2009, killing over 1,300 people (UNCTAD, 2009) – has been worst affected by the violence and economic repercussions.

In September 2005, Israeli unilaterally disengaged from Gaza, marking, according to former Israeli Prime Minister, Ariel Sharon, the 'end of Israeli control over and responsibility for the Gaza Strip' (Human Development Report, 2010). This 'gift' soured, however, as it was followed by a new regime of containment as Israel hermetically sealed Gaza's borders. The trade route between Gaza and West Bank was severed, while the supply of basic goods to Gaza has been so restricted businesses have been unable to operate (ibid).

Due to the blockade, data on business activity in Gaza is sketchy, however the Palestinian Federation of Industries estimates that 98% of Gaza's industrial operations had become inactive by 2010 (Human Development Report, 2010). Even activities that do not rely on outside resources have suffered under the blockade. Fishing, which accounts for 4% of Gaza's gross domestic product, is under threat due to shrinking of fishing grounds as the security ring around Gaza closed (ibid).

Economic survival

Against these odds, the Palestinian economy still continues to function and after the initial shock of the *intifada*, began to claw back ground and by 2007, unemployment had dropped to 28.9% – not far from its all time low, of 21.2%, in 1999 (Kawasmi and White, 2010). This level, however, varies widely between the regions, with 72% of business activity found in the remaining West Bank (ibid). Many of these jobs, however, did not come from enterprise but from the PA itself who increased the public sector by over 50%, from 103,000 people in 1999 to 159,000 in 2007 (ibid).

In the private sector, there is evidence to show that agriculture absorbed some of the shock of mass unemployment, employing around 16% of the labour force in 2004, compared to 13% in 1999 (Khan and Naqib, 2006).The change, however, shows a shift from higher paid, skilled industrial activity to low paid working the land, as in the same time period industries such as construction and manufacturing declined from 16% and 22% respectively, down to 13% and 12% (ibid).

This is downgrade is evident in the fact that, despite some job market recovery, in 2009 poverty was still 10% higher than 10 years before with 67% of Palestinians living below the poverty line and 48% of those in extreme poverty (Kawasmi and White, 2010).

Even the agricultural lifeline is under threat due to the continuous confiscation of Palestinian land by the Israeli authorities. For example by 2004, 86% of the land confiscated for the construction of the Separation Barrier was agricultural, leading to West Bank Palestinians employed in the sector to drop from 23% in 2004 to 14% in March 2005 (Khan and Naqib, 2006).

The ability of private enterprise to function amid such conditions can be, to a large extent, accredited to their size (particularly as most are self-financing), allowing them react more quickly to change.

In this way, businesses who survived the crisis have continued to function, despite restrictions imposed by internal barriers, as they have been able to downscale; localising operations by producing and selling goods in the same small territory.

However, the same time, they remain vulnerable – powerless to influence the environment in which they operate, and, while the barriers remain, having little hope of achieving economies of scale through expansion (Human Development Report, 2010; Kawasmi and White, 2010) – in turn, limiting their ability to generate employment.

Externally the growth potential for exporters looks no better. Exports continue to be handled by Israeli middlemen and since the Intifada this market is closing due to increasingly tighter and unpredictable boarder restrictions (Kawasmi and White, 2010).

A further barrier to development is that a high proportion– estimated at 50% to 60% (Kawasmi and White, 2010) – of businesses continue to exist informally; operating without registration or licensing. Before the establishment of the PA, Palestinian enterprises found ways to avoid paying tax to the Israeli authorities and evidence suggests that this culture has continued.

Attempts by the PA to move businesses to the formal sector have been hampered by its own licensing and registration process, which is expensive and highly convoluted. To set up a business, an investor must go to 17 different departments to secure approvals, in a process that is said to take up to a year and a half and costs between $4000 and $5000. Today, the World Bank business ranking for the oPt stands at 139 out of 183 economies[3].

Furthermore, due to Israeli security measures, many businesses are forced to operate beyond the jurisdiction of the government as it only possible to start a new business the areas administered by the PA; meaning that in the majority of the territory, including the entire Gaza strip, all new businesses must be run informally (Kawasmi and White, 2010). As these businesses operate outside of government jurisdiction, it is impossible to collect accurate figures, but the PA estimates that the informal sector employs around 180,000 people and generates $300 million annually (ibid).

The effect on business is to keep operations small, and income at subsistence level. Due to their lack of registration, they have no access to financing from banks or grants from donors. Employment is unregulated, operating outside safety laws and very low income. The PA has estimated that the average employee earns $800 annually, with wide regional variations (Kawasmi and White, 2010). Additionally, the PA acknowledges that child labour is a problem[4].

The importance of family and community

This chapter would not be complete if something were not said about the resilience, social cohesion and ingenuity of the Palestinian people to help themselves.

Despite terrible food insecurity, a food crisis has not materialised, thanks partly to the support of international aid, but also from the strong social ties and tradition of helping each other (Human Development Report, 2010). In addition, culturally, Palestinians place a high priority on education, showing ambition and optimism. In spite of the disruption and damage done to education institutions as a result of military action (ibid), Palestinians, by global standards remain well educated, with a literacy rate of 99.1% among 15 to 24 year olds in 2009 (Kawasmi and White, 2010).

Many businesses have continued to function thanks to these same support mechanisms – families often provide the labour for a business (and often unpaid – Human Development Report, 2010), as well as its security and financing. A survey conducted by the UN found that 80% of enterprises in the oPt relied on personal and family savings for their start up and operating costs (UNCTAD Secretariat, 2004).

The UN has noted a spirit of resilience, initiative, drive and optimism among oPt entrepreneurs observing that:

> Entrepreneurs have proven their willingness to assume the risks associated with new ventures, despite adverse market conditions. In so doing, they have demonstrated a remarkable capacity to harness their personal qualities (talents, education and previous experience) and available resources to exploit emerging business opportunities. (UNCTAD Secretariat, 2004, p. 23)

Personal will, however, is not enough to grow an economy. In a political climate where land can be confiscated and infrastructure destroyed, entrepreneurs – like outside investors – are unwilling to invest in long-term projects, preventing industrial growth (UNCTAD Secretariat, 2004).

Palestine and the social welfare debate with regards to SME Development

Since the establishment of the PA, donor aid has been an integral part of the Palestinian economy, accounting for 14% of GNI from 1994 up until the 2000 crisis (Khan and Naqib, 2006).

Pre-*intifada*, many of these contributions – in the form of donations, grants, and loans with generous interest rates and long repayment periods – were provided for economic development projects (Khan and Naqib, 2006).

Even before crisis, however, the economic impact of many of donor development initiatives were not as effective as hoped. For this, the UN has placed much of the blame on the donors themselves, arguing that they were creating projects more geared to serving their own commercial interests than to addressing industry shortfalls; undertaking initiatives with little research of the private sector's needs or knowledge of other donor projects in the area; and taking too long in their preparation and implementation[5].

With the onset of the crisis, donations grew (57% over the period between September 2000 and September 2002 (UNCTAD Secretariat, 2004)), but with the focus shifting from long-term development to emergency assistance, as conditions deteriorated. In 2000, the ratio between the two types of aid was approximately 7:1 in favour of development assistance. By 2002, however, the ratio had altered to almost 5:1 in favour of emergency assistance, with development assistance declining by 70% (ibid).

Evidence from The Rosa Luxemburg Foundation; a non-profit, socialist research organisation suggests that this policy has continued. As the means of self-sustainability have been eroded by the increased security measures, NGOs have continued to fill the 'need' gap with food aid and medical care. Development assistance is still active, but rather than helping people to start or continue independent businesses, NGOs *themselves* are said to be providing the employment through donor sponsored jobs in one of their many projects.

As a consequence, beyond conflict violence, people have not suffered as they have done in other crisis nations; from famine or disease, but are relatively healthy (Human Development Report, 2010).

The generosity of the international community means that this resource is not likely to run dry in the foreseeable future, but at the same time rather than advancing the Palestinian cause, it could providing a further obstacle.

Donor projects have been criticised by the UN, who has stated that, without a long-term development plan, Palestinians are prevented from creating a self-sustaining economy, and are becoming increasingly dependent on aid (UNCTAD, 2004).

In this way, the UN argues, aid becomes 'distorting'. Rather than helping Palestinians to overcome development problems, aid may actually be preventing it, as with food, basic necessities and even jobs provided for, one of the few tools the Palestinians have to assert their independence and resist the occupation; namely their own initiative, drive, resourcefulness and entrepreneurial spirit is being eroded (UNCTAD Secretariat, 2004).

Food programmes also act as unfair competition for local businesses, and even make the territory *more vulnerable* to containment, as with essential goods provided for, complete closure of borders becomes viable (Khan and Naqib, 2006). And while Palestine slips into a culture of dependency, economically the main benefactors of international aid is Israeli as the oPt buys almost 40% of its goods from the country (UNCTAD Secretariat, 2004).

Furthermore, the fulfilling of basic need serves to remove the stress factors that force change, creating a society in limbo; suffering in degradation, powerless to command its future, but without the urgency of a crisis to force a resolution. It also allows governments to take a step back from the issue as without a humanitarian disaster on-hand, they are excused, for the time being, from stepping into the fray.

As Peter Schaefer, Head of Office, Rosa Luxemburg Foundation, Palestine observes:

> The (Palestinian) people don't have to fight Israel and I think also the situation is convenient (for outside nations). I mean why should (the political situation) change course? Everything works fine. There is no conflict, there is no resistance. Nothing is happening. If (a conflict situation) happens, it's easily controllable, compared with other conflict areas. So everything is fine – why should anybody exert pressure?
>
> People get enough rice and cooking oil, what's lacking is of course the freedom to do what you want yourself. I feel that's always the biggest problem to explain to people: what it means to live for an extended period of time under foreign domination, how this changes a society[6].

So far, the major donors have placed themselves outside of the political debate; working in the country but remaining silent on the Palestinian cause. This is most likely because if their work became political, they may cause friction with their international sponsors and risk losing funding. Their silence, however, has been noted by the UN who has criticised them for seeing to the immediate need while ignoring its causes. In a report published in 2006, the UN urges donors not to underestimate their influence in international politics and 'exert all possible efforts to limit the extension of asymmetric containment strategies as a necessary part of economic recovery and long-term development' Khan and Naqib, 2006, p. 41). Whether this will ever happen, remains to be seen.

The PA and SME assistance

The PA recognised that SMEs are the bedrock of its economy, and has sought to support the sector by attracting foreign investment and improving exports.

Pre-*intifada*, the authority had attempted to widen its export market beyond Israel, with the Palestine Liberation Organisation, on behalf of the PA, signing several trade agreements with the US, the EU, the European Free Trade Association and the Arab Free Trade Area, to provide duty free access for Palestinian industrial exports (Khan and Naqib, 2006). Also, in the same time frame, the PA initiated nine industrial estates and free zones – six in the West Bank, and three in Gaza – to foster growth in its industrial sector. The estates, built with donor money, were planned to be constructed on the border between the oPt and Israel, to help ensure the free movement of people and goods, and agreements were reached with the Israeli authorities that they were to be exempted from closures and, in the future, from thorough security checks.

Sadly, the free zone projects never got off the ground. To-date, only one has been built; Gaza Industrial Estate which started operations in 1999 with 58 businesses. Two years into the intifada only 18 remained (UNCTAD Secretariat, 2004) and at the time of writing, the site is said to have been completely raised[7].

In the wake of the intifada, the PA split its initiatives into two categories: 'short-term', to alleviate poverty, and 'long-term', to reduce its economic dependence on Israel. Like its donor counterparts, the PA placed priority on the short-term, and sought to fulfil these objectives by focusing on sectors such as agriculture and food processing that – although they typically provide only low paid work – had 'stronger potential for growth and job creation than export oriented sectors', considering barriers to external trade (Khan and Naqib, 2006, p. 20).

The PA supported these industries by: granting priority treatment to labour intensive public investment projects; providing loan guarantees for new investments in the industrial sector; subsidising the purchase of fertilisers; and buying locally produced goods for donor funded poverty alleviation programmes (Khan and Naqib, 2006).

However, with the destruction of many of its infrastructure projects and others put on hold, the PA has seen its administrative powers shrink further. With external development out of its remit, the PA looked inward; into its own organisation to stimulate growth by improving its touch points with private enterprise.

The PA recognises the process of setting up and operating a business is expensive and bureaucratic, while the ministries the private sector has to deal with are inefficient and lack transparency. To address this problem, in 2002, it started a new reform agenda, the '100 Days Plan for government action', with a view to streamlining the civil service and modernising ministries, enforcing accountability, and creating a transparent legal environment (UNCTAD Secretariat, 2004, p. 32).

Meanwhile, to address the difficulties in licensing and registration, the PA plans to develop a one-stop-shop service where an investor can fulfil the necessary requirements in a single place, cutting the time and cost[8].
However, it has been argued by the UN that such reforms are overly ambitious and unworkable, unless the oPt achieves statehood, as it lacks the administrative capacity, human resources and political capital needed to put them into practice (Khan and Naqib, 2006). In addition, the PA currently has very little power to address business laws and regulation that are woefully out of date. At present companies must be registered under a law established in 1964 by the Jordanian and Egyptian governments when the West Bank was under the occupation of Jordan and Gaza, Egypt (Kawasmi and White, 2010). Furthermore, there are no new laws to cover modern industry such as intellectual property (IP) rights, internet law or patents[9].

New Palestinian business laws have been drafted, but have been awaiting approval since 1998 (Kawasmi and White, 2010), while IP laws are said to be in the pipeline[10]. However, presently no laws can be established, as for some years the legislative council (which authorises the laws) have been unable to function as its members 'are in prison', according to a PA spokesperson[11]. He added that under Palestinian law, the President can make new laws by decree, but this takes time and the legislative council always has final approval, meaning that new decrees can be overturned.

Further, enforcing laws already in existence is difficult in the areas the PA does control, due to lack of resources – and impossible in area 'C', as it has no jurisdiction.

The PA, however, as the closest the oPt has to a government, could and should have a large part to play its developmental future. It has been recommended by the UN that rather than pursuing individual projects, donor money should be considered a *national resource* and given to the PA who would play the lead role in project coordination. With the Ministry of Planning in charge, projects have a greater chance of being geared towards national objectives; linking with existing industries to create trade relationships and becoming strategically important for the economy at large. Resources for relief aid, should, where possible, be sourced locally to support domestic industry, while social aid in health, education and other welfare initiatives should complement each other and meet the requirements of an overall national strategy. In return, to assist donors, the UN recommends that the PA improves its financial, judiciary and support system, to foster transparency and accountability (Khan and Naqib, 2006).

However, without direct access to this resource (and with almost no foreign investment or public money of its own) it is not the PA who continues to set the development agenda, but donors, conceiving projects in isolation without wider objectives and even damaging the success of others by initiating rival projects.

The PA's position as the commander of its country is further undermined by the fact its very survival depends on donations from outside providers, which can be withheld if the oPt steps out of international party line.

This happened in 2006 when Hamas came to power in Gaza and although unrelated to the party the PA suffered a temporary but complete cut of US and EU funding (Wendland, 2006). As the oPt's principal employer, one can only imagine the devastating impact that with drawing funds had across the territory – or how the people and the PA itself have since modified their behaviour to avoid its repetition; downgrading the PA into not a representative of its citizens, but rather a pawn to manipulate them.

Conclusion

At the time of writing, the last segments of 'The Wall' are being erected. The resulting isolation, not only internationally but of enclaves within the territory, has driven an already weak economy to crisis point.

While the PA recognises the importance of business, it has not the jurisdiction to affect its most pressing problems. Without sovereignty and with it the power to halt the containment policy, make new laws, impose existing ones and its own public money, the PA is too restricted to steer its countries economic future which remains in the hands of its Israeli occupiers and the priorities of international donors.

Likewise, while donors have successfully filled the 'need-gap,' a decade later the economic crisis is no closer to being resolved as the underlying causes have largely been ignored. Donations although generous have not strengthened economic opportunities but arguably weakened them, creating a culture of dependency amongst Palestinians while taking away the stress factors that may force change. Moreover, this resource may have served to accelerate and strengthen the principal cause of the oPt's economic decline (the Israeli containment policy), as Israel does not need to consider how the state will provide for itself.

At the heart of the issue lies the Palestinian dream of an independent state, without which, the ability to create a self-sustainable economy will remain forever out of their hands. With sovereignty currently little more than a pipe-dream, think tanks such as The Palestinian Strategy Group (PSG) have put forward the suggestion of dissolving the PA and handing back responsibility for the oPt to Israel, creating a bi-nation state. Though seemingly a step back, (and not without problems practically and ideologically) the PSG argues the gains of returning to Israel may well outweigh the losses; taking the issue back to basics and releasing Palestine from the disastrous 'peace process' that Israel has exploited to further its occupation and control. More importantly, however, for the first time in over two decades Israel will bear the administrative responsibility for the human cost of its occupation, with the inference that the monetary expense alone will place a rethink of such policies firmly on the table.

Acknowledgements
The author would like to thank Richard Agnew for data collection and editorial assistance.

Notes
1. Interview with Hazem Shunnar, Assistant Deputy Minister at the Ministry of National Economy, Palestine (February 2012)
2. Interview with Hazem Shunnar, Assistant Deputy Minister at the Ministry of National Economy, Palestine (February 2012). The PA has full jurisdiction only in area A (17% of the territory), some jurisdiction in area B (24%) and no jurisdiction in area C was in the hand of the Israelis.
3. Interview with Hazem Shunnar, Assistant Deputy Minister at the Ministry of National Economy, Palestine (February 2012)
4. Interview with Hazem Shunnar, Assistant Deputy Minister at the Ministry of National Economy, Palestine (February 2012)
5. Gaza Industrial Estate, for example, was conceived in isolation from existing industries in the area, making it highly dependent on Israel for its trade linkages. Source: UNCTAD secretariat, (2004) 'Palestinian small and medium-sized enterprises: Dynamics and contribution to development' United Nations Conference on Trade and Development p. 36.
6. Interview Peter Schaefer, Head of Office, Rosa Luxemburg Foundation

Palestine, April 2012.

7   Interview Peter Schaefer, Head of Office, Rosa Luxemburg Foundation Palestine, April 2012.

8   Interview with Hazem Shunnar, Assistant Deputy Minister at the Ministry of National Economy, Palestine (February 2012)

9   Interview with Hazem Shunnar, Assistant Deputy Minister at the Ministry of National Economy, Palestine (February 2012)

10 Interview with Hazem Shunnar, Assistant Deputy Minister at the Ministry of National Economy, Palestine (February 2012)

11 Interview with Hazem Shunnar, Assistant Deputy Minister at the Ministry of National Economy, Palestine (February 2012)

9

The politics of welfare after revolution and war: The Imam Khomeini Relief Committee in the Islamic Republic of Iran

Kevan Harris

Introduction

In northeast Tehran, on an edge of the ever-expanding capital city and next to an amusement park, sits the sprawling and lavish new headquarters of the Imam Khomeini Relief Committee (IKRC).[1] As the largest of the self-described 'revolutionary' welfare institutions of the Islamic Republic of Iran, the IKRC provides a range of services to target populations, including financial aid and health insurance to low or no-income families, interest-free loans for housing, scholarships for young Iranians, and stipends for the elderly poor in rural areas. While it solicits donations from the public, the organization relies on the Iranian government for the majority of its revenue. It is colloquially known in Iran as *Komiteh-ye Emdad* (Relief Committee), and its blue octagonal collection boxes are spread out among the country's cities and towns. As with semi-public welfare organizations in other countries, such as urban Catholic federations in 1930s America or the Eva Perón Foundation in 1950s Argentina, Iran's welfare system contains a prominent place for 'charity' institutions that blur the lines between the public purse and the private sphere (see Dostgharin in this volume for further examples in Iran).[2] In doing so, they take part in the political construction of social boundaries between needy and undeserving populations. For Iran, this boundary has continually been contested through revolution, war, and reconstruction.

On a visit in late 2009 to IKRC headquarters, the institutional habitus of the organization was visibly apparent.[3] Its managers wear the oversized suit, conspicuous beard, and personal religious accoutrements that became popularized via a particular Islamic revolutionary 'counterculture' that spawned in the public sector after 1979. Not only are photographed visits from Hezbollah leader Sayyed Hassan Nasrallah and various Hamas dignitaries visible in the entryway of its main building, but the IKRC itself has branches in Lebanon, Syria, the Palestinian Territories, Iraq, Afghanistan, and Tajikistan. In the IKRC's own research journal, a symbol of global knowledge production for the organization slightly at odds with its revolutionary habitus, a recent article on the social ills of poverty is written by an in-house religious scholar. It quotes Imam Ali, the Shi'a-revered son-in-law of the Prophet, on the subject: 'It is very likely that poverty turns into blasphemy' (Jalali 2005: 45). Poverty alleviation is therefore presented as pious, something any Islamic state is beholden to engage in, even as it also fits with the well-known Millennium Development Goals of the United Nations.

Yet how did the makeup of such an organization evolve and intertwine with the trajectory of Iran's post-revolutionary state formation? After all, religious poverty charity organizations in Muslim-majority countries are often located outside the networks of the state.[4] The IKRC, as evidenced by its name, is associated with the main founder of the Islamic Republic of Iran, Ruhollah Khomeini. Created in the revolutionary turmoil of 1979, the IKRC was mandated to give aid to the 'deprived and excluded.' Its structure and duties, however, considerably expanded during the long war with Iraq from 1980-88. As in many European states in the first half of the 20th century (Goodin and Dryzek 1995), warfare formed a crucial conditioning mechanism for the ways through which the Iranian welfare system developed. Yet the State's survival amidst conflict also depended on how it was able to utilize the levers of social policy to maintain sufficient public support and participation.

From outside the country, it surprised most onlookers that the new revolutionary government even lasted a few years. Many reasoned that the State mobilized the population during the Iran-Iraq War through the exhortations of a martyr-laden Shi'a ideology, which alone could galvanize the human wave attacks of volunteer brigades that drove back the Ba'athist enemy. Others believed that the pre-1979 munitions and training of the Shah's army formed the edifice on which the country's survival rested. Yet few scholars and journalists at the time were aware of the manner in which welfare-making activities intertwined with State-making and war-making in the new Islamic Republic.[5] Just as organizations like the Islamic Revolutionary Guards Corps and the *basij* militia arose during the post-revolutionary period in parallel to the armed forces inherited from the Pahlavi Monarchy, a set of new welfare organizations emerged and played major roles in wartime Iran. As the first, and arguably most important, of these para-governmental welfare organizations, the IKRC was heavily engaged in re-organizing social life for those most affected by war, whether on the front lines or in the cities and countryside. Consequently, the ideological connection of social policy with revolutionary legitimation and the reorientation of welfare institutions towards new social strata replaced the social support networks of kinship and family with State-linked welfare to an extent previously not experienced in Iran.

After the war ended, the IKRC did not disappear. Instead, it became heavily relied upon by the Islamic Republic's post-war State-building project. The organization currently provides an array of welfare services to nearly ten percent of the country's population. In this chapter, I first focus on the IKRC activities which emerged in response to war exigencies. The outcome was a warfare-welfare organizational complex whose categories of 'needy' and 'deserving' were constructed in tandem with the State itself. Then, I analyze the social and political effects of the IKRC's activities, including how segmented groupings of beneficiaries and social cleavages that lasted well beyond the war period are embedded in the contested public discourse over social policy in Iran today.

The IKRC's origins and war activities

Although little documentation exists on the subject, the IKRC's revolutionary pedigree predates the fall of the Pahlavi monarchy. The original governing council of the welfare body, formed 22 days after the collapse of the Shah's government in February 1979, contained Khomeini loyalists who had participated in underground resistance movements for years. These men, such as Mehdi Karroubi and Habibollah Asgarowladi, coordinated relief for families of political prisoners during the Shah's reign. Amidst the revolutionary chaos of 1979, and as multiple political groups and networks contended for influence in the newly forming State, Khomeini established the IKRC as a manifestation of support for a symbolic grouping of those who had demonstrated against the Shah in the streets over the previous months. Khomeini referred to this collective social actor as the deprived, excluded, or dispossessed of society.

During a long process of resistance to the Shah's rule, as well as during the revolutionary mobilization itself, such linguistic terms for a 'people' became transformed from ones that connoted the passivity of the humble masses into words that signified the active agents of revolutionary upheaval (Abrahamian 1993: 47-8). As a result, this category of social actors became central to the legitimation of rule by the revolutionaries. Khomeini, who eventually assumed the position of Supreme Jurisprudent in the new government, told the public, 'Those who have been deprived their whole life should not be so in an Islamic Republic' (Kimiafar 2008: 28). Yet, given that the 'masses' of Iranian society were now spoken of as active participants in the creation of a new State, earlier relationships of charity could not suffice. Khomeini's successor, Ali Khamene'i, illustrated the IKRC's new position in Iranian State-society relations when he noted,

> 'With the formation of the IKRC in the early phase of the revolution, the Imam [Khomeini] conveyed the importance of the dispossessed for the opinions of government officials and *institutionalized it*' (*ibid*: 29, emphasis added).

The IKRC, in other words, was borne amidst revolutionary strife and absorbed the conflict-forged categories of the era into its operational rubric. Its organizational identity, including the habitus of its staff and volunteers, is bound up with these origins.

When the Pahlavi State collapsed, this surrounding conflict structured the role of the IKRC as a para-governmental entity, a parallel institution to the inherited structures of the old regime. Welfare institutions, under the auspices of ministerial bodies, certainly existed during the Pahlavi monarchy. Yet the dynamics of the post-revolutionary struggle for supremacy by Khomeini loyalists ensured that these organs were sidelined and new 'revolutionary' institutions acted as the auxiliaries of Khomeini's faction. This occurred for two main reasons.

First, as with any major social revolution, the incoming revolutionaries did not trust the bureaucracy of the *ancien régime*, and anything associated with the previous State was considered a possible fifth column. For Khomeini and his followers, it was a self-perceived truism that the Shah and his elite cared little for the population, and therefore any sort of new welfare body should be constructed *sui generis*. New incoming government cadres subsequently policed all of the existing ministries from within, and the daily routines of bureaucratic order were frequently upended by the chaos and violence of the post-revolutionary years.[6]

Second, a large amount of self-organization within communities occurred in the months following the revolution's victory. Self-appointed committees in city neighborhoods, often armed, took over the distribution of basic goods, the regulation of public order, and even the extra-judicial pursuit of 'revolutionary justice.' One of the priorities of the revolutionary government in 1979 was to corral these groups into a new State, or at least disband and disarm them. Yet the winning revolutionary coalition which toppled the Shah did not solely contain Khomeinists, but also a host of competing opposition groups with varying ideologies and social bases – Islamic liberals, secular Marxists, alternative radical Islamist organizations. The struggle for power between elements of this coalition consumed the domestic life of Iran for more than two years beyond the revolution, even after Ba'athist Iraq invaded in September 1980. Khomeini's followers continually created organizations parallel to the inherited bureaucracies in order to outflank their competitors in the political and social spheres.

From the local communes of Khomeini-supporting militants rose the Islamic Revolutionary Guard Corps, who, in Napoleonic fashion, refused to use the officer ranking system of the existing Armed Forces. *Ad hoc* courts for punishing Pahlavi officials with 'Islamic justice' were haphazardly organized under a revolutionary tribunal system, which often clashed in jurisprudence with existing civil courts. The 1979 constitution itself combined the Fifth Republic-inspired structures of Parliament and President with separate bodies of Islamic 'guidance' overseen by the quite unorthodox Shi'a position of Guardianship of Jurisprudence that Khomeini occupied. The IKRC took over the non-State networks of charity housed in urban bazaars that existed in pre-revolutionary days (Bhakhash 1986: chs 3-6, also see interviews by planning officials in Amouee 2002 on the subject of post-revolutionary parallel organs). In this way, the welfare push by Khomeini and the Islamic Republic was a method of containing and channeling the popular mobilization that emerged from the revolution into bases of support and legitimation for the State. This process would be broadened and deepened with the onset of war.

By the fall of 1980, the IKRC was present in most Iranian provinces and in both urban and rural sectors. As evidence of its rapid spread, when Iraqi forces bombarded the southwestern post city of Khorramshahr in their initial surprise raid, one of the buildings shelled was the local IKRC office (Kimiafar 2008: 33). The initial response to the war relied on provincial networks that had sprung up after the revolution, within which new elites had taken over from the fleeing Tehran-linked upper strata of the Pahlavi era (Ehsani 2009). Friday prayer Imams became major coordinators and political brokers of provincial life, and assumed chief roles in arranging the IKRC activities in their areas. The organization itself, along with the other new parallel institutions such as the Revolutionary Guard Corps, the volunteer *basij* militia, and the Construction Jihad, proved to be principal avenues for upward social mobility by individuals who possessed commitment to the new State and desired the social prestige and status attached to its cadres. Many of the initial casualties of the war were, in fact, IKRC workers who aided Iranian armed forces in the evacuation of civilians from areas under attack in southwest and western Iran.

Coordinated through Tehran, the IKRC became a logistical support organization as much as a social welfare institution.[7] Along with its initial mandate of supporting the deprived, needy, and weak strata of society, the organization took over the systematization and centralization of volunteer aid efforts. During the 1980s, the IKRC was engaged in the following activities (compiled from Kimiafar 2008):

- Gathering and transmitting public aid to war fronts to be distributed either via the military or through IKRC-manned charity stations behind front lines. Aid gathered included dried fruit and sweets, medicines, books and stationary, automobiles, trucks, and cash donations. IKRC collection caravans would roll through towns and villages across Iran soliciting aid. In 1982, for example, the value of all collected aid donated to the IKRC was estimated at over 2 billion rials, a bit under 0.1% of GDP at the time.

- Operating 350 charity stations for soldiers behind front lines, coordinated through four main IKRC centers in southwest and western Iran. These stations provided water, soup, soft drinks, sweet porridge, or ice cream, depending on the season. Also available were the services of volunteer tailors, cobblers, and barbers. In the Fao peninsula in southwest Iran, 3000-6000 soldiers used the station daily; while in Marivan in western Iran, 2000 soldiers used the station's services.

- Paying compensation to war injured and dead. Debts of soldiers were wiped clean in some cases, and fees for therapy care also covered. The largest cash transfers from IKRC in this era went to families whose property and lives were damaged by shelling and fires near the war front, or, as the war progressed, by missiles fired from Iraq into Iranian cities including Tehran. In 1987, during the 'war of the cities,' the IKRC compensated nearly 150,000 families around the country for damages due to war or natural disaster. Families of war dead were certified with 'martyr' status and received aid from IKRC until the establishment of the Martyrs Foundation, which took over this welfare function.

- Supporting war refugees who had fled the war fronts or lost homes in bombardments. The IKRC set up tent camps, arranged shared housing in cities away from the front lines, and provided food and medicine to the most indigent of the refugee population. This included not only Iranians from war-affected areas, but Afghans fleeing their own country's civil war as well as Iraqis who had been expelled by the Ba'athist State. A reported 34,000 refugees were covered by the IKRC by 1986, rising to 76,000 in 1987. The Refugee Foundation was also founded, separate from the IKRC, to subsequently handle the continuing problems of refugees. Yet individuals continued to utilize IKRC services in tandem after the war.

In sum, the IKRC became indispensible to the State's conduct of the war. In 1990, marking the eleventh anniversary of the welfare body's founding, then-Parliament head Mehdi Karroubi stated:

'Today we realize that if [the Committee and similar organizations] did not exist, there is no knowing what would have happened to the fate of the revolution and the country'.[8]

While there always exists constraints of guns vs butter, new welfare institutions can be borne from conflict due to States' attempts to maintain a mass mobilization procured earlier through volunteerism or conscription, for instance in the new pension systems of Napoleon's Grande Armée or the US' Union Army during the Civil War (Skocpol 1992). Conversely, warfare, but more specifically its aftermath, was central to the further development of Iranian welfare policy, as there now existed a status group known as 'martyrs and devotees of the revolution' that shaped political discourse, patronage, and policy decisions. The familiar historical link between war mobilization and social policy was perhaps best captured by historian AJP Taylor, who noted for England, 'The Luftwaffe was a powerful missionary for the welfare state' (1965: 455).

Post-war IKRC expansion in Iran and the politics of welfare policy

There was no shrinkage in the Iranian welfare apparatus after the war's end in 1988. The government was concerned with pent up demand for higher consumption and living standards among an exhausted population. Even though the State utilized economic levers of price, currency, and trade controls to keep consumption from dropping during the 1980s, the last few years of the war strained the government's ability to maintain such an effort (Amouee 2002). In post-war Iran, a group of liberal-minded technocrats surrounding President Hashemi Rafsanjani (1989-1997) attempted to implement a swift liberalization of the country's etatist economic structures. But the social demands for increased consumption belied their efforts at investment and price liberalization. After prices were freed on most consumer goods, a flurry of economic activity ratcheted up inflation rates to 50% by 1993. Food and housing riots occurred in poorer neighborhoods in Tehran and elsewhere. The State put the brakes on its economic liberalization plans, and a slower, sclerotic process of reform commenced. Amidst this tumult, Iran's welfare system was expanded by the State, cushioning the dislocations brought on first by the war and then later through the market. Unlike postwar European welfare States, however, the Iranian system remained fragmented due to the lack of a powerful centralizing political apparatus. Instead, an elite still rife with opposing factions could only veto the elimination of institutions rather than merge them.

Rafsanjani's first 5-year development plan promised to cover the basic needs of 570,000 elderly Iranians, 360,000 families and 1 million refugees partly by using IKRC resources.[9] The country's social security, pension, and health insurance programs were expanded via law. Although these programs were legally open to all individuals, in reality, as in most middle-income countries, a person's access to formal welfare institutions depended on their employment. Those in the public sector or in large industry enjoyed the benefits of the Social Security Organization. But workers in the informal sector, urban migrants, and villagers were outside of this system.[10] The IKRC and other organizations were utilized to provide some modicum of support for lower and excluded strata of the population as a matter of policy.[11] IKRC total declared expenditures went from 20 Billion Rials in 1991 to more than 110 Billion Rials in 1998; it reportedly increased its service provisions to cases involving 10% of the population in 1991 to 20% in 2001 (Salehi Esfahani 2005: 513-4).[12] In the economic recession of 1993-4, the IKRC proved to be a flexible agent of welfare support. As a semi-public institution, it operated outside of the budget constraints to which fully public welfare organizations (such as the State Welfare Organization) were being subjected.

This was an unplanned outcome of the dual welfare system of the post-revolutionary Iranian State. On the one hand, a corporatist system of pensions, health insurance, and formal sector job security existed for a segment of the labor force. On the other hand, an institutional complex of revolutionary welfare institutions, with the IKRC as its largest organization, catered to a variety of social groups that, most likely, would have been excluded from any corporatist welfare organization (see Harris 2010). This included families of war veterans, orphans, widows, the elderly, and families of debt prisoners. Unlike the State Welfare Organization, for example, the IKRC quickly extended its services to rural areas during the war and afterwards. It identifies beneficiaries in its Aid Project based on a series of questions that determine need, not through a pre-defined poverty line. These include collecting information on income, dependents, housing size, and ties to war veterans. Individuals can then be provided with pensions, cash, food, educational loans and grants, healthcare, housing repair grants, and marriage loans. The IKRC's separate Shahid Raja'i Project (named after the assassinated former Iranian President Ali Raja'i) specifically targets the rural elderly. Of the population covered by its Aid Project, 60% are women and 40% live in rural areas (Salehi Esfahani 2005: 518). Iran's urban-rural ratio is now 70%-30%, illustrating the targeting of rural areas by the IKRC. The organization also funds micro-loan projects and rural industry support programs for activities such as carpet weaving and animal husbandry.

On a field visit to IKRC offices in the Northeastern city of Tabriz in February 2010, supplicants were required to fill out a paper form that had changed little in 20 years, according to earlier IKRC forms seen in government archives.[13] IKRC employees and volunteers are responsible for verifying the accuracy of beneficiaries' statements about their income and living conditions. Volunteer workers far outnumber, by tens of thousands, the paid permanent staff of the IKRC. The staff, like many State-linked organizations in Iran, is populated with war veterans itself as a result of job quotas set in place after the war. Yet even within the organization there exist administrators formally trained in social work and social policy within Iran's higher education institutions (which also greatly expanded after the war). As in the habitus of most of the 'parallel' revolutionary organizations that lived well beyond the war, an initial emphasis on fervor at the expense of expertise eventually reverted back to a more sustainable tempo.

Interviews and house visits are conducted by staff and volunteers, but the system of supervision is far less advanced than the larger and more technically savvy administration of formal pensions and healthcare through the government's Social Security Organization. By 2001, over 6 million

(10% of the population) people were receiving some form of support from the IKRC, and this ratio has been maintained over the past decade.[14] While nearly 90% of the IKRC's budget comes from the Iranian government, it maintains a discourse of charity and independent public service. Blue boxes on most main streets exist for donating change and bills. During religious holidays or on specified weeks, IKRC tents are set up in major cities to collect public offerings. Like many of Iran's welfare organizations, the IKRC does also manage and garner revenue from a variety of business subsidiaries it owns.

After the 1980-8 war and the 1993-4 economic recession, absolute poverty in Iran experienced a gradual but steady decline, resulting in poverty rates far below anything seen under the pre-1979 Pahlavi monarchy – as seen in figure one. There is not one causal factor for explaining this trend, but IKRC's activities were instrumental in targeting the most deprived sectors of Iranian society – individuals that the welfare programs inherited from the Pahlavi monarchy to the post-revolutionary State were not adequately designed to reach.[15]

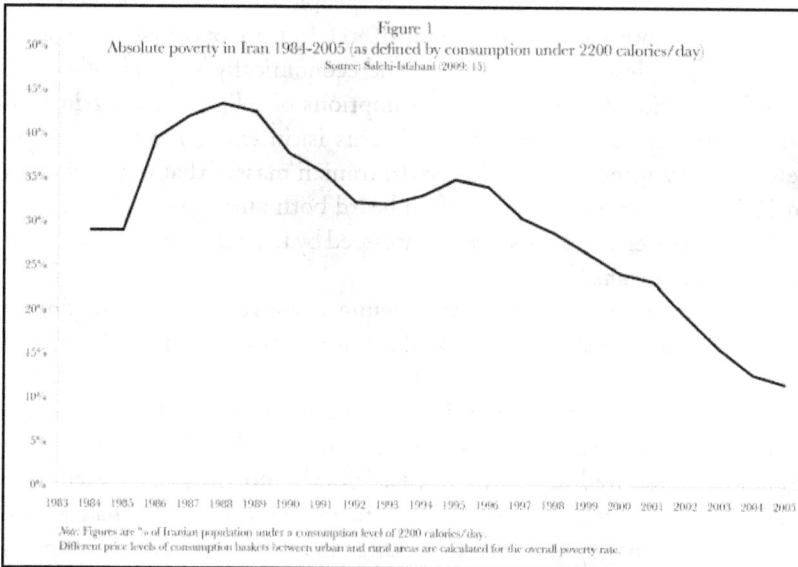

Figure 1

Absolute poverty in Iran 1984-2005 (as defined by consumption under 2200 calories/day)
Source: Salehi-Isfahani (2009: 13)

Note: Figures are % of Iranian population under a consumption level of 2200 calories/day.
Different price levels of consumption baskets between urban and rural areas are calculated for the overall poverty rate.

Nevertheless, the role of the IKRC as a semi-public or para-governmental welfare body remains controversial. There are two main criticisms of the IKRC and its associated 'revolutionary' organizations, both of which highlight the political and social cleavages that exist in contemporary Iran.

First, IKRC's activities have been accused of creating a dependent class of Iranians who remain unproductive and beholden to the Islamic Republic's largesse (see Messkoub and Doostgharin in this volume regarding dependency in Iran). Former President Rafsanjani and his aides often claimed the existence of a trade-off between economic growth and means-based welfare policy. Ayatollah Javadi Amoli, the conservative former Friday prayer leader of Qom, expressed a similar viewpoint when asked about current President Mahmoud Ahmadinejad's economic policies of increased cash spending for provincial rallies: 'One can't use the method of the Imam Khomeini Relief Committee to run the economy of the country.'[16]

Such economically liberal critiques in the Iranian public sphere, which are shared by a sizeable portion of its middle class, echo the much wider debates over the welfare state in wealthier countries, wherein means-tested welfare supposedly contributes to a 'cycle of poverty' and a 'culture of dependency.' This is what Margaret Somers and Fred Block describe as the shift of blame in ideational debates over welfare from 'poverty to perversity.' Instead of identifying social-structural reasons for poverty's persistence, the 'perversity narrative' attributes the cause of poverty to the 'corrosive effects of welfare's perverse incentives on poor people themselves' (Somers and Block 2005: 260; also see Hirschman 1991). In Iran, of course, the notion that poor people are psychologically and economically 'dependent' on the State is additionally tinged with assumptions of religious indoctrination and dogmatism among the deprived. This is, in effect, a reversal of the revolutionary agency bestowed upon the Iranian 'masses' that was celebrated in 1979. The Iranian poor, it is often heard both among some Iranians as well as in Western accounts, are easily duped by the State through spiritual and material means.[17]

Consider the observations of a young State-trained Iranian doctor who conducted her required medical service with a semi-nomadic tribe.[18] Many nomadic communities settled in permanent villages over the course of the 20th century, yet maintain nomadic migration routes seasonally. In this particular case in southwestern Iran, most families in the settled community received aid from IKRC. Elderly individuals were eligible, but even younger members with government connections also had access. This included money, rice, sugar, cooking oil, beans, and housing supplies. Loans were given for industrial activities such as bee-keeping and classes were held to teach carpet weaving for young girls. The doctor said that IKRC aid encouraged a sedentary lifestyle for these nomads, who reduced their own economic activities because of additional income accrued from the State. She expressed alarm at the end of their 'traditional' existence.

They participate less in agricultural production and animal husbandry than previously, she noted. Furthermore, the carpets produced by women tended to of poor quality and design, which made them unattractive to urban markets. These were the observations of a young educated Iranian who most likely possessed overly romantic notions of a socially autonomous, ahistorical nomadic life, as is widely celebrated in Iranian art cinema and other high culture. Nevertheless, the kernel of her observations is correct. The post-revolutionary Iranian welfare system has replaced kinship-based networks of social reproduction with State-based networks of welfare to a significant degree. This is evidenced by, and intertwined with, a drastically lowered family size, an increased entering of females into the labor force, and the shift in most rural sectors towards producing cash crops for urban markets (see the collected essays in Gheissari 2009). This cannot but alter social relations in some manner, but whether it can best be characterized as the creation of wholly 'dependent' State-society relations is another question.

IKRC officials, when interviewed, argued that the organization's goal is to end poverty, not perpetuate it. They admitted, however, that this outcome was unlikely in a developing country such as Iran. Their duties, then, should be to continually supply the poor's basic needs, whether the poverty rate goes up or down.[19] The rhetoric of 'social justice' is posited as a counter to the neo-liberal critiques of the Welfare State that, even in Iran, are prominently wielded by public intellectuals, economists and policy makers. This form of justice, however, is not transformational in the revolutionary sense that it would end poverty. IKRC and similar institutions derive their legitimacy from their revolutionary origins and their service during the war and the country's reconstruction. Yet that legitimacy can be undermined when other prominent ideological frameworks challenge its 'revolutionary' institutional habitus. From a comparative viewpoint, the organization is not radically different to recent development initiatives such as Bolsa Familia in Brazil and Progresa/Oportunidades in Mexico – small subsistence-level cash transfers to the poorest strata (Barrientos 2009).

A second criticism of the IKRC contends that the organization is heavily politicized along the Islamist lines of Iran's conservative political factions. This distorts its activities in two ways. The IKRC devotes resources towards proselytizing for the mix of nationalism and Shi'a theology that form the core ideological claims to legitimacy by the Islamic Republic. In addition, it maintains itself as a mostly independent para-governmental organization outside of the regulatory bodies in the executive or legislative branches. It is only accountable to the offices of the Supreme Leader, from where its public revenues are directly drawn. Such parallel organizations, as mentioned earlier, not only sometimes overlap with state ministries, but actively resist being incorporated or merged into more accountable structures. During the late 1990s, the liberal-reformist political faction, led by President Mohammad Khatami (1997-2005), engaged in a major attempt to centralize and streamline the various activities of the government. This was not simply a technocratic move, but a realization that their conservative competitors in the political field used such parallel bodies to continually stymie and overturn the actions of the democratic institutions of the State.[20] The rural development agency Construction Jihad, for example, was brought under the Ministry of Agriculture.

Yet, in the sphere of welfare, the Khatami government was less successful. While a new Ministry of Welfare and Social Security finally opened in 2003, neither the IKRC nor other, smaller foundations for the care of revolutionary martyrs and war veterans could be brought under its ministerial auspices (Saiedi 2004). During the 1990s, there were major accusations of corruption, nepotism, and lack of transparency against these bodies. They control large asset funds and manage privatized businesses. While the IKRC is not the most notorious of these para-governmental agencies, it is associated with the sector's cronyism. In sum, there are dual accusations against the IKRC: active zealotry for the conservative forces and ideology of the Iranian State, and corrupt practices that undermine democratic and transparent operations of the elected government. Critics argue it is a bastion of regime 'soft power' masquerading as an 'ordinary charity' (Majidyar and Alfoneh 2010). The Iranian State itself is responsible for a fair amount of this characterization, since IKRC charity events are often shown on television or described in large banners unfurled near town bazaars. The head of the IKRC in 2009, Hossein Anvari, even claimed that none of the families helped by the organization took part in the country's Green Movement demonstrations in the summer of that year, which he said was 'natural because [these families] have touched the warmth of people's donations' (*Financial Times*, 6/30/2009). While a statement like this is taken at face value by opposition activists and Western media organizations, a more nuanced reading is needed of the organization's history and position in Iranian State-society relations.

Conclusion

Unlike the portrayals by critics, the 6-7 million individuals who are beneficiaries of IKRC activities cannot realistically be conceptualized as a solid class of clients embedded in a patron-client relationship with the State, and not only for the reason that the organization is semi-autonomous from the government. For example, during three months in the spring of 2010 in the town of Babak, in Kerman province, with a population of 50,000, monetary allowances of $20-30/month were given to 3800 families, nearly 700 students received some form of stipend, $300,000 in micro-loans were given to 46 borrowers, 120 food baskets were delivered, 22 cases of rent arrears were covered, $1000 in medical bills were paid, food and energy coupons worth $500,000 were distributed to 4,000 families, dowry and funeral costs were financed for tens of families, and $64,000 in donations were collected.[21] This is hardly a political machine of the Peronist or Richard Daley type.

The continued fragmentation of Iran's welfare system does, however, condition the political categories through which social policy is discussed. Large segments of population over the past three decades have been excluded from various organizations due to class structure, the factional battles within the State, and the identification of some groups as either 'deserving' or 'dependent.' Poorer Iranians struggled to gain access to the new State-generated flows of prestige and status that would insure better livelihoods, such as 'martyr' or veteran affiliation for admission to educational institutions or jobs in provincial State offices. Concurrently, the target population of the old corporatist welfare system – formal workers, professionals, newly educated graduates - demanded access to the political and cultural capital that would allow for the creation and maintenance of middle class lifestyles free from the bureaucratic authoritarianism of a post-revolutionary State. In this social landscape, 'legitimate' welfare given to war veterans and the poor in the 1980s and 1990s morphed into 'undeserved' benefits for a group too young to have fought in the war, and in some cases (such as the *basij*), for youth actively engaged in preventing the middle class from enjoying autonomy from the hated paternalistic intrusions by the State. Meanwhile, it became apparent that political elites and officials possessed the means of protecting their own networks from downward mobility, while the new professional and formal working classes' 'fear of falling' became manifest. All of these factors are embedded in Iranian public discourse over social policy, and are easily manipulated by political entrepreneurs of various ideological stripes.

Yet this transformation reveals an important outcome of Iranian social policy since the 1979 revolution. As the philosopher Alasdair MacIntyre argued, 'the institutionalization of welfare, like all other rises in the standard of living, alters the horizons of possibility for different social groups and alters too the standards by which they assess their deserts and their rights. Not absolute but relative deprivation becomes crucially important' (2008 [1967]: 346). In Iran, this form of deprivation, or, as sociologists prefer to call it, social inequality, arguably underlies most of the main conflicts in the country currently. The onset of democratic challenge by social groups empowered through earlier rounds of State-led development and social policy is not exclusive to Iranian history. It is perhaps the overarching characteristic of the 'Third Wave' era of democratization, which took place mostly in middle-income countries in the world economy (Arrighi 1990). Politics in Iran today, therefore, can be partly and fruitfully understood as a consequence of the various and conflicting lineages of welfare efforts and the response to those efforts by newly empowered social classes.

Notes

1. The interviews and ethnographic fieldwork used for the preparation of this chapter occurred between June 2009 and May 2010 in Iran. This research was assisted by a fellowship from the International Dissertation Research Fellowship Program of the Social Science Research Council, with funds provided by the Andrew W. Mellon Foundation.
2. On the role of US Catholic charities in channeling New Deal welfare policy, see Brown and McKeown 1997; on Eva Perón's massive Foundation, which did much to maintain her husband's base among the *descamisados* but also was accused of operating as a personal slush fund, see Taylor 1979.
3. Habitus, for Bourdieu (Bourdieu and Wacquant 1992, Bourdieu 1998), refers to the social disposition of individuals as structured by their positions in particular social fields. Institutional habitus is often used to discuss such 'total' institutions as the educational system, but for Bourdieu is a method of understanding how social reality can be constructed through formation and regulation of specific social practices. I employ the term to call attention to the norms and practices that are reproduced within various state welfare organizations. These can be observed not only through bureaucratic actions of its managers, but also in architecture, pamphlets, dress, and the production of social knowledge via research and journals in these institutions.

4. For a general overview of non-state social policy providers in the global South, see Gough and Wood 2004, Cammett and Maclean 2011.
5. I allude here to Charles Tilly's (1985) celebrated article on Western European state formation.
6. For instance, the newly appointed head of the Central Bank of Iran, Mohsen Nourbakhsh, discovered bullets in his desk drawers on his first day in office (Amouee 2002: 77).
7. The IKRC's old headquarters are located in drab central Tehran on Somayeh street, in a dusty multi-floored building, but were accessible to all points of the city. The differing locations of IKRC headquarters, then and now, are a telling sign of the organization's enmeshed position within the political elite, since its new buildings in northeast Tehran are difficult to reach unless one is already wealthy or have plenty of time to spend in traffic.
8. Daily Report, Near East & South Asia, FBIS-NES-90-045, 3/7/1990, p. 50.
9. Daily Report, Near East & South Asia, FBIS-NES-90-039, 2/27/1990, p. 41.
10. The problematic of a European-inspired corporatist welfare system implemented in a middle-income country with a different class structure is not unique to Iran. See Haggard and Kaufman 2008 on similar instances for Latin America.
11. As enunciated by Finance Minister Mohsen Nourbakhsh in 1993. See Daily Report, Near East & South Asia, FBIS-NES-93-150. 8/6/1993, p. 39.
12. Transparency is not a strong suit of the IKRC – its reports are not independently verified or audited by outside actors. However, these numbers do give a sense of the trends of expansion in both social expenditure as well as beneficiaries of the organization.
13. Personal observation by author, Tabriz, Iran, February 2010.
14. Interviews with IKRC officials, Tehran, Iran, October 2009.
15. Poverty levels in Iran are a highly contentious topic among the politically factionalised elite and media. Critics of the government use higher poverty lines and, consequently, generate alarming poverty rates. Government supporters use the lowest possible poverty line, such as the World Bank's $2/day line, which places Iran's poverty level at 8% in 2005. There is no official national poverty line in Iran at all which would mandate state support for individuals falling under a particular income level. As a result, not only do estimates of Iranian poverty in Western media tend to be highly exaggerated, but also educated Iranians themselves believe that poverty is rampant in their own country. In doing so, they confuse absolute poverty with relative income inequality, which is a more pressing social problem in contemporary Iran.
16. Business news site *Emruz*, 11/21/2008.
17. The analogous nature of this criticism with the arguments of Charles Murray

and other detractors of the US welfare system are no accident. Much of the libertarian critique of a welfare policy associated with a bloated and overreaching state made its way to Iran in the 1990s through translations of newspaper columns and social science articles, becoming useful political fodder for any faction temporarily out of power.

18. Interviewed in Baltimore, MD, USA, January 2011.

19. Interviews with IKRC officials, Tehran, Iran, October 2009.

20. Plans on merging these parallel institutions into government departments were mentioned by Seyyed Reza Akrami, MP in the Fifth Majles (1996-2000) and still in the parliament in 2011. Daily Report, Near East & South Asia, FBIS-NES-96-117, 6/17/1996, p. 64

21. These statistics can be found on www.emdad.ir though the frequency and accuracy of statistical collection in the IKRC are unverified. My purpose in citing these numbers is simply to give a picture of the breadth of the organization's activities and the target population.

10

Developing professional identity and practice through professional supervision programmes in the Occupied Palestinian Territories

Jane Lindsay

Introduction

International impulses to respond to the psycho-social needs of regions experiencing war and conflict and emerging into post-conflict reconstruction can lead to funding and rapid development of social programming without due diligence being paid to equipping, developing and supporting national psycho-social workers to carry out such work (see Agnew in this volume for an analysis of the repercussions of civil conflict in Palestine). Such was the case in the Occupied Palestinian Territories (oPt) in relation to the donor-driven establishment of the schools counselling service in the period immediately after the Oslo Accords (1993-5) to meet the perceived needs of young people who had been affected by the first *Intifada* (Uprising).

Since 1996, school-based psycho-social workers (graduates in social work, psychology, sociology and education) have been appointed to all schools in the oPt, with many covering more than one large school. There are currently approximately 1200 school-based psycho-social workers in post and they form the largest group of psycho-social workers, providing a service which can be accessed by the majority of Palestinian children.

This chapter first outlines the development of this role and the emergence of recognition of their need for professional training and supervision. It then considers the approach taken by the Centre for Continuing Education of Birzeit University in partnership with the Palestinian Authority Ministry of Education to develop and deliver a locally relevant Professional Diploma in Professional Supervision and to create institutional and policy structures to support the appointment of professional supervisors for school-based psycho-social workers. The approach taken to evaluate the development of the Professional Diploma in Supervision programmes and key findings of the evaluation process are then presented and discussed, highlighting the changes that appear to have been achieved by this approach. A particular finding, that both school-based psycho-social workers and supervisors were able to articulate a clearer, more confident sense of professional identity is examined. A rationale as to why this model of programme delivery appears to have been successful is offered and the transferability of this approach to other contexts and settings is considered.

The development of schools counselling in the context of the Occupied Palestinian Territories

Since the Oslo Accords (1993-5) the Palestinian Authority has had responsibility for the provision of education, health and social services within the oPt and for the development of legislation, national plans and social programming to achieve these social goals. The region is characterised by chronic and at times acute political conflict and has a rapidly deteriorating economic situation. Before the donor driven establishment of the schools counselling service in 1996, there was no history of this service in the oPt. On appointment, school-based psycho-social workers were not provided with role-specific professional training though they were frequently targeted by international non-governmental organisations and provided with short training courses to implement donor-driven experiments (for example Classroom Based Intervention Save the Children (USA) (2004)). They were not provided with professional supervision though they were 'managed' administratively at a distance. School staff and school-based psycho-social workers were unclear about their remit and role.

Giacaman (2004) conducted a baseline survey of all social workers and psycho-social workers in the West Bank & Gaza which highlighted the ineffectiveness of short training courses and noted the supervision and development needs of school-based psycho-social workers, pointing out that their professional identity was contested and that this had led to highly divergent practice. Lindsay's (2007) study found that they were taking on much crisis intervention following political events and were experiencing stress and value conflicts. Exploring support needs of these psycho-social workers, she noted that they were professionally 'isolated' and highlighted the need for professional supervision and clarity in job role. A clear job description of the role of a school counsellor was eventually developed by the Ministry of Education in 2005 which included assessing problems experienced by individual students, classes or the school and dealing with these problems by providing counselling, referral and advice and by developing and implementing preventative activities with groups (eg how to avoid drug and alcohol problems, abuse, and violence). The majority of school-based psycho-social workers had not been trained to take on this full remit of work.

Responding to these needs, the Centre for Continuing Education[1] in partnership with the Ministry of Education developed a Professional Diploma in Schools Counselling to provide professional training for school-based psycho-social workers. School-based psycho-social workers were allowed day release from their work to undertaken the programme. In the period between 2002 and 2006, three Diploma in School Counselling Programmes were provided with 'training supervision' and live practice assessment through the observation of practice and regular field visits to assess the impact of these programmes school-based psycho-social workers practice.

Structured observation of practice was a new development in professional training programmes in Palestine. This proved to be one of the strongest elements of the programme in that it made school-based psycho-social workers ' practice visible and highlighted the range of different practices used, and school-based psycho-social workers' development needs including 'personal development' (dealing with the impact of the work and stress). Overall, these programmes which trained approximately 60 school-based psycho-social workers were positively evaluated (Lindsay, 2006) with increased role clarity found but there was concern that training effects would be lost without ongoing professional supervision of practice. There was increasing recognition that achieving 'critical mass' of all school-based psycho-social workers trained to a professional standard would take many years and of the potential of employment based professional supervision to meet this deficit.

Developing a locally relevant Professional Diploma in Professional Supervision and the institutional and policy structures

The Centre for Continuing Education and the Ministry of Education strongly felt that an 'off-the-shelf' import for a Professional Diploma in Supervision from another country would not be appropriate.(Lindsay and Baidoun, 1996, Lindsay, 2010) They reviewed the literature on supervision from a range of sources including local research and devised a year long programme (with 414 contact hours over the year) with the aim of providing a planned and systematic development opportunity both for the trainee supervisors and for those school-based psycho-social workers they would be supervising. In particular, the Ministry wanted school-based psycho-social workers to undertake more planned work with groups of school students. It was felt that direct observation of practice was an essential component of the supervision role and would promote more standardised practice.

The curriculum includes theory and approaches to supervision (informed by texts such as Kadushin (1992) and Hawkins and Shohet (2006)), supervision planning; assessment and providing feedback; providing personal development sessions and a review of approaches to school counselling practice in order to assist supervisors in their educative role. The Ministry agreed that trainees would be released from their substantive roles as school-based psycho-social workers for two days a week to undertake the programme and the practicum. For the practicum, each trainee supervisor was allocated eight school-based psycho-social workers chosen by each governorate[2]. Trainee supervisors were required to provide group supervision to their eight supervisees for four hours every two weeks, individual supervision to each group member monthly and to conduct two field visits of observation of practice to each counsellor. Those joining supervision groups were required to commit to provide an intervention programme of 10 sessions with a group of school pupils. Trainee supervisors were observed and assessed in all activities and were provided with individual and group supervision themselves.

The assessment for the Professional Diploma entailed a portfolio of work products and self-evaluative reflective commentary, identifying areas for future development. This seemed a challenging and intensive practicum. During the period 2006-9 was that 54 out of 55 trainee supervisors trained (28 men and 26 women) completed the practicum fully. Given the adverse political situation in the oPt at the time, with considerable restrictions on movement, the fact that almost all completed their courses was a tribute to the dedication, persistence and resilience of both trainers, trainee supervisors and their supervisees and their perception that this intervention was needed.

In tandem with these developments, the Centre arranged and funded a local consultant to work with the Ministry on strategic planning for the schools counselling service. After considerable negotiation and debate, this was included in national planning (Ministry of Education and Higher Education (2008) *Education and Development Strategic Plan 2008-2012* which signalled the Ministry's intention to 'adopt a professional supervision system in school counselling' (2008: 105) and 'to train 77 educational school-based psycho-social workers in the skills of vocational supervision' (2008: 145) (one supervisor per 15 school-based psycho-social workers). By July 2009, thirty-seven graduates of the Diploma in Supervision programme had been appointed to these new posts.

The approach taken to evaluate the development of the Supervision programme

An evaluation model was agreed which was informed by Carpenter's (2005) version of Kirkpatrick/Barr's model of Levels of Learning Outcomes of Educational Programmes. A range of evaluation instruments was used in order to generate detailed and comprehensive findings, facilitate a more detailed understanding of the processes underpinning the delivery and impact of the programme, and also enable triangulation between the different sources of data (see Lindsay, 2008).

The approach taken in line with Rossi & Freeman's (1993: 5) views that evaluation requires not only an accurate description of the processes under evaluation but also a systematic assessment of 'the conceptualisation, design, implementation and utility of social intervention programmes'. It also was informed by Pawson and Tilley's (1997: 214) 'new rules of realistic evaluation', namely that evaluators need to focus on reasons why programmes appear to be effective; that it is important to 'penetrate beneath the surface of observable inputs and outputs of a programme' (Pawson and Tilley, 1997: 216); and that evaluators need to develop an understanding of understand how outcomes are produced, to consider 'context-mechanism-outcome pattern configuration' (1997: 217) and test explanations.

It was agreed that the evaluation would utilise a participatory methodology in which the external evaluator would work closely with Centre to define the scope of the evaluation, agree evaluation instruments and that all parties would work together to analyse and interpret results and agree future courses of action. The external evaluator made six visits to the project during the period the programmes were delivered (2006-9). The methods used for the external evaluation process included semi-structured interviews with programme staff and Ministry staff on six occasions over 3 years; review of evaluation measures undertaken by the Centre, mid- programme and end of programme semi-structured interviews with a sample of trainee supervisors for each of the four cohorts taking the programme (2006-9) (36 interviews) and a sample of supervised school-based psycho-social workers (26 interviews). Interviews were taped and transcribed.

When it was not possible to interview in English, professional interpreters provided simultaneous translation in interviews (Arabic/English). It appeared from the interviews that key themes were emerging. In order to check the accuracy of these perceptions across all those who had undertaken the programme, two post-programme surveys was devised and translated into Arabic, approved by the Ministry of Education, and sent in 2009 to both trainee supervisors and supervised school-based psycho-social workers respectively. Responses were received from 44 of a possible 55 of trainee supervisors and from 53 school-based psycho-social workers of the 100 asked to complete survey.

The surveys were processed using SPSS and back translated into English and analysed. Open-ended questions were transcribed, translated into English, the accuracy of translation was checked and these were also analysed. The next sections present the some of the findings of the evaluation. Though the evaluation as a whole considered all aspects of programme design and delivery, this article focuses on one of the most interesting elements, namely engagement with the practicum and the process of becoming a supervisor.

Choosing to train as a supervisor

One of the challenges in providing the Diploma in Supervision programme in the period from 2006-9 was that the professional supervision system had not yet been established. This meant that most of those nominated for the programme had not had personal and professional experience of supervision of their own practice though interestingly by the third year of programme delivery a number of trainees had had some experience of being supervised by those who had taken the programme on previous years. Whilst those on the first years of the programme stated that they had been 'selected and sent' on the programme by their employer, those in the third year were more likely to state that actively sought to join the programme, an indication that the programme was gaining credibility. Most trainees indicated they wanted to progress in their career to be a supervisor and thought this course would help achieve this goal. This finding was not surprising when the educational and employment profile for respondents is considered. 80% of survey respondents had been employed as school-based psycho-social workers for eight years or more, with 50% (22 people) with twelve years service or more.

Becoming a supervisor:
Undertaking the practicum (group supervision)

Trainees were required to work with eight school-based psycho-social workers as supervisors in order to complete the required practicum elements. Evaluation interviews in the period 2006-9 noted similar processes and reactions which led to a sense of a set of predictable stages which trainee supervisors might go through in starting to provide group supervision. This was tested in post programme survey to see if a model of 'key messages' might be built which would be useful for future planning and development of the programmes. This is shown in Figure 1 overleaf.

Starting the group supervision process

The majority of trainees (93%) had found it easy to identity and set up their supervision group of eight school-based psycho-social workers as 'volunteers' for them to undertake the practicum of the programme. They were clear that this was possible because of Ministry support and direction. Most recognised that some of their colleagues might be suspicious of the process illustrated by one interviewee:

> This is a very new process here and people are still suspicious that they are being spied on and inspected rather than being enabled to grow and develop. The issue of observing someone else is still a very sensitive area, but the

requirements for supervised practice and what the supervisors are meant to do are clear and this can help lessen anxiety. The agreement and planning process helps people see that this in not an investigation (*Trainee Supervisor from Bethlehem, in interview, August 2008*).

Trainees and programme staff found that successful engagement in supervision process hinged on spending considerable time in discussing and drawing up the supervision agreement both for group and individual supervision to ensure full understanding of and commitment to the process. The agreement process also served to educate school-based psycho-social workers about the rationale for and approach to professional supervision. For some trainee supervisors, it took up to eight hours with a group to secure agreement. It appeared that the time spent on this activity may be critical to the success of the process as the agreement became meaningful and an act of commitment to the process.

Trainee supervisors recalled feeling initially nervous about their ability to manage the group. Some were worried that they might not be accepted by those with whom they work. These responses point to the importance

Figure 1
Key messages for trainee supervisors providing group supervision

Starting the group supervision process.
+ Institutional support for the programme is important
. Some degree of reluctance and suspicion of the supervision process from those supervised may be expected.
. It is important to spend sufficient time to draw up clear group supervision agreements.
. It is normal for some supervisors to feel nervous and unsure at the start of the supervision process. They will need support at this time.
. Planned deployment of team building skills will help.

Approaches and Issues which arise when working in a supervision group
. Help workers manage their work – develop a clear focus on a task.
. Enable the group to share experiences and ideas.
. Expect challenges from the group members and access support.
. Anticipate positive outcomes of group supervision.

Personal and Professional Learning will result from providing group supervision
. Be prepared to learn new skills
. Be committed to ongoing personal development and own supervision
. Expect positive outcomes.

of providing support, confidence boosting and assistance with problem solving for new supervisors. Personal development sessions which promote self awareness, observation of trainees' practice by tutors and planned deployment of team building skills seemed to be of particular importance in supporting trainees at this time, helping them learn to recognise their reactions when they encounter resistance and develop ways to overcome unhelpful reactions, as the following two examples illustrate.

> At the start of the supervision group there were some problems. I was nervous and did not come across as I intended. I became aware that I get angry easily and this shows on my face. I found team building tiring. My tutor told me that I did not listen to people. I had to develop my skills in this area. I practised this with my supervision group and we all practised listening to each other verbally and non-verbally. I then used a group drawing to help each group member learn their boundaries and limitations and to learn how to compromise and to make a picture which was a whole picture which connects (*Trainee Supervisor from Hebron, in interview, July 2009*).

> My tutor told me that I gave complements to others and did not express my feelings. I realised that this is because I did not want people to be angry with me. I realised I had to change some things. He [the tutor] helped me *to* be more open, reflect back and give developmental feedback (*Trainee Supervisor from Ramallah, in interview, July 2007*).

Approaches and issues which arose when working with a supervision group

Trainee supervisors were required to enable all those they supervise plan and implement a sequenced intervention with a class of students and to observe them carrying out this work. Most school-based psycho-social workers had never undertaken work of this nature before and it appeared that working on a task of this nature led to enhanced motivation in those being supervised. Interviews revealed that some supervision groups worked on the same intervention and supported each other in developing a plan of work and carrying it out. This appeared to be particularly helpful. Topics of intervention ranged from 'alternatives to violence', to 'study skills and time management'. Having a clear focus and task for a group work appeared to be important. If school-based psycho-social workers are able to see clear outcomes to their participation in group supervision, they may be more likely to commit to the process.

One of the important skills of a group supervisor is being able to facilitate a process in which the group acts supportively towards each member and shares experiences and ideas. This requires the supervisor to be able to step back from 'controlling' the process and create an environment in which group members can feel safe in sharing problems and difficulties they may encounter in their work, without incurring the judgement of their peers. The supervisor should also identify and promote learning from these accounts for all group members. Trainee supervisors considered that this was a skill they had been able to develop. This finding was supported by limited evidence from interviews with school-based psycho-social workers and from the positive feedback they gave to the supervisors in their training log-books. It is important to be aware that there is a strong potential for bias in these accounts, but it is clear that trainees recognised the importance of the deployment of these skills

Perhaps in most groups in any setting there will be those who challenge the leader. A significant proportion of trainees (42%) stated that they experienced challenge from a group member and needed support from their tutor. This highlights the need for supervisors to be provided with on-going support and supervision when they are in post as supervisors to enable them to deal positively with problems which perhaps will inevitably arise. Trainees identified that they had developed their skills in facilitating others' learning and how to challenge in a positive way. They had learned to be self-aware and be open to learning about themselves and to make any necessary changes. Almost all trainee supervisors felt that by the end of the group supervision process that their group was working well together and felt pleased with the outcome of their work. This appeared an important message for trainee supervisors which may help to promote motivation and endurance in difficult times and inspire them to promote confidence in the process and outcomes amongst group members. Brown and Bourne (1996) warn that there is a danger that group supervision may not achieve its goals. Factors which appeared to promote success in the oPt context were the support provided to trainees both from the programme and their employer.

Becoming a supervisor: Observation of practice and individual supervision

One of the aims of the Supervision programme is to promote more standardised practice in school counselling. It is believed that by making school-based psycho-social workers' work more visible, through repeated observation of practice and the provision of feedback using standardised approaches, more consistency in the standard of service will be achieved. Trainee supervisors visited and observed each of their eight supervisees twice in their school setting undertaking group guidance sessions. Providing structured feedback to school-based psycho-social workers is a key learning topic on the Supervision programme and a format for feedback on observations was provided, setting out clear behavioural criteria for observation. Almost all respondents considered that this format was useful in thinking about how to provide feedback to the counsellor, enabling supervisors to be clear and focussed in their approach to feedback, dealing with issues which are open to being changed. Over half of respondents felt that when they gave feedback to the school-based psycho-social workers, most workers accepted this positively, were not defensive and were able to use feedback. A significant number noted though that some school-based psycho-social workers were defensive and did not accept their feedback. This could be difficult as the following example from an interview shows:

> One worker was insistent that I change my evaluation of her to one which was more positive. She even mobilised her head teacher against me. She has been talking to the children very quickly and quietly and they could not hear her. The session she had prepared for the children lacked substance. She told me that because I was from the countryside I could not understand her accent. When I observed her the next time, she had more focused objectives for the session and she spoke more clearly and she involved the whole class. But she continued to find it difficult to receive feedback (*Trainee supervisor in interview from near Hebron, July 2008*).

On a positive note, all trainees detected change when they observed the school-based psycho-social workers for a second time, with all considering that most of those they supervised had acted on their feedback. This of course may be a biased response, as they may wish to be optimistic about the effects of their supervisory intervention. The interviews with school-based psycho-social workers gave an indication of their responses to observation and feedback. For the most part this was positive, as the following excerpt from an interview shows:

> My supervisor observed me working with a group of young people on the subject of violence. I felt very comfortable with him being there. He gave me positive feedback. I thought that I knew about reflecting back and asking questions, but I realised, when I got feedback, that I needed to develop my skills more. The supervisor had a nice way of looking at my written work, which made me feel he was looking at this as a colleague. I did not feel threatened (*Interview with school-based psycho-social worker, August 2009*)

In providing individual supervision, most felt that they have been able to help those they supervised plan their work (98%), that they had offered new ideas to those they worked with (100%) and enabled them to open up and talk about their feelings in supervision. All trainees thought that supervision might lead to better standards of practice in school counselling.

The supervised school-based psycho-social workers were generally positive about the supervision experience, considering that supervision helped to develop their direct practice and skills in planning and organising their work. Most considered that receiving feedback on their work following observation of counselling sessions was a benefit. They saw supervision is a source of personal/ and moral support and that it helped to boost their professional confidence. They noted also that supervision can provide support with working with the school administration staff.

Trainee Supervisors' experience of their own supervision on the programme also appeared to be a critical factor in determining how they themselves acted as a supervisor. Factors which they valued included learning new skills and practising them: including feedback, planning, and team building skills and group leadership. Others noted benefitting from feedback provided by the supervisor, being assisted in personal and professional development, being helped to apply theory to practice, being helped to manage difficulties in the supervisory process and becoming more confident as a 'professional'.

Trainees were asked if the programme had confirmed them in their motivation to be employed as a supervisor. Interestingly, five respondents (11% of survey respondents) expressed ambivalence about taking on a supervisor role. The majority of respondents hoped to proceed to take up a supervisor post (39%) or were already newly employed as supervisors (48%) and they saw undertaking supervision as a significant personal and professional achievement.

My greater achievement was the acceptance of my performance as a supervisor trainee by all school-based psycho-social workers. I appreciate the fact that professional supervision helps school-based psycho-social workers give value to themselves and to the fact there is a clear goal for their work that could be measured professionally through supervision. I have built a professional relationship with them and helped to develop them professionally in the field (*Survey respondent*)

An emerging sense of professional identity creation and formation

Trainee supervisors offered suggestions about what was needed to develop professional supervision and schools counselling. Most frequently mentioned factors were institutional support and advocacy about the role of the school-based psycho-social worker and their supervisors in order to create a positive environment for both professional groups. They also pointed to the need for improved working conditions and training. Ongoing support and further professional development, including meetings to examine progress in the field, further study, developing professional associations; and exchanges with other countries, including '*presenting our professional supervision experience on the Arab world level as an outstanding experience*' were suggested. Trainees called for local research on school-based psycho-social work and supervision and suggested that as supervisors they could learn to train others. The supervised school-based psycho-social workers also called for professional training for all school-based psycho-social workers, supervision, advocacy for their role and improvements in systems delivering services for children in the oPt.

It appeared that the supervision programme and the process of supervision had enabled these trainees and those they supervised to develop a stronger idea of the profession of school-based psycho-social work, a collective response rather than individualised position-taking found in Giacaman's (2004) baseline survey. The social interactive process of the supervision training and its practicum, including live supervision of school-based psycho-social workers in schools and the active involvement of the Ministry of Education at the national level, seems to have supported individual school-based psycho-social workers and supervisors with a variety of educational backgrounds to develop greater positive sense of both their personal and professional identity as oPt school counselling professionals in the sense of the development of an internally derived view of their role and in relation to other professions and systems (primarily teachers/education).

The programme seems to have promoted more standardisation of practice and role clarity. A stronger sense of professionalism, in terms of the practices of a professional and aspirations for 'the profession', was evident as is seen in their aspirations for further professional development, associations and research. The provision of supervision appeared to have played a role in legitimising the schools counselling service's identity as a distinct professional group within education settings, a form of 'identity politics' in the broad sense as suggested by Payne (2006). There was a common identification of problems in the institutional system, with supervision being viewed as a site for achieving acceptance of their emerging view of their role and position. This was solidified by the creation of institutional change, with the appointment of trained supervisors to posts and systematic planning within the Ministry of Education.

Contextual factors supporting change

The development of the Diploma in Supervision appears to have been instrumental in creating a significant shift in the oPt Schools Counselling Service. Three important contextual factors enabled this to occur.

First, the relationship between the Centre and the Ministry of Education was critical in ensuring institutional 'ownership' of the Initiative. Ministry staff in particular held a strong perception of 'working in partnership' with the Centre to develop and deliver the programme and felt they had genuine involvement in planning, selecting, investing in and supporting trainees and evaluating the programmes. The attention paid to ensure that the development of professional supervision was situated within national planning processes appeared critical. Interestingly, the Ministry also saw a measure of success of the programmes being the development of professional identity:

> This course takes a group of psychologists, social workers and teachers and turns them into school-based psycho-social workers and professional supervisors, with a common and distinct professional identity (*Head of*

Counselling of the Ministry of Education in interview, July 2009). (quoted in Lindsay (2011)

Secondly, the skill set of staff in the Centre was perhaps ideal for pioneering this type of programme. These included a strong policy and planning lead, experienced staff who had detailed knowledge of school counselling having both been employed in the sector and having delivered Professional Diploma programmes in School Counselling previously, and a charismatic and committed lead trainer. Centre staff were highly motivated and frequently articulated that they were 'doing something for Palestine'. This configuration may be hard to replicate.

Finally, the approach taken was driven by the impetus and recognition that it would not be possible in the immediate future, due to vagaries in donor funding, to provide all school-based psycho-social workers in the oPt with a Professional Diploma in Schools Counselling. The decision to implement the supervision programme with its demanding practicum was made in order to attempt to provide some measure of education and support to all school-based psycho-social workers. The model of programme implementation meant that over a third of all oPt school-based psycho-social workers received some form of supervision and professional development during the period supervisors were in training and almost half are now in receipt of professional supervision by employed supervisors who continue to use this model of supervision practice. Donor funding for the Diploma in Professional Supervision has now ended and funding is being sought to train more supervisors.

The Palestinian experience suggests that it is vital to consider professional supervision at the inception of any new role such as school counselling. The Diploma in Professional Supervision model has already been adapted for developing social workers in providing new child protection services in the oPt. The Palestinian approach to developing professional supervisors appears a promising model to enable professional development in contexts of limited resources and reliance on donor funding. It may be particularly useful in contexts where new professional roles are emerging.

Notes

1. Centre for Continuing Education is a non-profit, non-sectarian public-service organisation which is one of the community-service extension units of Birzeit

---

University in Ramallah, West Bank and focuses on developing human resources and upgrading skills and capacities of professionals.

2.   A governorate is an administrative district. Sixteen governorates under the jurisdiction of the Palestinian Authority were set up in the oPt after the signing of the Oslo Accords 1993 (11 in the West Bank and 5 in Gaza).

II

Social protection in Afghanistan: Between conflict, traditions and international aid

Martine van Bijlert

Introduction

Afghanistan is faced with several paradoxes. It is a desperately poor country, awash with money from a decade of international intervention and a booming drug business. The population has well-developed but very basic coping mechanisms, and after decades of conflict and drought it is unclear how much elasticity there is left. The high levels of international reconstruction and State-building assistance have had a limited impact on the nation's levels of poverty and have resulted in a very uneven mix of government policies, a complicated constellation of old and new elites, and an environment in which poverty reduction is explicitly not a priority. The resurgence of the Taleban and the ensuing violence has complicated the delivery of basic services, by both the Government and non-governmental organisations (NGOs), in large parts of the country (see Agnew in this volume regarding the impact on civil conflict on basic services in Palestine). The post-Taleban intervention in Afghanistan, in short, has brought wealth and opportunities to some, but it has not significantly decreased the vulnerability of large parts of the population. This is illustrated in all main development indicators: maternal mortality and child mortality rates remain exceptionally high, literacy and access to clean drinking water remain notoriously low, and half of Afghanistan's population continues to live under or just above the poverty line.[1]

Arrangements that help the population deal with risks, setbacks and calamities continue to be largely informal, through family and community solidarity. Market-based arrangements, such as targeted saving, insurance and microfinance, play only a very small role, while the country's public social protection programmes are either outdated or still in their infancy and have only a very limited reach. Most of the existing programmes are, moreover, not specifically designed to target the poor or most vulnerable. Donors and the Afghan government are seeking to redesign the country's social protection policies, but the efforts remain fairly modest and are taking place in the context of a massively aid dependent government, shrinking aid budgets, and an over-arching free market approach that is not explicitly geared towards poverty reduction.

The face of poverty in Afghanistan

The clichés that preface every article and project proposal about Afghanistan still hold true: the decades of war, destruction and massive displacement have degraded Afghanistan's already very limited physical and educational infrastructure, they have uprooted the country's political and political social structures, and they have skewed its economy, rendering it largely informal and conflict-driven.[2] The population has displayed a stubborn but very fragile resilience. The recent massive inflows of aid money have done little to seriously address the widespread vulnerability: around half of Afghanistan's population continues to live under or just above the poverty line (Ministry of Economy & World Bank (MoE & WB), 2010: 26). Many people, as a result, are highly vulnerable to even small, negative shocks such as a sudden loss of income or unexpected expenses caused by illness, death (including funeral costs), minor calamities or natural disasters.

> The everyday reality for the individuals obscured by poverty statistics is that the people are often hungry; they have limited access to health care; many cannot read or write; some may even sell a child, probably a girl, to feed the family; their children work instead of going to school; and, they are more vulnerable to violence as they lack the protection that patronage, corruption and alternative security arrangements (such as the hiring of private security or migration) may offer' (United Nations Office of the High Commissioner for Human Rights (UN OHCHR), 2010: 16).

Reliable quantitative data are notoriously hard to come by in Afghanistan; all figures – even from the most reputable institutions – should be treated with a fair amount of caution. But the available and generally accepted data on poverty and vulnerability indicate that around one third of the Afghan population (36%) live below the poverty line.[3] This means that around 9-10 million Afghans are not able to meet their basic needs. Up to half of the population was found to be either under or just above the poverty line (Central Statistics Office (CSO) 2009: 55; MoE & WB, 2010: 26).

Poverty was found to be most widespread among the landless rural poor and the *kuchis* (nomads).[4] The urban population was found to be relatively better off, although recent studies suggest that poverty is also on the rise among the urban poor (Afghanistan National Development Strategy (ANDS), 2008b: 2), possibly as a result of an increased migration from the rural areas to the cities, either in search of employment or greater security. Within the rural population, which accounts for an estimated 74 per cent all of Afghans, ownership of land was found to be an important mitigating factor, not just as a possible source of income but also as a safety net and a means to more easily obtain credit (UN OHCHR, 2010: 16).[5] The poorest households tend to be those relying on wage labour or transfers, such as loans or rental income, both in urban and rural areas (MoE & WB, 2010: 41).

Although the main poverty research – the Government's National Risk and Vulnerability Assessment (NRVA) – does not provide gender specific figures, it notes the large gender gap in education, access to health care, and participation in the labour force, with women engaging in far less economic activities, for fewer hours and predominantly in vulnerable employment (CSO, 2009: 19).[6] Field research moreover indicates that there is a significant difference between men and women's access to food, due to discrimination and exclusion (UN OHCHR, 2010: 17-8).

Figures on disability in Afghanistan are imprecise and estimates vary. The available data suggests that around 400-600,000 Afghans (around 2 per cent of the population) suffer from severe disability.[7] The figures seem relatively low, when taking into account the protracted and violent conflict and relatively poor levels of healthcare, possibly pointing to a strict definition of 'severe disability' or to considerable under-reporting. It is of course also possible that a relatively high number of people with disabilities do not survive, due to a lack of essential services.[8]

Whatever the real figures are, the prevalence of (severe) disability provides a considerable strain on often already struggling households. Field research found that two-thirds of disabled-headed households had extremely poor access to adequate food and that only one out of ten disabled-headed households had access to adequate food. Disabled people with land tended to depend on leasing or sharecropping for cultivation, which meant that they did not have full control over their produce. In terms of social protection, there were informal social safety nets with communities giving alms or assistance, but many people with disabilities failed to benefit from food aid programmes because of bureaucratic reasons, such as being unable to register with the relevant authorities (UN OHCHR, 2010: 17). For individuals disability often results in stigmatization, social exclusion and greater poverty: the probability that a disabled child will attend primary school is half that of a non-disabled child; disabled men are 50 per cent less likely to work than their non-disabled counterparts, while for disabled women this is one third (CSO, 2009: 88, note 4).

Food insecurity and poor nutrition affect a large part of the Afghan population. Afghanistan has one of the highest stunting rates in the world, with more than half (54 per cent) of Afghan children under age five stunted (chronically malnourished) and over a third (34 per cent) underweight. More than two-thirds (72 per cent) of children suffer from iodine and iron deficiency. These poor nutritional outcomes are closely linked to poor access and utilization of food in Afghanistan, both in terms of calorie intake and dietary diversity. The problem of food insecurity is compounded in leaner seasons, for example in spring, when a third of the population suffers from calorie deficiency and a quarter from poor diet (MoE & WB, 2012: 7).

Afghanistan's current aid and governance system

Despite the high levels of vulnerability, formal safety nets in Afghanistan remain very modest, both in terms of coverage and spending. This partly reflects the limited reach of the Afghan government in terms of geographical access and the difficulties it faces in delivering services to the population, but it also stems from the failure, both by the Afghan government and its international backers, to rein in internal wastage and corruption. The UN's Office of the High Commissioner for Human Rights has probably been the most outspoken and most succinct of all institutions that have published on poverty in Afghanistan:

A key driver of poverty in Afghanistan is the abuse of power. Many Afghan power-holders use their influence to drive the public agenda for their own personal or vested interests. ... The way power-holders emerge and how they use their power, in particular with respect to the use of resources, entrenches social exclusion, perpetuates unequal access to social justice, and undermines efforts geared to the enjoyment of human rights (UN OCHR, 2010: 4).

Although Afghanistan has been listed as both one of the poorest countries on earth and one of the most corrupt,[9] both poverty reduction and anti-corruption efforts, although often professed, have consistently been overshadowed by the seemingly more pressing concerns of rapid reconstruction, state-building, counter-insurgency and, more recently, the winding-down of the international engagement in Afghanistan under the banner of 'transition'. [10]

Out of the estimated 57 billion USD in international development assistance that was spent in Afghanistan between late 2001 and late 2010,[11] over 50 per cent was allocated to programmes related to the security sector, outweighing the investments in all other sectors combined (see Candland and Khan Qazi in this volume regarding similar priorities by the Pakistan Government).[12] Of the money that was allocated to reconstruction, development and poverty reduction – an estimated 28.14 billion USD – the social protection sector received 3.4 billion USD (out of an allocated 7.52 billion). This seems high, as it roughly equals the total disbursements received in the health and education sectors taken together,[13] but the figure is probably skewed by massive counter-insurgency spending in the insurgency-affected rural areas of the south and southwest. Such counter-insurgency spending often involved small and medium-sized infrastructure projects (reconstruction or repair of roads, buildings, irrigation systems) and short-term cash-for-work programmes. The idea was to 'win hearts and minds' and to compete with the presumed economic incentives provided by the insurgency.[14] Such 'stabilization programmes' often involved massive cash injections that led to a flare-up in local tensions, raised expectations and distortions of the local economy (US Senate, 2011: 11-12).[15]

This prominence of counter-insurgency objectives led to interventions that were often expensive and ill-targeted:

> The trend is to fund high value projects that are often implemented through large for-profit private companies, linked to military and political priorities, and targeting geographical areas where the donors have a military presence or political interest. The development and humanitarian needs of the Afghan people are not being met, despite significant donor funding to Afghanistan (UN OHCHR, 2010: 13, 17).

The progressive discussion on the so-called transition – the hand-over of responsibilities to the Afghan authorities – has put the spotlight on the immense aid dependency of the Afghan government: Since 2002, the entire development budget and, on average, almost half of the operating budget of Afghanistan was financed by external aid. Although there has been a steady increase in domestic revenue, expenditures have risen at an even higher rate, which means that the revenue ratio has actually decreased (Ministry of Finance (MoF), 2010a: 17).[16] The Afghan government has long complained about the fact that the bulk of external assistance – up to an estimated 80 per cent – bypasses the Government's budget and is managed by implementing agencies in what it often considers 'ill-conceived contracting and sub-contracting processes' (MoF, 2010a: 2). But although the criticism is in many ways justified, the proposed solution of avoiding wastage by channelling money through the government's budget remains highly unattractive to donors, given the twin problems of institutional corruption and the difficulty many ministries face to actually spend the allocated money.

Formal social protection policies

Afghanistan's government institutions continue to be highly fragmented and under-developed. A decade of technical assistance and capacity building has resulted in

> a fragmented 'second civil service' of an estimated 7,000 skilled Afghan consultants managing projects, without building sufficient government capacity (World Bank, 2011: 14).[17]

These consultants feed into a complex aid coordination structure that is mainly developed and adapted to meet evolving donor requirements. An example of such a process was the drafting and ratification in 2008 of an over-arching five year strategy: the Afghanistan National Development Strategy (ANDS). The process has resulted in a dizzying array of working groups and drafting sessions that feeds into high-profile donor conferences, as well as regular high-level meetings by a Joint Coordination and Monitoring Board (JCMB), which is a gathering of senior officials of all involved ministries, agencies and donor countries.

Although the Afghanistan ANDS was originally designed as a Poverty Reduction Strategy Programme (PRSP), the subsequent documents –

including most prominently the ANDS Prioritization and Implementation Plan – show a focus on economic development, illustrating the belief that this will probably automatically lead to poverty reduction.[18] The ANDS process itself has probably done much less to guide actual development spending or policy-making than often claimed, but it did result in the drafting of various strategic documents, including a Social Protection Sector Strategy (ANDS, 2008b). The document lays down a vision and policy guidelines in the fields of social protection, pension reform and disaster preparedness, but none of these policies feature in the subsequent ANDS Prioritization and Implementation Plan. The text of the social protection strategy, moreover, does not really seem to consider poverty reduction and social protection as ends in themselves, linking them instead to the goals of increased business activity and improved recruitment into the security forces.[19]

When designing its strategy the Government estimated that up to 80 per cent of the existing social protection cash payments were not targeting the most vulnerable. These payments concerned cash transfers to war victims and retired former military and civil servants, which were unrelated to economic status, while public subsidies such as those for fuel or electricity tended to disproportionately benefit the relatively well-off, who could more easily afford these services. According to the Government assistance in the field of what was loosely-termed 'public works and skill development' had the best chance of targeting the poor, but the track record of the existing programmes in doing so was patchy at best (ANDS, 2008b: 11).

The Government's Social Protection Sector Strategy is based on the premise that around 12 million people – or almost half of the population – require some form of public support.[20] In 2006 it was estimated that around 2.5 million people benefitted from public support, with the bulk of the beneficiaries (1.75 million) receiving assistance through 'public works and skills development' programmes.[21] These programmes were not specifically targeted at the poor and vulnerable, or failed to do so effectively. Participation among *kuchis*, for instance, one of the most vulnerable groups on all counts, was found to be very low; and although participation in the cash-for-work programmes was found to be higher among the poor than among the non-poor, the non-poor tended to receive higher wages (ANDS, 2008b: 7-9). Moreover, in over half of the households involved in cash-for-work programmes in 2006, the food situation did not improve as a result of the added income (CSO, 2009: 112-3). This suggests that many households either did not really need the assistance, or that the assistance was simply insufficient to address the shortfalls. In practice, the government's social protection interventions consisted of little more than the continued payment of government pensions and stipends to a limited group of people.[22]

In 2008 around 367 thousand individuals or households received direct cash payments: for having had a 'martyr', i.e. a registered war-related death, in the family (224,850), a war-related disability (87,717), or in the form of a government pension (54,000 – out of a total of 83,000 registered pensioners). The martyrs and disabled stipends are distributed irrespective of the economic situation of the beneficiary, and are basically a political subsidy; they were described in the sector strategy as an expression of 'societal solidarity with the victims of war [rather] than the instrument of social protection' (ANDS, 2008b: 7-9). These cash transfers are scheduled to be integrated into the pension system and will thus no longer be considered part of the welfare system (ANDS, 2008b: 22).

The cash transfers have been plagued by corruption, due to weak institutional capacity and the absence of oversight – even though the amounts are relatively small. The Social Protection Strategy euphemistically mentions that 'a number of individuals with false documents were given the entitlement' (ANDS, 2008b: 9). The potential extent of the abuse was illustrated when a pilot re-registration in 2006 resulted in the removal of around 20 thousand families from the list, in Kabul alone, because they were either ineligible or did not exist. This represented 9 per cent of the country-wide total, suggesting a seriously corrupted list of beneficiaries (ANDS, 2008b: 8-9, 14). The local misappropriation of the stipends for widows and the disabled by provincial officials is a common complaint, and seems to be considered one of the lowest forms of corruption, stealing from those who already have almost nothing and whom have suffered in the *jehad*.[23] The collection of pensions and stipends has always been weak and erratic, in particular since the very low levels meant that for some the (transport) cost of collecting the money was simply too high to make the effort regularly.

In 2006 the annual cost for pensions was 21 million USD (ANDS, 2008b: 10). This amount has since considerably increased – and is likely to increase even more – due a rise in the number of pensioners (given the relatively old civil service), a raise of the amounts paid, and the increased likelihood that pending payments are actually being claimed. Poor record keeping has meant that the Government has no records of eligibility until the claim is filed, which makes planning difficult and the system vulnerable to abuse. Due to the complicated registration process and the previously low pensions, many pensioners did not make an appearance for years and when they finally do come, they tend to present a consolidated claim. This has led to an accumulation of arrears, which complicates budget planning (ANDS, 2008b: 14).

The somewhat meandering discussions on pension reform and social protection policies, in the context of the Afghanistan National Development Strategy, gained some urgency after the 2008 food price crisis confirmed the need for improved safety nets. A pilot programme, jointly run by the World Bank and the Ministry of Labour and Social Affairs, involves local community councils (linked to the National Solidarity Programme) who locally select vulnerable households to be provided with cash grants. The programme aims to ultimately establish a credible and regularly updated database that can facilitate aid coherence and predictability in terms of the assistance provided. The programme is still at a very early stage, with cash grants having been provided in a handful of villages and only in the country's relatively safe and accessible areas (World Bank, 2009; personal briefings October 2011).

Market-based arrangements are very limited and dominated mainly by microfinance. According to government figures, in April 2007 34,000 people had borrowed a total of around 76 million USD from 15 microfinance institutions, with an average of 2,235 USD per loan.[24] The Government intends to encourage and strengthen the provision of microfinance, as well as the development of community-based insurance schemes, but it does not seem to have many concrete plans other than to work on a regulatory framework (ANDS, 2008b: 23).

The Government estimated that it would need around 2 billion USD annually to keep the poorest and most vulnerable above the poverty line (ANDS, 2008b: 20). However, given Afghanistan's political volatility, the Government's institutional problems and the current unpredictability within the aid sector, it seems unlikely there will be the funding, the donor confidence or the Government capacity for an effective country-wide safety net programme any time soon.

Among parts of the urban and the educated rural population there is a certain sense of nostalgia for some of the Soviet-era arrangements, including the cooperatives, the coupon system for government employees, the microloans provided by the Agricultural Bank, and the job security provided by state-led enterprises. At the height of the Soviet-era programme an estimated 80 per cent of the city populations benefitted from the distribution of food and fuel coupons, providing an important way of tying the population to the Government (Giustozzi, 2000: 190).[25] The rapid disbandment and privatization of government enterprises under the internationally-backed Karzai regime is viewed by many as having been done too soon and as having stripped the population of an important potential safety net.[26] There seems to be a general expectation among the population that an effective government looks out for the vulnerable groups in society; an expectation that is not met by the free-market orientation of the Afghan government and its international advisers.

Poverty in Afghanistan: Coping mechanisms

For large parts of the population their main coping mechanisms are based on social ties: patterns of reciprocity, patronage, social and religious obligation, and support within families and tribes have helped mitigate the worst consequences of decades of conflict and calamity. Afghanistan's social structures have however been severely tested under the pressures of war, migration and hardship, and the support based on social ties is clearly insufficient to lift large parts of the population out of poverty. When all else fails, the main other options available to the poor include internal displacement and borrowing money (UN OHCHR, 2010: 16).

> For those living in absolute poverty, there is no official safety net system, except for limited pensions for people with disabilities, and families of martyrs. While the extended family structure serves as an informal social safety net, community-based assistance tends to occur on a case-by case basis through voluntary contribution or, on occasion, a *shura* initiative. In sum, help in times of distress can be hard to come by; for the very poor, adverse events, including sickness or a death in the family, can be calamitou' (UN OHCHR, 2010: 16).

Patronage and reciprocal relations are important sources of support that however require a certain level of 'maintenance'.[27] Qualitative village-based field research found that the security provided by patronage became considerably less predictable in the absence of (potential) reciprocity. It found that social protection through patronage relations worked best in relatively equal settings, with wealthy and socially powerful local elites more likely to act in the interests of the community or to honour social obligations to help others in times of need. In contexts of greater inequality, a surplus economy and links to politically powerful actors led to more much self-interested economic behaviour among local elites. In these cases patronage ties became less predictable and the poor were more often left to fend for themselves. Where households were largely dependent on charitable relationships, it was found that such relationships were often in decline or highly variable, with harsh economic circumstances and modernisation processes slowly shifting interest away from collective needs. Those with more resources, who were for instance in a position to access credit or to reciprocate help, were enmeshed in stronger informal, mutual support networks, where they for instance could get interest-free loans. For the most poor and vulnerable this was significantly more difficult (Kantor & Pain, 2010b).

The main livelihood strategy for vulnerable households is the diversification of income sources. This is particularly pertinent in the rural areas, where seasonality greatly impacts income and poverty. For instance, an estimated 40 per cent of Afghan households, most of them in the rural areas, have no revenue from their principal income source during the winter months – illustrating the immense difficulties many households face to make ends meet in winter.[28] Spring tends to be the most difficult season, when reserves have been depleted but the new harvest is not yet in. In the spring 2007 almost half the population was found to be subsisting under the poverty line.[29] Diversification in income generating activities, obviously, does not always prevent households from falling into poverty and it may also be taken as recourse only after disaster strikes (CSO, 2009, 38-42).

The most prevalent strategies to deal with household shocks are the reducing of expenditures, food intake reduction, the seeking of community support, taking out loans or credit, and the sale of means of production (CSO, 2009, 111-13). Most of these strategies are problematic, as they represent a deepening dependency and a further depletion of resources, reducing the chances of recovery. This is particularly the case with high-interest loans and the selling of animals, tools and essential household items, such as for instance the family's rice cooker or winter clothes in spring. Other last resort strategies included (labour) migration, putting children to work, often in combination with withdrawing them from school, and if matters are very desperate the sale of a child. Many households depend to a large extent on remittances. Large parts of the Hazarajat in Central-Afghanistan, for instance, which continues to be among the poorest parts of Afghanistan, have become noticeably more wealthy (although this is still relative) due to the fact that many households receive money from family members residing in Iran and Pakistan, or further. The increase in relative wealth can be deduced from the growing number of households with cars, mobile phones, satellite dishes and school-going children. Conditions in the Hazarajat however remain harsh, particularly in winter when access roads are blocked. [30]

The Taleban have not moved into the social protection realm at all.

Although the leadership continues to harbour ambitions of establishing an expanding shadow administration, their reach remains patchy and contested and their focus remains on matters related to security and (rough) justice. They have no policies or activities that include service delivery – at the most they demonstrate a level of local tolerance for development projects or education activities (see also Clark, 2011) – and the informal religious taxes they collect are spent on their own fighters. Even when the Taleban regime was in power in the 1990s, it barely involved itself with social protection. It relied heavily on individual initiative, improvisation and *ad hoc* transfers of cash, to keep rudimentary government payments, such as salaries, going.

Conclusion

Despite the high levels of poverty and vulnerability, formal safety net programmes in Afghanistan are very modest, both in terms of coverage and spending, and are not really designed to target the poor or most vulnerable. The country's social protection reform is still very much in its infancy and will face huge challenges posed by shrinking aid budgets, institutional fragmentation, widespread corruption and political instability. This means that the Afghan population will continue to be left to largely fend for themselves, with the combination of resilience and vulnerability that has keeps large parts of the population surviving just under or around the poverty line, for the foreseeable future. A well-targeted social safety net programme could make quite a difference, but the odds seem stacked against it.

Notes

1. Per capita GDP was 528 USD in 2010/11, infant mortality was the highest in the world with 134 deaths per live births, life expectancy is very low at an average of 48.1 years and an estimated 75% of the population is illiterate (World Bank, 2011: 18).
2. According to an International Committee of the Red Cross (ICRC) survey in 2009, 96 per cent of the population had been affected by armed conflict; 76 per cent said they had at some point been driven from their homes; and 6 per cent had been separated from their families (ICRC, 2009: 2).
3. The national average poverty line was set at 1,255 AFG (the equivalent of around

25 USD) per person per month, representing the estimated cost of providing 2,100 calories per person per day and meeting some basic non-food needs. The CSO findings were based on measurements in 2007 (CSO, 2009: 55).

4. The incidence of poverty was fairly close to the national average in the rural population, relatively low in the urban population (29 per cent) and high in the *kuchi* population (54 per cent). The *kuchi* poor, moreover, tended to be on average much poorer than those in the other groups (CSO, 2009: 55-6).

5. The proportion of poor households among those owning land was estimated at 26 per cent, while among those who rent, sharecrop or have a mortgage on their land, it was found to be much higher at 42 per cent.

6. Participation in the labour force is estimated at 86 per cent for men and 44 per cent for women. Women's economic participation is highest in the poorer segments: the rural and *kuchi* populations (respectively, 61 and 70 per cent), where women engage in agricultural and pastoral activities (presumably largely unpaid). In urban areas, participation is a very low 21 per cent. Of the relatively few women who generate income themselves, only 20 per cent can decide on their own on how to spend the money (CSO, 2009: 19).

7. Handicap International estimated in 2005 that 2.7 per cent of the population, at the time almost 600,000 people, suffered from severe disabilities, translating into an average of one in every five households hosting a person with severe disability. It also estimated that around 10 per cent of those with physical disabilities also experienced mental disabilities (Woloszyn, 2008). The figures were based on a 2003/04 estimate by the Ministry of Public Health. A household survey in 2007/8 found 1.6 per cent of the population, or around 400,000 individuals, suffering from severe disability, with an estimated 10 per cent of the households having at least one severely disabled household member, and more than a quarter of households having at least one mildly disabled household member (MoE & WB, 2010: 59). An earlier household survey in 2005 had found that 14 per cent of all rural households had a disabled family member – without specifying severity (ANDS, 2008b: 5).

8. The UN estimates that 10 per cent of the world population lives with a disability, but this probably includes all kinds of relatively mild forms as well, http://www.un.org/disabilities/default.asp?id=18

9. Afghanistan was ranked 172 out of 187 countries and territories in UNDP's 2011 Human Development Index, and second to last, together with Myanmar in Transparency International's 2011 Corruption Index (only North Korea and Somalia scored worse).

10. The concept of 'transition', or its Dari equivalent *enteqal*, was introduced in 2010 to describe the joint Afghan-international process of gradual handover of responsibilities to the Afghan authorities, which was to begin in 2011 and end in 2014. The process that was largely driven by NATO, was designed to facilitate the gradual and 'responsible' draw-down of the international military presence, but also included

discussions surrounding the handover of responsibilities in the field of governance and development aid. For a brief discussion of transition see van Bijlert (2011).

11. The figure of 57 billion USD does not include the massive expenditure on contracting in the fields of construction, logistics, fuel and supplies, or the costs of security provision that have accompanied the military presence, some of which has been contracted locally.

12. Much of this money comes from the US that accelerated its spending, in particular to the army and the police, in an effort to make them ready for the security handover: 26 billion USD was spent by the US Department of Defence alone; 14.8 billion USD to the Afghan National Army, 8.16 billion USD to the Afghan National Police, 1.54 billion USD for the so-called Commander Emergency Response Program (CERP), and 1.4 billion USD to the Department of Defence's Counter-Narcotics activities (**Ministry of Finance**, 2010a: 23-5).

13. According to the Ministry of Finance figures, the education sector received 1.72 out of a total commitment of 4.13 billion USD and the health sector received 1.75 out of a total of 3.97 billion USD (Ministry of Finance (MoF), 2010a: 27).

14. In the 'Commander's Guide to Money as a Weapons System' the US Army Handbook of April 2009 explains how funds provided to the commanders could be used 'to win the hearts and minds of the indigenous population to facilitate defeating insurgents' (quoted in Wilder, 2009: 1). For a critical discussion of the 'hearts and minds' programming see Wilder (2009); for a critical discussion of ISAF's belief that the insurgency is largely economically driven see van Bijlert (2010).

15. For instance a USAID agricultural programme was significantly expanded in 2010/2011 after it was relabelled a stabilization intervention: from 60 million USD for a nation-wide development programme to 360 million USD for the southern provinces of Kandahar and Helmand alone. The programme included a considerable cash-for work component with 780 projects that employed a total of 103,000 labourers and paid 27 million USD in wages (US Senate, 2011: 11-12).

16. Although in 2010 revenue was estimated to have more than doubled from 619 to 1,422 million USD per year, it still accounted for less than 10 per cent of the total GDP, while at the same time expenditures had almost tripled from 884 to 2471 million USD (MoF, 2010a: 17). The World Bank (2011) has further estimated that Afghanistan will be facing a financing gap of around 25 per cent of its GDP post-2014 (based on a projection of revenues that reach 17 per cent of the GDP, which is quite optimistic).

17. Ministries lean heavily on externally funded staff to implement projects and meet the donors' reporting needs. They tend to be more expensive than the government will be able to fund in the future: in the nine mostly affected ministries externally funded staff made up 5% of the positions, but 40% of the payroll costs (World Bank, 2011: 14).

18. Azerbaijani-Mogaddam et al (2008: 5-6) refer to this as the 'rising tide approach' with economic growth firmly positioned as the cornerstone of the strategy. Kantor

and Pain (2010a: 3-5) criticise the lack of nuanced understanding reflected in these documents and point out that earlier documents, such as the 2004 National Human Development Report, that focused on human security (Tadjbakhsh, 2004) reflected greater understanding of for instance the role of inequalities, instead of treating poverty reduction mainly as a matter of increasing resources.

19. According to the Social Protection Sector Strategy '[p]reservation of human capital will be key contribution of the Social Protection Sector Strategy to the economic growth. Moreover, improved social protection will decreases uncertainty among the vulnerable and encourage them to take risk and get involved in small scale business activities resulting in higher employment and income for the poor and vulnerable. Apart from low salaries, non-existence of the effective social security in the case of death and injury discourages recruitment into the Afghanistan National Army (ANA) and Afghanistan National Police (ANP). Therefore, improved social protection together with social inclusion of vulnerable and minorities would lead to more stable Afghanistan' (ANDS, 2008b: 1).

20. The Social Protection Sector Strategy gives no source for the figure of 12 million. It is most probably based on the NRVA estimate that around half of the population lives under or around the poverty line.

21. The term 'public works and skills development' was not detailed or defined and seemed to capture a wide range of on-going programmes. The cash-for-work components involved in the grassroots development programmes such as the National Solidarity Programme (NSP) and the National Rural Accessibility Programme (NRAP), for instance, were thus also counted as social protection interventions. Other major 'public works' included various food-for-work programmes, presumably also food-for-education and the distribution of iodized salt (ANDS, 2008b).

22. Additional public social protection arrangements included land distribution programmes for returning refugees or certain categories, such as teachers or military pensioners. In practice, however, the land was often redirected and either given to friends of the officials distributing the land or sold to the highest bidder. Author's unpublished interviews in various provinces, 2004-2011.

23. Author's unpublished interviews in various provinces, 2004-2011.

24. Quoted in ANDS, 2008b: 8. The Afghan government claimed that around 70 per cent of the borrowers were women and that the repayment rate was 95 per cent, but the source (and veracity) of the information is unclear.

25. In 1983 over 250,000 families country-wide received food and fuel coupons; this was 340,000 in 1988; 450,000 in 1990 and 550,000 in 1992. In 1988 up to 700,000 households were receiving either government salaries, rations or coupons (Giustozzi, 2000: 190).

26. Author's unpublished interviews, 2004-2011. See also Paterson and Blewett (2006).

27. For wider discussions of the role of patronage and the commoditisation of influence in Afghan society, for instance in the field of governance or electoral campaigning,

see van Bijlert (2009a and 2009b).

28. In rural areas the first income source contributes on average for 71 per cent to the household's total annual income (the corresponding figure is 89 per cent in urban areas). Rural households on average engage in twice as many income generating activities as their urban counterparts. Sources of income that are not seasonally sensitive or that lie outside the agricultural sector help '[smooth] consumption throughout the year ... and prevent these households from depleting their assets and from contracting excessive debt' (CSO, 2009: 38-42).

29. In spring 2007 42 per cent of the population was found to live below the poverty line; 45 per cent of the population was not able to purchase a basic food basket providing 2100 calories per day; and an additional 20 per cent were concentrated just above to the poverty line and thus highly vulnerable (ANDS, 2008b).

30. Author's observations in 1997 and 2006-11. See also Monsutti (2010) for more background on labour migration in Afghanistan.

12

The Kurdish region of Iraq: Conflict and the role of adolescence in the democratization process

Elise Kipperberg

Introduction

While I was acting as a lay member of the Norwegian Immigration Appeal Board in 2001, a rejected application from an asylum seeking family from the small, ancient town of Amediya in the Duhok Governorate in Northern Iraq was one of the difficult cases to be solved. The family, belonging to Assyrian Christians, claimed to be threatened and persecuted by Kurdish Muslims who, together with some Jewish population, made up the inhabitants of what is believed to be home place of the Biblical 'Three Wise man'. Little did I know then that I would visit this very same place myself ten years later, accompanied by Kurdish colleagues from the University of Duhok, facing guns and tanks of the unofficial military presence of the Turkish army. And little did I know that I would come to do research about the democratization process in the area, focusing on religious and cultural tolerance as one of the issues. In the meantime, the 2003 invasion of Iraq had provided new possibilities for the Kurdish population of Iraq, for decades suppressed by the brutal regime of Saddam Hussein who since the 1970s had systematically tried to change the demography of Iraq and to exterminate Kurdish identity, culture and language. Forced removals of thousands of Kurds, gas attacks killing and chemical bombs were used to wipe out thousands of Kurdish villages during the Anfal campaign in 1988, thus violating the freedom and rights of the Kurdish people. The Supreme Criminal Court of Iraq has later declared the mass killing as genocide against the Kurdish people.[1][2]

Adolescents[3] are important stakeholders during war and conflict as well as resourceful participants in post conflict reconstruction phases and democratization processes. This is also the case regarding rebuilding of the Kurdish region after years of brutal conflicts. Many of the youth population in Kurdistan[4] belong to families who have survived the former Anfal campaigns in 1988, others have been directly exposed to the last Iraq war. Statistics document that 13, 4 % of the 182 000 victims from the Anfal campaigns were children below 4 years old, 13, 35 % between 5-9 years and 12.20 % between 9-14 years, which make young children the greatest numbers of victims of the mass killings.[5] The majority of all victims were women and children. What is their situation after Saddam Hussein's fall in 2003? How are their rights to provision, protection and participation met in the phase of post-conflict? What are their aspirations, and how can they contribute to the reconstruction and democratization process? What are the main challenges related to the national authorities' short time and long time goals concerning children and youth?

This chapter will look at the human rights and legal framework for youth participation in post conflict as expressed in the Convention on the Rights of the Child (CRC), with particular reference to the child's right to express his/hers own views and the obligations of the state parties to give the views of the child due weight in accordance with the age and maturity, as expressed in article 12. We will also look at political framework developed by Kurdistan Regional Government (KRG) to strengthen participation and empowerment of youth as expressed in the KRG Youth Road Map adopted in 2009. How adolescents in the city of Duhok view their opportunity to be heard, develop critical thinking and creativity within the family, at school and in the local community, and what they hope for in the near future for themselves as well as for their country, will be described with reference to extract of results from my ongoing study about Youth Participation in the Democratization Process in Kurdistan. Views from parents and local professional expertise will be included as well. My own understanding and comments are influenced by a western perspective, being an humble visitor and researcher from abroad, yet engaged in Kurdish issues through my work with asylum seeking Kurds in Norway.

Kurdistan 2012: From violent conflicts and war to post conflict reconstruction

The Kurdish region of Northern Iraq has had an autonomous rule since 1992. The three Kurdish governorates, Dohuk, Erbil and Sulaimaniya were recognized as a legal 'region' by the October 2005 Iraqi Constitution following Saddam Husseins fall, with the power to introduce new laws for the Kurdistan Region and also to amend Iraqi national legislation as it applies in the Kurdistan Region. A government for the Kurdistan Region, the KRG, was announced in May 2006.[6]

Today the Kurds are spread in four bordering countries in addition to Iraq: Iran, Turkey, Syria, Armenia and Azerbaijan, and amount to a total population worldwide of 30 million. About 800 000 live in exile in Europe, 250 000 in USA and 6000 in Canada[7]. The Kurds are still the largest ethnic group in the world without a state of their own. In total, 4 million of the Iraq population are Kurds. Kurdistan, as the region is called by the Kurds themselves, has its own Parliament, Government and Minister of State.[8] Kurdish political parties are also represented in the central Parliament in Bagdhad.[9]

Reconstruction after the fall of Saddam Hussein has brought dramatic changes to the Kurdish region which is now enjoying a far better safety than the rest of Iraq.[10] Diversity within the population is increasing. The main religion is Islam Sunni, but Shia Muslims as well as Yeazides and Christian groups settle in the area, many of them taking refugee there due to the principle of religious freedom stated in the Constitution. Large internal refugee families, suffering from poverty arrive from other parts of Iraq. The reconstruction phase demands new infrastructure and offers many job opportunities, especially in the engineer, trade and craft business. Kurds from neighbouring countries as well as Arabs move from other places within Iraq to work in the area, benefiting from the striking optimism among the growing population. With short gaps between, new block buildings and houses in sparkling colours of pink, yellow, blue and red, hotels, restaurants, shopping centres and public and private schools pop up. Several Kurdish as well as international, private universities have been established. Foreign countries have opened consulates in Erbil, and many international companies have established business there. On a daily basis, authorities as well as the public have to relate to noticeable social and cultural challenges, including challenges concerning the old, patriarchal value system based on a collectivistic family structure and clan rule. Many Kurdish families and political refugees who during years in exile have gained insight into a democratic culture now bring back new, modern ideas about gender equality and the role of children and youth. Some of them have taken up high government positions in this phase of transition. In the construction of Kurdistan, the Kurdistan government sees Sweden as its role model, the Ministry of Sports and Youth pointed out some years ago.[11] Several ministers are Swedish-Kurds, and astonishingly many employees in the Ministry of Youth and Sports are young Kurdish women brought up in Swedish, according to the Minister.[12]

Human rights for children in Iraq: Provision, protection and participation

Iraq ratified the Convention on the Rights of the Child already in 1994,[13] committing to the principles of provision, protection and participation for all children below 18 years, without any discrimination. By doing so, the authorities of Iraq agreed to ensure children specific human rights expressed in 40 articles related to civil, political, economic, social and cultural rights.

The CRC is valid in times of peace as well as during war. State parties which have ratified the convention are obliged to provide, to the maximum extent possible, a standard of living adequate the child's physical, mental, spiritual, moral and social development, free compulsory education, to recognize the child's right to a name and nationality, freedom of expression, thought, conscience and religion and to ensure the right to enjoy his/ hers culture and language.[14] Authorities are obliged to take all appropriate administrative and legislate measures to ensure the child protection and care which is necessary for the child's well-being. The child has, according to the CRC, the right to be protected from all forms of physical or mental violence, injury or abuse, neglect or negligent treatment, maltreatment or exploitation, including sexual abuse, while in the care of parent(s), legal guardian(s) or any other person who has the care of the child. By ratifying the CRC, Iraq committed to ensure that 'the best interest of the child shall be a primary consideration in all actions concerning children, whether undertaken by public of private social welfare institutions, courts of law, administrative authorities or legislative bodies, according to the CRC' as an overall principle.[15]

Iraq reported for the first time to UN on the status of child rights in 1996[16] and received the UN Child Rights expert committee's concluding observations and recommendations two years later.[17] At that time concerns were raised with regard to insufficient disaggregated data, lack of child budgetary resources and lack of awareness of the principles of the CRC, insufficient coordination among entities working for children, inadequate measures to ensure school enrolments of girls, especially in rural areas, and poor services for children with disabilities. The expert committee was also concerned about the absence of an independent mechanism to address child rights violations and improper investigations of case of abuse and ill-treatment, extensive child labour and street children. The need for strengthened law enforcement corresponding to international standards was underlined.

According to UNICEF Country Program Iraq 2011-2014,[18] virtually all concluding observations by the CRC committee in 1998 have still not been followed up. In the meantime, war has worsened the situation for children and youth. Furthermore, UNICEF states that no measures are yet in place to implement relevant provisions.[19] The Iraq Government has recently decided to prepare a second State report to establish a baseline for monitoring the Convention.

The right to participate in post conflict reconstruction processes

Article 12 in the CRC underlines the right of the child to be provided the 'opportunity to be heard in any judicial and administrative proceedings affecting the child,' the right to express his/hers own views freely in all matters affecting the child, and the obligations of the state parties to give the views of the child due weight in accordance with the age and maturity. This is a groundbreaking principle in the CRC and represents a new dimension compared to other human rights instruments.[20]

Children and youth's rights to voice opinions in all matters concerning them also include the right to be heard related to reconstruction and rehabilitation activities following war and conflict. In a general comment on article 12,[21] the CRC committee points out that children affected by emergencies should be encouraged and enabled to participate in analysing their situation and future prospects, and that adolescents in particular should be given the opportunity to play an active role related to assessments, design, implementation, monitoring and evaluation of programmes. Taking part in this kind of work might develop their organisational skills and strengthens a sense of identity, thus also helping them to regain control over their lives, the committee emphasized in 2009.

The KRG Youth Road Map: participation and empowerment of youth

In a sense, the Kurdish Regional Government has taken the idea of youth participation in the phase of transition seriously. Based on the third UN Millennium Goal[22] the Kurdistan Regional Government formally adopted the Youth Road Map January 2009, a strategic document dealing with youth related issues and how to tackle them.[23] According to the government, one of the main goals of the road map is to 'engage young people in the democratic process, empower them and encourage them to be active citizens who are aware of the environment, human rights and individual and public responsibilities'.[24] Another aim is to increase young people's interest in their roles in the decision –making organs.

The foundation of the road map was laid through consultations with a wide range of NGOs and civil society actors working with youth, and individual comments from youth and others responding to media's invitation to identify key issues and needs and wants concerning youth.

According to the Ministry of Sports and Youth (MOSY), the main problems per 2009 concerning youth in the region were:

1. Unemployment and poverty
2. Low level of education
3. Youth Immigration
4. Housing
5. Young people's low level of participation in the decision making process, and the attainment of democracy.

The ministry set as a mission to meet challenges of illiteracy, high level of unemployment, shortage of housing, migration and educational shortcomings within two years. By 2011, illiteracy among youth should be eliminated and every child in Kurdistan have nine years of elementary education, with the aim that 30 % of high school graduated go to university, 20 % of high school graduates know good English and that 50 % of the elementary graduates study computing. Regarding participation and democracy, the road map recommended that at least 30 % of employees in government sector jobs and decision making bodies should be below 25 years of age, and that the age limit for becoming a Member of Parliament should be reduced from 25 years of age to 18. In order to improve and strengthen the situation for children and youth, the KRG decided to establish two new institutions: An Ombudsman for Children to defend and tackle youth issues, and a Regional Board for Youth Affairs, acting as a consultation board representing all democratic youth organizations.

Critical voices from youth

On August 2011, 22 years old Banaz Jawad, a young woman from Erbil, burned herself to death, leaving an audio recording explaining to her family and to the world her reasons for her suicide. Coming from a deprived family, she graduated from the Technology College and spent 16 months of much efforts looking out for work. Having no success, she became increasingly disappointed and depressed. According to the Editor of *Kurdistan Tribune*,[25] case workers and researchers stated in interviews with local newspapers that Banaz Jawad committed suicide because of lack of job opportunities. Community researcher Hama Salih told a local reporter that 'the suicide of this young girl was because of *injustice and corruption*.' Reporters stated that the tragic event was a reminder of the tragic event of the young Tunisian fruit seller, Mohammad Bu Azizi, who burnt himself to death because of injustice, sparking the 2011 Tunisian revolution and the Arab Spring.[26]

Already half a year earlier, on 17th of February 2011, angry youth in Sulaymania voiced their discontent with the KRG traditional leadership, demonstrating against the authorities' unwillingness and incompetence to create job opportunities and stable salaries which could enable them to establish a decent future life. Despite blossoming economy and increasing job opportunities, between 35-45 % of Kurdish youth remain unemployed or underemployed, according to Maria Fantappie, analyst at the Carnegie Middle East Centre,[21] pointing out that political affiliation often regulates job access and job advancements. The demonstrations gave voice to a discontent that had been simmering in Kurdistan long before the wave of mobilization engulfed the Middle East region and revealed increasing disaffection toward a leadership that has anchored its legitimacy to past achievements and failed to fulfil the aspirations of its youth, Fantappie stated.

According to Mufid Abdulla[28], the average age of the demonstrators were between 15-25 years old. Problems related to education and work opportunities explain why the youth of Kurdistan at present is found to be in a revolutionary state of mind, he emphasized.[29] Education is limited as school buildings are few and poor. Often two- three shifts of pupils are forced to use the same school, strictly limiting their classes. Besides, authoritarian teaching methods cause alienation and frustration. Furthermore, a large part of the present youth bulge has grown up in poor conditions resulting in increasing anger and despair, he commented. Many children who are now reaching adulthood are still suffering from difficult conditions, resulting from the traumas of their parents and grandparents dramatic experiences. By now Kurdistan has the largest population of graduates without jobs, Abdulla pointed out, underlining the need for better leadership and a dynamic economy to deal with the youth's rebellious state of mind.

Research imperative: Youth participation in the democratization process in Kurdiŝtan

The long-term vision expressed in The Youth Road Map is to create a society where the youth are:

1. Free, peace-loving, and democratically oriented; where they have the opportunity to be creative; where they are educated and can play an important role as active participants.
2. Be aware of individual and public responsibilities, aware of gender, the environment and the rights of people with disabilities.[30]

In order to find out how adolescents themselves view their situation related to some of these issues today, the author initiated a research project about 'Youth Participation in the Democratization Process in the Kurdish region' in October 2011, in cooperation with a Kurd in exile in Norway, Sipan Sendi. Using a questionnaire consisting of 64 questions, data was collected from altogether 400 adolescents aged 16-18 years attending eight different high schools in Duhok and the neighbouring city, Zakho. Two of the schools were public schools of excellence, two ordinary public girl schools, two ordinary public boy schools and two ordinary public mixed schools. Pupils from private schools were not included in the research. The questionnaire contained a set of questions related to each of the goals of the KRG Youth Road Map, some of them formulated as multiple choice questions, others as open questions. Within the time frame of this chapter, it has not been possible to thoroughly study responses from all respondents, but answers from 40 boys and girls from the schools in Duhok are presented below related to specific visions formulated in the KRG Youth Road Map. Their answers seem to form a certain pattern. Combined with data gathered in 2009 from yet another ten girls and boys in the same age range from Alind youth organization,[31] from other children and youth of families we have met over the past two years as well as voices from youth expressed through media, the responses are interesting as they point in the same direction .

... 'To create a society where the youth are free, peace-loving and democratically oriented' ...

What do the adolescents associate with the idea of 'being free', and what are their hopes for themselves as well as for the future of the nation in this sense?

Do they respect people who differ from themselves regarding religion, ethnicity, colour of skin, income level, social group? How do the grown-ups around them support their attitudes? What needs to be done in order to develop Iraq to become a democratic state in which various cultural and ethnic groups live together in freedom and peace, side by side?

A large majority of the Kurdish girls and boys expressed that it is very important for them to feel independent and free to live as they wish. Only two persons, one boy and one girl, meant that this was of no importance to them. When asked about their hopes for themselves and for their country, the young girls mostly answered in general terms, underlining their wishes for progress, growth and happiness. Several mentioned the need for greater freedom, but it is not clear whether they mean individual freedom for themselves or freedom for the Kurdish region. Consensus and solidarity are the most used words in their answers. 'Freedom and brotherhood is important for our nation', one of the girls explained. To help the poor, to have reasonable salaries, honesty, sincerity and trust are also issues mentioned. *'I hope for a successful development without suppression and violence from enemies. I hope that knowledge and awareness will increase'*, a girl stated.

Many of the boys expressed that their personal hopes were related to getting a high education degree, becoming successful in their jobs and marry a nice wife. Regarding the country, several of the boys mentioned the need for a well-functioning federal system and a parliament which is honest and real and implements its duties. The governorates should be given stronger power instead of centralism, and the authorities must act faster and with less bureaucracy. Some of the boys pointed out that different religious beliefs and cultural backgrounds should not lead to separation or discrimination, and that criminals and terrorists must be dealt with. Several mentioned that Kurdistan should become free, separated from Iraq. *'I hope that my country will develop successfully into an independent and peaceful state. When a nation has peace, progress and prosperity follows'*. An independent Kurdish state should not exclude other cultures or ethnic groups, though, they pointed out.

By far the majority of girls and boys expressed that they regarded mutual respect to be of great importance. More than two thirds (70%) supported the idea of religious freedom and that people must be treated on equal terms, without discrimination. Girls as well as boys pointed out the need for just and good governance. Kurds and Arabs should be given equal status and stand strongly together in solidarity. *'They must find common interests and issues, and develop attitudes which link them together. The different groups need willingness and ability to forgive so that they can live together in freedom and peace'* one of the girls commented. *'Democracy, solidarity, friendship and maturity. Equal rights for all'* one of the boys commented, underlining that Arabs and Kurds are brothers and must be treated as such.

Almost all the girls and boys expressed that adults around them often/ very often encouraged them to respect people from other cultures, religions and backgrounds. In real life, however, they often experienced that the grown-ups talked about people with different backgrounds than themselves in a bad or negative way, many of them commented.

... 'where they have the opportunity to be creative' ...

Do the adolescents get sufficient attention and guidance from the grown ups around them? Do they get help and support to develop their talents, and do they have sufficient time to use their imagination? Do adults listen to their views?

Almost all of the girls and boys stated that they always got much attention and support at home, but at the same time half of them felt that they seldom or never had any time to use their own imagination and creativity in their home surroundings. Almost half of the group felt that they rarely got any attention and support at school to develop their talents, and a large majority of them felt that they very seldom did get any opportunities to use their imagination and creativity in school. Some of the boys expressed that they were never given any attention at school at all. Both girls and boys expressed that it was very important for them to get such attention and support to develop their talents and use their imagination at home as well as in the school context.

Nearly half of the girls expressed that adults at home listened to their views most of the time, and a large part of the boys experienced the same. This was not the case at school. Nearly half of the girls and boys expressed that adults at school seldom listened to them. Almost all girls and boys stated that it is important/ very important that adults at school listen to their opinions, however.

... 'where they are educated' ...

Does the family decide what kind of education their sons and daughters should choose, or are the adolescents free to make this choice and plan for their future independently? Is it important to be free to make such choices? What are their views about gender equality, and who are their role models? What kind of jobs to they plan to hold?

A little more than half of the girls and boys believed that they can decide themselves regarding choice of education. For nearly a fourth of the respondents the family decides in this matter. More girls than boys are free to plan for their future. Almost all the girls as well as the boys expressed that it is very important to them to make their own choices. We note, however, that the adolescents have a stronger wish to decide about their education more freely than the present situation allows them.

Almost all of the boys and girl expressed that girls and women should be treated with the same respect and rights as boys and men by the society. Everybody identified this issue to be of great importance to them. But which type of jobs do the adolescents hope to obtain as grown-ups? To become an engineer seemed to be the most popular profession for girls as well as the boys; even more girls than boys hoped to get such a job. To become a doctor, or a lawyer, was the second sought after profession, with no differences among the genders. Some girls also wished to become teachers, while this was the case for just a couple of boys.

A few boys and girls wanted to become police or politicians. Some boys and a few girls wished to become a businessman. Very few of the girls wanted to become a nurse or a housewife. To become an imam was mentioned by one of the boys, while another boy wanted to become a diplomat and yet another to become an artist.

Almost all of the forty adolescents considered their mothers and fathers to be their role models. A few of them mentioned siblings or grandparents. Friends and teachers were mentioned by two of the boy respondents, and sports idols or popstars was mentioned by two other boys. Their plans about future jobs differ rather much from the jobs of their parents.

••• 'A society where they can play an important role as active participants......to be aware of individual and public responsibilities' •••

Are the adolescents satisfied with the democratization process in their region? How can they influence and contribute to the process themselves? Do they trust the politicians? What is needed in order to have a good life, and how can the municipality contribute in this matter? What might their future look like, 10 years ahead?

Only four out of the 40 adolescents, all of them girls, expressed that they considered the democratization process in Kurdistan to be on good track, while more than half of them viewed the process to be negative or bad. Concerning their own contribution, half of the group of girls did not answer this question. Almost all of the remaining commented with words of resignation that they could do nothing in this matter. Only three girls pointed out that they can contribute by expressing their opinions based on knowledge obtained through studies.

The resignation was also tangible among the boys. More than half of them responded that they can do nothing. However, a few of them commented that while being in no positions at present as youth/ pupils, they must, as citizens, contribute to defend democracy, fight corruption and theft by the politicians and contribute into making Kurdistan prosper and develop in the best direction. More than half of the girls and boys had no trust in the politicians; only about 25 % had some faith in them.

In order to have a good life, youth should be respected and taken seriously, the girls pointed out. It was important to have places where they can feel safe, relax and enjoy themselves, for instance in special youth centres or parks. A large part of the girls suggested that the municipality should build (amusement) parks for girls only. Freedom, security, education and job opportunities were mentioned as the most important factors to obtain a good life within the municipality, according to the girls.

The boys underlined even stronger the need for more and better education, including special education, to take care of children and youth with special needs. The youth should be secured job opportunities with decent salaries in government positions and business enterprises. The need for more and better schools facilities, better housing, access to psychological/ psychosocial support and respect for diversities, individual human rights and rights for youth in particular, was underlined by the boys. Law and order, freedom and no unemployment would bring good solutions for the youth. A few of the boys suggested that the municipality should improve roads, strengthen tourism attractions, build parks and improve the environments by establishing special places for garbage. Local authorities should listen to recommendations from the youth about good living conditions, provide possibilities to develop skills, creativity and take part in sport and art activities. The municipality should establish a library and more places where youth can meet and not get bored. Poor people living nearby should be taken care of as well, for example should the authorities build housing units for them, some of the boys suggested.

The question about how they imagined their lives 10 years ahead from now was formulated as an open question, encouraging the adolescents to reflect about jobs, family and place of living. Some of the respondents reflected about all of these issues, while other's responses were limited. Eight of eighteen girls who answered stated specifically that they planned to stay on in Kurdistan, while only two said that they wished to study and work abroad. Seven out of twenty girls imagined that they had established their own family within the next ten years. A couple stated that they did not want to marry at all. Nine of the girls expressed that they probably had completed studying and taken up a job as engineer, doctor, professor or working for the government. Expressing frustration, a few of them emphasised that their lives depended on Gods will and help, or whether the government would provide them with some guaranties to secure their lives, stating that such safety was lacking now. One of the girls specifically mentioned that she would look after her parents in the future. Several of the girls expressed general phrases about future hope and happiness, while several of the boys put a weight on good economy, safety and hoping to avoid problems and tragedies.

Eight out the seventeen boys underlined that they would continue living in Kurdistan. Some of them wished to go abroad and return after having completed their studies, while two of the boys planned to live in a foreign country. Several of the boys imagined that they would still be studying for the next ten years.

Three of the boys mentioned that they planned to establish a family, while some more stated that they had no plans in this direction. One of the boys underlined that, providing the region developed in a safe and peaceful way, he hoped to become a successful and important person for the society. Another put his trust in God. 'God knows what my life will be. God owns heaven and earth and He decides what we get and what will happen in our lives', he wrote.

Comments from local expertise and parents

During our stay in the Kurdish region in Autumn 2011, we discussed the situation for adolescents and challenges ahead with various institutions and people, among them Vice Governor Behzhad Ali Adam, Duhok, representatives from UNAMI Iraq, university staff, school rectors, politicians, parents and others. Most of the parents had lived in exile with heir families in Iran or in Europe and Scandinavian but had returned to Duhok during the past five years.

The parents expressed deep concern about the authorial regime of yet many school teachers. Verbal abuse and other disciplinarian ways of reprimands unknown to them from their Scandinavian experiences, crowded schools, packed classes, lack of English language classes, lack of sports and lack of creativity in general had made many of them send their children to new private schools instead of ordinary Kurdish schools, as planned. The risk of establishing a class 'cash' society and widen the gap between the rich and the poor, represented a great dilemma, they pointed out. However, all rectors and school staff we met at the public schools expressed energy and optimism, enjoying the possibility to contribute creating a new, tolerant and skilled generation. Most of the school administrators felt the burden of coping to do so with too little funding and too small schools, though. Neither had they been trained to exercise the new school curriculum stemming from the Swedish School curriculum, nor to implement democratic teaching methods adopted by the KRG some years ago, and made known to them by distribution of handbooks only. 'How can I know how to implement this new way of education as long as I never have visited any countries outside Iraq?' one of the school rectors questioned. 'How can I train my staff to teach and deal with the pupils based on democratic values when none of us have experienced democracy or pupil centred teaching ever before?'

Staff at another school was concerned about thee need for some of their students to work long hours outside schools hours to help the family to cope financially. Many families had returned from other parts of Iraq with no money and had to rely upon government assistance to establish themselves. Sometimes the lines to receive financial support from the government through local authorities were too long, and while looking for other opportunities, or receiving some temporary funding from the Kurdish Democratic Party (the dominant political party in the region), the children had to find odd jobs to help the family to survive. However, one of the schools visited had been able to implement parts of the Swedish system. In the corridor, for example, a proud rector showed us a blackboard full of colourful pictures, including photos of The Annual Pupil's School day. On this day, the pupils themselves were in charge of running the school, holding positions as rector, teachers etc, enjoying the power of organizing all lectures and events on that specific occasion.

Participation and patriarchy

During a discussion on youth issues with Dr. Chnar Saad Abdulla, former Minister of Martyrs and Anfal Affairs, presently Head of Vocational Organizations KDP Political Bureau, she emphasised that although Kurdistan society has become much more open and flexible compared to ten years ago, the social system in Kurdistan is still a Patriarchal society.[32] 'In the Kurdish family, the father or an older member of the family makes decisions about the fate of the family and its members. But now we must talk about the change of the role of youth within the family and about the freedom which they did not have before. These changes and freedom also include the right to choose whom they want to marry, the right to choose their work, and the rights for girls to travel,' she underlined, pointing out that Kurdistan still needs more time to get rid of the patriarchal system.

One of the mothers was deeply concerned about traditional patriarchal values and ways of behaviour meeting modern European customs and traditions. While in exile, her young daughter of 11 years old had worn the same kind of T-shirts, jeans and other outfits common among children her age. Returning to Kurdistan, however, the family's older uncle, who had stayed in Kurdistan all the time, 'advised' the child and the mother not to use such T-shirts but to cover up her sleeves and dress according to the Muslim customs. Receiving such instruction from an elderly in the family, the mother stayed up crying all night, realizing how the clash among old traditional values and beliefs might suppress her young daughter's life to come. If so, she would rather return to exile, she said, facing how the understanding of 'the best interest of the child' varies between collectivistic cultural values and those of western, individualistic cultures regarding perspectives on children.

Regarding school environments, both Dr. Abdulla and the parents worried about the fact that many teachers are not capable of handling the students outside the old patriarchal control systems, and about teachers threatening students. On the other hand, adolescents and youth at school know more about their rights now and wished to be freer, Dr. Abdulla commented. This has caused many problems between teachers and students and in some cases even led to students hitting their teachers. All this is happening because the role of youth is incomplete and unclear within the family and in school, she remarked, adding that the patriarchal, authoritarian style also affects the possibilities for the youth to contribute to positive changes on the level of the municipality as well as on governmental level.

To establish arenas for youth to play, rest, discuss and develop themselves, has been a short term goal for the Duhok Governorate, the Vice Governor assured us, when we asked him about the situation in Duhok city.[33] He referred to the establishment of the Youth Centre in Duhok city, admitting that it was not only possible to offer enough attention to the situation of the youth. Still too many internal refugees were arriving asking for help, and he felt that his office suffered from a precarious need to prioritize development of infrastructures and to establish offices to take care of many new tasks in this phase of transition. Besides, many youth organizations offered different activities. The governorate regarded cooperation with political youth organizations and humanitarian NGOs as a key to youth development in a long term perspective, and organized monthly meetings to be updated on their activities and action plans.

Trust and tolerance

As we note from the study, the adolescents widely supported the right to religious freedom and the need to strengthen mutual respect and tolerance between the various groups, many of them underlining that Arabs and Muslims should stay together to achieve lasting peace and future prosperity. On a governmental level, too, the Kurdish authorities officially welcome diversity, allowing various ethnic groups and others, for instance different religious or international communities, to build elementary schools and universities according to their own aims and intentions. In this way, families in disposal of money become able to choose among a variety of schools for their children. The government provides financial support to Arab schools as well as to American schools, Kurdish public schools, Kurdish private schools and others. New steps are made every day to develop Kurdistan into a united, diverse nation. We sensed, however, a certain unspoken resistance among Kurdish parents and local politicians to fully accept this arrangement. Some found it strange and uncomfortable to welcome the other ethnic group, Arabs, to their neighbourhoods, while Kurds may still risk their lives visiting cities populated by Arabs, such as Kirkuk and Mosel. In this situation, why should they treat their former enemies as their equals? Is it reasonable to include the Arabs in the Kurdish society as long as the Kurds are suppressed by the Arabs? Wouldn't such arrangements threaten Kurdish culture and identity, they asked.

Another aspect to be handled is the problem of corruption, they pointed out. The traditional clan rule system favours collective values which strengthen clan network, thus enabling persons and families belonging to certain tribes to have easier access to facilities, jobs and public and private services etc rather than others. Combined with the aftermath of war, the clan system creates good conditions for increasing corruption. In this regard the Kurdish region makes no exception. International and local business investors and politicians are often accused of being arrogant and corrupt, they underlined. While listening to their worries, I recalled a recent situation visiting the Kurdish capital which had made me reflect about my own attitudes related to values and behaviours among people in different countries, and how our various experiences affect our relationships with others. On the way back from Erbil to Duhok we had stopped for a meal, parking outside a restaurant in a street overcrowded with cars and people. Out of old habit I had desperately started to grab my small suitcase full of completed questionnaires, which until then had been placed on the open platform of our pick-up. I was struggling to put it inside the car and lock up, only to discover that the driver was laughing loudly at me. What was I doing? Didn't I trust the pedestrians or other drivers and passengers to leave my luggage alone? Absolutely not. Not even in safe, little Norway did I risk losing goods by placing my bags that much available. The driver's convincing words were completely lost on me, despite his assurances referring to the Kurdish culture, which would not allow this kind of theft.

Tolerance and respect, or opposition and hatred? One of the mothers reflected on this everyday dilemma illustrating incidents occurring in the summer holidays. Very often Arab families from other parts of Iraq bring their families to Duhok for vacation, enjoying the beautiful landscapes, historical places and museums of the city and its surroundings. Her own children were fond of visiting the new amusement park nearby. But as long as the Arabs stayed around, the Kurdish mother would not bring her children to the park, as she usually did on Sundays throughout the year, she confessed. She found it uncomfortable and difficult to let her children mix with Arabs who had harmed her family so much in recent years. And even if she tried to control herself intellectually, she could not control her feelings, she said. Her mixed feelings illustrate that expectation and demand of reconciliation might still be too much to ask for on the level of the individual person. However, on a national level, development of formal systems and structures cannot depend upon individual, personal approval from all citizens. It can only act as a frame for the citizens to exist within. Besides, reconciliation strategies and reconstruction efforts seem to follow another pathway and timetable on the level of the nation. This has also been the case in other conflict areas in the world, like for instance in South Africa.[34]

Conclusion

Adolescents have particular capacities and can make significant contributions in reconstrucction and development processes. The adolescents in our study on some occasions clapped their hands when given an opportunity to express themselves outside their own, narrow circles at home within the family. They communicated optimism and energy. They expressed strong and concrete wishes about their future education and jobs, and clear visions about the need of making Kurdistan a peaceful, democratic and including society. They hoped for a well-functioning federal system which makes it possible for different beliefs and cultural groups to live together in freedom and solidarity. At the same time, they experienced lack of attention in school and felt that no arena was available in which to develop their creativity and capacities.

The KRG Youth Road Map invites youth to participate in making Kurdistan a place of democracy and stability, and to be involved in solving the social challenges ahead. But do the authorities really want to include the youth in decision-making and policy development, or is the invitation to do so just an act of tokenism? Generally it is a tendency to overlook resources of children and youth related to societal safety and democracy building in post conflict phases. Adolescents in our study experience that they have almost no possibilities to contribute towards reaching such a goal, either in school or on the level of the municipality. Critical voices from youth and severe acts to attract attention to their cause and conditions support the need to increase awareness about their rights and roles in the region. By ignoring their voices today, and neglecting their demands for democratization and social justice, the authorities increasingly risk unrest and upheaval instead of trust, tolerance and stability.

Notes

1. Human Rights Watch. (1993). *Genocide in Iraq. The Anfal Campaign against the Kurds. A Middle East Watch Report*. New York. Accessed 10 January 2012 at http://www.hrw.org/legacy/**reports/1993**/iraqanfal/
2. Kurdish Television news. (May 31, 2011) Supreme Court Acknowledged Halabja attack as Genocide. Accessed 20 August 2011 at http://www.kurdsat.tv/news.php?id=1&type=anfal
3. UN documents speak about "youth" as the age group between 15-24 years. The Convention on the Rights of the Child uses the term "children" about young people between 0- 18 years old. To narrow down the group of children and youth included in my own research I have therefore chosen to use the term "adolescence", focusing on the group between 13 – 18 years of age.
4. Various sources use different names about this region. The author will do the same.
5. Barzani, N., & Abdulah, C. S.(2008). Crimes of Mass Murder against the Kurdish People and their Consequences. In Hussein F. (ed.), *International Conference on Genocide Against the Kurdish People* (p. 11-35). Erbil, Kurdistan: Aras Press, Serial no 03.
6. Amnesty International. (2009). *Hope and Fear: Human Rights in the Kurdistan Region of Iraq*. London, UK.
7. Bird, C.(2005). *A Thousand Sighs, A Thousand Revolts: Journeys in Kurdistan*. New York: Ballantine books.
8. The present KRG cabinet is made up of members of the Kurdistani List coalition, which won the region's parliamentary elections in July 2009, together with other

parties. The coalition government consists of the Kurdistan Democratic Party (KDP), Patriotic Union of Kurdistan (PUK), Kurdistan Islamic Movement, the Chaldean Assyrian Syriac Council, Turkmen representatives, Communists and Socialists. The government has 19 ministries. For more information about the Kurdistan region and the structure of the Kurdistan Regional Government, see webpage accessed on 10 June 2012 at ***http://www.krg.org/articles/detail.asp?lngnr=1 2&smap=03010300&rnr=140&anr=23911***

9. UNAMI Publication Information Office.(June 2010). *Iraq Election 2010.* Accessed 15 February 2012. at http://unami.unmissions.org/LinkClick. aspx?fileticket=PGVyYGKl_NQ%3D&tabid=2873&language=en-US

10. UNAMI Human Rights Office/OHCR, Bagdhad. (January 2011). *Human Rights in Iraq 2010.* Accessed 20 February 2012 at http://www.ohchr.org/Documents/ Countries/IQ/UNAMI_HR%20Report_1Aug11_en.pdf

11. *Focusing on Honour.* (7 December 2007). Statement issued by the Ministry of Sports and Youth, citing T. Barwary, Minister of Sports and Youth. Accessed 29 December 2011 at http://www.mosy-krg.org

12. ibid

13. See status of ratification of the Convention of the Rights on the Child for all State Parties. Accessed 10 May 2011 at http://www.bayefsky.com/pdf/crc_ratif_table. pdf

14. The Convention on the Rights of the Child. Adopted by UN 20 November 1989, entered into force 2. September 1990. Accessed 8 May 2011 at http://www2. ohchr.org/english/law/crc.htm

15. CRC Article 3. Accessed 8 May 2011 at http://www2.ohchr.org/english/law/ crc.htm

16. Iraq Initial State report on the CRC. (1996). CRC/C/41/Add.3 Accessed 8 May 2011 at http://www.bayefsky.com/reports/iraq_crc_c_41_add.3_1996.php

17. Concluding observations by the UNCRC committee on Iraq State report (1998). CRC/C/15/Add 94. Accessed 9 May 2011 at http://daccess-dds-ny.un.org/doc/ UNDOC/GEN/G98/190/39/PDF/G9819039.pdf?OpenElement,

18. United Nation Children's Fund, Executive Board (15 July 2010).*Revised Country Programme Document Iraq 2011-2014.* Accessed 20 August 2011 at http://www. unicef.org/about/execboard/files/2010-PL.13-Iraq-revised-English-26July.pdf

19. Ibid

20. Smith, L.(2010). FNs konvensjon om barnets rettigheter. Kap. 1 in : N. Høstmælingen,& E. Saga Kjørholt& K. Sandberg (eds.), *Barnekonvensjonen og barns rettigheter i Norge* (p 17 – 30). Norway: Universitetsforlaget.

21. General Comment no 12, 2009: The Right of the Child to be heard. CRC/C/ GC/, UNCRC Committee 12. July 2009. Accessed 10 May 2011 at http://www. coe.int/t/dg3/children/participation/CRC-C-GC-12.pdf

22. The Millennium Development Goals (MDGs) are eight concrete targets to

reduce poverty and increase development and stability, aimed to be achieved by 2015. Altogether 147 heads of states and governments signed the Millennium Declaration during the UN Millennium Summit in 2000. Resolution adopted by the UN General Assembly 18 Sept 2000. A/RES/55/2.The third goal concerns promotion of gender equality and empowerment of women in particular. Accessed 10 January 2012 at http://www.un.org/millenniumgoals

23. Ministry of Sports and Culture, Kurdistan Regional Government. (2009).*The Youth Road Map*. Adopted by the KRG Council of Ministers meeting on January 21st 2009 as part of the KRG programs. Accessed 10 January 2012 at http://www.mosy-krg.org/doc/youth_road_map.pdf

24. Ibid

25. Kurdistan Tribune, lead article by editor. (18 September 2011). *Banaz Jawas is a symbol of Revolution*. Accessed 20 January 2012 at http://kurdistantribune.com/2011/banaz-jawad-symbol-of-revolution/

26. Ibid

27. Fantappie, M. (2011) Iraq: In country's north, a youth-led "Kurdish spring". *Los Angeles Times, May 4th 2011*. Accessed 22 January 2012 athttp://latimesblogs.latimes.com/babylonbeyond/2011/05/iraq-in-countrys-north-a-youth-led-kurdish-spring-blooms.html

28. Abdulla,M. (2011). Why the Mood of the South of Kurdistan Youth is in a State of Revolution. *Kurdistan Aspect*, 20 February 2011. Accessed 10 March 2012 at http://www.kurdishaspect.com/doc022011MA.html

29. ibid

30. *The Youth Roadmap*. Op.cit. p. 8.

31. Kipperberg, E., Lind, A. W.(2009). *Feasibility Study Northern Iraq, Kurdistan*. Internal report, University of Stavanger, Norway.

32. Personal communication between Dr. Chnar Saad Abdulla and the author. Erbil, 10 October 2011.

33. Personal communication between the author and the Duhok Vice Governorate Office. Duhok 4 October 2011.

34. Kipperberg, E.(2007). The structures of the TRC in South Africa and resulting violence among children and youth. In: Burton, P.(ed.), *Someone Stole my Smile. Violence among Children and Youth in South Africa today.* (p. 69-89). Cape Town, South Africa: Centre for Justice and Crime Prevention.

13

Social welfare provisioning in MENA: Religious or secular?

Mahmood Messkoub

Introduction

The 2009 post-presidential election mass demonstrations in Iran, along with the sporadic yet frequent protests elsewhere in the Middle East and North Africa (MENA) region, and following 2010, the so-called 'Arab Spring', has brought into sharp focus not only the democratic deficit and deep inequalities in the region but also inadequate public social provisioning of regional poorer countries. Recent political movements in the region have not been in direct response to these inequalities and lack of social provisioning that have been going on for decades, but are a response to blatant abuse of power, lack of accountability and the naked suppression of dissent. Yet the desire for a less inequitable and just society, as well as an end to poverty, have been the promised goals of almost all political movements in the region.

Both secular and religious opposition groups and individuals have been subject of the systematic and brutal repression in the region. Religious political organisations have not been on the forefront of the protest movements, yet they have been the main beneficiaries wherever the protests, popular movements and international pressure and involvement brought down dictators, and changed the political map of countries in the region. In the 2011 parliamentary elections in Tunisia and Egypt Islamic religious parties won more seats than secular parties; and in Libya the emerging power structure, following the deposing of Gaddafi regime, has a strong religious leadership and backing. The question remains whether these avowedly Islamist parties will be able to live up to their promises of reducing poverty, improving living standards and creating a more just and equitable societies. Or more generally, is Islam, or other religions,the answer to the social inequalities, economic stagnation and lack of democracy in the region?

Given the variety of social and economic structures present across MENA countries one should not look for a single model to answer the above questions. Besides, the specific historical and cultural heritage as played out in different parts of MENA have shaped the role of Islam, its interpretation and influence on the social and political life of each country. However, it is legitimate to search for a pattern in or record of an Islamic approach to poverty alleviation and social justice in the region. As well as asking whether control of State power would bring any changes to the Islamic approach (as in Iran) to welfare provisioning, as well as inquiring whether such control will become more religious or secular.

To address the above issues, this chapter will provide a brief account of economics and poverty in the region. It will seek to locate the role of religiously based institutions in providing social support for the population, and discuss how this support is formalized in State social policy when religious parties come to power.

The religious approach to poverty alleviation has a long history and has been dominated by what is called, in the modern language of poverty studies, 'targeting of the poor', which combines the principle of 'inability to support oneself' by eg being an orphan, too young or too old to work, having some kind of disability, being victims of war and acts of nature – with an implicit or explicit 'means testing' to identify the poor.

Being a victim of circumstance is an important criterion in qualifying for support that puts the emphasis on the 'conjunctural poor' rather than the 'structural poor'(Iliffe, 1987). This distinction is important when it comes to tackling the underlying causes of poverty. Much religious and charity work on poverty has focused on conjunctural poverty that stems from the fact that religious establishments, in the main, have had an important stake in maintaining the status quo when it comes to distribution of assets such as land and other general distributional policies. Having said that, one should not ignore the radical religious interpretations of holy texts (combining religious thoughts with modern socialist ideas, e.g. radical priests advocating Liberation Theology in Latin America and the Islamic socialism of Mujahedin Khalgh Organisation in the 1960s and 1970s in Iran) that have often brought radical religious groups into conflict with the established order and religious hierarchy the world over.

Poverty and vulnerability in the MENA region

The social and economic backdrop to the movements for democracy and equality in the MENA region is one of high poverty, unemployment (especially youth unemployment) and vulnerability, despite the region's wealth and good record of economic growth. MENA countries, on average, have experienced a steady annual real GDP growth in the range of 4 – 6 % for much of the past 20 years. (Messkoub, 2009, Appendix Tables 1-2.) These are respectable rates of growth that should have helped MENA countries to attend to some of the urgent needs of the population such as job creation and alleviation of poverty. All countries in the region, whether resource-rich (in oil, gas and other minerals):labour importing or resource-poor: labour abundant, have shared in the high growth era of late 20th and early 20th century, in part because of the widespread links, through trade, finance and labour migration, between the two groups of countries. As will be demonstrated, all these countries have achieved very modest gains in reducing poverty and increasing employment.

With regards to other basic macroeconomic indicators, real per capita GDP in constant US dollar has also increased in all countries in the past 20 years, with inflation being brought down from double digit figures of the early 1980s to a single digit by 2000.

In broad terms, on the eve of the Arab Spring the macroeconomic situation looked rather healthy. There was no runaway inflation in MENA countries, public finances seem to be under control; and under the guidance and pressure of international financial institutions and sections of the local elite, all countries had opened up *(infitah)*[1] their economies, in various degrees, to market forces at national and international levels. Given the increasing role of private sector and integration of MENA countries in the world economy it is useful to consider the forces that shaped the opening up of these economies. According to Richards and Waterbury:

> 'Infitah' should be seen as the outcome of three interacting set of forces: class actors, often fostered by earlier state-led growth policies; serious economic difficulties, generated both by state-led growth policies and by the international conjuncture; and pressure from international actors.... [that] does not mean that the public sector is about to be dismantled... [nor] state ceding to 'civil society'. Rather than a *retreat* of the state, *infitah* is better conceived as a *restructuring* of state activity, always mediating between society and international actors, still responsible for the basic welfare of the population, and continuing to formulate the goals and strategy of economic development and structural change' (1990: 261).

These developments have taken place against the background of structural transformation of MENA that has been under way for decades. Industry and service sectors have long replaced agriculture as the main source of GDP. By 2004 the share of agriculture in GDP in most MENA countries had dropped to less than 20 %, except in Sudan (39 %) and Syria (23 %). However, in most countries agriculture employs a sizable proportion of the labour force ranging from 27% in Egypt to 54% in Yemen. In general the employment share of agriculture is larger than its GDP share (Messkoub 2009, Appendix Tables 6 and ILO, 2006).

The upshot of the above figures is that a large proportion of the population working in agriculture has had to rely on a proportionately small share of GDP for its livelihood, and that carries implications for the incidence of poverty among the rural population. The data on poverty reveal that in most countries of the region poverty rates are higher in rural areas than in urban areas.

According to the national poverty lines in the MENA countries, 22% of Algerians were considered to be poor in 1998. A similar indicator in Egypt revealed that 16% of the population were poor in 2000. Corresponding figures in other countries were: 19% in Morocco in 1999, 35.4%in Yemen in 1998 and 7.6% in Tunisia in 1995. In all MENA countries a larger proportion of the poor lived in rural than in urban areas. In Tunisia, for example, four times as many poor people were living in rural areas than in urban areas. In Morocco, more than twice as many poor were living in rural areas in 1999 than in urban areas (Iqbal, 2005: 18).

The scale of poverty in some of these countries increases dramatically if we use an international poverty line of the percentage of people whose income is below $2 a day, which in the case of Egypt in 2000 would be 43.90%. The corresponding figure for Tunisia in 1995 is 12.7%. However, apparently in other countries there is not much of a gap between the national and international criteria since the percentage of the population who are poor does not change much when the international poverty line is used.

Where Jordan is concerned, only those studies that use the international poverty line are available. According to the $2 criterion, the proportion of the population who were poor in Jordan in 1997 was 7.4%, but another source (ILO, 2006) reported a higher poverty rate of 21.3% for 1997. The same source also reported a higher incidence of rural poverty compared with urban areas, as observed in other countries. Despite the difference in headcount poverty rates, both sources agree on the reduction in poverty – by 2002 Jordan experienced a 33% drop in the poverty rate.

An important aspect of poverty in most developing countries is that the poor are working, but their earnings are not sufficient to provide them with the most basic needs necessary for survival in terms of nutrition, sanitation and health (which is usually measured by an absolute poverty line of say $1 or $2 per day). The number of the working poor rises if we use the more appropriate measure of relative poverty (that takes account distribution of income and expenditure as well as capability to participate in the society by having a voice in the running of ones' affairs). In this chapter absolute poverty measures are used since the relative poverty measures that are country specific are not available for all countries concerned.

Evidence on the working poor in MENA is quite striking. Among the MENA countries in the late 1990s, Egypt and Yemen had the highest share of the working population who were poor: 71.5% in Egypt (1999 figure) and 73.70% in Yemen (1998 figure). In the case of Yemen there was a doubling of the number of working poor since 1995. The lowest percentage of the working poor belongs to Tunisia at 11.90% in 2000 and Jordan at 12.80%; and those figures were lower than the corresponding figures in the early 1990s. Morocco and Algeria, in contrast, recorded quite a high percentage of working poor at 23.50% (in 1998) and 30.50% (in 1995) respectively. (Messkoub 2009, Appendix Table 3)

Poverty among employed people could be due to many factors such as labour market conditions, as well as low productivity and low skills. An excess supply of labour, especially of the unskilled type, often pushes wages down and people in the lower end of the labour market into poverty. Where minimum wage regulation exists, it is often set at too low a level to prevent people falling below the poverty line. Low productivity could also result in low wages and income. This is often the case of the working poor who eke out a meagre living in the informal sector.

An important aspect of measurement of poverty based on a poverty line is the treatment of those who are just above the poverty line. These are the people who are vulnerable to poverty because any changes in the economy (e.g. increase in inflation that will have price and income effects) would push them below the poverty line. Any anti-poverty policy that is based solely on a poverty line, and does not address the problem of vulnerability, fails to address the structural causes of poverty that are related to, for example, to distribution of assets, human capital and skills, ethnic/race/caste, gender and other discriminations.

To have a measure of vulnerability in the MENA region, let us look at the percentage of poor in the population at different poverty lines of $1, $2, $3 and $4. Sharp increases in the percentage of the poor can be observed as we move up from $1 a day mark. The jump is most dramatic in cases of Egypt and Yemen where the rates of poverty at $1 are respectively about 3 and 10% increasing to about 42% for both countries at $2. Further jumps in the percentage of the poor can be observed at $3 and $4 but the rate of increase declines. For the richer MENA countries the jump in the percentage of the poor is lower as we move up from $1 to $2, than it is for a move from $2 to $3 and from $3 to $4. In Jordan, for example, the percentage of the poor is below 5% at $1 and goes up to about 5% at $2, but then jumps to about 22% at $3 and 42% at $4. (Iqbal, 2005)

The difference in the rate of increase of poverty in the poor and rich group of countries is, in the first instance, due to differences in per capita income and a purely statistical one at that. In other words the high per capita income puts more people above the basic international poverty lines of $1 to $4. The lower the per capita income in the country the sharper is the increase in the percentage of the poor as the poverty line is moved up. The MENA countries not only need anti-poverty policies to deal with the sizable number of the poor, they also need to have policies that will monitor and provide cover for the substantial number of people who are just above the poverty line, whatever the threshold, and who could join the ranks of the poor with slightest shifts in the economy affecting the poor. In Syria, for example, Islam (2006) estimates that about 19% are considered vulnerable and go through periods of poverty that is almost double the percentage of the people who are poor - 11%. In Egypt, in 2001, the number of the poor at $2 was 28.6 million jumping to 47.6 million at $3. This vulnerable population of just under 20 million people should be taken into account in the design of pro-poor social policies. At the MENA level, with the use of higher threshold of poverty line - at $3 – the number of poor rises to 95.3 million, indicating that the vulnerable population at the lower poverty line of $2 is 43 million. Given that the vulnerable population in Egypt accounts for about half the vulnerable population in the MENA region, Egypt should have a strategic position in regional poverty alleviation programmes of international organizations working in the region.

To sum up, the oil and mineral-resource poor countries of the region where most of the poor live are beset with large scale of poverty and vulnerability in the region.

Social needs in the region

High rates of poverty and vulnerability in the region are, unsurprisingly, matched by poor social indicators and high social needs, in particular in countries where a large percentage of population lives in rural areas (e.g. 58% in Egypt and 70% in Yemen, World Bank, 2011), which, as is noted above, is home to a large number of poor people. This is despite the improvement in macro-level social indicators in the regions since the 1970s. Infant (below one-year-old) and child (below five-year-old) mortality rates, adult literacy, and life expectancy improved following the rise in oil revenues, limited land reform, large scale government investment, public spending on social programmes, and rapid urbanisation with its concomitant development of urban-based industrial and service sectors and general increase in urban demand.

By the 1990s the MENA countries narrowed the gap in social indicators with other countries with similar levels of per capita income. Yet gender gaps remain, especially in relation to female literacy and educational attainments, between the MENA and comparable countries (Karshenas and Moghadam, 2006). The other major problem has been the slow growth of job creation relative to supply of labour in general, and educated school and university graduates in particular. Despite the fertility decline in most MENA countries, the population momentum and youth bulge has ensured high growth of labour force; a factor, which combined with the low growth rate of demand for labour, explains the growing youth unemployment problem in the region(Messkoub, 2008).

Income poverty also reflects itself in poverty in terms of access, *inter alia*, to health, education, housing, adequate nutrition, and social and political power. Without coordinated intervention and collective action poverty and vulnerability become entrenched and deepened in any society. Social indicators of health and education and State social expenditure are the most important indicators of outcomes of collective action on the part of the State.

Indeed the social rights to education, health, housing, land, freedom and so on have always been important objectives in the nation-building agenda in the post-colonial era, and have found their way into the manifestos and declarations of religious and secular political and social movements in the MENA and elsewhere in the developing world. The failure of the State to meet its obligation to citizens has been the most important reason for the activism of Islamic religious movements in the region, not only in terms of providing social services to the poor but also challenging the ruling elite and the State (see Jawad and also Aboulhassan & Abdel-Ghany in this book for further analyses on this point).

Having said that it may be surprising to find that social indicators in the region are on a par with countries of similar per capita income. From the 1960s to 1990s the median social expenditure (as a percentage of GDP) on health (0.9%) and education (4.4%) have been above those in East Asia, 2.6 and 0.6 percentages respectively. However, the aggregate figures on spending conceals the poor record of the region compared with East Asia, in terms of quality of education, enrolment in tertiary education and the gender gap in education. For example, despite improvement in female school attendance and literacy the region is still far behind comparator countries (Karshenas and Moghadam, 2006). The region also has a poor record in job creation and employment for its young labour force. In fact the steady decline of fertility rates since the 1970s has opened up a demographic window in the region that has hardly been planned for and utilised, unlike the situation in the East Asian countries which successfully used their young and educated labour force to integrate their economies into the emerging global economy.

An upshot of this failure has been the rise in unemployment in most MENA countries in the post-oil boom era of the 1980s and sharp decline in economic growth. Moreover, States in the region also failed to develop coherent social policy measures to cushion the impact of rising unemployment, and to help the labour market to adjust to the shock of decline in oil prices. Decline in oil prices reduced the capacity of States to create sufficient jobs in the State sector for the fast rising youth labour supply. Whilst the private sector had limited ability to absorb the labour supply of both the retrenched State sector employees following various structural adjustment programmes and the young entrants into the labour market. Neither has the so-called '*infitah*' , or opening up of economy to market forces, led to the expected rise in job creation. It is important to emphasise an earlier point that '*infitah*' did not mean withdrawal of state and total dominance of the market, rather a restructuring of the relationship between the two in which state would still be responsible for social welfare.

But this has not translated into concrete policy measures to protect the poor and the vulnerable. What social benefits and welfare measures existed were, by and large, the privileges of State and corporate sector employees, whose jobs were relatively well protected but at the expense of declining real wages. The most dramatic example is that in Egypt, where between 1985 and 1992 real product wage in the manufacturing sector declined at an annual rate of 9.5%, with the corresponding figures for Morocco and Tunisia being 5.7% and 1.4% (Karshenas and Moghadam, 2006: 16). Declining real wages were a result of low growth of output and declining labour productivity, and did not lead to higher demand for labour as the market oriented policies of the IFIs suggests.

Whilst the clientalist and patronage-oriented social policies were being questioned by market-oriented policies of international financial institutions and donor communities, increasing number of NGOs were calling for a rights based/citizen oriented approach to social welfare and social development. States simply could not deliver, neither economically nor socially and politically. Small wonder that :

> ... the space between social aspirations and developmental requirements on the one hand and the existing realities and capacities of the states on the other is [has] being rapidly filled by a plethora of NGOs – both of a traditional type, usually controlled by Islamists, and the more modernist externally financed type (Karshenas and Moghadam, 2006:18).

'Infitah' and the restructuring of State – market relationship increased the vulnerability of the working poor and the unemployed whilst those in State employment or working in industry were facing declining living standards; and all that in the absence of meaningful social insurance policies to cushion the impact of liberalisation, reduction in food and other subsidies, together with the clampdown and suppression of any organised protests against worsening economic conditions. These developments seriously undermined the informal family-based social welfare model of the oil-boom era, which has deteriorated further as a result of worsening employment situation and the impact of the financial crisis of 2008.

Employment and labour markets in the MENA

An important social and economic backdrop to the Arab Spring has been the high levels and persistent unemployment in the resource-poor countries, and even in the populous resource-rich countries like Algeria. Job creation and gainful employment is a major problem in the region. The high natural growth of the population due to a concomitant former high fertility rate and the more recent population momentum in the region has ensured an increase in working age population and labour supply that has outstripped labour demand in all MENA countries. The labour force in the region has been growing at an annual rate of 3-4% since the mid-1980s. The high population growth of the recent past also accounts for the young age structure of the population. At least 30% of population in the MENA countries are below the age of 15. Thus a critical challenge in the region is to increase labour demand in public and private sector.

Unemployment has been a major problem in the region. In countries for which data are available the aggregate unemployment rate for males in 2003 varied between a rather low figure of 7.3% in Egypt to a high of 23.4% in Algeria. In between are Morocco at 11.5% and Jordan at 14.7%. The aggregate rates for females are in most cases higher than those for males, with female unemployment rate in Algeria being 25.4%, in Egypt at 23.2%, in Morocco at 13.0%, and standing at 19.7% in Jordan. A similar picture emerges in Syria where female unemployment is slightly higher than male unemployment, with the largest gap being at the 20-24 age group (Islam, 2005).

Since 1980 the trend in male unemployment rate has been on the increase in Egypt and Jordan while that in Morocco has been relatively stable. Interestingly enough, female unemployment has either been relatively stable, as in the case of Egypt, or has had a moderate downward trend as in Algeria, Morocco and Jordan.

An important feature of unemployment in the region is a very high rate of youth (15-24 age group) unemployment. According to the latest UNDP estimates (UNDP, 2012) a quarter of the 15-24 years old are unemployed, accounting for 50% of the total unemployment in the Arab MENA countries. Country specific data are only available for few countries. In Morocco youth unemployment rates are respectively 17.4% for males and 15.9% for females. In Jordan youth unemployment rates are respectively 28.0% for males and 43.2% for females (ILO, 2009).

ILO's country studies reveal that a large proportion of young unemployed people are educated at least to secondary level. In some cases the higher the level of education the higher the unemployment rate. In Jordan female unemployment rate has been highest for those with a bachelor degree (ILO, 2006, p. 3). In Egypt both males and females with 'intermediate' education had the highest rates of unemployment. (Laithy and El Ehwany, 2006:10). The UNDP notes that:

> ... one of the main reasons for a high youth unemployment rate is the problematic transition from school to work, particularly among university graduates. (UNDP, 2012: 41).

Both supply and demand factors have been responsible for the rise in unemployment. On the supply side the rapid population growth of earlier periods, as noted above, has increased the size of the labour force, especially in the younger age groups, and on the demand side, economic growth and job creation have fallen far behind the labour supply. An interesting feature of labour supply in the Arab MENA is the decline or stability of male labour-force participation rate (LFPR) in most countries, as against the rise, albeit modest, of the female LFPR. This is the pattern in Algeria, Morocco, Tunisia and Syria (see Messkoub, 2009) that poses an important question regarding the problem of female unemployment in these countries. Labour market and job creation policies in the MENA region rarely take note of such gender difference in unemployment rates.

On the demand side it is important to know the growth of employment by sector in order to investigate whether sectoral distribution of employment has changed, and whether a shift of labour from sectors with low productivity to those with higher productivity has been taking place that could, in turn, help in reducing poverty. As noted earlier there has been a sectoral shift away from agriculture, but the gain in employment in the industrial sector has been very modest in most MENA countries for which data is available. Within the industrial sector the manufacturing sector employment has had a very disappointing employment record. ILO (2009). provides data for the manufacturing employment in very few (Egypt, Iran, Morocco) of the larger countries of the MENA region. In all of them, the share of manufacturing in total employment, as well as the volume of employment in the manufacturing sector, has been stagnant over the years. It is interesting to note that female employment in manufacturing has gone up, albeit modestly in all the countries concerned.

The service sector, which has absorbed much of the increase in the labour force in the MENA region, is composed of a diverse range of activities – ranging from high productivity and high-return sectors such as banking, insurance and finance at one extreme to very low productivity and low-return street vendors on the other. To investigate whether the service sector can, or will, be able to play a major role in poverty reduction we need to see which sub-sectors of the service sector have been growing and have the potential to provide high productivity and high-wage jobs to the unemployed and under-employed labour force. The available data for the larger countries of MENA that have the most serious unemployment and poverty problems indicate that the high productivity, high-return sectors are a very small sub-set of the growing service sector, and have also been growing very slowly. The trade and small-scale repair shops (motor as well as household goods) are the only sub-sectors that have been showing some sign of growth. A large proportion of this sub-sector could be considered informal with low productivity and low returns. However, it would be of interest to know the composition of this sector both in terms of products and skills, as well as its linkages with other sectors, in order to investigate its potential for productivity growth. Very little information is available on these aspects of the informal sector.

Let us now turn to the role of the public and private sectors in the labour market and changes over time. There is a large variation in the MENA region in the share of public sector employment in total employment. On the high end of the spectrum are Egypt (with a figure of 60% in 1998) and Jordan (56% in 1998), and on the low end are Algeria (25% in 2004), Syria (26% in 2003) and Yemen (11% in the 2003). In all these countries the share of public sector employment has either been falling over the years or, at best, has been fairly stable (as is the case in Syria and Jordan). The mirror image represented by these figures is the private sector employment that employs 89% of the labour force in Yemen, at one extreme, and 40% in Egypt, at the other. This raises very important questions with regard to the role of public and private sectors in creating good quality jobs in the future; particularly when one considers the pressures on the public sector finances. How to improve the capacity of the private sector to increase its supply of high quality jobs would depend on a range of factors and policies: the level of demand in the economy, government tax and subsidy policies, labour market rules and regulations, and level of and complementarity between public and private sector investments in particular in the areas of education and infrastructure.

As noted governments can influence the labour market by adopting a range of policies but the time needed to plan and implement them varies by the type of policy. For example, providing tax incentives to promote job creation take a short time to implement, but others such as investment in infrastructure would take longer both in terms of planning and implementation.

Labour market and job creation policies should also take note of two important features of the Arab labour market: higher female unemployment compared with males, informal employment and the working poor. In the Arab MENA female unemployment is 16% compared with 8% for male, with the problem being most pressing for those women who enter the labour force for the first time. Expansion of and participation in higher education and delayed age of marriage has contributed to this trend. As a result 35% of the young Arab women were unemployed in 2004-2011 compared with 20 % of young Arab men. This not only reflects the failure of Arab States to create sufficient jobs, but also reflects a gender bias in filling the available jobs, and gender differences in the jobs carried out by men and women, with the latter being mainly employed in social, personal and community services (UNDP, 2012, p. 41).

Informality defined by OECD as 'non-coverage by social protection' is another feature of the labour market in developing countries in general and MENA in particular, where the resource-poor Arab countries are closely associated with self-employment and working in the informal sector. Vulnerability to shocks due to, market conditions and health problems, for instance, is an important characteristic of informality. In most of the resource-poor Arab MENA at least 50 % of the employed people could be considered as active in the 'informal' sector, with women having a significant share of it.

Poverty, unemployment and gender discrimination are only few of the social and economic problems facing the Arab MENA countries. Following the downfall of long established Arab rulers the incoming regimes have a huge task ahead of them with the added pressure of justifiable high popular expectations. The question is whether the answer to these problems are going to be found within the agenda of the Islamic political forces, which have come to prominence in the Arab world, or whether solutions have to be found through democratic dialogue among secular and religious political forces.

Policy responses: Religious or secular?

What are the policy options for the post-Arab spring to reduce poverty, unemployment and vulnerability in the region? The answer lies less in the Islamic ideology and more on the fiscal capacity of the State and on the support policy of aid donor countries and international financial institutions (IFIs).

Almost all labour-abundant countries, whether resource-rich or not (Algeria being an exception) have had fiscal deficits since the 2006, particularly in the resource-poor labour abundant countries. This raises the all important question of fiscal capacity of the State and the associated social policy space to alleviate the worst effects of the crisis on the population by increasing employment, maintaining access to basic consumption goods, maintaining social expenditure on health and education, and in general preventing poverty from increasing even further.

What States in the region can do in this regard depends to a large degree on the fiscal space and policy space that they have, and the way such a space is interpreted. An orthodox neoclassical interpretation of fiscal space, as favoured by the IMF and other IFIs, is put in terms of

> the room in government's budget that allows it to provide resources for a desired purpose without jeopardising the sustainability of its financial position or the stability of the economy. (Cavallo and Izquierdo, 2009, quoted in Islam, 2009)

This approach usually focuses on the short term stability of the economy, which may be at the expense of the long term development goals of increasing investment in infrastructure and meeting the basic needs of population in the areas of health, education, etc. An alternative interpretation of the fiscal space rooted in the structuralist/heterodox macroeconomics, and associated with UNDP, does not negate the importance of economic stability (avoidance of runaway inflation and ballooning of balance of payments deficit) but focuses instead on the development objectives.

The fiscal and policy space then is as much about the priorities of State and the economic and development model that it adopts. For example, the orthodox approach recommends cuts in public expenditure during a financial crisis because tax and other revenues will be on the decline, whilst its expenditure remains static if not rising in the short to medium term. The alternative approach requires a shift in expenditure away from areas like defence and focuses on health, education, social protection and infrastructure. Countries that have the possibility of accumulating reserves during the boom could pay for their expenditure in the downturn (Islam, 2009). This is the path that East Asian countries followed after the East Asian financial crisis of the 1990s.

The resource-rich countries of the MENA countries have sufficient national and international reserves to cope with a changing political map if they choose to. It is in this connection that social policy space should be added to the fiscal policy space. That is, how fiscal policy space could be translated into social policy goals to ensure that universal social protection is available especially for the poor and vulnerable, with a focus on the vulnerable. The resource-poor countries of the region on the other hand have a more difficult task because of their budget and balance of payments deficits, whilst having to provide for a larger proportion of their population being poor.

In the short-term the resource-poor countries would certainly need support to stabilise their external balances, but without the usual orthodox strings of cuts in public spending; and in general pro-cyclical policies that would worsen the impact of crisis. Given that unemployment in the region is expected to increase, of particular concern is the share of 'vulnerable employment' in total employment, which in the MENA region has been put at 33% in 2008, and is expected to increase to 39% in 2009, according to the worst case scenario. The corresponding figures in North Africa are 37% and 42%, respectively (Tzannatos, 2009:25). Maintaining social expenditure on food subsidies, education and health is not only important from a social and humanitarian point of view, but also owing to its contribution to demand in the economy.

At a more general level policies should be put in place to maintain employment. In the public sector investment in infrastructure (water, sewage, roads and the like) would boost demand and have a counter-cyclical effect on the economy while increasing demand for labour, at least in the short-term. Private sector would also need support to maintain employment. In all financial crises private sector will face cash flow problems as a result of the general decline in economic activities and an ensuing credit crunch. Not only should the State step in to provide short-term finance, it could also help by giving tax holidays and help to reduce labour costs through social expenditure on health, nutrition and education.

Labour market policies in the region have taken variety of forms. They range from early retirement in Tunisia (to boost demand for labour and hiring of younger workers) to support for small and medium size enterprises in, for example, Egypt and Jordan. Other strategies include tackling youth unemployment through employment of graduates, introduction and expansion of training programmes; to job sharing as in Tunisia; and finally, measures to tackle child labour, as in Egypt, and offers of cash transfers to families if they keep their children at school.

In the medium-to-long-term job creation and the raising of the income of the working poor, as a policy to reduce poverty, remains the main challenge facing the MENA countries. This is perhaps one of the most difficult areas of policy, not only in response to crisis but also in general (For further details see Messkoub, 2008, especially sections 4 and 5).

Before the Arab Spring religious and secular opposition political forces had a very limited role and influence over the social and economic policies, but provided limited support for the poor through various charity and NGO networks mainly in areas of health and education. Religious involvement in provisioning social and welfare services have to a large extent been due to the failure of State to provide basic services in deprived urban and rural areas in many of the poorer Arab MENA countries, especially after the liberalisation of the economy – *infitah* – that led to cut backs in food subsidies, and health and education spending.

Before coming to power the religious and secular opposition movements challenged the State power and the corrupt practices of the existing regimes in order to influence and shape policies for what were considered to be 'justice' for the people and for the development of the country, with explicit egalitarian and nationalist objectives. For the religious opposition, however, this is no more than a vision for a future Islamic State. Islamist used such discourses to garner support from the mass of poor and middle class people without 'offering a viable realistic programme of a future Islamic state' (Abdelrahman, 2001:116). This vagueness in relation to having a clear plan is at the heart of the flexibility of the Islamist governments after they come to power; and goes a long way to explaining the Islamists' pragmatism and use of the legal and administrative infrastructure of the previous regimes, particularly in relation to the management of the economy. Islamists, however, have always argued for the supremacy of the Islamic legal system – *sharia* – and tried to use their influence to ensure that secular laws conform to it. It is in social areas where the influence of *sharia* is mostly felt, areas such as the justice and penal system, and family law that have always had a strong gender bias against women. In economic areas it is finance and interest rate which have usually come under close scrutiny by Islamic jurists because of the outlawing of usury in Islam. But even here the flexibility and creativity of Islamists reveals itself in re-formulating financial contracts of savings and lending (the core activities of any banking system), so that the interest rate is not recorded as a return on money but as a return on productive business activities.

With the overthrow of the old order the incoming power faces the harsh realities of running a modern State. It is here that the limits of an Islamic approach to govern and manage a modern State will be tested to the full.

The experience of Iran is a case in point. Before the revolution of 1979 the Iranian religious establishment had its own means of finance through its control of endowed (*vaqf*) properties and religious dues/taxes (khoms and zakat) that were voluntarily paid by some of the richer religious sections of the population. The financial independence of the religious establishment was somewhat dented by the pre-revolution Iranian land reform of the 1960s and 1970s that seriously undermined, indeed in most cases removed, the control of the religious establishment over the endowed agricultural land. However, in other areas the religious establishment continued to maintain its financial independence.

In coming to power, the religious establishment in Iran actively used its power to channel and appropriate public/State resources to a variety of institutions under its control. These included the so called 'revolutionary institutions' or foundations (*boniyads*) such as the Martyr Foundation (*Boniyad Shahid*) and *Boniyad Mostaz-afan* run by these bodies and not accountable to the elected bodies of the State (see Harris' chapter in this book for an extension of this discussion). An important activity of the Martyr Foundation is to provide support for those who fought in the Iran-Iraq war and their families. The finances for their support come from direct claims on State budget and a legal requirement that ensures salaries of state employees who lost their lives or who cannot work because of the war injuries are paid through the Martyr Foundation. This has extended to a new generation the clientalist relationship between Martyr Foundation and those supported by it (for further details see Messkoub, 2006). But by far the largest welfare provisioning and social support institutions are still State financed and run through the ministries of Welfare and Social Affairs, Health, and Education. The successive governments in the Islamic Republic of Iran have used the administrative and legal infrastructure that they inherited to widen the scale and scope of social policy in Iran. Herein lies the contradiction faced by the incoming Islamic regimes across the MENA. In some social matters they would try to assert and indeed impose their Islamic ideology, in particular in areas of justice and penal system, family law, culture /education, and gender relations. Yet it is not certain that they will succeed, given the strength and opposition of secular social movements who were the driving force behind the recent changes. In other matters Islamists who may well come to power would have to adapt to a secular legal and administrative structure.

If the experiments of a particularly *shi'iat* and Iranian Islamists is anything to go by the Islamism in power in other MENA countries will also unravel, hopefully sooner rather than later.

Note

1. For an excellent discussion of comparative macroeconomic study of *infitah* and other macroeconomic issues of MENA see Richards and Waterbury (1990).

Part III

Globalisation, Urbanisation and Social Transformation

This book concerns countries that profess Islam, either through the number of people within that country of the Islamic faith or through that State's explicit assimilation of Islam as part of government. This third section expands the purview, exploring the global context in which socio-political developments occur within Islamic countries. In globalisation, urbanisation and social transformation the wider contextual settings and meanings are considered.

This chapters in the third section focus on the impacts of globalisation and transformations within societies from the rural to the urban, examining the ways in which social life plays out global realities within a localised context. Sara Ashencaen Crabtree, Margaret Wood and Belkeis Altareb explore juvenile delinquency and youth justice in the United Arab Emirates, considering the attitudes of professional practitioners working with youth offending towards rehabilitation and include an analysis of the perceptions of Emirati social work students towards perceived deviant conduct in young people.

The impact of urbanisation and globalisation processes are clear within Nabil Aboulhassan and Abdel-Ghany's critical analysis of social welfare policies in Egypt prior to the tumultuous changes resulting from the removal of Mubarak in the Arab Spring. The chapter considers some of the rapid changes in the Egyptian society at the economic, social and cultural levels that result from the processes of globalisation, and identifies some of the social problems that have led to agitation for change.

Hew Cheng Sim and Azlinda Azman provide the final chapter of this section in which we return to Malaysia and explore some of the implications of globalisation for women's health and vulnerability, recognising that maternal mortality has decreased. Gender relations, power and health care are considered within this context and the global problem of human trafficking, predominantly sexually focused and concerning women, reflects the negative side of these otherwise enviable advances in women's health.

14

The social construction of juvenile delinquency and social welfare responses to youth justice in the United Arab Emirates

Sara Ashencaen Crabtree, Margaret Wood, and Belkeis Altareb

Introduction

The accelerated trajectory of the youthful United Arab Emirates (UAE) from a traditional Arab, rural and subsidence-based economy to a powerhouse of materialism and affluence in the Middle East and global arena, has matured; and the country is now witness to problems of high inflation, national skills shortages, significant numbers of cross-cultural marriages, and a perception of the rise of social problems, including that of youth crime. The speed of change may potentially result in fear and uncertainty and a fraying of the social fabric as a manifestation of anomie. The UAE is not immune to this dynamic, where many traditional families in the United Arab Emirates might well believe that the social fabric of society has been detrimentally affected by the forces of globalisation and the extensive reliance upon expatriate labour, often confused with Westernisation (Turner & Khondler 2010) .

The cohesiveness of society is duly influenced by globalisation, technological and demographic pressures and the implications of this must be grappled with, in particular as it affects juvenile delinquency. UAE Nationals currently make up less than 15% of the population and represent a minority group within their own society. Accordingly, it may be hypothesised that the traditional values of society have become weakened, especially for younger generations. Cultural beliefs provide standards of behaviour that are internalised; and adherence to cultural tradition therefore offer social 'knowns' and a sense of continuation and security. The challenge for the UAE lies in its efforts to remain firmly rooted in localised Muslim traditions and beliefs, while managing complex social interactions across diverse cultures and associated practises that may offer a threat to its indigenous culture. These inter-cultural tensions may ultimately lead to weakened social cohesion, and has been found by the authors to present itself as a relevant issue for juveniles 'at risk' of perceived delinquent behaviour in the UAE (Ashencaen Crabtree, 2005; Hirschi, 1969).

The UAE offers a comprehensive welfare system to support the local Emirati population, and one where occasionally locally-resident, non-citizens may also benefit, as, for example, in relation to child developmental disabilities (Ashencaen Crabtree and Williams, 2010). However, all residents who are not Emiratis, from labourers to executives, are required to have health insurance; and while emergency care is provided by public hospitals this is at a cost reclaimed from the insurance companies. Commensurately, it would appear that an increasingly sophisticated system of youth justice is emerging in the UAE in which, although useful lessons may be drawn from Western models, a far greater emphasis is placed on developing indigenised interpretations and welfare responses that owe much more to a traditional cultural and religious framework.

In this chapter the authors offer an analysis of statistics in the public domain pertaining to juvenile delinquency in the UAE. These are considered in the light of our research findings into this phenomenon, where the social construction and implications behind the responses of the local judicial and rehabilitative social welfare systems are correspondingly examined. Although an important topic, youth crime in the UAE is a neglected area of academic interest in this region. It is also considered to be a rather sensitive one as well, in implicating both Emirati youth as well as migrant, non-Emiratis, in a dominant culture where family reputation and honour together with national prestige are fiercely protected. Although the scope of the topic has been explored in relation to available data, many issues regarding legalities, welfare service provision and future outcomes for young people await further examination.

Data collection concentrated on two emirates of the UAE, that of Dubai, a commercial hub in the UAE, and the nearby but distinctly different Emirate of Sharjah, which specialises in the preservation of Islamic culture and art. Sharjah, however, is also responsible for processing youth offenders across a wide catchment area, and also covers cases from the small Emirate of Ajman and Umm Al Quwain. The analysis of the social construction of 'delinquency' and youth crime in the UAE offer a number of divergent interpretations. These might be framed within essentialised constructions, such as a primarily Anglo-Saxon, Westernised discourse, or alternatively from within an Islamic schema.

The context of juvenile delinquency in Arab society

The issue of juvenile delinquency and crime in Arab societies is highly complex and differs markedly from Western contexts, where for some members of the former civil strife and military aggression has been the dominant feature of life. For example, in a study of 225 Palestinian schoolchildren Qouta *et al.* (2008) hypothesise the intuitive connection of warfare begetting child aggression in relation to children living in the Gaza Strip. The authors conclude that the witnessing of military violence does indeed lead to higher rates of aggressive and antisocial behaviour among these children. However, an interesting finding emerges that this was correlated to the trauma of witnessing such occurrences towards family members and neighbours, as the following quote illustrates:

> War and military violence signify a shattering and nightmarish reality for children: life threat, loss of home, killing and detention of family members, and witnessing humiliation of trusted and admired adults. (Qouta *et al.*, 2008: 241)

Yet, as we know, Palestinian children are often the casualties of such violence as well. However, the findings indicate that while directly experienced aggression to their own person was also traumatic, these could more easily be reframed by victims as constituting a demonstration of personal heroism.

Additionally, in Iraq violence has been a quotidian experience that both adults and minors have been exposed to, where 'People are afraid of children, who instead of playing with toy guns, use real machine ones to kill them' (Younis *et al.*, 2008: 131). In Iraq we learn that a mandatory psychiatric assessment is made of all minors accused of delinquency. In one study of 100 minors (with a heavy preponderance of boys) under judicial detention for delinquency in 2001, the majority were reported to suffer from abnormal psychopathology (Younis *et al.*, 2008). In this sample the most prevalent crime was reported as theft, followed by fighting and thirdly, murder. Gender differences were made apparent here, where murder was solely committed by boys, but where fighting was slightly increased in girls compared to theft. Alcohol abuse constituted one of the lesser crimes with an even lower prevalence of substance abuse – with both offences confined to male minors alone.

The examples of Palestine and Iraq are particularly extreme and the situation relating to the social construction of youth offences in other societies experiencing civil turmoil might offer fascinating new interpretations. For example, the use of a liberation discourse to further analyse youth revolt in the popular uprisings of the so-called 'Arab Spring' (see Jawad, Al-Krenawi, Messkoub, Aboulhassan and Abdel-Ghany in this volume for further references to this even). To-date, however, the phenomena of youth offences in Arab societies remains at best obscure.

However, we do know that the judicial system in the UAE is governed by a dual system of Islamic law (divine, revealed law) that confines itself to family and religious issues; and a secular Penal Code for dealing with criminal and civil matters. Many criminals who in a Western context might otherwise go to court are dealt with in direct negotiation between the police and the family. In these respects therefore the UAE is quite different from some other Arab nations, like Saudi Arabia, where the legal system is entirely based on Islamic law, encompassing *Shariah* law.

The criminal system in the UAE has been partially formulated with a degree of consciousness towards the nation's close ties with the West. Being in addition secular, the law may apply less stringent forms of punishment than those meted out in other Arab states. In addition, it has successfully begun to harness the growing professional basis of social work to child and youth welfare services, with the intent of active intervention by social workers in both school and clinical settings, as well as in terms of youth justice. The shortage of social workers educated to IFSW standards is recognised by the Ministry of Social Affairs in the UAE. However, enhancing the skills of current practitioners, together with that of promoting more rigorous training of social workers to deal with the growing issues of disruption to family social cohesion, is a government priority. In the case of youth justice this is commensurate with the considerably more established involvement of qualified social work in criminal justice cases in Egypt, from where many of the UAE's professional, migrant work-force originate (Ali et al., 1966).

However, the definition of crime, as well as the State response in the

UAE, has at times created consternation in the international community (Amnesty International 1998: 1). Unusual and cruel forms of punishment in the UAE, by Western standards at least, notoriously include lashing as well as amputation, for instance. The latter, however, is not applied to juveniles. Yet the list of typical crimes, as perceived by its victims across ages, would be familiar to most readers, with car content theft (rather than theft of cars), shop lifting and common assault being most prevalent, although far less so than 'harassment' and 'harassment by beggars' standing at 32.6 and 28.1% respectively (Alomosh, 2009). An interesting point is the discrepancy between actual crimes and the perception of the most feared, imaginary crimes of an adult sample of 1,530 respondents, where the fear of 'riots by young people near one's home' (25.2%) was only outweighed by fear of 'susceptibility to deception, fraud, swindling' (27.2%) (Alomosh, 2009). It would appear therefore that perceived fear of youth crime ranks highly in terms of the social construction of anti-social behaviour and offences. In this respect, such discourses can equally be found universally and frequently signal a certain demonisation of youth, youth culture and perceived social permissiveness.

Such fears are by no means a recent phenomenon, historical studies of social and media reports reveal that fear of the young, mobile proletariat coloured the imagination of the bourgeois German public during revolutionary turmoils of the early twentieth century (Weinhauer, 2010). Earlier, public outcry in Victorian and Edwardian Britain was targeted at the corrupting influence of new forms of unlicensed or mass entertainment accessible to children and adolescents, through *ad hoc* stage shows and later, silent film – the power of new media over the masses having historically been socially disquieting (Springhall, 1998) Furthermore, a scoping study of media representations of youth crime in Canada from the 1930s to the 21st Century indicates a shift in attitudes towards young offenders. Whereas reporting in the earlier twentieth century took a more paternal but liberal tone of portraying such juveniles as 'misguided' youngsters, by the 1990s a conservative and harsher discourse prevails, where adult standards of conduct and responsibility have been applied (Faucher, 2009). Equally though, articulated fear of the young offender in Britain, accompanied by tough sentencing, has drawn condemnation from the National Youth Agency, in calling for an end to the presumed persecution of vilified and marginal youth, which it is argued, escalates the likelihood of offending (National Youth Agency, 2010).

In Britain the causal link between perceived disorder and fear of crime has been recast into an alternative question of whether it is 'perceptions of disorder that shape fear or whether fear drives perceived disorder' (Brunton-Smith, 2011: 885). However, while the causes of crime remain contested, fear of crime is commonly assumed to increase with age and presumed vulnerability; an assumption fuelled by emotive labelling and descriptions of elderly victims of crime in the media. Yet, early research findings from the USA failed to note an elevated fear of crime (Akers *et al.*, 1987). Furthermore, an interesting study of older people in the Caribbean additionally found no such correlation (Chadee, D. & Ditton, J., 2003). A curious feature, however, is noted by Brown and Benedict (2009) in reference to the USA where fear of gang crime by young people is apparent; and additionally carries gender (as well as ethnic) overtones, with females being more fearful of such activities, which appear to be correlated with their fear of rape (Brown and Benedict, 2009). A final noteworthy point relates to the fear of crime in relation to its form, where Brown and Benedict (2009) comment on research findings that indicate that while mugging or being threatened with a gun have not escalated fear of crime in the USA, burglary has. This raises the question therefore whether such direct assaults fail to escalate fear due to being highly elevated in the first place; or whether the sinister invasion of one's home, as a sanctuary, causes a greater sense of vulnerability and hence fear among victims. An issue that may resonate with attitudes towards burglary in the UAE. In the UAE youth crime typically corresponds with that familiar to Western readers: including theft, substance abuse and assault, for example. However, the issue of sexual immorality, as variously defined in this region, also carries a strong presence in the list of juvenile offences (Committee on the Rights of the Child, 2002, Ministry of Social Affairs, 2008, 2009).

Although youth offending in general has been subject to much theorising, few studies resonate with the particular circumstances of the UAE, where although it is not particularly high, it is on the increase and is a source of genuine social concern (Murad, 1996). There are some exceptions to this situation in the research literature documenting risk factors for delinquent behaviour, such as urbanisation (particularly where overcrowding exists), and insufficient social control and weakened social bonds (Brennan-Galvin, 2002, Clinard & Meier, 2011). In addition there is a reported tendency for adolescents to drift towards juvenile delinquency within societies undergoing rapid social change (Boehnke and Bergs-Winkels, 2002).

This latter point has a particular bearing on the UAE as being quintessentially a region of extremely accelerated social change due to the sudden affluence generated by the oil boom over the past three decades. The immediate environment has been transformed from a subsidence-based, rural economy to a dense, urbanised, cosmopolitan one within the lifetime of a generation. The effects upon family cohesion and shared values have only lately been scrutinised, but it is argued that the divide between the generations, based on life experience and future aspirations, is a yawning one (Schvaneveldt *et al.*, 2005). Additionally, the influx of globalising trends in the UAE, in association with a high percentage of expatriate workers, growing access to media and technology, and the opening of progressive Western-led educational institutes has been critiqued as a contaminating factor upon the morals of local youth (Murad, 1996; Wood, 2011).

Despite social changes some aspects remain the same, like polygamy, which is common in Arab societies, whereby a man is entitled to take up to four wives, provided that he attempts to treat them equally. In reality, research findings indicate that polygamy is associated with increased mental health problems for senior wives, and delinquent behaviour in their offspring, specifically in adolescent boys (Al-Krenawi *et al.*, 2002). Al-Shamsi and Fulcher (2005) report that a study of youth offending in the Emirate of Sharjah indicates that polygamy, as well as the effects of parental divorce, was associated with nearly 95% of reported cases. However, while divorce and polygamy is often blamed in the UAE society for the increase in social problems, statistics in 2008 and 2009 provide evidence that in 2008 70% and in 2009 50% of the boys arrested in Sharjah were from homes where parents were married with only one wife. Furthermore, only 2% of the girls arrested came from divorced homes. In the same period only 6% of the boys arrested came from divorced homes. However, the second largest group of boys 15% were from married families living with their father (Ministry of Social Affairs, 2008, 2009).

In relation to the role of the family with regards to delinquency, Ryan and Yang (2005) for example, identify two main threads in youth offending: that of social learning and social control. Family members, as well as peer groups, may be the role models of undesirable behaviour. By contrast social control of youth, particularly in connection with parental involvement and appropriate care, reduces the risk of delinquency in the first place and later, recidivism (Ryan and Yang, 2005).

In reference to this point, research findings undertaken with UAE adolescents of either sex indicate that their main concern relates to a 'lack of family guidance and care' (Russell *et al.*, 2005: 198-199). Paradoxically however, adolescent girls only rated parental restrictions on their freedom as being a significant problem (Russell *et al.*, 2005). Family functioning, as defined by emotional fulfilment and behavioural control, was evaluated by participants in a study of 181 offending and non-offending youth (Alnajjar and Smadi, 1998). Interestingly, offending youth more positively evaluated family functioning than non-offending youth. Whilst males were more likely to positively evaluate family functioning than female counterparts. The authors suggest that this finding relates to the centrality of males in UAE society, in comparison to the marginal status of females. In addition, they posit that male participants would consequently feel a greater investment in upholding the reputation and honour of the family by deflecting any blame away from parenting styles. This is somewhat counter-intuitive in that in patriarchal Muslim societies, similar to those of Catholic ones, family honour at the micro level and religio-cultural integrity at the macro level is embodied in the icon of the pious and chaste woman (Ashencaen Crabtree and Husain, 2012). Therefore close supervision of girls is a normal process of socialisation in Arab societies that continues to extend a high level of sociosexual control of females in general through the exercise of patriarchal guardianship (*qiwamah*) (Haj-Yahia, 2003; Minces, 1982; Schvaneveldt *et al.*, 2005). However, Azaiza argues that parental control of adolescent Arab females result in more family conflict than is found in the relationship between male adolescents and their parents (Azaiza, 2005).

Regardless of this, it is argued that the preservation of the family reputation is a very important consideration in Arab families in general (Abu Baker and Dwairy, 2003). Some light may be thrown on this discrepancy by understanding the process of socialisation of young children in Arab families. This serves to intervene in the mother's direct sphere of influence as the main carer of children, in which boys from five-years old have traditionally been increasingly absorbed into the male world (Bouhdiba, 1977; Dahl, 1977). Accordingly, adolescent boys may not expect to be under the authority and supervision of mothers to any significant degree; and where autonomy is granted to them commensurate with the male prerogative (Ashencaen Crabtree, 2007; Russell *et al.*, 2005).

It could be argued that cultural differences permit male minors more autonomy from parental controls than is the norm in the West. An alternative interpretation would be that the acceleration of change, with its attendant problems, has overwhelmed the normal, traditional, coping strategies of many parents. In either case, delinquency in the UAE occurs within a society that has been rapidly transformed into a particularly vivid example of a heterogeneous, fast-paced and cosmopolitan one, and with all the temptations of a laissez-faire capitalism directly to hand.

Methodological Strategies

A number of different research strategies were used to develop a more incisive, critical understanding of the social construction of youth crime in the UAE; and how these were responded to at a judicial and social welfare level. Accordingly, qualitative data was collected over the course of two separate periods (2003-2004) and (2010-2011), which constituted aspects of a longitudinal study.

Primary data: Fieldwork

Data collection used a qualitative approach in which multiple data collection methods were used. Thus in the first data collection period twelve open-ended, in-depth interviews were conducted with a variety of professional stakeholders from a number of formal youth justice resources, based in Dubai and Sharjah. The existing and official statistical data on young offenders were analysed to reveal points of comparison and divergence. In addition, formal interviews were supplemented by a greater number of informal sessions with professionals at the centres, alongside the use of critical observation techniques.

The analytical process utilised ethnographic techniques, in which data were analysed through coding strategies (Hammersley and Atkinson, 2007). Here data are subjected to coding strategies at multiple levels, where both single and recurring codes are noted. Codes cluster into nested concepts from which themes begin to emerge, which in turn form the findings of the study. Saturation of the data is achieved once no new codes have been identified (Ashencaen Crabtree, 2011).

Interviewed staff included senior managers and directors, social workers, psychologists and other allied professionals. A number of interviews were carried out at the Male and Female Rehabilitation Centres run under the Ministry of Labour and Social Affairs at Sharjah. Similarly this was the case in Dubai; however, here youth justice services differ in being run under the auspices of the police authorities. Resources are less centralised geographically than in Sharjah and are located at local police stations. It was not possible to interview staff at every identified resource, as permission was not always forthcoming. Additionally this study was unable to provide a user perspective, as permission was also withheld from interviewing juveniles in custodial care for confidentiality reasons.

In the second phase of data collection period three focus groups each with fifteen participants were conducted with 'at risk' juveniles. Youth in the focus groups volunteered in the knowledge that their behaviour was putting them at risk of potential criminal action if caught. This was supplemented by three qualitative interviews with each of four participants from the focus groups who volunteered for further interviewing, as well as four social workers and three Government Officials.

Secondary data: Scoping of statistical data

This exercise included the sourcing of relevant statistical data from a number of government documents, which were then professionally translated into English for the purpose of secondary analysis. We are also indebted to the Ministry of Social Affairs for giving us access to examine further statistical data held on juvenile offences across the Emirates, in relation to developing a clearer perspective of how delinquency is defined and classified in the UAE. Finally, analysis of these data provided a level of triangulation by which to evaluate our primary data.

Research findings

Studies undertaken by Government-run youth justice facilities, such as that of the Sharjah resource in the following Table, indicate that young male offenders aged between approximately ten and eighteen years, greatly outnumber female counterparts.

Table 1
Youth offenders by sex (Sharjah, 2008)

Sex	Number of Cases	%
Male	90	91.5
Female	16	8.5
Total	106	100.0

(Ministry of Social Affairs, Dubai, 2008)

The situation in Sharjah is characteristic of that in Dubai, as data served to confirm that the male/female ratio showed a similarly marked preponderance of male offenders. This situation is also commensurate with the more limited resources established for female juvenile offenders in Dubai, in comparison with those for males. To our best knowledge these appear to be one custodial centre designated for male youth, and one for females locally.

In relation to the Sharjah statistics, it should also be noted that 31% of boy and 69% of girls are UAE Emirati Nationals, the remainder being a diverse group of expatriates. In interview, an anonymous high-ranking respondent based at the Dubai Police Headquarters in charge of juvenile offending, confirmed that in the Emirate of Dubai, 60% of offenders are Emirati. Returning to the Sharjah figures, the greatest majority 27% of the male expatriates originate from neighbouring Arab States such as Oman, Yemen, Iraq and Iran. In relation to the Indian subcontinent, Pakistani offenders make up the greater majority at 13% of male minors, but only 6% of female minors. Only 19% of females are expatriates from Morocco, Iran and Pakistan, while Westerners are not represented (Ministry of Social Affairs 2008).

These findings are interesting in indicating how high the percentages are with regards to offences committed by Emirati youth, given the low population figures for Nationals in the UAE (Russell *et al.*, 2005).

Juvenile offending in the UAE

To put matters into better context, the most recent statistics in the public domain, which refer to the year 2008, provide a breakdown of the number of cases of delinquency in the UAE for that given period.

Table 2
Ages and nationalities of male youth offenders in Sharjah 2008

Ages	11	12	13	14	15	16	17	18	Total
Nationals	0	0	1	0	5	9	16	0	31
Non-nationals	0	0	2	7	11	10	19	10	59
Total	0	0	3	7	16	19	35	10	90

Table 3: Ages of female youth offenders in Sharjah 2008

Ages	9	10	11	12	13	14	15	16	17	18	18+	Total
Offenders	1	1	0	1	1	2	1	2	3	1	3	16

Table 2 relating to female offenders, unfortunately does not record the ethnicity of these young offenders, although interview data confirms that Emirati girls make up 12 of the numbers reported here. In Table 4 we see the number of alleged offences reported in the year 2000.

Table 4
Number of Alleged Offences Reported to Police in the UAE, 2000

Emirate	Youth under 10	Youth 10-18
Abu Dhabi	0	440
Dubai	4	364
Sharjah	72	484
Ajman	164	234
Umm al-Quwain	3	41
Ras al-Khaimah	6	43
Fujairah	46	194
Total	295	1800

(Committee on the Rights of the Child, 2002: 11)

Two noteworthy factors emerge from the Sharjah tables: insignificantly small though the figures are for female minors, 25% are aged 13 and under. Of the male minors 3% are aged 13 or under. Thus female offenders have a much larger distribution of ages, ranging from 11-18+ years, however 55% of the male youth offenders are 17-year-olds. The age of offenders encompasses very young children of both sexes, as the following quote from a research publication disseminated from Dubai Police General Headquarters makes clear:

> The juvenile delinquent is hence the one who commits an offence punishable by effective laws if he or she is seven and under 18 years old, unless he or she is mentally retarded or lacks consciousness or discernment. (Murad, 1996:1)

Our findings indicate that this situation has remained unchanged to-date. We learn that children from the age of seven upwards may be held accountable for offences, although in reality police charges of this age group are rare occurrence. Nevertheless, in the UAE the age of responsibility is therefore younger than that found in Britain, where ten is considered the age of criminal responsibility, notably lower than in most other European states (Haydon and Scraton, 2000). In Britain this situation thus conforms to the imposition of more adult sanctions on children that have become a feature of some contemporary Western societies

A second point of interest is that although a respondent based at the Dubai Juvenile Association claimed in interview that juvenile offences are decreasing at a rate of 3-5% annually, the demographic pattern of such offending across the emirates remains intriguing. Dubai, for instance, has long since promoted itself as a centre of tourism with an abundance of highly sophisticated, easily accessed leisure outlets. Consequently it would be natural to assume that this would be matched by high levels of youth offending, in comparison with less urbanised and cosmopolitan emirates. Sharjah, by contrast, boasts of being an emirate governed by comparatively strict rules of Islamic conduct. These include the prohibited purchase of alcohol, as well as the imposition of a Public Decency dress code for males and females, applicable to Emiratis and expatriates equally. Yet, Table 2 indicates that at this period of time Sharjah has carried a higher number of youth offending cases than Dubai.

One explanation may lie in the small size of the UAE and the proximity of Sharjah to Dubai. Another might be a higher incidence of the construction and labelling of delinquency operating in Sharjah. However, looking further afield towards the congested, oil-driven economy of the capital city, affluent Abu Dhabi has fewer cases of reported offences than Sharjah. Finally, the remaining less developed, rural emirates like Umm al-Quwain, Ras al-Khaimah and to a lesser extent, Fujairah have, as might be expected, the least number of cases.

Types of youth offence

According to the figures in Table 5 below, theft appears to be the most common offence. However, according to our data, in relation to males, this varies from year to year, and at other times substance abuse or perceived sexual immorality may be more prevalent. The crime of theft, as one respondent argues, is not perhaps an unsurprising finding in view of the abundance of material temptations surrounding adolescents. In Table 6, is contrasted with figures for charged crime in 2008.

Table 5
Charged crime in 2001, both genders

Charge	Number	%
Theft	178	46.5
Sodomy	68	17.7
Unlawful intercourse	10	2.6
Glue-sniffing	2	0.5
Public decency offence	6	1.5
Rape	8	2.1
Affray	13	3.4
Assault	10	2.6
Driving without licence	2	0.5
Manslaughter	2	0.5
Immigration transgression	31	8.1
Recidivism	19	5.0
Other	34	8.9
Total	383	100.0

(Committee on the Rights of the Child, 2002: 12)

Table 6
Charged crime Sharjah, 2008

Charge	Boys	Girls	%
Theft	52		49
Sodomy	10		9
Unlawful intercourse	12		11
Incitement to debauchery	1		1
Adultery	2	2	4
Rape	2	2	4
Fighting	3		3
Assault	2		2
Driving without licence	3		3
Forgery	1		1
Possession of firearm	1		1
Credit card fraud	1		1
Escaping from home		5	5
Alone with foreigner		2	2
Alleging rape unjustly		1	1
Human trafficking		1	1
Prostitution		1	1
Other		1	1
Total	90	16	100

In comparing the 2001 figures with those of 2008 an interesting finding emerging is that relating to illicit sexuality in terms of 'sodomy' and 'unlawful intercourse', where sodomy was reported at a higher rate in 2001 than in 2008. By contrast these rates were reversed for unlawful intercourse. In regards to male delinquency, sodomy, as a product of homosexual encounters, is forbidden under most interpretations of the Holy Qur'an (Ashencaen Crabtree and Baba, 2001; Ashencaen Crabtree *et al.*, 2008). Despite a secular Penal Code, the UAE conforms to cultural and Islamic religious principles in regarding homosexual acts, whether performed by adults or minors, as criminal. However, according to our investigations no distinction appears to be made by the UAE Authorities between sexual experimentation (typical of pre and early adolescence with same-sex partners) and consenting sex between partners or non-voluntary sexual acts.

In terms of the increase in figures for unlawful intercourse over a seven-year period it is open to speculation whether this represents an insignificant statistical anomaly, or whether there is a direct correlation between the drop in illicit homosexual acts and the rise in assumed illicit heterosexual acts. This leads to a further hypotheses regarding whether this phenomenon in turn corresponds to a change in social behaviours among young people in the UAE. Furthermore, an additional issue lies in the reporting of rape in the 2008 statistics, which although small in numbers, were equally reported across the sexes. Although there appears to be a drop in percentages from the 2001 figures, which are undifferentiated in terms of gender.

While statistics in the public domain do not tend to analyse crime in terms of gender differentials, a respondent at the Sharjah Female Rehabilitation Centre noted that the range of offences dealt with, in relation to female offenders, were predominantly categorised as morality issues. A variety of behaviours and allied offences by girls spanned those associated with *zina* (the definition of fornication and adultery under *Shariah* law), and unlawful association with men. In addition to this were added 'leaving the family home without parental permission'; and 'bad morality', which is loosely defined as behaviours that are not suited to Emirati culture and society. Offences pertaining to *zina*, and public decency, tend to carry feminine overtones, if only because apparently females are more likely to be found transgressing the law through this than through other punishable offences.

Anecdotal evidence relating to past cases were offered by staff in interview, where the following example is particularly illustrative of how a fairly innocuous incident, by Western standards, may be interpreted very differently within the moral parameters set out in the UAE:

A young (age unknown) Emirati girl was discovered sitting in a car alone with a boy known to her for some unspecified period of time. No evidence was brought forward of any illicit sexual act having taken case. However, the girl was guilty of indecent behaviour and duly taken into custody while matters were investigated.

The development of youth justice

A study of judicial responses to youth offending in the UAE provides some interesting insights into the sophisticated and highly complex teamwork that has developed between the UAE judiciary and youth welfare services. Although precise details vary slightly across the emirates, the general principles underlying legal systems remain similar. Therefore from the outset it can be seen that statutory efforts are made to avoid custodial care due to the stigmatising effect of this outcome. Indeed we learn from a respondent, based at the Dubai Police Authorities, that delinquent behaviour, which can be handled by parents or by social welfare practitioners, should not be charged, due to the possible ramifications on the young person's future. Thus the charge may be dropped immediately by the police, usually with a formal agreement by the parent to undertake full responsibility of their child.

Table 7
Sharjah Report of Court Decisions for males minors in 2008

Sentence	Number	%
Innocent	5	6
Reprimand and release	14	16
Written undertaking not to offend	25	28
Home detention	10	11
Deportation	5	6
Jail	15	17
Jail and then deported	4	4
Case awaiting sentence	6	6
Sheikh released	3	3
Released with criminal record	3	3

Table 8
Sharjah Report of Court Decisions for female minors in 2008

Sentence	Number	%
Innocent	1	6
Reprimand and release	2	12
Jail	2	13
Released to parents	7	44
Home detention	3	19
Case awaiting sentencing	1	6

Of the two female minors jailed, the recorded offence was for indulging in sexual relations outside of marriage. By contrast, the four males were jailed and deported because sexual intercourse outside of marriage resulted in inpregnation. The case of the seven girls recorded here were released into the care of the family, all having offences of an implied sexual nature. The data represented in the above tables indicates an attempt to find alternative solutions to punitive custodial measures, and an attempt to restore both girls and boys back into the family home.

If, however, the police decide to pursue matters a 'social report' is ordered: this being essentially a comprehensive social work-type assessment of the personal, family and social circumstances of the apprehended minor. This is a similar procedure to the sophisticated social work intervention strategies that have operated in the field of youth justice in Egypt for several decades (Ali, *et al.*, 1966). The outcome of this assessment procedure is to ascertain whether to detain the minor in question in custodial care or to recommend a 'judicial test'. This 'test' enables minors to remain at home under the care of their guardians during a period of intensive, remedial social work intervention designed to rehabilitate the offending youngster back into the community.

The judiciary is also empowered to designate certain areas forbidden and therefore inaccessible to offending juveniles, if this is viewed as increasing the risk of re-offending. In addition the judiciary is empowered to enforce other prohibitions designed to protect their welfare, and to avoid corruption and recidivism (Committee of the Rights of the Child, 2002).

Custodial care of delinquents

If the judiciary decides in favour of a custodial sentence, juveniles may be detained in jail, normally pending a placement in a Juvenile Social Care Unit. The UAE Penal Code states that the duration of custodial sentencing of minors to these centres should be no more than eighteen months. Life imprisonment cannot be applied to juveniles in the UAE, unlike the indeterminate tariff handed to a pair of ten and eleven-year child murderers in the Britain in 1993 (Haydon and Scraton, 2000). Commensurately, capital punishment cannot be applied to juveniles in the UAE, unlike the USA (James, 2001). However since murder, unlike manslaughter, does not appear on the list of offences committed by minors in the UAE, it is difficult to evaluate whether future judicial responses would be revised towards juvenile offenders guilty of committing such serious crimes.

However, juveniles of both sexes, like adults, can still be subjected to corporal punishment, although as will be discussed further this appears to be becoming a rarer recourse. Nevertheless, research findings based on cases at the Sharjah facilities, indicated that of approximately 171 adolescents dealt with over the course of a year, 82 were lashed (the severity of which is unknown) and then returned to their guardians (Comprehensive Social Care Report, Sharjah, 2005: 8).

In relation to educational needs however, Article 3 of the Federal Act No. 9 of 1976 (UAE) states matters clearly. This specifies that apprehended minors must be held in a special institution that provides appropriate social welfare, as well as educational facilities (Committee of the Rights of the Child, 2002). This latter emphasis on education is not an internationally adopted view towards children, but is enshrined in Islamic principles that education should be extended to both males and females of all ages, as a demonstration of *Imaan* (religious faith) (Haw, *et al.*, 1998: 150). However in an interview senior officials in Sharjah noted their concern that the cuts in educational funding means that accessibility to formal education for both male and female cases is now proving difficult. A lack of funding for teachers to teach at various levels is a major obstacle for juveniles gaining education at the centre.

A similar situation exists for male adolescents in Juvenile Centres in Dubai, however, no such educational facilities are offered to youths detained in police care prior to sentencing, other than medical care. Finally, it is not known what kind of welfare and educational resources are offered to girls detained at the Dubai Women's Prison or the police stations, due to a lack of available data.

The influence of families

Parental example and guidance is considered to be a very important factor in preventing youth crime, despite the perceived differences in parenting children of different sexes. Indeed the attitude towards parents of delinquent youth places the greatest responsibility for offences upon the shoulders of parents, as these quotes from three respondents convey, the first working with male and the other two with female delinquents:

If families were good, youngsters would not be here.

First families must teach young girls from an early age the rules of being Arab.

The family becomes the regulator, the powerful system that maintains control.

One social worker described a case of an 'educated' father who wished his aggressive son, whose fighting he couldn't control, to be taken into the Centre, under staff protection. This respondent observed that in many other cases it was paternal serious physical chastisement of sons that was believed to lead to such behaviour in these juveniles.

Social workers and allied social welfare professionals accordingly attempt to strengthen family and community relationships. They offer advice to parents on how to relate to, and monitor their children more effectively; and seek to develop programmes facilitating relationship-building in the community, all of which serve to reinforce the rehabilitation process. Our research indicates that poor parental communication and a lack of understanding by parents towards the needs of young people are regarded as risk factors for delinquency, as are uncensored satellite television programmes, access to multiplex cinemas, unsuitable peer groups and undesirable activities like smoking. Other risk factors include accessibility to drugs and a family with limited social cohesion allowing freedom and time to experience Western norms of behaviour, such as meeting up with boys in shopping malls.

In one interview, however, a professional respondent discussed parental support of young offenders and the future prospects of such children. It was conveyed that the sex of juveniles, taken in relation to the nature of the offence within the cultural context, can have a heavy bearing on how far families are willing to re-engage with and support their child through the rehabilitation process, as will be discussed further.

In the focus groups with 'at risk' juveniles, female respondents discussed the tensions between traditional values of UAE and modernity. Contradictory discourses are evident in the respondents' claim that their behaviour was guided by religious values. Yet, they also spoke of being able to manipulate and deceive their families to get what they wanted, in order to explore and experiment in illicit lesbian encounters in places and venues forbidden by Islam. Such encounters are facilitated by internet social networking and accessing of chat rooms and forbidden sites, all of which are deemed inappropriate, and where discovery would result in criminal charges for delinquent behaviour.

As one respondent said

> My secret life is about pushing the boundaries sexually, in the chat room the way we talk is so different, we are easily aroused, so then we can be as deviant as we can.

Finally, parents are often seen as culpable for delinquent behaviour by their offspring, and especially so if one parent, specifically the mother, is foreign-born and therefore, viewed as inherently lacking in insufficient knowledge about the prevailing values of the UAE. Because Arab mothers are traditionally the primary care-givers of young children, (heavily assisted by maids) they are expected to transmit Islamic and cultural values to the younger generation. This, as one respondent stated, was a factor in female delinquency, where half of the cases 'had mothers who were not local'; whereas with the Emirati male cases, 84% the boys had local mothers (Ministry of Social Affairs, 2008). This is not a solitary opinion: non-UAE mothers are regarded as problematic, even if they are nevertheless Arabs. This is seen as a notable risk factor for delinquency, particularly in girls, due to gender normative parenting, if mothers (or maids who have become primary care givers) are, to quote:

> Asians (meaning non-Arabs) that do not have a good way of raising (children) and thus (permit) children to fall prey to ambiguities, psychological and social pressure, which leads them to bad behaviour (Comprehensive Social Care Unit, Sharjah, 2005).

Concluding discussion

Based on the collated data several interesting points emerge in relation to juvenile delinquency in the UAE. Firstly, there is a wide disparity of crime committed by juveniles based along gender divisions. Additionally, the nature of the offence itself is subject to gender differentials. There appears to be an interesting tension discernable between the traditional autonomy bestowed upon adolescent boys, as seems to be indicated by the types of crime committed, and the concern of the judiciary and welfare authorities to place the responsibility for youth supervision directly back with parents.

These policy trends require some interpretation: once social control was wielded by family, tribal and community sanction, but due to modernisation this has become much more fragmented and therefore far less effective. Social welfare professionals, as well as the judiciary and the police, now appear to be reframing customary parental permissiveness towards boys as a form of parental neglect. Yet a different interpretation could be that because girls are more protected in Emirati culture, they are not equally represented. Furthermore boys are at a higher risk of being charged with juvenile delinquency, due to the fact that the social bonds of the Emirati family are weakening, and are under threat from globalisation within contemporary UAE society (Wood 2011).

These differing views are not necessarily mutually incompatible but are likely to form fragments of a larger picture concerning the tension between traditional cultural values governing social and gendered interaction, against the inexorable encroachment of the multiplying, polymorphous 'meta-society' typified by social media and the call to both a self-constructed anonymity and yet paradoxically irresistible intimacy with strangers

The research literature does indicate that adolescent males in the UAE appear to want more parental attention, which may also imply an unvoiced need for greater guidance and supervision in the face of dangerous freedom (Russell *et al.*, 2005). However, due to gender norms, adolescent girls can continue to expect to be closely monitored in the home situation, where it is possible that social networking sites may offer access to virtual locations and relationships, forbidden in the tangible world (Ashencaen Crabtree, 2007; Azaiza 2005; Schvaneveldt *et al.*, 2005). When, however, an offence is committed of a sexual nature, severe social norms governing the conduct of females in the UAE, may serve to militate against the family support of female juveniles undergoing rehabilitation. These girls may therefore be left in a highly vulnerable situation, in which, unlike boys, they risk losing an entire supportive network, thus making reintegration into the community a more difficult task to achieve.

Yet, as the data shows, illicit sexuality is a common offence in terms of juvenile delinquency amongst girls. An implicit assumption prevailing in the West is that the circumstances under which an offence takes place, are likely to weigh heavily in the judicial decision. Within the UAE, as a practising Muslim nation, the issue of illicit sexuality is often not sufficiently considered within the context in which the act took place. Consequently, it was reported by the New York Times (2007) that a fourteen-year-old French minor returned to the UAE to testify against three men who had raped him, despite the very real risks of being prosecuted in turn of participating (albeit forcibly) in a forbidden homosexual act. Although in this case prosecution of the minor did not take place, the blurring of the boundaries between consent and coercion in respect of illicit sexual acts represents a dangerous omission for child protection issues.

A further development of great importance to the international community is that lashing is no longer applied to juvenile transgressors. Accordingly in the past few years there have been no such incidents. This is especially noteworthy, as corporal punishment of children in general continues to form a contentious and ongoing legalistic debate among European nations.

This form of retribution for adults, however, is compatible with both Islamic principles and remains embedded in Emirati cultural practice; although Islamic scholars would argue that the UAE does not offer an example of an Islamic society as such.

What can be gathered from research literature, together with statistical data held in the UAE and reported here, is that the abuse of children and young people, which is considered a factor in delinquency and subsequent offending in the West, is regarded as a very sensitive topic in Arab countries (Baker and Dwairy, 2002).Accordingly, it is not possible to gain statistical data on any correlation between children and young people who have been abused and subsequently offended.

Thus, at its best the UAE offers an emerging model of youth justice and welfare service of juvenile delinquents, being progressive and enlightened towards the rehabilitation and with attempts to bring restoration of the offender back into the community. Its emphasis on parental responsibility, in association with professional support of young offenders, offers a most encouraging example of how one particular Arab nation has responded to the challenging problem of youth crime. That said, many of the responses towards youth crime will remain both unfamiliar and anomalous to

Western readers, particularly in relation to gender issues and sexuality, crime and punishment, therefore and provides a fascinating glimpse into the social construction of crime and the social responses meted out to minors within a progressive Muslim nation. It is to be hoped therefore that further research will be generated within the UAE, in order to explore the ontologies of youth justice and welfare provision, together with other unanswered questions that pertain to culture, religion and indigenised responses towards juvenile delinquency in this region.

15

The impact of urbanization and globalization on social welfare policies in Egypt: A critical analysis

Nabil M. Aboulhassan and Tamer M. Abdel-Ghany

Introduction

The world around us has changed rapidly and reflects changes in the economic, social, cultural and political dimensions of developing countries. One example of these changes is the speed of urbanization, which means the increasing establishment of cities and migration from the countryside to the city. These changes include changes in habits, traditions, values and consumption patterns, and absorbing new information; as well as the growing movement of technological and scientific innovations, especially in the field of transport, communications and information (Mustafa Seruji, 2004).

All of these aspects have caused social policy changes in Egypt. For instance, in 1984, the State stopped appointing graduates, which had been the case since the 1950s. Consequently not even educated people could find sufficient jobs to prevent a rise in the unemployment rate in the country.

With the advent of the new world order, whose features crystallized in the 1980s and were more clearly defined in the early 1990s, a system based on the rule of market mechanisms and the prosperity of economic relations between States was established. This saw the emergence of multinational companies, of global and international economic blocs, competition and communication networks, along with the information revolution. These features have transformed the world into a global village with competing parties dependent on the internationalization of production and global markets (Zaki Abu Al-Nasr, 2008).

To manage these local and global changes, the trend in Egypt has been to embrace market economics with a reduction of government employment and the sale of many government-run companies in the move towards privatization, thus increasing reliance on investment from the private sector to create jobs in the community. This has led the labour market in Egypt to become characterized by diversity, where there are more labour markets such as in the government and private sectors, as well as irregular labour market, and foreign project labour markets. Unemployment rates, however, remain high, with Egypt ranking 117 in the country listings according to the Human Development Report (2007).

Unemployment in Egypt

The causes of unemployment have been the result of an increasing annual population rate of nearly one million people, compounded by the scarcity of economic resources available to the country in achieving development. This is particularly the case due to the major transformations experienced by the global economy and its impact on the Egyptian economy (Zaki Abu Al-Nasr, 2010). In addition there has been an inability of the labour market to absorb graduate jobseekers, especially with the lack of alignment between the quality and efficiency of the graduates on the one hand and the needs of the labour market on the other.

Increased unemployment in the 1990s in Egypt reached unprecedented levels, when the rate rose from 8.6% of the labour force in 1990 with an estimated number of about 1.3 million unemployed, following at the rate of 12.2% of the labour force in 1992, and reaching a total of 2. 7 million unemployed in 1995. The rate dropped to 11.5 of the labour force in 1998 with 2.02 million unemployed. Numbers then rose to 15.3% in 2000 to number 3.5 million – resulting in a huge rate of unemployment and creating significant political, economic and social problems (Central Agency for Public Mobilization and Statistics, 2005).

It is therefore important to confront the phenomenon of unemployment in Egypt and to formulate programmes and services, underpinned by relevant social welfare policy, in order to address the impact of urbanization and the increased rates of internal migration of people in search of jobs in the city. There has been a need for further efforts to activate traditional safety nets, such as widening the social insurance system, and the social role of Nasser Bank – a productive families project; and 'Shrouk' - the national programme for rural development. All of these services have added to the development of modern safety nets as a social development fund, and to improve the level of public services.

In addition to these projects, the Ministry of Social Solidarity has called for programmes that target groups deserving of social care. These include those who are least able socially and economically to meet their needs and to be able to access effective services to meet those needs, including social security pensions, ration cards, health insurance and education at all levels (Abou-al-maaty, 2007).

It could be argued that since the beginning of its activity in 1993 up to 2000, the Social Fund for Development has achieved a total employment of about 803,000 including over 515,000 permanent jobs and 288,000 temporary jobs. Compared to the number of the targeted job openings, we find that the Fund has achieved an overall employment rate of 96.1% of the stated target, with permanent jobs increasing by 91.2% and temporary jobs by 106.2% (Ministry of Social Solidarity, 2008). With the opportunities provided by the Social Fund for Development it is reasonable to say that the fund has not achieved all its goals, despite such high unemployment, which worsened after the application of the economic reform program in 1991.

Given employment opportunities provided by the Fund compared to the scale of unemployment in Egypt, we find that these opportunities have not exceeded 6% for the number of unemployed from 1993 to 1998. This has been similar to the number of permanent jobs provided by the Fund, which did not exceed 3.6% for the numbers of unemployed for the same period. Instead, the numbers went down considerably if these ratios are to be compared with estimates by International labour Office (ILO) experts on the numbers of unemployed in 2000, in which 3.5 million unemployed people found employment provided by the Fund, which represents only 3.3% of the total number of unemployed (Mustafa, 2008).

This very modest rate may not have been due to a failure of the Social Fund, but may be a result of the scale of unemployment that saw 9% unemployment in a population of 82.5 million in 2010, which the labour market was unable to absorb. Thus a temporary entity like the Social Development Fund, funded by limited and diverse programmes does not have the capacity to fully address unemployment in Egypt.

Gender indicators: Egyptian women

Women represent 48.83% of the total population of Arab Republic of Egypt. The proportion of women able to undertake paid work includes those aged 20 up to 49-year-old. Despite this, these statistics indicate a diminished contribution from women in social development (Abdel Rahim, 2007). In 2004, the percentage of women represented only 23.9% in work force, which means women contributed by a third, compared to men. Women also suffer from illiteracy to the rate of 51%. Accordingly, the Ministry of Social Solidarity (2008) holds the remit to:

1. Ratify all international treaties and pay due attention to Arab women and the elimination of all forms of discrimination against women in Egyptian society.
2. Offer necessary legislation for the protection of children and females, such as the articles mentioned in the Egyptian Children›s Act No. 12 of 1996.
3. Passing the Egyptian Act No 78 of 2000 for Social Security, this guarantees a minimum income for families who do not have a breadwinner.
4. Establish specialized national councils such as the National Council for Motherhood and Childhood to deal with issues and problems relating to women.
5. Create a unit for Equal Opportunities in ministries to overcome obstacles that prevent women›s participation in the work force.
6. Establish centres to support and develop the skills of women in small enterprises.
7. Establish women's clubs in all governorates
8. Participate in national and local seminars and conferences to debate issues relating to women in Egypt.

Regarding social welfare policy planning for women in Egypt, we find that, The Five-Year Plan (2002 / 2003 - 2006 / 2007) promoted the aim to achieve full equality between men and women, in order to bridge those gaps as defined in development indicators. As well as aiming to reduce illiteracy rates to less than 10%; and reducing the proportion of low-income groups to less than 5 % of the population.

Health care services for women

There is an integrated national project to care for women, with the creation of 650 health care units for local women and staff training to provide high quality health services. Additionally a thousand women's clubs have been established to support social and cultural development of rural women, through health awareness, education in crafts, as well as mobile clinics to connect all health services, including reproductive health and family planning to Egyptian women living in disadvantaged areas. Furthermore, the provision of reproductive health services has led to a higher rate of life expectancy at birth for females from 71.9 years in 2002/ 2003, rising to 72.3 years in 2003/ 2004. A lower rate of maternal deaths per 100,000 births has been recorded from 84 in 2000. Fertility rates fell from 5.2 children per woman in 1980, to 3.5 in 2000, and down to 3.2 in 2003. The percentage of married women who use family planning methods rose from 24.2% in 1980 to 56.1% in 2000, rising to 60% in 2003 (Central Agency for Public Mobilization and Statistics, 2004).

Women and the labour force

The Five-Year Plan (2002 / 2003 - 2006 / 2007) aimed at increasing the growth rate of females in the labour force to 4.47%, which is equal to double the rate of males standing at 2.18%, and where the percentage of female participation in the labour force has increased from 18.4% in 2003/ 2004 to 18.75% in 2004/ 2005.

Women's education

Attention to women's education is one of the most important aspects in reducing the gap between male and female in this respect. Illiteracy rates have declined among women from 51% in 1996, to 40.7% at the end of 2003, and down to 28.1% in 2004/ 2005. There are increased opportunities for females in the pre-university enrolment rates, which have risen in 2003/ 2004 to 96.9% for primary education, 94% middle school education, to 76.4% for secondary education and up to 98%, 98%, 87.95% in 2004/2005 respectively (Yousef, 2008).

In spite of the efforts made by social welfare policies, the rate of improvement in social conditions for women remains weak, and this seems to be reflected in official statistics concerning the deteriorating status of women at the economic, social and political levels. Looking at the situation in Egypt in terms of the Human Development Index, it occupies a low rank among the countries of the world. It also occupies a low ranking for gender empowerment, which stands at 75 of the 87 countries, and that the Gender Empowerment Measurement (GEM) applied to Egypt carries a very low value at 0.266 compared to Norway at 0.908, which occupies the top rank (Al-Fawal et al., 2000).

Women's waged work

Official indicators point to the increased participation of women in the workforce, where from 18% in 1996 to 31.4% in 2004 women represented 23.9% of the workforce in the age group 15-years-old and over, while the unemployment rate among females was 24% in 2004. These statistics indicate that the participation of males is double that of female participation in the workforce, with a corresponding higher unemployment rate among females compared to males.

Educational levels

There is an increased enrolment rate in pre-university education in general. However, poverty has lead to widening gender gaps, where the female literacy rate stands at 51% compared to 29% of men, and is even worse in rural and slum areas. The gap in the illiteracy rate is 16% among children from poorer families, compared to 5% of children from higher socio-economic brackets. The illiteracy rate among households headed by women in rural areas is about 85% as compared to 57% in the urban areas (Central Agency for Public Mobilization and Statistics, 2004).

Health indicators

Despite the rise in female life expectancy at birth, there are health risks associated with gender, such as the phenomenon of female genital mutilation, a tradition that has been practiced in Egypt since the Pharaonic era. Recent evidence suggests that the phenomenon is declining among girls and women of the new generation. According to the Demographic and Health Survey of Egypt in 2008, the prevalence of female genital mutilation is 91.1% among women aged 15-49 years; while it is 74% among girls between the ages of 15-17 years. The average will decline over the next fifteen years to 45%. This phenomenon associated with cultural, educational, economic and place of residence factors. Urban women are less likely than those from rural communities to practise female genital mutilation, and the percentage of female genital mutilation among girls of mothers with no education is up to 64.7%, while the incident for girls from mothers with a university degree stand at 22.3%. The Egyptian Shura Council in (2000) has reported that women's access to the provisions of the Conventions and International Declarations and human rights conventions remains out of their reach. This is because women are either unaware of their rights or cannot even claim or defend them due to the high rate of illiteracy and economic hardship, unemployment, poor educational attainment, as well as a lack of alternative cultural constructs relating to the values of equality and non-discrimination, justice and tolerance.

The status of women within the slums communities have been subjected to many changes that have contributed heavily to their economic, social, health and cultural deprivation, where basic needs cannot be met to any reasonable degree. The current economic and social conditions prevent women from having sufficient opportunities to acquire adequate food and safe drinking water, proper housing, social services, education at all levels, recreation and transportation, leading to an inability to meet their basic needs in the community.

Poverty in Egypt

In order to understand the phenomenon of poverty in Egypt, the demographic characteristics of the poor in the 1990s needs to be reviewed, including educational, health and employment characteristics, as indicated by Tarek Farouq (2007).

Demographic characteristics

1. Large family size: the size of families in low-socioeconomic brackets is 6.8 in urban areas and 7.2 per capita in rural areas, as compared to the size of higher-income families, which were 4.8 per capita in urban areas and 5.6 per capita in rural areas in 1995/1996.
2. People with disabilities: the percentages have increased among poorer families from 30% in 1990 as compared to the ratio in richer households at 3% for the same year.
3. Women-headed households: at the national level the proportion of these households was 17% in 1993, of which 18% were in urban areas and 16% in rural areas. They were characterized by low-income households compared to households headed by men.

Educational characteristics

1. Illiteracy rates: the rate of illiteracy was 44.5% overall in Egypt in 1996, including the proportion of 56.5% for females, a rate ahead of previous years. However, these percentages indicate that about half of the people of Egypt can barely read or write.

Health characteristics

1. Housing is characterized by a lack of minimum cost housing for the middle classes and poor alike. This has led to the proliferation of slums in all the governorates of Egypt to address the scarcity of cheap housing. Health and environmental problems are typical of these areas among low-income residents (Presidency of the Republic, 1998).
2. The percentage of slum housing in Egypt consists of 81% in urban areas and 89% in rural locations. According to estimates by the World Bank, in the Cairo area there are 79 slums areas, including 12 squatters housing areas or slums, which require removal. The number of slum dwellers in Egypt is more than 20% of the total population and because they are concentrated in the cities, they make up about 37% of the total urban population. This percentage is apparent in the Giza governorate standing at approximately 62%; and in the Sohag governorate at 6.4%. In

the Minya governorate this stands at 49 %, and in the Cairo governorate at 35.9%. There are 1,172 slums distributed over Egypt in the 24 governorates. These areas have appeared in response to the population increase in Egypt. Internal migration has taken place of newly displaced people from rural to urban areas seeking new job opportunities. Upon being faced with housing issues they then are obliged to live with their families in city-based slums areas (Ministry of Local Development, 1998).

3. Clean water and sanitation services: it is estimated about 18% of the population in Egypt in 1996 do not have access to clean drinking water, and about 57.3% of the population have no access to sanitation services. This has meant the deterioration of health and environmental conditions for about half of all Egyptians, and of course, most of these are impoverished individuals (Mustafa, 2008).

4. Malnutrition: The number of undernourished people in 1995 is about a million, where the percentage of underweight individuals stood at 12.4% of the Egyptian population in 1995, and most of these were from low-socioeconomic groups.

Employment indicators

The unemployment rate reached 15.5% of the labour force in 1995, where the numbers of unemployed people reached 2.7 million; again the majority of those who are unemployed are poor (Farouq, 2007).

The measurements of poverty after the economic reform in Egypt during the 1990s demonstrated the increasing rates of poverty, where poverty rates stood at 39% and 39.2% in 1990 | 1991 in urban and rural areas respectively. These rose to 45% and 50.2% in 1995/1996, which led to an increase in the number of poor people from 9.7 million to 12.5 million people. This has meant an increasing number of people surviving below the poverty line, at 6.7% and equalling a million people in the period following the application of the economic reform programme, in addition to the presence of large incomes gaps between the rich and poor (Mahmoud, 2003).

Disability indicators

Statistics indicate that the rate of disability in Egypt in 1996 is around 3.4%, meaning that there were more than 2 million disabled people accounted for in this year. A total of 73% of the population has intellectual disabilities, followed by motor impairment at about 14.5%. Visual and hearing disabilities account for approximately 12.5% of the total number of disabled persons in Egypt. Although Egypt is considered one of the countries with both established government and non-governmental organizations (NGOs) addressing the problems of disability through prevention and treatment, the efforts of these institutions currently covers only 1% of the total number of disabled persons in Egypt. This indicates the seriousness of the situation and the problems for people with disabilities in Egyptian society (Central Agency for Public Mobilization and Statistics, 1998).

The number of disabled individuals doubled in Egypt by 2011 to 4 million disabled people experiencing various types of disabilities. Egypt has adopted a set of programmes for the implementation of a strategic plan for the care of disabled people, and these programmes were reported by the Ministry of Social Solidarity (2008) to offer the following services:

Programme for prevention and early detection

1. A project to develop skills in health teams.
2. A project to support a referral system for children with special needs.
3. A community-based rehabilitation project
4. The support and establishment of 100 community-based rehabilitation projects via NGOs.
5. A development programme providing institutional support to organizations and units working in the field of disability.
6. A specialist training project for practitioners in the field of disability.
7. Draft rules on data banks and integrated information on disability and people with disabilities.

National programme to care for the disabled at the provincial level

1. Construction of integrated care centres for persons with disabilities (26 centres, with a centre in each province.
2. Construction of central agencies for the rehabilitation of people with disabilities in major cities (100 centres in 100 major cities).

Educational rehabilitation programme for people with disabilities

1. The construction of more special education schools (200 schools).
2. The construction of more classrooms for children with disabilities in mainstream schools and equipping them with the latest equipment required.
3. Preparation projects for trainers and teachers.

National programme offering work opportunity to people with disabilities

1. A technological development of work systems and appropriate mechanization to expand employment opportunities for people with disabilities.
2. The construction of offices and special agencies in the governorates to follow up on the employment of people with disabilities (26 agencies, one in each governorate).
3. The establishment of research centres on disability issues.
4. The construction of the National Centre for Research on Disabilities (National Centre).

Childhood indicators

Children constitute a significant figure in the population pyramid of Egypt. The total percentage of children less than 5 years-old is about 14.8% of the total population. Children in the age group of 5-15 years constitute 24.6% of the population; where 39.4% of the total population are in the age group 0 to 15 years, and represent all children in Egypt up to the age of 15 years-old (Abdul Fattah, 2008).

Child poverty in Egypt is concentrated more in rural areas and is higher in Upper Egypt than Lower Egypt, where the poverty rate hit 30.5% in rural areas in 2009, compared to 12.6% in urban areas, and 21% in Upper Egypt. As indicated in the national survey of child labour in Egypt in 2004, there are approximately 2.76 million working children in Egypt, representing approximately 20.5% of children in the age group of 14 up to 16 years-old, and where the ratio of males is 73% to females at 27%. This represents a rate of 13.8% of the total labour force in Egypt. The number of homeless children is around 2 million children, despite the existence of the National Council for Motherhood and Childhood, and the passing of certain legislation that supports the protection of children's rights, such as the Egyptian Child Law (Hanna, 2007)

The elderly in Egypt

The number of elderly residents of the provinces of Lower Egypt is about 2 million, which is about 45% of the elderly in Egypt, and up to 1.4 million in the provinces of Upper Egypt; and where the number of elderly people in the border governorates numbers at least around 50,000.

The total number of elderly people in Egypt is 4.4 million. 493,000 of them are literate and represent a percentage of 11% of the elderly in Egypt. There are also 81,000 elderly people with various disabilities, representing 2% of elderly people, comprising of 46,000 males and about 35,000 females, and where the number of elderly people with disabilities continues to increase yearly from 25,000 in 1996 to 81,000 in 2009 (Central Agency for Public Mobilization and Statistics, 2010).

Most of the elderly in Egypt, whether male or female suffer from some kind of chronic disease, especially cardio-vascular diseases, and where the percentage of elderly males suffering from such diseases is about 39% of the total elderly males who suffer chronic diseases. The percentage of female elderly who suffer from the same disease is about 42% of the total female elderly who suffer chronic diseases, followed by high rates for diabetes, which is more prevalent among elderly females than elderly males, at approximately 30% and 28%, respectively.

There are only 120 residential homes for the elderly in Egypt, where there is a need for more resources to care for the elderly, especially in relation to health, social and psychological care, as well as additional resources required to finance pension funds. It is evident that there is a decline in the care for the elderly, including the provision of elderly residential homes, clubs, care units and physical therapy centres serving the elderly. There are only 170 clubs for 23,000 elderly people, and equally the number of physiotherapy centres is low at 52 serving a population of 1258 elderly persons (Khouzam, 2010).

Surveys into Egyptian family conditions demonstrate that 83.6% of the total number of older people are elderly male breadwinners for families with more than two dependents, with 25.5% having one dependent individual. 48.3% of older females live alone and are therefore subject to psychological and social problems. The percentage of elderly widows is about 91% of the total older heads of households.

The report points out that there are a number of problems facing the elderly such as health insurance issues, where 20.7% of the total elderly males suffer from a lack of available health services, as compared to 16.5% of the total elderly females experiencing the same problem.

There are several services provided by the Ministry of Social Solidarity to care of the elderly. However, there are many needs that need to be addressed, including the need for the establishment of residential homes to care for the elderly aged 60 years-old and above who cannot receive care within their own families. There is also a need to establish clubs and day care for the elderly, serving as day centres offering different services to elderly people. Additionally domiciliary services have recently been started to serve elderly people who live alone or reside with their family.

The Ministry of Social Solidarity provides security assistance to those who meet the criteria under the Social Security Act. It also provides rehabilitation services and prosthetic devices, and assists poor families to benefit from small family-industry projects and preparation of exhibitions marketing products to the elderly.

Based on the circumstances of different groups in Egyptian society, we offer a discussion of social welfare policy strategies that could counter the negative effects of urbanization and globalization; as well as those changes that have resulted from various transformations of rural and urban areas. These strategies include:

Recent safety social network in Egypt (SFD)

1. The Social Fund for Development (SFD) is a recent safety network in Egypt addressing the social impact of the economic reform programme, the Egyptian name of the Emergency Social Fund (ESF). This was previously applied in 16 countries, and is characterized by temporary provision, as an entity subject to a temporary transition period towards a free market economy.

2. The SFD is an entity that temporarily fills the financial resources of international and local projects to provide opportunities for productive employment, and alleviates the burden of economic reform on low-income groups. The aim is to achieve the basic goal of supporting the economic reform programme (Social Fund for Development, 1997).

3. The SFD in Egypt was established by the Presidential Decree No. 40 of 1991 and was implemented in 1993. The aim of the fund is to address the social impact of the economic reform programme that was applied in Egypt in 1991. It aims at reducing high rates of unemployment, widespread poverty, and to increase the disparity in income distribution (Mona Khouzam, 2010).

The target groups of the SFD are reported as the following (Social fund for development, 2000):

1. The groups most affected by the economic reform programme
2. The labouring classes and the low-income workers
3. New university graduates
4. Women
5. Less developed communities and residents of underprivileged communities

In spite of the importance of a safety social network (the SFD), and the transformation in Egypt to a market economy, the role of this fund in tackling the social and economic impact resulting from these changes seems to be limited. If we look at the role of the SFD in reducing poverty, it appears that the bulk of the financing of SFD projects are allocated to poorer regions in general, while the least funding has been directed to the poorest provinces. Consequently it can be said that the Social Fund, with its limited finances of 5.1 billion pounds over 1993 to 2000, has not effectively combated the multi-dimensional phenomenon of poverty.

Hence it is clear that modern welfare programmes and safety nets have not been able to adequately deal with the effects of economic reform policies in the 1990s. This situation has become worse with the deterioration in the first decade of the new century in terms of the increasing rate of poverty, unemployment and falling living standards. As well as the disappearance of the middle class and increasing wide disparities in income between groups. There has been a prevalence of crime, including money laundering, theft, the smuggling of money out of Egypt, and finally, fraud in the parliamentary elections in 2005 and in the last elections in 2010. Furthermore there has been political repression of opposition groups as well as political arrests after military trials and torture of detainees. The corruption of political life and the absence of democratic practices, as well as the impoverished economic and social circumstances in the country, was the impetus for the revolution of the Egyptian people on Tuesday, January 25, 2011 against the regime, which carried the slogan 'freedom, democracy and social justice' (see Messkoub, Al-Krenawi, Jawad and Ashencaen Crabtree et al in this volume for further discussion of the Arab Spring events).

The (Shrouk) project for integrated development

This project was established in 1994 due to the need for a national program for integrated rural development based on the concept of a specific and clear strategy embedded in every civil and governmental effort for the advancement of rural communities. Shrouk means 'sunrise' in English, and the project was carried out in 26 rural local councils with each governorate represented by one council. Work commenced in 1995/1996 in 78 rural councils. The project was implemented in 1996/1997 as well as planning further projects in 104 new councils. In 1997/1998 the project was implemented across 208 new councils. Since 2001/2002 the numbers of councils that have benefitted from the project have numbered 1060. Development of Egyptian villages was undertaken with the help of foreign international agencies. The benefits of this project reached 35 million people in 1046 rural councils; In addition this has also provided further benefits for 21,000 people in the 26 provinces in Egypt (Shehata, 2007).

Project objectives

These strategic goals represent continuous progress towards improving the quality of life for all members of society; and the increase of active participation towards these aims. These empirical goals are defined as:

1. *Development of the local environment through*
   + Increasing and promoting greater efficiency in the use of material resources.
   + Conserving physical resources available in order to serve future generations.
   + Continuous improvement of living standards for citizens.

2. *Economic development through*
   + Increasing income averages of citizens and diminishing income differentials.
   + Increasing opportunities for continued employment.

3. *Human development through*
   + Increasing citizen participation in development processes.
   + Raising the efficiency of NGOs.
   + Improving quality of life of citizens.
   + Improving the health system.
   + Promoting effective participation by women in strategic development efforts and in improving child care systems.

Shrouk developmental projects

The Shrouk development projects focus on 78 areas as follows:

1. *Basic environment*
   + Drinking water, sanitation, roads, electricity and energy.
   + Hygiene and environmental care, mail services and communications, urban planning.
   + Public shopping centres, civil defence, security services and protection of the environment.

2. *Development of human resources and projects*
   + Educational services, health services, religious services, popular arts.
   + Maternity and child care, nurseries, women's clubs.
   + Cultural Centres, vocational training centres, literacy.

+ Family planning, care for the disabled, social security supplement, youth centres.

3. *Economic development projects*
+ Improvement in soil fertility, drainage, agricultural mechanization.
+ Veterinary services, livestock fattening, feed manufacture.
+ Poultry production, cooperative marketing, honey production.

Despite the importance of Shrouk projects in tackling the impact of the transition to a market economy and in terms of the alleviation of suffering experienced by different members of the community, the outcome of this project does not seem to have significantly improved the standard of living or quality of life for the poor. This may not indicate that the project has failed but points to the exacerbated social problems and the magnitude of the phenomenon of poverty, unemployment and the high rate of illiteracy in the Egyptian society. Additionally, the State's interest in providing facilities to wealthy legitimate and illicit business leaders has lead to the neglect of the poor or poorest citizens. This was reflected in the rejection by the majority of Egyptian people to continue with the current situation, where they have refused to accept policies that are not based on the principle of social justice and democracy.

Projects of the Ministry of Social Solidarity (2008)

Productive family project

This is a social project aimed at developing the economic resources of low-income families. The total number of beneficiaries is 1,003,824 households. The mechanisms of this project are as follows:

+ Centres for productive families: offering training and technical supports; so far there are a total of 3,512 centres.
+ Marketing services: creating 137 exhibitions to market family produced products.

Vocational training centre

This targets school 'dropouts' and trains them in appropriate skills to prepare them for the workforce.

Women's development projects

The Ministry of Social Solidarity promotes the advancement of Egyptian women in general and rural women in particular. This is in order to facilitate their ability to perform their essential role in social development and in relation to the associated projects run by the Ministry of Social Solidarity as described:

+ Rural Women Development Project: a project that aims to provide rural women a range of skills and experiences in 135 villages.
+ Training project for rural women in development and housing: this project aims to increase awareness of rural women in 139 villages.
+ Project to develop the role of women in food production. This project seeks to increase the capacity of rural women in food production in 9 villages.
+ Training project promoting basic life skills in women. This project aims at increasing women's awareness of their ability to practice basic life skills in 5 villages.
+ Women's Initiatives Project. This project is one of the pilot projects in the field of integration of rural women in economic development. This project was implemented in 49 villages in the governorates of Qena and Aswan.
+ Project to development the awareness of rural women. This project aims to empower rural women to prepare feasibility studies for small industry projects. It was implemented in 3 villages of the Menofia governorate.
+ Centre for Working Women Services. There are 32 centres spread over 13 governorates with the aims of providing services for working women to enable them to perform their family functions, such as child rearing and education or domestic work.
+ Women's clubs: aims at enhancing women's cultural and social awareness.

Despite these efforts, 15% of the lowest-income groups in Egyptian society survive on an average income of less than two dollars per capita daily, and where approximately 20% of the population of the Egyptian society live under the poverty line (with an average per capita income of three dollars daily). This indicates the extent of poverty in Egyptian society, which requires considerable political and civic effort and cooperation to address this problem. The Human Development Report 2006 indicated that the rate of poverty in Upper Egypt (southern Egypt) and in the desert and border areas are greater than the rate in the governorates of the Delta and the coastal provinces (northern Egypt). These problems require planning to encourage investment and economic development in those areas where the proportion of low-income families has increased. Serious efforts are required to not only provide employment opportunities and increase average incomes, but also to improve quality of life. In addition to promoting the social, cultural, educational, and health standards among these groups; and enabling them to participate in decision-making processes and decisions relating to the efforts and activities of the comprehensive development strategies in Egyptian society (Ahmed Yousef, 2008).

Concluding discussion

It is clear that social welfare policies in Egypt have not achieved best results in relation to the effects of urbanization and globalization; and have not coped sufficiently well with the economic and social transformations that have occurred in society. Instead, social policies have failed for decades to achieve the hopes and aspirations of the Egyptian people. They have also failed to bring social justice to those in the lowest income groups, where the gap between rich and poor is dramatic, as are the vast disparities in access to better resources.

Health care services have worsened, despite the growing number of patients, especially for those with chronic diseases such as renal failure and infections of the liver. As reported in WHO statistics, Egypt has the largest epidemic of hepatitis C virus (HCV) in the world, in addition to a high drop-out rate from basic education, in addition to a high rate of child labour to the rate of 2.76 million working children. At the age of less than 15 years-old, the increased rate of street children, numbers two million. An increasing migration rate of rural residents to big cities in search for a better life has led to the accumulation of large urban city populations and the emergence of slums, and overlapping and mixed sub-cultures within these communities or slums. In Cairo the number of slums communities numbers 82 with a high rate of crime found in these communities, which lack the basic foundations for a decent life. This indicates the failure of social welfare policies in Egypt, in response to the effects of globalization and urbanization and those societal changes that have resulted from economic reform programmes in Egyptian society during the last two decades.

16

Globalisation and women's health vulnerabilities in Malaysia

Hew Cheng Sim and Azlinda Azman

Introduction

Malaysia has made impressive strides in the health of women. In fact, maternal and child healthcare constitute the twin pillars of the health services in the country. The maternal mortality rate has steadily decreased from 2.1 per 100,000 live births in 1963 to 0.3 in 2008 (Ministry of Health, Malaysia 2003; SUHAKAM, 2011). The infant and toddler mortality rate have shown significant improvement over the same period, from a high of 55.5 deaths per 1,000 live births in 1963 to a low of 6.3 per 1,000 live births in 2008 (Department of Statistics Malaysia, 2003; SUHAKAM, 2011). Such figures are the envy of many other developing nations. In fact, Malaysia has achieved the 4th and 5th Millennium Development Goals (MGDs) on reducing child and maternal mortality.

Additionally, male and female life expectancies do not reflect sex discrimination and neither do nutritional studies indicate a preference for male children (Chee and Wong, 2009). In other words, the health situation of women in the country is good when compared to other countries in the region. This was further borne out by the Malaysian Gender Gap Index (MGGI). In May 2007, the Ministry of Women, Family and Community Development launched the Malaysian Gender Gap Index (MGGI), which is a new index designed to measure the extent of gender inequality in Malaysia. Without going into the technicalities of the MGGI, it suffice to say that it works very much like the Human Development Index (HDI): that is, when there is no gender inequality in a society, the MGGI takes on a value of 0 and when gender inequality is at a maximum, it takes on a value of 1. It is a composite index and does not take into account the complexity of gender inequality and other factors such as legislations and gender-based violence. Although it is based on a simplistic value of a relative gender gap, it is a working tool and a beginning. The MGGI looks at four dimensions covering the area of health, education, economic activity and the empowerment of women. The last means women in positions of decision-making power. The MGGI indicated that women were doing well in health and education but doing very poorly in labour force participation and even worse in empowerment of women. This said, as Malaysia's economy becomes more and more globalised, not only will there be various groups of women who will fall through the gaps of the mainstream health system, but new health issues have presented themselves. For the purpose of this chapter, the WHO definition of health as 'state of complete physical, mental and social wellbeing and not merely the absence of disease or infirmity' will be used (Narimah, 2004). This chapter will examine globalisation and the health impact on four groups of people and women in particular. An understanding on the context of the globalizing processes in the region is required and is discussed in the following section.

Globalisation and the feminisation of transnational migration

Much ink has been spilt on defining globalisation. For the purpose of this chapter, globalisation is referred to as the intensification of global flows of people, capital, technology and commodities and the compression of the world in terms of time and space. Although the movement of people on a global scale is not a new phenomenon, what makes it different in contemporary times is the scale in which it is occurring and the feminisation of the transmigration of labour. Since the 1980s, there has been an unprecedented rise in international migration in the Asia-Pacific region (Chow, 2002). The international division of labour and the export of labour intensive industries from the matured economies in the North to the emerging economies in Asia meant that many countries faced accelerated urbanisation as rural migrants take up newly created jobs in the new economic priority zones (EPZs) in their countries. The rapid growth in export-led industrialisation has resulted in an increased participation of women in the work-force and a tightening of the labour market as wages increased. The depletion of labour reserves in the rural areas meant that cheap labour had to be imported from neighbouring countries to fuel the expansion. However, by the late 1990s, vibrant economies in the region attracted not only unskilled labour but also professional and highly skilled migrants. It has been estimated that guest migrants workers accounted for 20% of the total labour force in Singapore and Malaysia, over 10% in Hong Kong and 6% in Thailand by the mid-1990s (Chow, 2002). This would have risen over the last decade. Although traditionally, male workers were the active migrants and women followed as dependent wives and daughters, recent studies showed important changes in transnational migrations (ibid). There is a feminisation of transnational migration where women are autonomous migrants. In other words, there is a shift from traditional male migration or family migration to the migration of individuals and that of women.

Global estimates by sex revealed that from 1960-2000, female migrants have reached the same number as male migrants. By 2000, female migrants constituted more than half (51%) of all migrants in the developed world and about 46% of all migrants in developing countries (Piper, 2005). This trend is particularly acute in Asia where it has been reported that 70% of women migrant workers globally are Asian (Matsui, 1999). Statistics from Indonesia revealed that out of every 100 female migrant workers there were only 36 male migrant workers (Wee and Sim, 2004). The major sending countries include the Philippines, Indonesia, Thailand, Malaysia, Myanmar, Laos, Vietnam and Sri Lanka and the major receiving countries have been Hong Kong, Japan, Taiwan, Singapore, Malaysia, Brunei, Saudi Arabia, Kuwait, Canada and the European Union. Southeast Asia is thus a region that includes both sending and receiving countries. Malaysia for instance, sends workers to Singapore in particular and receives from Indonesia in particular, while Thailand sends workers to Hong Kong, Singapore and Taiwan and receives workers from Myanmar and Laos. In the Malaysian state of Sabah, it has been estimated that 24% of its population in the year 2000 were foreigners (Jones, 2004). In addition, the number of illegal migrants has been estimated to be equal to or even greater than the number of legal migrants.

In Malaysia, male migrants mainly work in the construction, industrial, plantation and fisheries sectors while women migrants are to be found in domestic services and the manufacturing industries. For example, many Indonesian women work in the saw mills of Sarawak. As Matsui (1999) pointed out, many Asian women migrants are employed as domestic workers and a large proportion also work in the sex-related entertainment industry. Employment in these sectors is invisible and exploitative and women are vulnerable to physical and sexual abuse. A large proportion of migrant women in the region are forsaken by their own governments and marginalised by the host governments, both of whom benefit greatly from their labour – in terms of remittance to home countries and economic development of recipient countries. Apart from work migration, women also migrate for marriage. With globalisation and the ubiquitous use of the internet, the phenomenon of mail-order bride is an area of emerging research interest. As this is not yet a major issue in Malaysia, it will not be addressed in this chapter.

To contextualise the magnitude of the phenomenon, the authors suggest a conservative estimate of tens of millions of Asian women on the move (Wee and Sim, 2004). Having set the stage to show the regional flows of people, the following sections will focus on the health vulnerabilities of the four groups of women in Malaysia.

Women migrant workers

Malaysia is home to two million Indonesian workers of which 200,000 are maids in Malaysian homes and 3,000 are professionals (Borneo Post, 9/11/09). The invisibility of domestic labour makes Indonesian maids particularly vulnerable to abuse. Recently, there has been a spate of reports in the media of domestic violence and horrific assaults on Indonesian maids, which led to public outcry and strained relations between the two countries. In December 2009, there were 140 domestic workers and six children in the Indonesian embassy shelter in Kuala Lumpur waiting for their court cases to be resolved. The situation was deemed serious enough for the Indonesian government to impose a moratorium for sending workers to Malaysia in June 2009 (Borneo Post, 3/12/09).

In a 2006 Memorandum of Understanding (MoU) between Indonesia and Malaysia which covered the employment of Indonesian domestic workers in Malaysia, employers could hold the passport of their workers until their work contracts expired. Workers were also to be paid directly although many employers withheld payment for up to six months in order to recover payment to labour recruiting agencies (US State Department, 2009). In addition, domestic workers were supposed to have time off but it was not uncommon for them to work 14-18 hours a day, seven days a week, sometimes in both the employers' homes and business premises. Others hired out their maids to work in the homes of others. Employers also have to pay a government levy to employ foreign workers and the cost of this is often passed on to the workers by way of lower wages. There are no trade unions to protect foreign workers and often they are put to work in the most dangerous and unhealthy sectors that locals avoid. In addition, there is an unspoken policy that public hospitals and clinics, which are already badly stretched in terms of resources, should not be expected to treat non-Malaysian nationals unless it is a life-threatening situation. Thus all foreign nationals have to pay for private health care, which can be exorbitant. As there is no mandatory health cover for foreigners, employers often do not want to bear the cost of expensive health care. Foreign wives of local men whose application for residency and citizenship is protracted and uncertain also face the same fate.

This is a short sighted policy as migrants can reintroduce infectious diseases into their host countries. For example, Indonesian workers have reintroduced diseases such as leprosy, filariasis, tuberculosis and diphtheria into Malaysia (Phua, 2004). In Sarawak, the opening up of agricultural land schemes for large-scale oil palm plantations have also led to a huge jump in the outbreak of malaria. The porous border between Sarawak and the Indonesian state of Kalimantan has made malaria control particularly difficult. For instance, the total reported cases of malaria in Serian district in 1999-2000 were three times higher than the previous year. Jamail Muhi of the Sarawak State Health Department pointed out that:

> Constant and unchecked population movement along numerous unofficial crossing points … illusive nature of 'illegal' border-crossers…have made malaria screening and other follow-up control activities operationally very difficult. (2004: 3).

Although this health issue affects both women and men, given the gendered nature of poverty and the circumscribed nature of women's mobility to access health services, women are likely to be disproportionately affected.

Victims of human trafficking

In the June 2011 publication *Trafficking in Persons Report* by The Department of State, United States of America, Malaysia was placed in the Tier 2 Watch List, among 16 other countries, such as Burma, North Korea, Papua New Guinea, whose governments do not yet comply with the minimum standards for the elimination of human trafficking, and are not making any significant effort to address this issue. Malaysia was regarded as a destination, a source and transit country for the many men, women, and children who were subjected to sex trafficking and forced labour. Women and children were mainly trafficked for sexual exploitation.

The trend has always been that women, especially from Indonesia, Thailand, Philippines, Cambodia, Vietnam, Burma, Nepal, India and China, willingly migrate to Malaysia for better economic opportunities. However, many ended up as forced labour with some forced into prostitution after being lured into Malaysia with promises of legitimate employment. Evidence for such activities include police reports of rescuing 2,000 foreign women and children forced into sex work in brothels in 2008 (US State Department, 2009: 199). Young foreign women were recruited to work in restaurants and hotels using 'guest relations officer' visas, but were eventually coerced into the commercial sex trade (US State Department, 2011: 243). Many who were brought into the country to work in the plantations, construction sites, textile factories and as domestic workers were subjected to various threats including restriction of their movements, wage frauds, passport being confiscated as well as debt bondage at the hands of either the agents or employers (US State Department, 2011: 243).

In fact, the Ministry of Women, Family and Community also runs two shelters for women who are the victims of trafficking, one in Kuala Lumpur and another in Kota Kinabalu, Sabah. Two other temporary shelters in Johor and Sarawak are being planned. Since March 2008, 386 women had been placed in the shelter in Kuala Lumpur for three months before being sent back to their respective countries (Borneo Post, 26/11/09). The rest were sent to their respective embassy shelters and housed at immigration detention centres pending repatriation. All of these reported cases show that there is little effort in screening in order to prevent vulnerable migrants becoming possible trafficking victims. Instead, many of the victims are quickly deported and in cases involving land borders, as in the Sarawak-Kalimantan border, victims are vulnerable to being re-trafficked. The Malaysian women too, primarily Chinese and also those from indigenous communities and rural areas were also vulnerable and trafficked to other countries like Singapore, Hong Kong, France and the United Kingdom for sex work. They suffer physical and sexual abuse, forced drug use, debt bondage, non-payment of wages, threats, confinement and confiscation of passports (US State Department, 2009; 2011).

Labour trafficking is so serious that Malaysia has been blacklisted as a country harbouring modern slavery. It was also reported that in August

2008, 1,000 foreign workers were victims of forced labour in a garment factory manufacturing for the United States. They lived in squalid conditions, had their passport and wages withheld and were forced to work under very exploitative conditions (ibid: 199). In February 2009, a national daily newspaper exposed the case of 140 Bangladeshi workers locked in a small apartment. The workers each paid labour recruiters US$5,000 to secure jobs in Malaysia only to have their passports confiscated on arrival and where wages were not paid for three to six months, and in some instances, they did not see a cent of their wages for a year. In 2008, police in Sarawak rescued 17 Cambodian men who were forced to work on a commercial fishing vessel and repatriated them back to Cambodia without prosecuting any of the employers who confined them (ibid). It was also reported that men from the Philippines were kidnapped and forced to work in plantations in the Malaysian state of Sabah (Chow and Pathmawathy, 2009). What is even more damning is the allegation that Malaysian immigration officials sold Burmese refugees to traffickers along the Thai-Malaysian border (*Malaysiakini*, 17/6/09). Although Malaysia has an anti-trafficking law enacted in 2007 with heavy penalties for human trafficking, there has been few arrest and prosecution. In July 2008, the director general of Immigration and his deputy director-general were arrested for corruption involving the acceptance of bribes for issuance of visas and visit passes for mainly Bangladeshi workers and Chinese nationals. Human trafficking is of course implicated in these cases (US Department, 2006: 199).

Although the Government of Malaysia was reported to fail fully to comply with the minimum standards for elimination of trafficking (US State Department, 2011), there is evidence of significant effort being taken towards more effective anti-trafficking and protection measures. For example, The People's Volunteer Corps (RELA) was introduced to rigorously conduct raids targeting illegal migrants and to consequently prevent or reduce the likelihood of these workers being coerced into forced labour or forced sex activities. Other efforts include the frequent raids on entertainment outlets to reduce the demand for sex and prevent labour trafficking. These actions by RELA have also increased awareness of the general population about the campaigns on anti-trafficking, which encompasses both labour and sex trafficking.

Indigenous women

Let us now turn our attention to the indigenous women in Sarawak. With globalisation and increasing penetration of a highly monetised economy, indigenous people have experienced these ramifications as never before. Large scale cash cropping through plantation agriculture, deforestation through excessive logging and expansion of urban centres have all led to an encroachment on customary rights land. In fact, foreign critics have labelled Sarawak as one of the worst environmental offenders (Anon, *Borneo Post*, 9/12/09). Commercialisation of forest products for example, wildlife meat, ferns, fruits, rattan and scented wood have all led to an over-exploitation of forest resources, resulting in a deteriorating environment. Deer and wild pigs, which are the traditional sources of protein in the rural areas, are now extinct over wide areas. Diminishing food resources as a result of deforestation has led to under-nutrition. For example, a total of 27 Dayak women and 24 Dayak men in Sarawak were studied for food intake versus energy expenditure and were found to be in 'negative energy balance' that is, they were not eating enough to sustain them. Iban women over forty years of age in Song and Kanowit district in Sarawak were found to be showing signs of chronic energy deficiency (Baer, 2007).

Pesticide run-offs from cocoa or pepper gardens and chemical effluents from oil palm plantations not only kill fish in rivers but also present health problems to humans. Some major rivers have been rendered unusable for drinking or bathing. Although many villages have gravity-feed tap water from nearby mountains, in the dry season, women collect water from rivers or swamps even when the water source is unhealthy. In addition, logging in the interiors of Sarawak has caused severe soil erosion, silting and flash floods (ibid). Environmental upheaval in Sarawak have also been the result of the siting of two hydroelectric dam projects – the Batang Ai dam in the Sri Aman division and the Bakun dam in the Upper Rejang River basin. The resettlement of communities to make way for the dam thrust people, who were from a mainly subsistence and partially cash economy, into a totally monetised economy. One Iban woman in Batang Ai commented:

> We work very hard, rain or shine; but still we don't earn enough to eat. We can't grow vegetable here because of the stony soil. We have to walk for two hours to find paku and then we still have to ask for permission from others. (Hew and Kedit, 1987)

Almost two decades later, the same narrative is heard when a woman resettled as a result of the Bakun dam said:

> Everyone has bills here. Move an inch, you have to pay for something. Before, we could sell our fish and save the money for the few bills that we had to pay. Now, I need at least RM 10 to take my ailing mother to the clinic. She has been lying here, unable to rise for three days already. (ibid: 48-49)

Rapid urbanisation in Sarawak has also led to rural women's increasing workload. Women left behind in the villages faced greater hardship as they struggle to support themselves and their children on exhausted land and depleted forests. Amongst the Bau-Lundu Bidayuh, a third of the breadwinners were women and many were pepper farmers (ibid). Over two decades ago, this is what two rural women had to say about being left behind by their husbands when they sought waged work elsewhere (Hew and Kedit, 1987).

> When they go, we have to look after the small children by ourselves. When they fall sick, we have to cope on our own. When the children are unwell, we cannot go out and work.

> My husband went to Brunei for five years. He wrote once or twice a year but never sent any money. I didn't know what work he had. He didn't even come home for a holiday and I was worried. I thought he would marry another and would never return. I supported our two children single-handedly.

As a result of such hardships, women are refusing to be left behind and family migration is increasingly the trend in Iban migration. The exodus out of the rural areas began with the young who had some schooling. They left to seek employment in towns and some went even further afield to the Middle East and elsewhere. In 1970, only 16 % of Sarawak's population was urban. By the year 2000, the figure had jumped to 48 per cent (Hew, 2007). The longhouses in rural Sarawak are slowly being emptied of their inhabitants, except for the old and some retirees who have returned to hobby farming in their villages. The picture of rural-urban migration is complex and the subject of other publications (Hew, 2007; Soda, 2007). When these indigenous women migrate outside of their communities, seeking employment to meet their increasing dependence on cash, they face discrimination because of their gender and ethnic minority status. In other words, discrimination, which they encounter outside of their communities is two-fold – both on the grounds of ethnicity and gender. For those who stay, their status and position within their own communities are eroded as their important role as food producers and custodians of rites and rituals associated with their belief systems are diminished by a shrinking subsistence agricultural base and increasing outside influence.

Another health related issue amongst indigenous communities is their remote location in the interiors of Borneo and the skewed development policies which favoured unsustainable exploitation of the forest with little regard to indigenous land rights and livelihoods. The Penan is a minority indigenous community in Sarawak, very much dependent on forest resources, while some are still semi-nomadic. In September 2008, an NGO, the Bruno Manser Foundation (BMF) revealed the sexual abuse of Penan women who fell prey to timber camp employees. On the 6 October 2008, the Star newspaper reported the rape of teenage Penan school girls by loggers (Chiew, 2008). The students were boarders in a secondary school and because of their remote location, they depended on loggers to provide transportation for them to return to their villages during the school vacation. According to a Bulan Laing, a female elder in a Penan village, the sexual exploitation of Penan women started around 1996 (Chiew, 2008). The exposé stunned the nation and the national task force formed to investigate found the allegations to be true. How did this human right abuse come about? The Penan has long resisted encroachment on their ancestral land by logging concessionaires but they fight a losing battle given that the force of the government is behind timber interest. However, their remote geographical location in the interiors of Borneo also meant that they were dependent on logging companies for water, electricity and transportation. Furthermore their natural forest paths were destroyed by logging. Such dependence on the logging companies have made them vulnerable to sexual abuse. In addition, there is the problem of accessing health care for remote indigenous communities. The Penan and other ethnic minorities depend on the flying doctor service and visiting health teams who travel by longboats to their settlements. However, such provision is limited due to the expensive nature of such travel and at times due to unfavourable weather. As a consequence, the needs of these interior people have not been met (SUHAKAM, 2011).

As they struggle to maintain their livelihood and traditional way of life, the pressing concern of ethnic minorities is to battle against encroachment and total incorporation into wider society and with it, a loss of cultural pride and identity. From the hill tribes of northern Thailand to the Orang Asli in Peninsular Malaysia and the various ethnic groups in Sarawak, Sabah, Indonesia and the Philippines, the threat to the socio-economic structure and the break-down of the cultural fabric of indigenous people are real and serious. Semai women in Peninsular Malaysia articulated their encounters with the State and globalizing forces as such:

> ... the outright acquisition of more and more Semai lands for 'development' projects that are invariably for others. The other is the imposition of a global culture, with its in-built male bias which replaces the indigenous social structure and worldview. (Nicholas et al., 2003: 122).

Women and HIV/AIDS

Women are often perceived to be a vulnerable group and globally women are 2.5 times more likely to be infected with the HIV virus. It was estimated that in 2007, of the 33 million people currently living with HIV around the world, five million are living in Asia and of this total, about 29% or a third of the population were women. In Malaysia, women remain as one of the fastest growing populations to be infected with HIV. As of December 2007, less than 10% of 80,938 of reported HIV cases were among women and girls. The statistics confirms a worrying trend as the new HIV infection cases amongst women have been increasing from a relatively low 1.2% in 1990 to 9% in 2002, rising to 10.8% in 2004 and reaching 15% in 2006 and 16% in 2007 (Ministry of Health Malaysia and UNICEF, 2008).

Men used to outnumber women among those infected in the early years of the AIDS pandemic. From a comparative studies of six countries in Southeast Asia (Malaysia, Indonesia, Thailand, Cambodia, the Philippines and Singapore), statistics indicate that, except for Singapore, in all these countries there has been an overall trend of increasing numbers of women newly infected with HIV. This feminisation of the HIV epidemic is rapidly spreading through unprotected heterosexual relationships as only a small proportion of women are drug users in Malaysia. Statistics published by the Ministry of Health Malaysia, reported that in 2002, 63.9% of the HIV infections among women occurred through heterosexual intercourse, with a large number of these women being housewives. It is also reported that women infected with HIV in 2002 showed that the highest percentage of HIV infected women was among housewives (26.3%), followed by industrial workers (4.1%), sex workers (2.8%), private sector workers (2.0%), public servants (1.8%) and students (1.0%) (Ministry of Health Malaysia & UNICEF, 2008: 32). Women as victims of human trafficking remain a hidden dimension of the HIV epidemic in Malaysia (Suhakam, 2004).

However, to date there is no available statistics on the HIV incidence rate amongst trafficked women.

Women were once believed and perceived to have low HIV infection risk. Recent statistics have now disproved this assumption as many women were reported to be infected via their spouses. Most of the infected housewives were unfortunately unaware that they were at risk of acquiring or being exposed to the HIV virus. These women living with HIV (WLHIV) often become distressed when they themselves are sick and vulnerable while caring for themselves and for their families. Although there has been much development in the position of women in Malaysia in terms of higher literacy rate, better access to education, increased labour participation in different work sectors, women continue to face challenges in protecting themselves and their families due to their subservient role and position in society (Ministry of Health Malaysia & UNICEF, 2008). Women have less power to negotiate for safe sex in their relationships. In many ways, commercial female sex workers are in a better position to bargain for the use of condoms during sex.

HIV infected women face many daily challenges, especially stigma and discrimination. They are more likely to avoid disclosure of their HIV status due to fear of rejection by their families, friends and society. Often this group suffers alone, while living with the fear of being unemployed; and the risks of being beaten, ostracised and abandoned. The silent plight of these women has resulted in the establishment of many support groups and non-government organisations (NGOs).

While there are many support services in Malaysia which offer a multitude of services such as providing information and counselling, basic medical treatment, shelter, care and support groups for women with HIV, the relentless struggles for this population are challenging. One of the major obstacles is the financial burden in obtaining needed but expensive treatment. Transportation to access much needed health care services is also a problem for these women (Sulaiman & Azman, 2010). With the lack of economic power, women become more vulnerable to the male partners on whom they rely. They fear being divorced, abandoned or subjected to domestic violence and this further contributes to their inability to negotiate for safer sex (Gupta, 2000).

The vulnerable position of women at risk of being exposed to the HIV/ AIDS pandemic needs to be looked at more seriously. More research needs to be done to understand women's vulnerabilities and their risks to HIV, its prevention, care and treatment. Many research gaps need to be quickly addressed particularly on heterosexual transmission of the HIV virus, as well as exploring the situation of women in marginalised communities, women as victims of human trafficking and the effectiveness of existing and numerous interventions programmes related to HIV/AIDS. The multifaceted dimension of women and HIV/AIDS requires strong multi-sectorial collaboration and commitment from families as well as various government and non-government agencies in the country (Azman, 2010). This has become more vital with the global phenomena of human trafficking.

Conclusion

Malaysia's healthcare for its citizens is good. However, as Malaysia's economy becomes increasingly globalised, more and more groups of women are at risk. The transmigration of labour, human trafficking, the abrogation of the rights of indigenous peoples and the spread of HIV/AIDS present major challenges to the health and welfare of people and women in particular, given the gendered nature of these issues. Transnational cooperation, the strengthening of civil society, a development agenda which respects human rights, and political will and commitment is urgently required to address these health issues brought about by globalisation.

17

Embroidered lives and tapestries of violence

Sara Ashencaen Crabtree and Jonathan Parker

Introduction

An unashamedly expansive canvas has been employed to capture as much of the subtle tones and complex motifs of the social contexts depicted here as is possible within the confines of this inevitably restricted medium. A panoptic depiction of diverse craftsmanship, uneven in contour and texture, has been the result, but one where each fragment reveals both intricate detail as well as overlapping patterns that are repeated throughout the text. In this concluding chapter therefore we seek to focus upon and magnify some of these motifs, drawing them into a synopsis of distinctive but interwoven themes that cut across chapters and encompassing sections.

The irregularly weighted scaffolding of this canvas in specific reference to the three major middle sections of the work, *religion, sectarianism and identity*, the *impact of direct civil conflict* and finally, *globalisation, urbanisation and social transformation*, has not led to self-contained, mutually exclusive categories of analysis. Instead, the sections have acted as porous meshes revealing crucial facets that yield to a higher level of understanding and appreciation of particular case studies, as well as those interlocking issues and politics of welfare that may be found more commonly across other Muslim countries. Although equally, a purview may reveal some predictable if intriguing comparisons with non-Muslim nations; as well as highlighting patches that are threadbare of detailed data, and await population through future research. However, sections plush with rich detail, show overarching patterns that form the major themes from which subsidiary ones flow relating to gender, ethnicity, class; and where, moreover, powerful international politics and international interventions are spun tightly into the fabric of Muslim nations and national autonomy.

Accordingly this concluding chapter attempts to gather together some of the main points developed in each chapter that bear comparison to and synthesis with others. Thus the reader may view the text in terms of the framework of the chosen scaffolding, which has formed our supporting, horizontal warp; or in terms of our vertical weft: relating to the themes and patterns, both robust, subtle and variegated that are now discussed.

Figure 1
Warp and weft: the integration of themes and sections

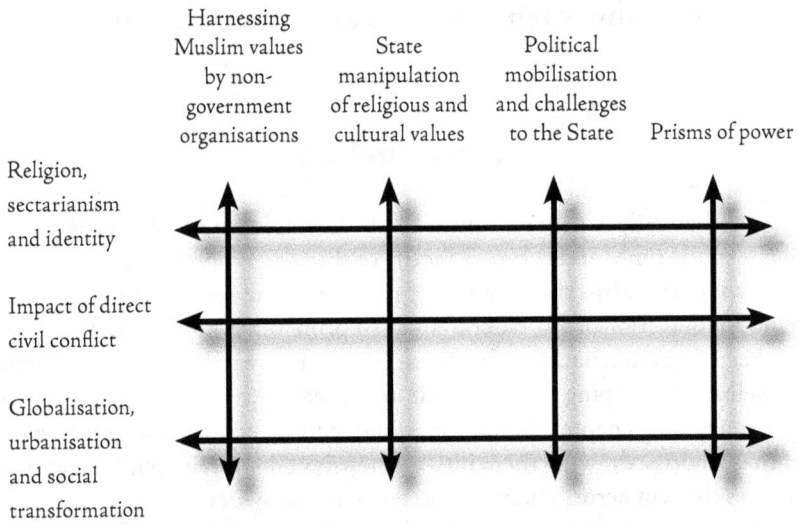

Theme: Harnessing Muslim values by non-government organisations

This first emerging theme delineates an interesting and unresolved tension between the State, as hegemonic provider of welfare resources; and those independent bodies who seek to offer competing or alternative services, but which, significantly, also carry an overt allegiance to defined Muslim religious and cultural values. Such independent populist movements form the basis of Jawad's discussion in this volume, where she moves away from the classic rentier construction to bring to bear a new analytical lens to the countries of the Middle East in reference to a renaissance of politicised, religio-indigenised reframing of citizenship in response to perceived social needs.

Jawad notes that the main challenges in Arab countries relate to distribution of wealth, income issues and the meeting of basic needs where effective structures are required to support these aims. Thus a potential power vacuum may occur where the ability and right to address these aspects effectively may be hotly contested by the State and independent Islamic-inspired groups, acting in competition for tangible and ideological control of the public sphere. The State is thereby forced to compete with these populist groups in order to maintain its existing but threatened status quo; while for the latter groups such contestations attempt to tip the power-balance away from the State.

The moral appeal to Muslim cultural values is exploited by such groups who seek to harness these sentiments in order to speak to and for a rising grassroots resistance to the State, which is seen as both secular and ineffective. Thus, Jawad comments that while populist (religious) movements may be regarded with suspicion in the West, such groups may be well received in Arab countries as speaking on behalf of the dispossessed.

Messkoub in turn also notes how such tensions play on the perceived inability of the State adequately to meet the general welfare needs of the populace. This key point is one that is additionally noted in reference to Egypt by Aboulhassan and Abdel-Ghany who pull together an impressive array of statistical data in relation to unemployment and poverty, including child poverty. An exploration of related indicators for female health, education and civic and labour participation are offered by the authors, in addition to those relating to the condition of the elderly population and that of disabled people in the country. A comprehensive overview is therefore provided regarding the level of social development in contemporary Egyptian society and the effectiveness of social policy strategies to-date.

In reference to Pakistan, Candland and Khan Qazi extend this theme by examining four Islamic philanthropic organisations with differing denominational features, mission-based agendas and relationships to the State - extending from militant opposition to distant involvement in political affairs. The authors draw an acute distinction between the issue of national security, which preoccupies the Pakistani government in relation to insurgent groups and Al Qaeda - and human security, relating to the vulnerability of the people and their need for protection from harm. Such distinctions are also suggested by van Bijlert in her chapter on Afghanistan. In Pakistan, it is on this fulcrum that the pendulum of ideological ascendancy pivots. These authors describe the perceived contrasts between these two points, where, as an example, due to military manoeuvres to combat insurgency hundreds of ordinary people were displaced from their homes and placed in makeshift camps. Candland and Khan Qazi comment that humanitarian groups were obliged to heavily subsidise the most basic level provision provided by the State to these people through international assistance. The authors also refer to the flaccid response by the State towards the needs of earthquake victims and the muscular, philanthropy of religiously conservative, zealous NGOs, who tend to share an overt aim of establishing *Shariah* law in Pakistan.

By contrast to these examples, however, van Bijlert's discusses the anomaly of Afghanistan's extreme poverty weighed against its great wealth acquired primarily through the illicit drug trade. She offers an analysis of the headlong political rush to embrace the discourses and practices of a free-market economy in a nation described as one of the poorest and most corrupt countries in the world, in contrast to stark paucity and unevenness of welfare provision provided by the State. While in contrast to some of the Islamic humanitarian organisations discussed so far, the Taliban in Afghanistan, who have fanatically pursued their own interpretation of Islamic rule with the aim of imposing this on the majority of Afghans, choose to refrain from championing underprivileged communities, and instead divert monies gained back into their organisations with a view to benefitting their own members.

The critiques offered in these chapters, however, should not lead the reader to assume the simplistic position that governments in Muslim societies as a rule occupy a polarised position with independent organisations in the contested sphere of welfare policy and provision. On the contrary, it is evident that some States are well versed in appealing to Islamic cultural sentiments in the attempt to construct harmonious relationships with sectors of society in the interests of political expediency.

Theme: State manipulation of religious and cultural values

As Jawad notes certain States in the Middle East, typified by Lebanon and Morocco, seek to form alliances with religiously-based welfare organisations in social service-type provision. Indeed, the example of Iran offers some interesting case studies in this respect, as discussed separately by Harris, Doostgharin and Messkoub. Post-revolution Iran has witnessed significant and diversified investment in social welfare in keeping with Doostgharin's point that insistent demands for reform served to fuel the Islamic Revolution and the deposition of the Shah. He seeks to demonstrate discursively the theological and historical source of the centrality of welfare in Islamic societies that underpins contemporary Iran's provision in this area, where charitable organisations like the Imdad Committee are fiscally supported by the Iranian government.

A diverse platform of welfare provision is offered in Iran, through both traditional, religiously-based charitable responses as mentioned, and the attempts by the State to distribute assets, privatised or nationally-owned to low-income groups in the form of stocks and shares, and through social insurance measures. Such innovations resonate with Messkoub's point that Islamic States when required will negotiate the ambiguous and slippery paths between pragmatism and dogmatism in adopting standard financial and banking strategies, by reconstructing and reframing such activities in order to achieve a more acceptable Islamic complexion. Accordingly, as Doostgharin notes, that although conspicuous areas of need remain apparent in Iranian society gains include a notable fall in malnutrition rates among low-income groups.

Harris deploys a penetrating critical ethnographic lens to the profiled Imam Khomeini Relief Committee in Iran to cast light on its opaque relationship with the State and how its publicly benevolent agenda is intimately tied to constructed ideology that served the aims of the Revolutionary State-building enterprise. This point is further developed by Messkoub, who also notes the pragmatic fluidity of governments who come to power with the agenda of establishing an Islamic State, but where the realties of uncompromisingly difficult aspects of economic and social policy governance in fact demand hard-headed secular development and management. Finally Harris, Doostgharin and Messkoub all note the dependency of citizens on enmeshed government-run and government-patronised networks of welfare provision that underpin post-revolution Iranian society.

Malaysia provides a very interesting example of how State politics are used to negotiate and harnesses religio-ethnic populist appeals to strengthen the Government's electoral appeal and power-base within a modern, multicultural society. Hew and Ashencaen Crabtree explore this aspect in conjunction with the phenomenon of the Islamic resurgence in Malaysia and its perceived increasing encroachment into the public sphere. The continuation of Malaysia's arguably anachronistic and controversial social policy of overt positive discrimination towards Malay-Muslim citizens via the New Economic Policy of 1969 is viewed as directly connected to these ethnic politics. The authors rehearse arguments that although social policies have successfully served to equalise the wealth and professional polarisation of ethnic groups in favour of the Malay population, this has come at a heavy social cost. Deemed anachronistic, given that the original objectives have now been reached, such social policies serve to disenfranchise citizens of other ethnic groups by creating significant disadvantages in terms of employment, education, housing and general advancement.

More worrying is that this form of nationalism is tied to cultural-religious hegemony, where the Islamic resurgence supported by the Malaysian government serves to increasingly police the conduct of any identified Muslim in the country, practising or otherwise, and where severe penalties for apostasy are imposed. In his valuable discussion on Islamic principles and social welfare Al-Krenawi argues that imposing criminal punishment for apostasy is incompatible with basic human rights.

The Islamic resurgence in Malaysia has additionally and regrettably resulted in numerous examples of religious intolerance and oppression towards non-Muslims. This, yoked to discriminatory social policy, forms a significant and conspicuous challenge to contemporary ideologies of multiculturalism as ideally being no bar to equality among citizens.

Theme: Political mobilisation and challenges to the State

A number of references have been made in this book to the issue of political mobilisation among citizens in response to the need for reform in or the reconstruction of nation States. The turbulent events of the 'Arab Spring', a grassroots-level populist protest that has spread across several countries of the Middle East are especially noted as an important and iconic example of mass uprising against authoritarian regimes. Aboulhassan and Abdoul-Ghany describe the phenomenon as an almost inevitable backlash against State corruption and incompetence, and rising crime in Egyptian society. Messkoub and separately Jawad bring to bear an economic-based critique of the MENA region to understand the socio-economic political context, which has given rise to the Arab Spring events. Arguing that poverty and unemployment, precarious economic health and a lack of effective planning at social policy levels have created vulnerability and uncertainty Messkoub notes where modern nation States will face considerable challenges in meeting the justifiable expectations of their citizens. Al-Krenawi in turn uses graphic imagery to convey the inexorable progress of the populist juggernaut wresting democracy from autocracy. Finally, Ashencaen

Crabtree et al. locate the Arab Spring uprising as an enacted, embodied liberation discourse utilising the idealism and energies of largely (but clearly not entirely) socially alienated Muslim youth actively resisting social and political anomie.

In the latter example, the need to engage and direct the latent political energy of young citizens is the focus of the chapter by Kipperberg. She explores the autonomous Kurdish Regional Government's efforts to involve Kurdish youth in developing democratic rule inspired by the Swedish model. Today, following the fall of Saddam Hussein, the Kurdish region enjoys greater security than the rest of Iraq and where religious tolerance is constitutionally promoted. In the aftermath of the overthrow of the former regime active reconstruction of the region is taking place, where growing diversity in the population in relation to religious affiliations is a feature in relation to Muslim denominations, Christianity and the formerly persecuted Yeazides.

In connection with the focus of the chapter on Kurdish youth, Kipperberg reports the harrowing detail that the majority of the Kurdish victims of Saddam Hussein's unspeakable genocidal oppression were in fact, Kurdish children, survivors of whom are the youth referred to. Although a gap exists between the rhetoric of participation and actual mechanisms to involve young people, a successful partnership would represent a fitting tribute to their sacrifice and a highly expedient manoeuvre towards harnessing the power of Kurdish youth during a significant social and political transition.

Theme: Prisms of power

Power relations and power dynamics have formed the contextual backdrop throughout the majority of the chapters presented in this volume. Power may be played out in terms of State control of re sources, local populations and groups, ideological conceptions and the identification of certain issues as social problems or alternatively as not constituting social issues requiring redress. The contested terrain across religious sects and religious constructions and their influence within society form another area where power is played out, which may additionally form a challenge to the State or may work in collusion with prevailing vectors of religious hegemony or social control. Power also informs religio-cultural and social constructions of gender, age, ethnicity and class; and therefore forms both a major category of analysis as well as a main theme emerging across the breadth of chapters offered here.

In respect of class, as we have learned, the social conditions found in many Arab countries prior to the Arab Spring events have resulted in a social insecurity, tension and wide-spread social discontent. The control of limited resources long held by an autocratic elite have been dispensed to the populace with varying degrees of social effectiveness: the United Arab Emirates and Egypt taking up the polarised positions of such a continuum, as both Ashencaen Crabtree et al and Aboulhassan and Abdel-Ghany illustrate. These structural hierarchies are clearly implicated in recognisable class factors that the events of the Arab Spring and grass-roots Islamic popular movements seek to overturn. However, as Messkoub points out Islamic revivalists, who appeal to the class element in appealing for justice for the underprivileged, seek to recreate an Islamic State through *Shariah* rule, which dictates family law and penal codes. Messkoub argues that *Shariah* has been implicated in sanctioning inequalities between the sexes, and ideologically stands apart from the secular and democratic moves that have driven the recent uprisings. Demands for material improvement and coordinated, accessible social protection represent a sphere around which States and Islamic revivalists oscillate in a dance for power.

Muslim nations, such as Malaysia and the United Arab Emirates offer a compromise in this respect, in running a parallel legal system of penal law and *Shariah* law and arguably therefore act as hybrid Islamic States. Both countries are highly developed and affluent with large multicultural populations, albeit living under very different circumstances. As Ashencaen Crabtree et al. point out the United Arab Emirates hosts a large number of expatriate resident non-citizen workers that reduce Emirati nationals to an ethnic minority group in a small country that tends to conforms more closely to a traditional rentier system. Accordingly, national conditions and needs on the home front, in conjunction with the powerful influence of modern global politics and market economies tend to demand prosaic expedient compromises for modern, highly developed Muslim nations.

The struggle for ideological hegemony is not merely confined to the secular and the religious, or between autocracy and democracy, but with respect to how the Islamic worldview relates to the authority of the Holy Qur'an and additionally how this is to be comprehended. Commensurately Al-Krenawi separates this issue into two theological approaches: the 'textualists' and the 'contextualists' (humanists). The former adhere to the belief that the word of the holy text and its hadiths as immutable to time and place. It therefore behoves believers to accept a literal interpretation (although this is by no means lacking in contention in itself among such adherents), but in so doing may support archaic and extremist practices that

Al-Krenawi believe are incompatible to an international understanding of human rights and social work values. By contrast the contextualists accept the socio-historical location of the holy text as inescapable and therefore that the Qur'an and hadiths are fluid and open to interpretation. This latter perspective, the author argues, enables Islam to evolve as a thriving religion, relevant to the modern world, by permitting contemporary discourses of rights and justice to be adopted, as well one assumes, as adapted to the local context.

In her study of small and medium-sized business enterprises in Palestine, Agnew considers power in relation to direct civil conflict. Here she draws our attention to the essential relationship between economic health at the micro and meso levels and welfare provision at the local level. Disruptions to the first two levels militate against the development of systematic and coherent responses to welfare needs of vulnerable and needy groups.

The armed control over the territory by Israeli forces has resulted in deliberate policies to ensure that high levels of surveillance are maintained and that free movement among Palestinians in designated areas is both strictly curtailed and hazardous. These controls have deleteriously impacted on the ability of smaller businesses to function in any normal fashion. Through interview data with local Palestinians Agnew records that despite these tangible and incredibly challenging barriers smaller businesses have managed to retain a tentative, precarious foothold to-date. Yet she also observes that the competitive edge of these ground-level businesses is blunted by international aid programmes supplying food and other necessities to the local population. Agnew reviews the argument that although such agencies offer important humanitarian aid this serves to reinforce dependency in the contained population. In the case of Palestine this may serve to maintain the current impasse and thus prevents a move towards a political solution to the conflict with Israel.

How far or how quickly local businesses would be able to contribute to building a more sustainable infrastructure from the current, degraded base level is debatable. In the meantime Agnew suggests that there is some evidence that through individual ingenuity in negotiating very difficult obstacles small enterprises may even have grown. However, what remains apparent based on the findings of this chapter is that while sustained damage to the infrastructure continues through civil conflict and the stifling of ordinary civil life, welfare needs will grow exponentially through resultant human casualties, as well as quotidian vicissitudes of life as experienced by ordinary Palestinian people,

In conjunction with this chapter, Lindsay adds a new dimension to our understanding for the recognition of formal social services support of Palestinian children by school psycho-social work. The strengthening of the professional basis of supervision of social workers through the partnership of the Palestinian Authority Ministry of Education and Birzeit University forms the focus of this chapter. Accordingly Lindsay describes and discusses the development of an innovative Diploma in Supervision. The training programme serves to equip trainee supervisors with enhanced professional knowledge and skills required to guide teams of school social workers in managing complex case loads. Although Lindsay does not specifically discuss the types and nature of psychosocial needs among school children, the continued conflict and collateral damage to the Palestinian environment forms the dominant and sinister backdrop to social work concerns relating to children and families in the territories.

Moving away from welfare considerations in conflict-ridden Palestine and the concomitant needs of the local population, we consider power in terms of gender. Hew and Azman examine the contradiction between very effective mainstream health policies in Malaysia targeting the heath needs of women and children, and gaps in service provision for marginalised groups. Thus while maternal and child health has improved across a number of indicators in relation to mortality, nutrition and increasing longevity, poorly-met or unmet needs are apparent elsewhere.

Having set the context in relation to health care Hew and Azman focus on gendered power relations in terms of three specific groups: indigenous women, female migrants (or trafficked workers), and finally, Malaysian women in cohabiting, heterosexual relationships.

Firstly, the authors argue that health services are failing to meet the needs of some of the smaller indigenous ethnic groups living in the remote interior regions of East Malaysia where access is difficult. The displacement and disruption of indigenous groups for commercial exploitation of customary held land through logging and dam building has long been the cause of concern by environmental protestors both nationally and internationally. The deterioration of the environment and the disruption of traditional practises appear to be endemic and has resulted in significant repercussions on the health and nutrition status of indigenous peoples. The scandal of the rape of Penan schoolgirls by loggers makes explicit the connection between the violation of native-held territories and that of native females by predatory incomers seeking to exploit vulnerable natural resources and the people that live with this fragile infrastructure.

The second group considered, refers to the significant numbers of migrant workers of both sexes arriving in Malaysia to service gender-specific industries. Both males and females may be victims of human trafficking, yet few prosecutions have to-date been achieved in Malaysia. For women migrants, voluntary or otherwise, the main areas of work lie in domestic service or in the sex entertainment industry. The health needs of such migrant workers are neglected by the Malaysian health services as falling outside of their remit, despite the contagious nature of some of these carried diseases. Apart from the humanitarian considerations towards individual sufferers, Hew and Azman point out this carries important implications for public health considerations in the country.

The final group discussed in relation to gender and power in this chapter are those Malaysian women in cohabiting relationships made vulnerable to infection with the HIV virus through contact with their infected partners. It is noted that women form the fastest growing group to be infected with the virus in Malaysia through unprotected sexual intercourse, owing in part to their inferior negotiating power in heterosexual relationships.

Parin Dossa develops the theme of gender and power in a chapter on the interweaving of violence in the lives of Afghan women. Taking an anthropological, ethnographic, moral position of 'witness' she offers a broad analysis linking micro realities to overarching socio-political structures structure in considering the oppressive context of Afghanistan. Here the dominant, oppressive, constant reminder of militarisation through heavy security surveillance are played out through the continuing resistance of Taliban insurgents, the visible presence of international armed peacekeeping forces, urban bombing and the rising numbers of dispensable, 'unrecorded' civilian causalities.

Dossa argues that lesser forms of violence are experienced daily through gross insecurity, severely damaged infrastructures and the ramifications of poverty and trauma upon children and adults alike. International 'donor agencies' serve to offer limited assistance to certain groups, but this is limited or highly selective and therefore inevitably exclusionary and inequitable. Research into a women's shelter established by a German agency enables Dossa to be explore the essentialist discourses surrounding how Afghan girls and women are perceived, which emphasises their deficits, benightedness and victim status at the hands of a particularly oppressive patriarchal system where child marriage and domestic violence is rife. This essentialist motif of violence attached to symbolic Afghan women, however, offer simplistic Manichean dichotomies; and thus fail to acknowledge other stories of family support, female success or the courage and resourcefulness of local women.

Concluding remarks

In conclusion, this collection does not claim to be representative of the many varied lives of the people and nations presented by our authors. However, the rich weave of experiences and emotions, sacrifices for others' needs and to beliefs, principles and traditions (Halbertal, 2012), develop an understanding of a social fabric that runs through and around diverse peoples. In this final chapter we have sought to pull together some of those core strands, hoping not to unravel our cloth but to examine our albeit rough rags, illuminating some of the key statements that bind humans together through crisis, conflict and political violence, and rolling out a tapestry connecting welfare and conflict in those Muslim countries that often gain cursory and ideological treatment from hidden political perspectives.

In our globalised world, lives are embroidered from many sources. The economic context forms our experiences of the social, and the social develops our political selves, whilst tradition, religion, values and families colour the fabric of our lives. The interweaving of welfare and social protection at times of conflict and crisis stems from many of these sources. At times one may be more pronounced than others, but the patterns of our vital tapestries derive from these complex and nuanced experiences.

Contributors

Dr Tamer M. Abdel-Ghany is a professor in the Faculty of Social Work, Helwan University, Cairo, Egypt. He has enjoyed a varied career in school social work and public relations management. His academic area of research lies in the participatory interface between schools and the community.

Andromeda Agnew is a freelance journalist and writer on international business and current affairs. She has contributed articles for quality broadsheet newspapers in the UK and prior to this held a number of editorial posts in magazine publishing and online media in the United Arab Emirates. A resident of Spain for the past few years she is interested in examining social and economic developments in the region, as well as internationally, relating to topics on poverty and social exclusion.

Professor Alean Al-Krenawi (PhD) is President of Achva Academic College and Professor of Social Work at Ben-Gurion University of the Negev, Dr. Al-Krenawi's research interest includes social work with indigenous people, political violence, mental health and Polygamy, he has authored several books, numerous book chapters and over 95 journal articles on several areas including culturally relevant social work and mental health services in the Middle East and North America Arab communities. Together with Dr. John Graham he is completing a book *Social Work with Muslims Communities* which will be published by Columbia University Press. His writing has recently honored as among the top 50 most cited in the English speaking world in the social work discipline.

Dr Sara Ashencaen Crabtree is the Deputy Director of the Centre for Social Work & Social Policy at Bournemouth University, UK and is series editor of 'Critical Studies in Socio-cultural Diversity' for Whiting & Birch. She has enjoyed a fascinating international academic career, where she has held academic posts at The Chinese University of Hong Kong, Zayed University, United Arab Emirates and finally, Universiti Malaysia

Sarawak, East Malaysia. Her research interests include vulnerable adults and diversity; faith and social work, with a focus on Islam; mental health, gender and ethnicity, and international social work. She has published widely in all these areas.

Dr Belkeis Altareb, a Counseling Psychologist, is Associate Dean of University College at Zayed University, Dubai, United Arab Emirates. Her teaching and research interests are in mental health, women, youth, and identity. Currently she co-leads General Education at Zayed University and serves as program developer for numerous other university initiatives. Prior to moving to the UAE, she practiced within university counseling centers in the US.

Dr Azlinda Azman is the Chair of the Social Work Programme and Convenor of the AIDS Action Research Group (AARG) at the School of Social Sciences, Universiti Sains Malaysia, was a Fulbright Scholar and obtained her doctoral degree in Clinical Social Work from New York University, United States of America in 2005. Currently, she chairs the National Joint Consultative Committee on Social Work Education in Malaysia, is an executive committee member of the Malaysian Association of Social Workers and is a member of Steering Committee for the development on Competency and Social Workers' Act in Malaysia. Her field of expertise is social work education and practice. Her research interests include sexuality, HIV/AIDS and substance abuse related issues, poverty, and community engagement and development.

Martine van Bijlert is a researcher and writer with a main focus on Afghanistan. She spent her early childhood in (pre-revolutionary) Iran and studied Sociology of Non-Western Societies at Leiden University. A Farsi-speaker, she has spent most of the last 20 years in Afghanistan, Iran and Pakistan, where she worked as researcher, aid worker, diplomat and independent analyst. She is currently co-director, and co-founder, of the Afghanistan Analysts Network, an independent, non-profit research organisation focusing on the analysis of political developments in and around Afghanistan. region.

Dr Christopher Candland is an Associate Professor of Political Science and was the Founding Director of the South Asia Studies Program at Wellesley College. He has worked in the United Nations and in the U.S. Congress and Department of State and has been an international fellow of the Council on Foreign Affairs and a fellow of the Woodrow Wilson International Center for Scholars. His scholarship relates to human development in South and Southeast Asia. His publications include *Labor, Democratization, and Development in India and Pakistan.* His current book project is on human security and religious philanthropy in Pakistan.

Dr Taghi Doostgharin is a senior FAST (Families and Schools together) trainer, working for FAST UK at Middlesex university. Dr Doostgharin was formerly an Associate Professor in social work. Dr Doostgharin's research interests are : Children and Families and working with individuals.

Professor Parin Dossa is Professor of Anthropology at Simon Fraser University. Her teaching and research interests include migration, gender and health, structural violence in war and peace, qualitative methods and anthropological theory. Her ethnographic work has focused on Muslim women in Canada, Afghanistan, Pakistan and on the coast of Kenya. She is the author of (a) Politics and Poetics of Migration: Narratives of Iranian Women from the Diaspora (2004); (b) Racialized Bodies, Disabling Worlds: Storied Lives of Immigrant Muslim Women (2009). Currently she is exploring the relationship between structural violence, gender and politics of memory in Afghanistan.

Dr Kevan Harris is a post-doctoral research fellow in the Department of Near Eastern Studies at Princeton University. His Ph.D. dissertation at the Department of Sociology at The Johns Hopkins University is entitled *The Martyrs Welfare State: Politics and Social Policy in the Islamic Republic of Iran* and is based on fieldwork conducted in Iran from 2009-11. Kevan has written broadly about economy and society in contemporary Iran, including articles on labor movements, intellectuals, and economic policy in the Islamic Republic.

Dr Nabil Aboulhassan is a professor in the Faculty of Social Work, South Valley University, Aswan, Egypt. A postgraduate of Helwan University, Cairo and Laval University, Quebec, Canada. His research areas include family mediation in Arab families, social welfare policies and people with disabilities in the Middle, and blended learning pedagogy in social work education.

Dr HEW Cheng Sim, PhD, is an Associate Professor in the Faculty of Social Sciences at Universiti Malaysia Sarawak (UNIMAS). Her research interests include gender relations, urbanization, marriage, family and work with a focus on Sarawak. She has published widely and her books include *Women Workers, Migration and Family in Sarawak* (London and New York: RoutledgeCurzon, 2003), *Village Mothers, City Daughters* (Singapore: Institute of Southeast Asian Studies, 2007) and *Tra Zehnder: Iban Woman Patriot of Sarawak* (Malaysia: UNIMAS Press, 2011).

Dr Rana Jawad is a lecturer in social policy in the Department of Social and Policy Sciences at the University of Bath. Her areas of research interest are social policy in the Middle East and the role of religion generally in social policy. Her publications include Social Welfare and Religion in the Middle East: A Lebanese Perspective (2009) and Religion and Faith-based Welfare in the UK: From Well-being to Ways of Being (2012), both by The Policy Press.

Raza Khan Qazi is a Pashtun political analyst and commentator based in Peshawar. He has done research in some of the most volatile regions of the Federal Tribal Administered Areas, Balochistan, and Khyber-Pakhtunkhwa and has written extensively on development, political economy, and religious radicalism in Afghanistan and Pakistan. His work has been published by *The News*, *The Washington Times*, *Global Politician*, the New America Foundation, and *World Politics Review*. Raza has earned a BA in Law and Economics and MAs in Political Science, Journalism, and International Relations. He is writing a Ph.D. thesis on 'Islamic Extremism-Terrorism in Pakistan: Causes and Counter-Strategy' at the University of Peshawar. He has taught in the Department of International Relations of the University of Peshawar and has held senior positions in Pakistan government ministries and departments, including in the Pakistan Ordinance Factory, the Pakistan Science Foundation, and Islamabad Policy Research Institute.

Elise Kipperberg is Associate Professor at the Department of Social Studies, University of Stavanger, Norway. She has for the past 20 years been engaged in international refugee issues and post conflict challenges regarding children and youth in particular. She has studied children's participation in the Truth and Reconciliation Commission in South Africa and done research on the situation for Maya youth in Guatemala after the civil war. For the time being she is in charge of a cooperation project between the University of Stavanger and the University of Duhok, Kurdistan. Her ongoing research projects focus on Youth Participation in the Democratization Process in Kurdistan and on Human Rights for Children belonging to Ethiopian Asylum seekers living in Norway without a stay permit.

Jane Lindsay is Acting Head of School of Social Work in the Faculty of Health and Social Care Sciences, Kingston University and St George's University of London. From 1997-2009 she acted as an independent monitoring and evaluation consultant (pro bono) for courses in psycho-social counselling and professional supervision offered by Birzeit University in the Occupied Palestinian Territories.

Dr Mahmood Messkoub is senior lecturer at International Institute of Social Studies (Erasmus University of Rotterdam, the NL) teaching on social policy and population issues. As an economist he also taught for many years in the UK (at universities of Leeds and London). His publications include articles on the social impact of adjustment programmes, population ageing in developing countries, and social policy. His current research interests are in the area of economics of social policy and population ageing, migration and universal approach to social provisioning. His recent publications on MENA are related to social policy in Iran, the impact of recent financial crisis on the region, poverty and employment policies. He has also acted as a consultant and advisor to Handicap-International, ESCWA, ILO, UNFPA and the World Bank.

Professor Jonathan Parker is Deputy Dean for Research and Knowledge Exchange and Director of the Centre for Social Work and Social Policy in the School of Health and Social Care at Bournemouth University. He is a past Chair of the Association of Teachers in Social Work Education 2002 to 2005, Vice Chair of the higher education representative body, the Joint University Council for Social Work Education from 2005-2010, and was elected as an Academician with the Academy of Social Sciences in 2008. He has published widely, including 18 books and over 80 academic papers, chapters and research reports. Jonathan is the co-editor of the highly successful series of Social Work text books Transforming Social Work Practice, published by Learning Matters/Sage and is Editor-in-Chief of the *Journal of Practice Teaching and Learning*.

Margaret Wood worked in Social Work Faculty in a large Tertiary Institute in United Arab Emirates, she now is completing her PhD in Education and Social Work and working in the Disability Sector in New Zealand and in intersection of this with Criminal Justice. Margaret's research interests include youth deviance, disability and criminal justice, and women caught between tradition and modernity in the Middle East.

References

Abdel Rahim, A.R., 2007. 'Requirements for the Integration of Women in Development', *International Scientific Conference* of Social work, 11-12 March 2007, Faculty of Social Work, Helwan University, Cairo.

Abdelrahman, M. M., 2001. *State and civil society relations: the politics of Egyptian NGOs*. PhD thesis. the Hague, NL: Institute of Social Studies.

Abdul Fattah Nagy, A., 2008. 'Activating community support networks for the protection and care of children at risk under the global and local variables', *The International Scientific Conference XVIIII*, 23-24 April 2008, Faculty of Social work, Fayoum University, Fayoum Governorate.

Abou-almaaty , M., 2008. 'A Social policy for caring of populations at risk in the Egyptian society', *International Scientific Conference XVIIII*, 23-24 April 2008, Faculty of Social work, Fayoum University, Fayoum Governorate.

Abu Baker, K. and Dwairy, M., 2003. Cultural norms versus State law in treating incest: A suggested model for Arab Families, *Child Abuse & Neglect*, 27 (1), 109-123.

Achtar, A., 2010. Challenging Al-Qa 'ida's justification of terror. *In*: D. Fisher and B. Wicker., eds. *Just War on Terror? A Christian and Muslim response*. Farnham: Ashgate, 25-36.

Afifi Abdul-Fattah A., 2007. 'Slums as one of the challenges faced by urban development', *International Scientific Conference XVIII*, 2-3 May 2007, Faculty of Social work, Fayoum University, Fayoum Governorate.

Afghan Independent Human Rights Commission, 2009. *Fourth Report on the Situation of Economic and Social Rights in Afghanistan*. Kabul: AIHRC, December 2009.

Afghanistan National Development Strategy (ANDS), 2008a. Kabul: Islamic Republic of Afghanistan.

Afghanistan National Development Strategy (ANDS), 2008b. Social Protection Sector Strategy 2008-2013. Kabul: Islamic Republic of Afghanistan, 14 February 2008.

Agency Coordinating Body for Afghan Relief (ACBAR), 2008. Afghanistan Pilot Participatory Assessment (APPA), Kabul: ACBAR.

Akbarzadeh, S. and MacQueen, B., 2008. Framing the debate on Islam and human rights. *In*: S. Akbarzadeh and B. MacQueen, eds. *Islam and Human Rights in Practice: Perspectives across the Ummah.* New York, Routledge, 1-11.

Akers, R.L., LaGreca, A.J., Sellers, C. and Cochran, J., 1987. Fear of crime and victimization among the elderly in different types of communities, *Criminology*, 25(3), 487-505.

Al-Fawal, N., Halim, N., & Adli, H., 2002. Symposium on Egyptian women and the challenges of community. *The National Centre for Social and Criminological Research.* Cairo, Egypt.

Al-Krenawi, A. and Graham, J., 2000. Islamic theology and prayer: Relevance for social work practice, *International Social Work*, 43(3), 289-304.

Al-Krenawi, A.; Graham, J.R. and Slonim-Nevo, V., 2002. Mental health aspects of Arab-Israeli adolescents from polygamous versus monogamous families, *The Journal of Social Psychiatry*, 142 (4), 446-460.

Al-Krenawi, A and Graham J., 2003. Principles of social work practice in the Muslim Arab world, *Arab Studies Quarterly*, 25(4), 75-92.

Al-Krenawi, A., & Graham, J. (Forthcoming). *Social work with Muslim communities.* Columbia: Columbia University Press.

Al Islam, 2010. *Sermons of the Commander of the Faithful, Imam Ali b. Abi. Talib. An order to Maalik al-Ashtar.* Letter 53. Available at: http://www.al-islam.org/ nahjul/letters/letter53.htm. [Date accessed, 28th October 2010]

Al-Shamsi, M.S.A. and Fulcher, L., 2005. The impact of polygamy on United Arab Emirates' first wives and their children. *International Journal of Child and Family Welfare*, 1 8 (1), 46-55.

Ali, B.-E.-D, Mattar, M. and Asfour, F., 1966. Treatment of juvenile delinquency in the United Arab Emirates, *Criminologica*, 4(2), 33-40.

Allen, J.G., 2007. Evil, mindblindness, and trauma: challenges to hope, *Smith College Studies in Social* Work, 77 (1), 9-31.

All India Council of Muslim Economic Upliftment (AICMEU), 2009. *Islam and Social Service.* Available at: http://www.aicmeu.org/Social.htm. [Date accessed, 26th November 2009].

Almihdar, Z., 2008. Human rights of women and children under the Islamic law of personal status and its application in Saudi Arabia, *Muslim World Journal of Human Rights*, 5 (1), 1-15.

Alnajjar, A. and Smadi, A., 1998. Delinquents' and non-delinquents' perception of family functioning in the United Arab Emirates, *Social Behavior and Personality*, 26, (4), 375-382.

Amnesty International, 1998, Annual Report 1998: United Arab Emirates. Available at: http://www.amnesty.org/ailib/aireport/ar98/mde25.htm [Date accessed, 23rd March 2012].

Amnesty International, 2009. *Hope and Fear – Human Rights in the Kurdistan Region of Iraq.* Report April 2009.

Amouee, B., 2002. *Political Economy of the Islamic Republic* [in Persian]. Tehran, Iran: Gam-e No Press.

Anderson, T., 2011. Bush's Wars, Oxford: Oxford University Press.

Afshar, H., 1996. Islam and feminism: an analysis of political strategies. *In*: M. Yamani, ed. *Feminism and Islam*. New York: New York University Press, 197-217.

Anon., *Borneo Post* 9th November, 2009; 26th November, 2009; 3rd December 2009 and 9th December 2009.

Anon., 2009., *Malaysiakini* 17th June 2009. Available at: http://www.malaysiakini. com/news/106614, [Date accessed, 8th December 2009].

Anon., 2011. Borneo Post, May 10, 2011. Available at: http://www.borneopost. com/2011/05/10/minister-disappointed-non-bumiputera-status-issue-crops-up-again-latest/#ixzzlec31gKOw, [Date accessed, 2nd Feb 2012].

Antonopoulos, G.A. and Winterdyk, J.A., 2003. The British 1998 Crime and Disorder Act: A 'restorative' response to Youth Offending?' *European Journal of Crime, Criminal Law and Criminal Justice*, 11 (4), 386-397.

Anwar I., 2006. Nation no longer competitive, *Malaysiakini*, Dec. 11, 2006. Available at: www.malaysiakini.com/new/60764, [Date accessed, 14th March 2012] Arrighi, G., 1990. The Developmental Illusion: A Reconceptualization of the Semiperiphery. *In*: B. Martin, ed., *Semiperipheral States in the World Economy*. New York: Greenwood Press, 11-42.

Ashencaen Crabtree, S., 1999. Teaching anti-discriminatory practice in Malaysia, *Social Work Education*, 18(3), 247-255.

Ashencaen Crabtree, S. and Baba, I., 2001. Islamic perspectives in social work education: Implications for teaching and practice, *Social Work Education*, 20 (4), 469-481.

Ashencaen Crabtree, S., 2007. Culture, gender and the influence of social change amongst Emirati families in the United Arab Emirates, *Journal of Comparative Family Studies*, XXXVIII (4), 575-587.

Ashencaen Crabtree, S., 2011. Gendered discourses of coping strategies and perceived cultural challenge for low-income Pakistani families in Hong Kong, *European Journal of Social Work*, 14(3), 363-378.

Ashencaen Crabtree, S., Husain, F. and Spalek, B., 2008. *Islam and Social Work: Debating values, transforming practice*. Bristol: Policy Press.

Ashencaen Crabtree, S. and Williams, R., 2010. Inclusive education and children with disabilities in the Gulf Cooperation Council Member States. *In*: Mazawi, A.E. and Sultana, R.G., eds., *Education and the Arab 'World': Political Projects, Struggles and the Geometries of Power*. New York/London: Routledge, 196-213.

Aspalter, C., 2002. *Discovering the Welfare State in East Asia Westport*. Connecticut: Praeger.

Aspalter, C., 2011. The development of ideal-typical welfare regime theory,

International Social Work, 54, 6, 735-750.

Atran, S., 2010. *Talking to the Enemy: Violent extremism, sacred values and what it means to be human,* London: Allen Lane, Penguin.

Attia Khouzam, M., 2010. *Globalization and Social Policy.* Modern University Office: Alexandria.

Auer, P. and Islam, R., 2006. Economic Growth, Employment, Competitiveness, and Labour Market Institutions. *In:* A. López-Claros, M. E. Porter, X. Sala-i-Martin and K. Schwab, eds., *The Global Competitiveness Report 2006-07.* Basingstoke (UK): Palgrave Macmillan: The World Economic Forum, 105-116.

Azaiza, F., 2005. Parent-child relationships as perceived by Arab adolescents living in Israel, *International Journal of Social Welfare,* 14, 297-304.

Azerbaijani-Mogaddam, S., Pinney, A., and Mansfield, A., 2008. *Understanding Afghanistan. Poverty, Gender and Social Exclusion Analysis,* DFID Development and Recovery Consortium, London: DFID.

Azman, A., 2010. Nurturing care in HIV/AIDS response in Malaysia. *In:* A. Azman, I. Baba, J. Sulaiman and J. Paramaswari, eds., *Sustaining HIV/AIDS - Prevention, treatment and care: The way forward.* AIDS Action and Research Group, Universiti Sains Malaysia, 1-8.

Azmi, H., 1991. Traditional Islamic social welfare: its meaning, history and contemporary relevance, *Islamic Quarterly* 35(3), 165-180.

Baba, I., Ashencaen Crabtree, S. and Parker, J., 2011. Future indicative, past imperfect: a cross cultural comparison of social work education in Malaysia and England. *In:* Stanley, S., ed. *Social Work Education in Countries of the East: Issues and Challenges.* New York, Nova, 276-301.

Baderin, M., 2007. Islam and the realization of human rights in the Muslim world: A reflection on two essential approaches and two divergent perspectives, *Muslim World Journal of Human Rights* 4(1), 1-25.

Baer, A., 2007. Women and Health. *In:* Hew, C.S., ed., *Village Mothers City Daughters: Women and urbanization in Sarawak,* Singapore: Institute of Southeast Asian Studies, 42-70.

Balasubramaniam, V., 2006. Strengthening ethnic identity consciousness and the role of tactical voting in multi-racial Malaysia, *Asian Ethnicity,* 7(1), 75-88.

Banks, S., 2006. Ethics and Values in social work. 3rd edition. Basingstoke: Palgrave.

Banton, M., 1994. Modelling ethnic and national relations, *Ethnic and Racial Studies,* 17(1), 1-19.

Barrientos, A., 2009. Labour markets and the (Hyphenated) welfare regime in Latin America, *Economy and Society* 38 (1), 87-108.

Barrientos, A., 2011. Poverty, the crisis and social policy responses in developing countries. *In:* K. Farnsworth and Z. Irving, eds., *Social Policy in Challenging*

Times: Economic crisis and welfare systems, Bristol: The Policy Press, 119-138.

Barzani, N., Abdulah, Chnar, S., 2008. Crimes of Mass Murder against the Kurdish People and their Consequences. *In:* Hussein F.,ed. *International Conference on Genocide Against the Kurdish People.*Erbil, Kurdistan: Aras Press, 11 - 35. Serial no 03.

Baum, N., 2007. Social work practice in conflict-ridden areas: Cultural sensitivity is not enough, *British Journal of Social Work,* 37(5), 873-891.

Bayat, A., 2006. The Political Economy of Social Policy in Egypt. *In:* M. Karshenas and V. Moghadam, eds., *Social Policy in the Middle East.* UNRISD Social Policy in a Development Context Series, New York, Palgrave Macmillan, 135-155.

Beblawi, H., 1990. The Rentier State in the Arab World. *In:* G. Luciani ed., *The Arab State,* London, Routledge, 85-98

Beh, L.Y., 2006. Bumi equity hit NEP target 10 years ago, *Malaysiakini,* Nov. 1, 2006. Available at: www.malaysiakini.com/news/58885. [Date accessed, 14th March 2012].

Beijing Declaration and Platform for Action, 1995, Fourth World Conference on Women, 15September1995, A/CONF.177/20 (1995) & A/CONF.177/20/Add.1

Bhutto, F., 2007. *8.50 A.M. 8 October 2005: Stories of Hope and Courage from the Earthquake in Pakistan,* Karachi: Oxford University, 40.

Bilgen, M., 2009. *Great Islamic ethics.* Available at: http://www.islamicethic.co. [Date accessed, 26th November 2009]

Bin Talal, Prince El Hassan, 2004. Musa ibnMaymun and the Arab-Islamic education, *European Judaism,* 37, 2, 5-18.

Bird, C., 2005. *A Thousand Sighs, A Thousand Revolts: Journeys in Kurdistan.* New York: Ballandtine books.

Boehnke, K. and Bergs-Winkels, D., 2002. Juvenile delinquency under conditions of rapid social change, *Sociological Forum,* 17 (1), 57-61.

Borger, J. and Pearse, D., 2012. Assad tells Annan: no political solution while rebels are 'spreading chaos'. Syrian president meets former UN leader in Damascus for talks denounced by opposition as pointless while killing continues, Sunday March 11 2012, *The Guardian,* Date accessed, at: http://www.guardian.co.uk/world/2012/mar/10/kofi-annan-talks-syria [Date accessed, , 10th March 2012].

B'TSELEM, 2012. B'TSELEM: The Israeli Centre for Human Rights in the Occupied Palestinian Territories. Date accessed, at: http://old.btselem.org/statistics/english/Casualties.asp?sD=29&sM=09&sY=2000&eD=26&eM=12&eY=2008&filterby=event&oferet_stat=before [Date Date accessed, , Date accessed, June 2012]

Bouhdiba, A., 1997. The child and the mother in Arab-Muslim society, *Psychological*

Dimensions of Near Eastern Studies, 1997, 126-141.

Bourdieu, P.,1998. *Practical Reason: On the Theory of Action*. London: Polity.

Bourdieu, P. And Wacquant, L., 1992. *An Invitation to Reflexive Sociology.* Chicago, IL: University of Chicago Press.

Brandsma, J. and Bajourjee, D., 2004. *Microfinance in the Arab World*. New York: U.N. Capital Development Fund.

Brennan-Galvin, E., 2002. Crime and violence in an urbanizing world, *Journal of International Affairs*, 56 (1), 123-145.

Brown, A. and Bourne, I., 1996. *The Social Work Supervisor: Supervision in community, day care and residential settings*, Buckingham: Open University Press.

Brown, B. and Benedict, W.R., 2009. Growing pains and fear of gangs: A case study of fear of gangs at school among Hispanic high school students, *Applied Psychology in Criminal Justice*, 5(2), 139-164.

Brown, D. and McKeown, E., 1997. *The Poor Belong to Us: Catholic Charities and American Welfare*. Cambridge, MA: Harvard University Press.

Brunton-Smith, I., 2011. Untangling the relationship between fear of crime and perceptions of disorder: Evidence from a longitudinal study of young people in England and Wales. *British Journal of Criminology*, 51(6), 885-899.

Burgoon, B., 2006. On welfare and terror: Social welfare policies and political-economic roots of terrorism, *Journal of Conflict Resolution*, 50 (2), 176-203.

Cambanis, T., 2007. Dubai: Court hears French boy's rape testimony, *New York Times*, November 8th 2007.

Cammett, M. and MacLean, L., 2011. Introduction: the Political Consequences of Non-state Social Welfare in the Global South, *Studies in Comparative International Development* 46 (1), 1-21.

Camroux, D., 1996. State responses to Islamic resurgence in Malaysia: Accommodation, co-option and confrontation, *Asian Survey*, 36(9), 852-868.

Carpenter, J., 2005. *Evaluating outcomes of social work education*, Dundee and London, Scottish Institute for Excellence in Social Work Education /Social Care Institute for Excellence.

Case, W.F., 2000. The new Malaysian nationalism: Infirm beginnings, crashing finale, *Asian Ethnicity*, 1(2), 131-117.

Cavallo, E. and Izquierdo, A., ed., 2009. *Dealing with an International Credit Crunch: Policy Responses to Sudden Stops in Latin America*. Washington DC: Inter-American Development Bank.

Central Agency for Public Mobilization and Statistics, 1996. *Summary of the General Census of Population and Housing and facilities for the Arab Republic of Egypt*. Cairo.

Central Agency for Public Mobilization and Statistics, 1998. *Disability Statistics*.

Central Agency for Public Mobilization and Statistics, 2004: *Women in Egypt*,

Cairo.

Central Agency for Public Mobilization and Statistics, 2005. *Egypt in Numbers*: Cairo.

Central Agency for Public Mobilization and Statistics, 2010. *Aging Statistics*, Cairo.

Central Statistics Office (CSO), 2009. *National Risk and Vulnerability Assessment (NRVA) 2007/08*, Kabul: CSO, October 2009.

CFRPL, 2009. *Mapping the global Muslim population: A report on the size and distribution of the world's Muslim population*. Washington, D.C.: Pew Research Center's Forum on Religion & Public Life (CFRPL).

Chadee, D. and Ditton, J., 2003. Are older people afraid of crime? *British Journal of Criminology*, 43(2), 417-424.

Chee, H. L. and Wong, Y.L., 2009., Women's access to health care services in Malaysia. *In*: Chee, H.L. and S. Barraclough, eds., *Health Care in Malaysia: The Dynamics of provision, financing and access*. London and New York: Routledge, 137-153.

Chen, S. and Ravallion, M. 2008. *The Developing World is Poorer than we Thought, but no Less Successful in the Fight against Poverty*. Policy Research Working Paper, No 4703, World Bank.

Chiew, H., 2008. Violated by loggers, *The Star* newspaper, 6th October 2008.

Chow, E. and Pathmawathy, S., 2009. Blacklist – Gov't has head in the sand, *Malaysiakini*18th June 2009. Available at: http://www.malaysiakini.com/news/106698 [Date Date accessed, , 8th December 2009].

Chow, E. N.-L., ed., 2002. *Transforming gender and development in East Asia*, New York and London: Routledge.

Chua, L., 2007. Fixity and flux: Bidayuh (dis)engagements with the Malaysian ethnic system, *Ethnos*, 72(2), 262-288.

Clark, J.A., 2004. *Islam, Charity and Activism: Middle-class networks and social welfare in Egypt, Jordan, and Yemen*, Bloomington IN: Indiana University Press.

Clark, K., 2011. *The Layha: Calling the Taleban to Account*. Kabul: Afghanistan Analysts Network, 4 July 2011.

Clarke, J., 2004., *Changing Welfare, Changing State – New Directions in Social Policy*. London: Sage Publications.

Clarke, G. and Jennings M., 2008. Introduction. *In*: G. Clarke and M. Jennings , eds., *Development, Civil Society and Faith-Based Organizations - Bridging the Sacred and the Secular*, Hampshire: Palgrave Macmillan.

Clinard, M., Meier, R.F., 2011. *Sociology of Deviant Behavior*, 14th ed. Belmont, CA: Wadsworth.

Collier, P. and Hoeffler, A., 2004. Greed and grievance in civil war, *Oxford Economic Papers*, 56, 4, 563-595.

Committee on the Rights of the Child, 2002. *Written replies by the Government* of the United Arab Emirates concerning the list of issues (CRC/C/Q/UAE/1) received by the Committee on the Rights of the Child relating to the consideration of the initial report of the United Arab Emirates. The Permanent Mission of the United Arab Emirates, Geneva, 1-16.

Comprehensive Social Care Unit, 2005. *Annual Report for Comprehensive Care Unit*. Sharjah Ministry of Labour and Social Affairs, Sharjah, UAE.

Convention on the Elimination of All Forms of Discrimination against Women, December, 1979. New York: CEDAW.

Convention on the Rights of the Child U.N., 1989. General Assembly Document A/RES/44/25 UN.

Convention on the Rights of the Child, 1989. Adopted and opened for signature, ratification and accession by General Assembly resolution 44/25 of 20 November 1989. Entry into force 2nd September 1990.

Cooley, J., 1999. *Unholy Wars: Afghanistan: American and international terrorism*. London: Pluto Press.

CRC General Comment No. 12., 2009. *The Right of the Child to be Heard*. Fifty-first session Geneva, 25 May-12 June 2009

Dahl, T. S., 1997. *The Muslim Family: A study of women's rights in Islam*. Oxford/ Norway, Scandinavian University Press.

Das, V., 2003. Trauma and testimony: Implications for political community. *Anthropological Theory* 3(3), 293-307.

Das, V., 2007. *Life and Words: Violence and the descent into the ordinary*. Berkeley: University of California Press.

Deacon, B., 2011. Global social policy responses to the economic crisis. *In*: K. Farnsworth and Z. Irving, eds., *Social Policy in Challenging Times: Economic crisis and welfare systems*. Bristol: The Policy Press, 81-100.

Dedeoglu, B., 2003. Bermuda triangle: comparing official definitions of terrorist activity, *Terrorism and Political Violence*, 15, 3, 81-110.

Dekel, R., Hantman, S., Ginzburg, K. and Solomon, Z., 2007. The cost of caring? Social workers in hospitals confront ongoing terrorism, *British Journal of Social Work*, 37, 1247-1261.

Dinstein, Y., 2011. *War, Aggression and Self-Defence*, Cambridge: Cambridge University Press.

Doolittle, A. A., 2007. Native land tenure, conservation, and development in a pseudo-democracy: Sabah, Malaysia, *The Journal of Peasant Studies*, 34(3&4), 474-497.

Doostgharin, T., 2002. Poverty and Lone Parenthood: the case of Iran. *Journal of International Development*, No 14 (6), 881-886.

Doostgharin, T., 2010a. Inequalities in health care and social work intervention: The case of Iran. *International Social Work*, 53(4), 556-567.

Doostgharin, T., 2010b. Social Work in Iran. *In*: S. Stanley, ed., *Social Work*

Education in Countries of the East: Issues and Challenges. USA, Nova Publishers, 151-170

Dossa, P., 2005.Witnessing Social Suffering: Testimonial narratives of women from Afghanistan. *B.C. Studies*, 147: 27-49.

Dossa, P., 2009. *Racialized Bodies, Disabling Worlds: Storied lives of immigrant Muslim women.* Toronto: University of Toronto Press.

Dupree, L., 1997. *Afghanistan.* Oxford: Oxford University Press.

Dwyer, P., 2004. *Understanding Social Citizenship,* Bristol: The Policy Press.

Egyptian Shura Council, 2000. *Women Committee Report,* Cairo.

Ehsani, K. 2009., The Urban Provincial Periphery in Iran: Revolution and war in Ramhormoz. *In*: A. Gheissari, ed. *Contemporary Iran: Economy, Society, Politics,* ed. by Ali Gheissari. Oxford, UK: Oxford University Press, 38-76.

El-Ghonemy, R., 1998. *Affluence and Poverty in the Middle East,* London, Routledge.

Elsaidi, M. H., 2011. Human rights and Islamic law: A legal analysis challenging the husband's authority to punish 'rebellious' wives. *Muslim World Journal of Human Rights,* 7(2), pp. 1-25.

Erickson C.D. & Al-Timimi N.R., 2001. Providing mental health services to Arab Americans: Recommendations and considerations, *Culture Divers Ethnic Minor Psychology,* 7(4), 308-827.

Esping-Andersen, G., 1990. *The Three Worlds of Welfare Capitalism,* Cambridge: Polity Press.

Fantappie, M., 2011. Iraq: In Country's North, a Youth-led Spring Blooms. *Los Angeles Times,* May 4th 2011

Farouq Al-Housary, T., 2007. *The Social Impact of Economic Reform Programs.* Mansoura: Modern Library for Publishing and Distribution.

Faucher, C., 2009. Fear and loathing in the news: A qualitative analysis of Canadian print news coverage of youthful offending in the twentieth century, *Journal of Youth Studies,* 12(4), 439-456.

Financial Times, 2010. The dog that hasn't barked, *International Business Insight,* October 22.

Fisher D. and Wicker B., eds., 2010. *Just War on Terror? A Christian and Muslim response.* Farnham: Ashgate.

Focusing on Honour. Kurdistan Regional Government Official Webpage. Ministry of sports and Youth. Date accessed, at http://www.mosy-krg.org [Date Date accessed, , 29th 12, 2011]

Furness, S. and Gilligan, P., 2010. *Religion, Belief and Social Work,* Bristol: The Policy Press.

Ghafour, H., 2007. *Sleeping Buddha: The story of Afghanistan through the eyes of one family.* London: Constable and Robinson Ltd.

Gheissari, A., ed., 2009. *Contemporary Iran: Economy, Society, Politics.* Oxford, UK: Oxford University Press.

Giacaman, R., 2004. *Psycho-social/ Mental Health Care in the Occupied Palestinian Territories: the Embryonic System*, Ramallah, Birzeit University. Available at http://icph.birzeit.edu/Books/Psycho-Social.pdf [Date accessed , 30th July 2010].

Giustozzi, A., 2000. War, Politics and Society in Afghanistan, 1978-1992, Washington: Georgetown University Press.

Human Rights Watch, 1993. *Genocide in Iraq. The Anfal Campaign Against the Kurds*. A Middle East Watch Report. New York: Human Rights Watch.

Goodin, R. and Dryzek, J., 1995. Justice Deferred: Wartime Rationing and Postwar Welfare Policy. *Politics & Society* 23 (1), 49-73.

Goodson, L., 2007. *Afghanistan's Endless War: State Failure, Regional Politics, and the Rise of the Taliban*. Seattle: University of Washington Press.

Gough, I. and Wood, G., eds., 2004. *Insecurity and Welfare Regimes in Asia, Africa and Latin America: Social Policy in Development Contexts*. Cambridge, UK: Cambridge University Press.

Guan, L.H., 2005. Affirmative action in Malaysia, *Southeast Asian Affairs*, 2005, 211-228.

Guan, L.H., 2000. Ethnic relations in peninsular Malaysia: The cultural and economic dimensions, *Social and Cultural Issues*, 1, 1-43.

Gupta, G.R., 2000. 'Approaches for empowering women in the HIV/AIDS pandemic: A gender perspective', paper presented at the Expert Group Meeting, *HIV/AIDS Pandemic and its Gender Implications*, 13-17 November 2000, Windhoek, Namibia. Available at: http://www.un.org/womenwatch/dow/csw/hivaids/Gupta.html. [Date , 24th February 2012].

Haggard, S. and Kaufman, R., 2008. *Development, Democracy, and Welfare States: Latin America, East Asia, and Eastern Europe*. Princeton, N.J.: Princeton University Press.

Haj-Yahia, M. M., 2003, Beliefs About wife beating among Arab men from Israel: The influence of their patriarchal ideology, *Journal of Family Violence*, 18(4), 193-206.

Habertal, M., 2012. *On Sacrifice*. Princeton: Princeton University Press.

Habertal, M. (2012) On Sacrifice, Princeton, Princeton University Press.

Hamid, A.F.A., 2000. Political dimensions of religious conflict in Malaysia: State response to an Islamic movement, *Indonesia and the Malay World*, 28(80), 32-61.

Hanna Ibrahim, M., 2007. 'Poverty and child labour', *International Scientific Conference XVIII*, 2-3 May 2007, Faculty of Social work, Fayoum University, Fayoum Governorate.

Harris, K., 2010. Lineages of the Iranian Welfare State: Dual Institutionalism and Social Policy in the Islamic Republic of Iran. *Social Policy & Administration* 44 (6), 727-745.

Hashemi-Najafabadi, S. A., 2010. Has the information revolution in Muslim societies created new publics? *Muslim World Journal of Human Rights*, 7 (1), 1-16.

Hassan, R., 2005. Women's rights in Islam: Normative teachings versus practice. *In:* Hunter, S. and Malik, H., eds., *Islam and Human Rights: Advancing a US-Muslim dialogue.* Washington, DC: Center for Strategic and International Studies, 43–66.

Hayden, P., 2001. *The Philosophy of Human Rights.* USA: Paragon House.

Haydon, D. and Scraton, P., 2000. Condemn a little more, understand a little less: The political context and rights implications of the domestic and European rulings in the Venables-Thompson Case, *Journal of Law and Society*, 27 (3), 416-48.

Haw, K. F., 1998. *Educating Muslim Girls: shifting discourses*, Buckingham: Open University Press.

Hawkins, P. and Shohet, R., 2006. *Supervision in the Helping Professions*, 3ʳᵈ ed. Maidenhead: Open University Press.

Henry, C. M. and Springborg, R., 2001. *Globalization and the Politics of Development in the Middle East*, Cambridge: Cambridge University Press.

Hew, C.S., 2007. *Village Mothers City Daughters: Women and urbanization in Sarawak*, Singapore: Institute of Southeast Asian Studies.

Hew, C.S., 2010. Praying together, staying together: Islamisation and inter-ethnic marriages in Sarawak, Malaysia, *International Journal of Sociology of the Family*, 36, (2), 199-215.

Hew, C.S. and Kedit, F., 1987. The Batang Ai dam, resettlement and rural Iban women. *In:* N. Heyzer, ed., *Women farmers and rural change in Asia: towards equal access and participation*, Kuala Lumpur: Asian and Pacific Development Centre,163-219

Heyman, Janna C., Buchanan, R., Marlowe, D. & Sealy, Y., 2006., Social workers' attitudes toward the role of religion and spirituality in social work practice, *Journal of Pastoral Counselling*, 1, 13-21.

Hirschi, T., 1969. *Causes of Delinquency*, Berkley, California.

Hirschman, A., 1991. *The Rhetoric of Reaction: Perversity, Futility, Jeopardy.* Cambridge, MA: Harvard University Press.

Hosseinpoor, A.R., Naghavi, M., Alavian, S.M., Speybroeck, N., Jamshidi, H., Vega, J., 2007. Determinants of seeking needed outpatient Care in Iran: Results from a National Health Services utilisation survey, *Archives of Iranian Medicine*, 10 (4), 439 – 445.

Human Development Report., 2010. *Occupied Palestinian Territory 2009/2010: Investing in Human Security for a Future State.* Available at http://hdr.undp.org/en/reports/nationalreports/arabstates/palestine/name,14112,en.html [Date accessed, March 2012].

Hundeide, K., 2005. *Psychosocial care for disadvantaged children in the context of poverty and high risk*: Introducing the ICDP Program. University of Oslo, Norway. Available at: http://www.icdp.info/ICDP%20introduction%20in%20context%20of%20 poverty%20and%20high%20risk.pdf [Date accessed, October 10th 2011]

Ife, J., 2001. *Human rights and social work: Toward rights-based practice*. Cambridge: Cambridge University Press.

IFSW, 2002. *Definition of Social Worker*, International Federation of Social Work. Available online at: www.ifsw.org/publications/4.5.3.pub.html [Date accessed , July 21, 2009].

Iliffe, J., 1987. *The African poor: a history*. Cambridge: CUP.

ILO, 2005. *World Employment Report 2004-05: Employment, Productivity and Poverty*. Geneva: ILO.

ILO, 2006. *Employment Poverty Linkages and Policies for Pro-poor Growth in Jordan (1990-2003)*. Geneva: ILO. Second Draft. Mimeo (restricted document)

ILO, 2009. Key Indicators of the Labour Market (KILM). Fifth edition. Geneva: ILO.

International Committee of the Red Cross (ICRC), 2009. *Afghanistan Opinion Survey*, Kabul: ICRC.

ISESCO, 2008.Why the West fails to understand the Islamic world, *Journal Islam Today* [Online] Available at: http://www.isesco.org.ma/english/publications/ Islamtoday/25/Index.php [Date accessed, December 8th 2009].

Iqbal, F., 2005. *Sustaining Gains in Poverty Reduction and Human Development in the Middle East and North Africa*. Washington, D.C.: World Bank.

Islam, I., 2005. *Managing without Growth: Challenges Confronting the Syrian Labour Market*. Geneva: ILO. Unpublished manuscript

Islam, I., 2009. *The Global Economic Crisis and Developing Countries: Transmission Channels, Fiscal and Policy Space and the Design of National Responses*. Geneva: ILO, Employment Sector, Working Paper No. 36.

Islam, R., 2004. *The Nexus of Economic growth, Employment and Poverty Reduction: An Empirical Analysis*. Geneva: ILO.

Jalali, S. M. F., 2005. *A Study of the Relationship Between Poverty and Social Crimes and the Ways to Remove it by Emphasizing the Imam Khomeini Relief Committee* [In Persian]. *EmdadPazhoohan*, 3 (9), 37-54.

James, A., 2001. Capital punishment: The execution of child offenders in the United States, *The International Journal of Children's Rights*, 9, 181-189.

Jawad, R., 2009. *Social Welfare and Religion in the Middle East: A Lebanese perspective*. Bristol: Policy Press.

Jawad, R. and Yakut-Cakar, B., 2010. Religion and Social Policy in the Middle East: The (re)constitution of an old-new partnership, *Social Policy and Administration*, 44, 6, 658-672.

Johnson, C. and Jolyon, L. 2004. *Afghanistan: The Mirage of Peace.* London: Zed Books.

Jomo, K.S., 1994, *U-Turn? Malaysian Economic Development Policy After 1990.* Townsville, Queensland, Australia: Centre for East and Southeast Asian Studies, James Cook University of North Queensland.

Jones, G., 2004. 'Asian demographic transitions: transitions to what?' Paper presented at the *12th Biennial Conference of the Australian Population Association*, 15-17 November, Canberra, Australia.

Kadushin, A. 1992. *Supervision in Social Work,* New York, Columbia University Press.

Kahl, S., 2005. The religious roots of modern poverty policy: Catholic, Lutheran and Reformed Protestant traditions compared, *Archives Européennes de Sociologie (European Journal of Sociology),* XLVI, 1, 91-126.

Kamali, M.H., 2007. Shariah and civil law: Towards a methodology of harmonization, *Islamic Law and Society,* 14(3), 391-420.

Kandiyoti, D., 2005. *The Politics of Gender and Reconstruction in Afghanistan, Occasional Paper 4.* United Nations Research Institute for Social Development. Geneva: UNRISD.

Kantor, P. and Pain, A., 2010a. *Poverty in Afghan Policy. Enhancing Solutions through Better Defining the Problem.* Kabul: Afghanistan Research and Evaluation Unit (AREU).

Kantor, P. and Pain, A., 2010b. *Securing Life and Livelihoods in Rural Afghanistan. The Role of Social Relationships,* Kabul: Afghanistan Research and Evaluation Unit (AREU).

Karshenas, M. and Moghadam, V., 2006. Social Policy in the Middle East: Introduction and Overview. *In:* M. Karshenas and V. Moghadam, eds., *Social Policy in the Middle East.* UNRISD Social Policy in a Development Context Series, New York, Palgrave Macmillan, 1-30.

Khan, A., 2001. *Employment Policies for Poverty Reduction.* Geneva: ILO.

Khan, H and Naqib, M., 2006. *The Palestinian War Torn Economy: Aid Development and State Formation,* (2006) United Nations Conference on Trade and Development. Available at: http://unctad.org/SearchCenter/Pages/Results.aspx?k=The%20Palestinian%20war-torn%20economy%3A. [Date accessed, March 2012].

Kawasmi, H and White S., 2010. *Macro, Small and Medium-sized Enterprises Assessment Report: Towards a Policy Framework for the Development of Micro, Small and Medium-sized Enterprises in the Occupied Palestine Territory.* Ministry of National Economy, Palestine.

Kee, A., ed., 1974. *A Reader in Political Theology,* London: SCM Press Ltd.

Khan, S. *From Rescue to Recognition: Rethinking the Afghan Conflict.* (Unpublished paper).

Kheng, C. B., 2003. Ethnicity, politics, and history textbook controversies in Malaysia, *American Asian Review*, XXI (4), 229-253.

Kiely, R., McCrone, D., Bechhofer F. and Stewart, R., 2000. Debatable land: National and local identity in a border town, *Sociological Research Online*, 5 (2), Available at: http://www.socresonline.org.uk/5/2/kiely.html. [Date accessed, . 8th May 2012]

Kimiafar, S. M., 2008. *KomitehEmdad and War* [In Persian]. Tehran, Iran: ShahidBeheshti Cultural Center.

Kipperberg, E., 2008. The structures of the TRC in South Africa and resulting violence among children and youth. *In*: P. Burton, P., ed., *Someone Stole my Smile*. Monograph on Violence among Children and Youth in South Africa today. Cape Town, S. Africa: Centre for Justice and Crime Prevention, South Africa, 69-89.

Kipperberg, E., Lind, W.A., 2009. *Feasibility Study Northern Iraq, Kurdistan*. Internal UiS report.

Kipperberg, E., and Lind, W.A., 2011. *Social Developments in the Kurdistan Region, Iraq. Universal Values. Local challenges. In*: S. Stanley, ed., *Social Work Education in Countries of the East: Issues and Challenges*. New York: Nova Science Publishers, Inc., 171-190.

Kortteinen, T., 2007. Islamic resurgence and the ethnicization of the Malaysian State: The case of Lina Joy, *SOJOURN*, 23(2), 216-233.

Kronstadt , K. A., Pervaze A.S. and Vaughn, B., 2010. *Flooding in Pakistan: Overview and Issues for Congress*. Washington DC: Congressional Research Service.

Kuppusamy, B., 2006a. Apex court's ruling on Joy pivotal, *Malaysiakini*. Available at: http://76.164.232.35/opinions/54115. [Date accessed, , 14th March 2012]. Kuppusamy, B., 2006b. Racism rife in Malaysia's melting pot, *Inter Press Service* (IPS) 22 March 2006. Available at: http://ipsnews.net/news.asp?idnews=32593. [Date accessed , 14th March 2012].

Kurdistan Tribune, 2011. Banaz Jawas is a symbol of Revolution, *KRG Youth Editor*, September 18, 2011.

Lee, H.G., 2005. Affirmative action in Malaysia, *Southeast Asian Affairs*, 11-228.

Lindsay, J., 2007. The impact of the 2nd Intifada: An exploration of the experiences of Palestinian psycho-social counselors and social workers, *Illness, Crisis and Loss*, 15 (2), 137-153.

Lindsay, J., 2008. Dilemmas, opportunities, obstacles and achievements in training Palestinian social care workers and social workers. *In*: S. Ramon, ed., *Social Work in the context of Political Conflict*, IASSW, Venture Press: Birmingham, UK, 217-243

Lindsay, J., 2011. Equipping ourselves for practice: The Continuing professional development of social workers in the Occupied Palestinian Territories. *In*:

S. Stanley, ed., *Social Work Education in Countries of the East: Issues and Challenges*. New York: Nova Science Publishers, Inc., 369-388.

Lindsay, J. and Baidoun, M., 2006. Professional supervision in Palestine: a participatory evaluation of a development project. *Proceedings of the Global Conference on Social Work;* Sep 2006, Santiago de Chile, Chile. Available at: http://eprints.kingston.ac.uk/2732/ [Date accessed, 3rd July 2010].

Liu, J.H., Lawrence, B., Ward, C. and Abraham, S., 2002. Social representations of history in Malaysia and Singapore: On the relationship between national and ethnic identity, *Asian Journal of Social Psychology*, 5, 3-20.

Lock-Pullan, R., 2010. Challenging the political theology of America's 'War on Terror'. In: D. Fisher and B. Wicker, eds., *Just War on Terror? A Christian and Muslim response*. Farnham: Ashgate, 37-52.

Loewe, M., 2004. New avenues to be opened for social protection in the Arab World: the case of Egypt, *International Journal of Social Welfare*, 13, 3-14.

MacIntyre, A., 2008. *Alisdair MacIntyre's Engagement with Marxism: Selected Writings 1953-1974*, edited by P. Blackedge and N. Davidson. Leiden, The Netherlands: Brill.

Majidyar, A. and Alfoneh, A., 2010. Iranian Influence in Afghanistan: Imam Khomeini Relief Committee. *Middle Eastern Outlook #4*. Washington, DC: American Enterprise Institute.

Malott, J., 2011. The price of Malaysia's racism, *The Wall Street Journal*, Feb. 8, 2011.

Mamdani, M., 2004. *Good Muslim, Bad Muslim: America: The Cold War, and the roots of terror*. New York: Pantheon Books.

Manow, P. and van Kersbergen, K., 2009. Religion and the Western Welfare State – The Theoretical Context. In: P. Manow, Philip and K. van Kersbergen, eds., *Religion, Class Coalitions and Welfare States*, Cambridge: Cambridge University Press, 1-38

Marshall. C. and Rossman, G.B., 1995. *Designing Qualitative Research*. California: Sage.

Marx, K., 1990. *Capital: a Critique of Political Economy*. Translated by Ernest Mandel. Harmondsworth (UK): Penguin.

Matsui, Y., 1999. *Women in the New Asia: From pain to power*. London: Zed Books.

Mauzy, D.K. and Milne, R.S., 1983-84. The Mahathir Administration in Malaysia: Discipline through Islam, *Pacific Affairs*, 56(4), 617-648.

Mayer, A.E. 2005. Evolving concepts of human rights. In: S. Hunter and H. Malik, eds., *Islam and Human Rights: Advancing a U.S.-Muslim Dialogue*. Washington: Center for Strategic and International Studies, 8-26.

Mayer, A. E., 2008. The reformulation of Islamic thought on gender rights and roles. In: S. Akbarzadeh and B. MacQueen, eds., *Islam and human rights in practice: Perspectives across the Ummah*. New York: Routledge, 12-32.

McKinley, T. and Mehran, F., 2006. *Strengthening the Employment Impact of an*

MDG-Based Development Strategy for Yemen. Brazil: UNDP, International Poverty Centre, Country Study No. 4, September.

MENAFN, 2010. http://www.menafn.com/qn_news_story_s. asp?StoryId=1093365023 [Date accessed , 8th August 2010].

Messkoub, M., 2006. Constitutionalism, modernization and Islamization: A political economy of social policy in Iran. *In*: M. Karshenas and V. Moghadam, eds., *Social Policy in the Middle East. UNRISD Social Policy in a Development Context Series*. New York, Palgrave Macmillan, 190-220. Messkoub, M., 2006, Social Policy in Iran in the 20th Century, *Iranian Studies*, 39(2), 227-252 Messkoub, M., 2008. Social Policy in Iran: Islamic or secular? *Policy World* British Social Policy Association, Spring, 17-21. Messkoub, M., 2008. *Economic Growth, Employment and Poverty in the Middle East and North Africa*. ILO Working Paper Series, No. 19.

Messkoub, M., 2009. 'The impact of global financial crisis on employment and poverty in the MENA region,' UN-ESCWA expert meeting on the global financial and economic crisis: *The Social Impact and Responses in the Region*. 8th December, Beirut, Lebanon.

Messkoub, M., 2011.   Crisis, Employment and Poverty in the Middle East and North Africa. In: P. A.G. van Bergeijk, R. van der Hoeven and A. de Haan., eds, *The Financial Crisis and Developing Countries*. Cheltenham (UK): E. Elgar.

Mills, S., 1979. *Discourse*. Abingdon: Routledge.

Minces, J., 1992. *The House of Obedience: Women in Arab Societies*. London: Zed Press.

Ministry of Economy and the World Bank (MoE& WB), 2010. *Poverty Status in Afghanistan*. A Profile based on National Risk and Vulnerability Assessment (NRVA) 2007/08, Kabul: Islamic Republic of Afghanistan, July 2010.

Ministry of Economy and the World Bank (MoE& WB), 2012. *Poverty and Food Security in Afghanistan*. Analysis based on the National Risk and Vulnerability Assessment (NRVA) of 2007/08, Kabul: Islamic Republic of Afghanistan, February 2012.

Ministry of Education and Higher Education, 2008. *Education and Development Strategic Plan 2008-2012: Towards Quality Education for Development*, Ramallah: Ministry of Education and Higher Education.

Ministry of Finance (MoF), 2010a. *Development Cooperation Report 2010*, Kabul: Islamic Republic of Afghanistan.

Ministry of Finance (MoF), Department of Policy, 2010b. *Prioritization and Implementation Plan mid 2010-mid 2013*. Volume 1, Kabul: Islamic Republic of Afghanistan. Available from: http://mfa. gov.af/Content/files/ANDS.pdf [Date accessed, 8th May 2012]. Ministry of Health Malaysia and UNICEF, 2008. *Women and girls confronting*

HIV and AIDS in Malaysia. Malaysia.

Ministry of Health and Medical Education, 2005. *Report of Utilisation of Health Services Survey.* Tehran.

Ministry of Local Development, 1998. *A Weekly Report to the Prime Minister on the Development of 283 Slum Areas in 11 Province.* Cairo, Egypt.

Ministry of Social Affairs, UAE Government, 2009. *Annual Report of the Sharjah Boys Social Education House.* Dubai.

Ministry of Social Affairs, UAE Government, 2008. *Annual Report of the Sharjah Girls Social Education House.* Dubai.

Ministry of Social Solidarity, 2008. *The Project to Target Priority Groups of Social Welfare.* Cairo, Egypt.

Mir, A., 2007. *A to Z of Jihadi Organizations in Pakistan*, Lahore: Mashal Publication.

Mohamed Mahmoud, M., 2003. 'The role of civil society organizations to satisfy the needs of poor women in slum communities', *International Scientific Conference XVI*, 19-20 Mars 2003, Faculty of Social Work, Helwan University, Cairo.

Monshiouri, A., 2002. Islam and human rights in the age of globalization. *In:* A. Mohammadi, ed., *Islam encountering globalization* London: Routledge, 91-110.

Monsutti, A., 2010. The Transnational turn in migration studies and the Afghan social networks. *In:* D. Chatty and B. Finlayson, eds., *Dispossession and Displacement. Forced Migration in the Middle East and North Africa.* Oxford: University Press, 45-68.

Moshe, M., 2001. Peace building: A conceptual framework, *International Journal of Social Welfare* 26(14), 69-68.

Moyo, D., 2009. *Dead Aid: Why aid is not working and how there is another way for Africa.* London: Allen Lane.

Mufid, A., 2011. Why the mood of the South Kurdistan's Youth is in a State of Revolution, *Kurdistan Aspect*, February 20, 2011.

Muhi, J., 2004. 'Combat Malaria', Seminar paper, *Human Rights and the Millennium Development Goals*, 12 -13 October 2004, Kuching, Malaysia.

Murad, M., 1996. 'Police studies, juvenile delinquency indicators', *Security Indicators Conference*, Research & Studies Centre, 5-6 November, 1996, UAE.

Mustafa Hassan, H., 2008. 'Assessing the social care needs of the construction workers', *International Scientific Conference XIX*, 12-13 Mars 2008, Faculty of Social Work, Helwan University, Cairo.

Mustafa Seruji, T., 2004. *Social Policy in the Context of New Global Variables.* Dar- Alfekr Al-Arabi: Cairo.

Nah, A., 2003. Negotiating indigenous identity in postcolonial Malaysia: Beyond being 'not quite/not Malay', *Social Identities*, 9(4), 511-534.

Narimah, A., 2004. 'Human rights and Millennium Development Goals: Lessons from Malaysia's experience in reducing maternal and child mortality', *Human*

Rights and the Millennium Development Goals, 12 -13 October 2004, Kuching, Malaysia.

Nasr, S. V. R., 1994. *The Vanguard of the Islamic Revolution: The Jama☒at-i Islami of Pakistan*. Berkeley: University of California.

National Committee for Reducing Malnutrition of Families with Low Income (NCRMFLI), 2010. Available at http://www2.refah.gov.ir/c/portal/layout?p_l_id=PUB.1.592. [Date accessed, 27th October 2010]

National Youth Agency, 2010. *Children and Young People Now*. Haymarket Business Publication. Date accessed, at:

http://web.ebscohost.com/ehost/pdfviewer/pdfviewer?vid=53&hid=123&sid=a48141b6-f42d-47c6-aec4-6f1bc4f902b8%40sessionmgr114 [Date accessed , 1st February 2012].

NCB, 2009. Media portrayal of young people, *Children & Young People Now*, 29 Jan-4 Feb.

Neo, J. L.-C., 2006. Malay nationalism, Islamic supremacy and the Constitutional bargain in the multi-ethnic composition of Malaysia, *International Journal on Minority and Group Rights*, 13, 95-118.

Nicholas, C., Tuah, Y.C. and Tiah S., 2003. *Orang Asli Women and the Forest: The impact of resource depletion on gender relations among the Semai*. Subang Jaya, Malaysia: Centre for Orang Asli Concerns.

Oko, J., 2008. *Understanding and Using Theory in Social Work*. Exeter: Learning Matters Ltd.

Ong, A., 2006. Study: 30% bumi equity target exceeded, *Malaysiakini*, Sept. 23, 2006. Available from:www.malaysiakini.com/news/57219. [Date accessed, 12th March 2012].

Osmani, S.R., 2003. *Exploring the Employment nexus: Topics in Employment and Poverty*. New York: UNDP and Geneva: ILO.

Osmani, S.R., 2005. *The Role of Employment in Promoting the Millenium Development Goals*. New York: UNDP and Geneva: ILO.

The Palestinian Strategy Group., 2011. *Palestinian National Liberation: Options for Achieving Palestinian National Objectives in the Light of the Breakdown of Bilateral Negotiations*, The Palestinian Strategy Group.

Parker, J., Ashencaen Crabtree, S., Wing, H.C., Kumagai, T., Baba, I., Azman, A., Haselbacher, C., Ridha, H. and Szto, P., 2012. WAVE: Working with Adults who are vulnerable – A comparison of curricula, policies and constructions.

Paterson, A. and Blewett, J., 2006. *Putting the Cart Before the Horse? Privatisation and Economic Reform in Afghanistan, Kabul*, Afghanistan Research and Evaluation Unit (AREU).

Pawson, R. and Tilley, N., 1997. *Realistic Evaluation*, Sage: London.

Payne, M., 2006. Identity politics in Multi-professional Teams. Palliative Care Social Work, *Journal of Social Work*, 6 (2), 137-150.

Philanthropy Today, 2006. Victims of Pakistan Disaster Still Require Aid, *Philanthropy Today* October 5, 2006.

Phua, K.L., 2004. Globalisation: Possible effects on health and the health sector in Malaysia. *In:* Mohd Hazim Shah and Phua, K.L, eds., *Public policy, culture and the impact of globalization in Malaysia,* Kuala Lumpur: Persatuan Sains Sosial Malaysia.

Piper, N., 2005. *Gender and migration.* Singapore: Global Commission on International Migration, Asia Research Institute, National University of Singapore.

Qouta, S., Punamaki, R.-L., Miller, T. and El-Sarraj, E., 2008. Does war beget child aggression? Military violence, gender, age and aggressive behaviour in two Palestinian examples, *Aggressive Behavior,* 34, 231-244.

Quek, K., 2006. Bite the bullet, Malaysia, *Malaysiakini,* Sept 26, 2006. Available at: www.malaysiakini.com/news/57305. [Date accessed, 12th March 2012].

Qureshi, A.J., 2011. Rights of non-Muslims in Islamic State according to the Hanifi jurisprudence, *Research Journal of International Studies,* 18, 114-117.

Report of the Secretary-General on Children and Armed Conflict in Iraq, 2011. S/2011/366.

Report of the Secretary-General pursuant to paragraph 6 of resolution on UNAMI Iraq., 2011. 201., 2011. S/2011/736

Revised country programme document Iraq 2011-2014, 2010. UNICEF Executive Board15 July 2010.

Richards, A. and Waterbury, J., 1990. *A Political Economy of the Middle East: State, Class and Economic Development.* Boulder, Colorado: Westview Press.

Rogers, S. and Sedghi, A., 2012. Afghanistan civilian casualties: year by year, month by month, *Guardian,* 12 March 2012, Available at: http://www.guardian.co.uk/news/datablog/2010/aug/10/afghanistan-civilian-casualties-statistics. [Date accessed, 1st May 2012]

Rosler, M., 1983. *A Simple Case for Torture, or How to Sleep at Night,* video.

Rossi, P. and Freeman, H., 1993. *Evaluation: A systematic approach,* 5th ed. Newbury Park CA: Sage.

Roy, S., 1995. *The Gaza Strip: The Political Economy of De-development,* Institute for Palestine Studies, Beirut.

Rubin, B., 2000. *The Political Economy of War and Peace in Afghanistan.* World Development 28 (10), 1789-1803.

Russell, A., Coughlin, C., EL Walily, M. and Al Amri, M., 2005. Youth in the United Arab Emirates: Perceptions of problems and needs for a successful transition to adulthood, *International Journal of Adolescence and Youth,* 12, 189-212.

Ryan, J.P. and Yang, H., 2005. Family contact and recidivism: A longitudinal study of adjudicated delinquents in residential care, *National Association of Social*

Workers, 29(1), 31-39.

Said, E., 1978. *Orientalism*. New York: Vintage Books.

Said, E., 1979. *The Question of Palestine*. New York: Vintage Books.

Saikal, A., 2006. *Modern Afghanistan: A History of Struggle and Survival*. London: I.B. Tauris.

Salamey, I. and Pearson, F., 2007. Hezbollah: A proletarian party with an Islamic manifesto – A sociopolitical analysis of Islamist populism in Lebanon and the Middle East', *Small Wars and Insurgencies*, 18 (3), 416-38.

SalehiEsfahani, H., 2005. Alternative Public Service Delivery Mechanisms in Iran. *The Quarterly Review of Economics and Finance* 45, 497-525.

Salehi-Isfahani, D., 2006. 'Revolution and redistribution in Iran: Poverty and inequality 25 Years later', *Third Annual World Bank Conference on Inequality*. Washington D.C 2006. Available at: http://www.filebox.vt.edu/users/salehi/Iran_poverty_trend.pdf. [Date accessed, 27th October 2010]

Salehi-Isfahani, D., 2009. Poverty, Inequality, and Populist Politics in Iran, *Journal of Economic Inequality* 7, 5-28.

Sanford, V., 2006a. Excavations engaged observer: Anthropology, advocacy, and activism of the heart: Reflections on truth, memory, and structures of understanding. *In*: V. Sanford and A. Angel- Ajani, eds., *Engaged Observer: Anthropology, Advocacy, and Activism*. New Brunswick: Rutgers University Press, 19-41.

Sanford, V., 2006b Introduction. *In*: V. Sanford and A. Angel- Ajani, eds., *Engaged Observer: Anthropology, Advocacy, and Activism*. New Brunswick: Rutgers University Press. New Brunswick: Rutgers University Press, 1-18.

Save the Children (USA), 2004. *Impact assessment to measure the impact of the Classroom-Based Intervention (CBI) Program(Boston Center for Trauma Psychology) implemented in the West Bank and Gaza*. Available at: http://www.savethechildren.org/publications/technical-resources/education/CBI_Impact_Evaluation.pdf. [Date accessed, 30th July 2010].

Scheper-Hughes, N., 1992. *Death Without Weeping: The Violence of Everyday Life in Brazil*. Berkeley: University of California Press.

Schvaneveldt, P. L., Kerpelman, J. L. and Schvaneveldt, J., 2005. Generational and cultural changes in family life in the United Arab Emirates: A comparison of, others and daughters, *Journal of Comparative Family Studies*, 36(1), 77-91.

Shah, Z., 2009. Jihad and terrorism: a comparative study, *The Dialogue*, 4, 4, 527-554.

Sharom, A., 2006. A critical study of the laws relating to the indigenous peoples of Malaysia in the context of Article 8(j) of the biodiversity convention, *International Journal on Minority and Group Rights*, 13, 53-67.

Shehata Habib, G., 2007. 'General directions for the sustainable development policy in light of social contemporary', *International Scientific Conference*

XVIII, 2-3 May 2007, Faculty of Social work, Fayoum University, Fayoum Governorate.

Shenker, D., 1995. The challenge of human rights and cultural diversity. United Nations. Available online from: http://www.un.org/rights/dpi1627e.htm [Date, May 26ᵗʰ 2009].

Sherwood, H., 2011. Israel Unfreezes Palestinian Authority Tax Millions, *The Guardian*, 30ᵗʰ November 2011.

Shwany, N., 2012. *The Relationship between Kurdish Youth and KRG with Reference to Political Participation, Kurdishaspect.com*. Available at: http://www. kurdishaspect.com/doc040110NS.html [Date accessed, 3rd February 2012].

Siddiqui, S., 2007. *Social work according to the Quran Sound Vision Foundation*. Available online at: http://www.soundvision.com/socialservice/quran.shtml [Date accessed, July 8ᵗʰ 2007].

Singer, A., 2005. Serving up charity: The Ottoman public kitchen. *Journal of Interdisciplinary History*,35, 3, 481-500.

Singh, G. and Cowden, S., 2011. Multiculturalism's new fault lines: religious fundamentalisms and public policy, *Critical Social Policy*, 31, 3, 343-364.

Skocpol, T., 1992. *Protecting Soldiers and Mothers: The Political Origins of Social Policy in the United States*. Cambridge, MA: Harvard University Press.

Skytte, M., 2001. *Etniske minoritetsfamilier og sosialt arbeid*. Norway: Gyldendal akademisk.

Smith, L., 2010. The basic principles of Child Right. *In*: N. Høstmælingen, E. Saga Kjørholt, K. Sandberg, K., ed., Barnekonvensjonen og barns rettigheter i Norge. Universitetsforlaget: Oslo, Norway, 17-30.

Social Fund for Development, 1997. *Annual report*, SFD, Egypt.

Social Fund for Development, 2000. *Annual report*, SFD, Egypt.

Soda, R., 2007. *People on the move: rural-urban interactions in Sarawak*. Kyoto: Kyoto University Press and Trans Pacific Press.

Somers, M. and Block, F., 2005. From Poverty to perversity: Ideas, markets, and institutions over 200 years of welfare debate, *American Sociological Review* 70 (2), 260-287.

Springhall, J., 1998. Censoring Hollywood: Youth, moral panic and crime/gangster movies of the 1930a, *Journal of Popular Culture*, 32(3), 135-154.

Stark, J., 2006. Indian Muslims in Malaysia: Images of shifting identities in the multi-ethnic State, *Journal of Muslim Minority Affairs*, 26(3), 383-398.

Stivens, M., 2010. Religion, nation and mother-love: The Malay Peninsula past and present, Women's Studies International Forum, 33, 390-401.

Subbarao, K., 2003. *Systemic Shocks and Social Protection: Role and Effectiveness of Public Works Programs*. Washington, D.C.: World Bank, Social Protection Discussion Paper Series.

Sulaiman, J. and Azman, A., 2010. The economic cost of HIV/AIDS and the policy implications. *In*: A. Azman, I. Baba, J. Sulaiman and J. Paramaswari, eds., *Sustaining HIV/AIDS - Prevention, treatment and care: The way forward.* AIDS Action and Research Group, Universiti Sains Malaysia, 73-84.

Sundaram, K. and Tendulka, S.D., 2002. *The working poor in India: Employment-Poverty linkages and Employment Policy Options.* Geneva: ILO.

Supreme Court acknowledged Halabja attack as genocide. Kurdish Television reportage about May 31st 2011. Date accessed, at: http://www.kurdsat.tv/news.php?id=1&type=anfal [Date accessed , August 20th 2011].

Sutton, P. W. and Vertigans, S., 2005. *Resurgent Islam: A Sociological Approach.* Cambridge: Polity Press.

Sweifach, J., LaPorte, H.H. and Linzer, N., 2010. Social work responses to terrorism: balancing ethics and responsibility, *International Social Work,* published online 12 July 2010, DOI:10.1177/0020872809360036.

Tadjbakhsh, S., ed., 2004. *National Human Development Report, Security with a Human Face.* Kabul: United National Development Programme.

Tagore, Rabindranath, 1918. *Lectures on Nationalism.* London: McMillan 1918.

Tan, E.K., 2001. From sojourners to citizens: Managing the ethnic Chinese minority in Indonesia and Malaysia, Ethnic and racial studies, 24(6), 949-978.

Taylor, A.J.P. 1965. *English History, 1914-1945,* Oxford History of England Vol. 15. Oxford, UK: Oxford University Press.

Taylor, J.M. 1979. *Eva Perón: The Myths of a Woman.* Chicago, IL: The University of Chicago Press.

Teoh, S., 2008. Polls shows most Malaysians want NEP to end, *Malaysian Insider,* Oct. 9, 2008. Available at: http://www.themalaysianinsider.com/litee/malaysia/article/Poll-shows-most-Malaysians-want-NEP-to-end/. [Date accessed, 9th March 2012].

The Human Rights Commission of Malaysia (SUHAKAM), 2011. *Report on human rights and access to equitable healthcare: A report on the dialogues.* Kuala Lumpur, Malaysia.

The Human Rights Commission of Malaysia (SUHAKAM), 2004. *The importance of developing a National Plan of Action.* 4th October 2004. Kuala Lumpur, Malaysia.

The National Specialized Councils, 1998. *Report of the National Council for Culture, Arts, Literature and Media,* the 19th Session, the Presidency of Republic office, Cairo, Egypt.

The Youth Road Map, 2009. KRG Ministry of Sports and Youth.

Thien, T., 2004. Sarawak Iban remain poorest community, *Malaysiakini,* Sept. 25, 2004. Thien, 2004. Available from: www.malaysiakini.com/news/30329. [Date accessed, 9th March 2012].

Thobani, S., 2003. *War and Politics of Truth Making in Canada, Qualitative Studies in Education,* 16(3): 399-414.

Tilly, C., 1985. War Making and State Making as Organized Crime. *In:* P. Evans, D. Rueschemeyer and T. Skocpol, eds., *Bringing the State Back In.* Cambridge, UK: Cambridge University Press, 169-91.

Titmuss, R., 1956. *The Social Division of Welfare,* Michigan: University of Michigan Press

Tripp, C., 2006. *Islam and the Moral Economy, The Challenge of Capitalism.* Cambridge, Cambridge University Press.

Turner, B. and Khondler, H., 2010, *Globalization East and* West. London, Sage.

Tzannatos, Z., 2009. *The Global Financial, Economic and Social Crisis and the Arab Countries: a Review of the Evidence and Policies for Employment Creation and Social Protection.* Beirut: ILO Regional Office for Arab States.

UNAMI Human Rights Office, 2011. *Human Rights in Iraq 2010.* Baghdad: UNAMI Human Rights Office/ OHCHR.

UNDP, 2007. *Human trafficking and HIV: Exploring vulnerabilities and responses in South Asia.*

UNDP, 2012. *Arab Development Report 2011.* Cairo: UNDP.

UNIDO (United Nations Industrial Development Organization), 2001. *Integrating SME subglobal value chains: Towards partnership for development.* Vienna: UNIDO.

UN Millennim Development Goals. Resolution adopted by the UN General Assembly 18 Sept 2000. A/RES/55/2, Available at: http://www.un.org/millennium/declaration/ares552e.pdf [Date accessed, May 2011].

UNCTAD Secretariat, 2004, *Palestinian Small and Medium Enterprises Dynamic Contribution and Development,* United Nations Conference on Trade and Development.

UNCTAD secretariat, 2006. *Palestinian small and medium-sized enterprises: Dynamics and contribution to development,* United Nations Conference on Trade and Development. Available at: http://unctad.org/SearchCenter/Pages/results.aspx?k=Palestinian%20small%20and%20medium-sized%20enterprises%3A%20Dynamics%20and%20contribution%20to%20development%E2%80%99 [Date accessed, March 2012].

UNCTAD, 2009. *Report on UNCTAD assistance to the Palestinian people: Developments in the economy of the occupied Palestinian territory.* United Nations Conference on Trade and Development. Available at: http://unctad.org/SearchCenter/Pages/results.aspx?k=Report%20on%20UNCTAD%20assistance%20to%20the%20Palestinian%20people%3A%20Developments%20in%20the%20economy%20of%20the%20occupied%20Palestinian%20territory [Date accessed , March 2012].

United Nations, 1948. *Universal Declaration of Human Rights*. Geneva, Switzerland. Available online at: http://www.un.org/Overview/rights.html [Date accessed, Jan 1st 2010].

United Nations Development Programme, 1994. *Human Development Report 1994*. New York: Oxford University Press, 22-23

United Nations, 2003. *Arab Human Development Report*, Oxford, Oxford University Press.

United Nations Development Program, 2007. *Human Development Report*, Cairo, Egypt.

United Nations Office of the High Commissioner for Human Rights (UN OHCHR), 2010. *Human Rights Dimensions of Poverty in Afghanistan*, Kabul: UN OHCHR, March 2010.

U.S. Department of State, Bureau of Democracy, Human Rights, and Labour July-December, 2010 *International Religious Freedom Report*.

US State Department, 2009 *Trafficking in Persons Report*.

US State Department, 2011 *Trafficking in Persons Report*.

US Senate Committee on Foreign Relations, 2011. *Evaluating US Foreign Assistance to Afghanistan*, Washington: US Government Printing Office, 8 June 2011. Date accessed, at: http://www. foreign.senate.gov/imo/media/doc/SPRT%20112-21.pdf [Date accessed, 15th August 2011].

Van Bijlert, M., 2009a. *How to Win an Afghan Election; Perceptions and Practices*. Kabul: Afghanistan Analysts Network.

Van Bijlert, M., 2009b. *Imaginary Institutions; State Building in Afghanistan. Doing Good or Doing Better?* Development Policies in a Globalising World. The Hague: WRR/Dutch Scientific Council for Government Policy.

Van Bijlert, M., 2010. London Conference (2), 'Peace, Reconciliation and Reintegration', *Afghanistan Analysts Network website*. Date accessed, at: http://www.aan-afghanistan.com/index.asp?id=600 [Date Date accessed, ,15th August 2011]

Van Bijlert, M., 2011. Davos 2011 Open Forum: Handing over responsibilities in Afghanistan, *The Global Herald*, 27 January 2011. Date accessed, at: http:// theglobalherald.com/davos-2011-open-forum-handing-over-responsibilities-in-afghanistan/10072/ [Date accessed ,15th August 2011]

Vase, I., 2010. *Justice Shares*. Date accessed, at: http://www.vase.ir/index. aspx?siteid=81&pageid=214 [Date accessed, 26th November 2010]

Veblen, T., 1899. *The Theory of the Leisure Class: An Economic Study of Institutions*. London: MacMillan.

Vertigans, S., 2011. *The Sociology of Terrorism: People, places and processes*. London: Routledge.

Walker, A. and Wong, C.-K., 2005. Introduction: East Asian Welfare Regimes.

In: A. Walker, Alan and C.-K Wong, eds., *East Asian Welfare Regimes in Transition: From Confucianism to Globalisation.* Bristol: The Policy Press, 3-20.

Wasseem, M., 2010. Institutional reforms debate and FDI flows to MENA region: Is debate relevant? Date accessed, at: http://www.hecer.fi/Conferences/NCDE_2010/papers/Mina.pdf [Date accessed, 8th August 2010]

Wee, C.H., 1995. *Sabah and Sarawak in the Malaysian Economy,* Kuala Lumpur: Institute of Social Analysis (INSAN).

Wee, V, and Sim, A., 2004. Transnational networks in female labour migration. *In:* A. Aris and E. Nurvidya Arifi, eds., *International Migration in Southeast Asia,* Singapore: Institute of Southeast Asian Studies, 166-198.

Weinhauer, K., 2010. Youth crime, urban spaces, and security in Germany since the 19th Century, *Historical Social Research,* 35(4), 86-101.

Wendland, J., 2006. Decision to cut aid to Palestinian Authority criticized, *Political Affaires.net* [Date accessed at: http://politicalaffairs.net/decision-to-cut-aid-to-palestinian-authority-criticized/ [Date accessed, March 2012]

Wilber, C. K. and Jameson, K. P., 1980. Religious Values and Social Limits to Development, *World Development,* 8 (7/8), 467-80.

Wilder, A. & Gordon, S., 2009. Money can't buy America love, *Foreign Policy.* Date accessed, at: http://www.foreignpolicy.com/articles/2009/12/01/money_cant_buy_america_love?page=full [Date accessed, 1st December 2009].

Williams, C., Haluk S. & Johnson, M., eds., 1998. *Social Work and Minorities: European perspectives.* London: Routledge.

Winter, T., 2010. Terrorism and Islamic theologies of religiously-sanctioned war. *In:* D. Fisher and B. Wicker, eds., *Just War on Terror? A Christian and Muslim response.* Farnham: Ashgate, 9-25.

Woloszyn, R., 2008. NGO voices on social protection, Kabul: *ACBAR Advocacy Series,* April 2008.

Wood, M., 2011. *Identity work: Students making meaning between tradition and modernity* (unpublished work).

World Bank, 2009. *Afghanistan Pension Administration and Safety Net Project,* Emergency Project Paper. Washington/Kabul: Human Development Unit, South Asia Region.

World Bank, 2009. *2008 Economic Development and Prospects: Regional Integration for Global Competitiveness. Middle East and North Africa Region.* Washington DC: IBRD.

World Bank, 2011. *Afghanistan in Transition. Looking Beyond 2014* (presentation), Kabul: November 2011.

World Bank, 2011. *World Development Report, 2011.*

World Health Organization-Country Office in I.R. Iran, 2004. *Country Cooperation Strategy for World Health Organization and Islamic Republic of*

Iran. Tehran.

Younis, A.A., Al-Admawi, W.I., Yousef, S. and Moselhy, H.F., 2008. Psychiatric disorders in Iraqi juvenile delinquents during sanction period, *International Journal of Criminal Justice Sciences*, 3(2), 129-137.

Yousef Oliek , A., 2008. 'The relationship between education and rural women's attitudes toward consumption', *International Scientific Conference* XIX, 12-13 Mars 2008, Faculty of Social Work, Helwan University, Cairo.

Zaki Abu Al-Nasr, M., 2008. *Social Work between the Local and Global*, Dar Al-Fateh: Alexandria.

Zaki Abu Al-Nasr, M., 2010. *Alienation of Social Welfare in the Welfare Society*, Modern University Office: Alexandria.

Zarowsky, C., 2004. Writing trauma: Emotion, ethnography, and the politics of suffering among Somali refugees in Ethiopia, *Culture, Medicine and Psychiatry*, 28:189-209.

Index

Italic page numbers indicate figures.

www.ingramcontent.com/pod-product-compliance
Lightning Source LLC
Chambersburg PA
CBHW060140280326
41932CB00012B/1574